INVESTIGATIVE JOURNALISM

INVESTIGATIVE JOURNALISM

Proven Strategies for Reporting the Story

William C. Gaines
University of Illinois

CQ PRESS

A Division of Congressional Quarterly Inc.
Washington, D.C.

CQ Press
1255 22nd Street, NW, Suite 400
Washington, DC 20037

Phone: 202-729-1900; toll-free, 1-866-4CQ-PRESS (1-866-427-7737)

Web: www.cqpress.com

Cover photo and design: Jeffrey Miles Hall, ION Graphic Design Works
Composition: Judy Myers

⊗ The paper used in this publication exceeds the requirements of the
American National Standard for Information Sciences—Permanence of
Paper for Printed Library Materials, ANSI Z39.48-1992.

Printed and bound in the United States of America

11   10   09   08   07   1   2   3   4   5

Library of Congress Cataloging-in-Publication Data

Gaines, William C.
  Investigative journalism: proven strategies for reporting the story /
William C. Gaines.
      p. cm.
  Includes bibliographical references and index.
  ISBN 978-0-87289-414-3 (alk. paper)
  1. Investigative reporting. I. Title.

PN4781.G274 2007
070.4'3—dc22

                                                              2007013749

Contents

Tables and Figures   xi

Preface   xiii

C h a p t e r 1

The Investigative Reporter   1

    What Is Investigative Journalism?   2

    Investigative Reporters: Who Are They?   3

    Legal Issues: Investigative Reporters and the Law   5

    Tools of Investigative Reporting   5

    Case Study: A Public Document Denied   11

    Choosing a Subject for an Investigative Report   16

    Chapter Recap   20

    Class Assignments   20

C h a p t e r 2

How to Investigate and Pitch a Story   23

    Using Documents   24

    Gaining Access to Public Documents   28

Searching Databases for Previous Stories   30
Case Study: Mayor Mixes Public and Private Business   34
Rubbing Two Documents Together   39
Getting Attribution   42
Promoting a Story Idea   43
Winning Support for an Idea   44
How Not to Do It   47
Chapter Recap   48
Class Assignments   48
Notes   49

C h a p t e r 3

Investigating a Person, Place or Entity   51

Investigating a Private Person   52
Investigating a Public Official   56
Investigating a Business Entity   58
Investigating a Place   61
Ethics: Written and Unwritten Rules   61
Case Study: Waste in City Government   63
Chapter Recap   75
Class Assignments   75
Notes   75

C h a p t e r 4

Using the Internet During Investigations   77

Where to Look Online   78
Surfing the Net   84
Attribution   86
E-Mail   87
The Internet Audience and Bloggers   87
Case Study: Military Guns Sold on the Internet   88
Chapter Recap   98
Class Assignments   99
Notes   100

C h a p t e r   5

Investigating Those Who Guard the Public   101

Issues of Safety   102
Fire Protection   110
Case Study: The Firehouse   113
Children   118
The Investigative Interview   121
How Not to Do It   126
Chapter Recap   128
Class Assignments   128
Notes   129

C h a p t e r   6

Examining the Police and the Courts   131

The Police   132
The Courts   136
Case Study: A Look Behind the Judicial Robe 144
Chapter Recap   151
Class Assignments   151
Notes   152

C h a p t e r   7

Investigating Charities, Nonprofit Organizations
  and Foundations   153

Regulating Nonprofit Organizations   154
Case Study: Everybody Loves a Carnival   156
Charting an Investigation Project   166
Chasing Telemarketer Complaints—How TV
  Presents Investigative Findings   169
Chapter Recap   175
Class Assignments   175
Notes   176

C h a p t e r 8

Investigating Government 177

Investigating Voting and Elections   178
Investigating Local Misbehavior   179
Reviewing Documents, FOIAs and Open Records Acts   181
Finding and Understanding Political Campaign
   Reports   183
Reviewing Minutes of Meetings   185
Researching Property Ownership   187
Case Study: A Stolen Document   193
Chapter Recap   200
Class Assignments   200
Notes   201

C h a p t e r 9

Reporting on Consumer Fraud 203

The Defenders   204
Fraud Schemes   207
Survey and Undercover Investigations   211
Case Study: The Deal of a Lifetime   214
How Not to Do It   220
Chapter Recap   221
Class Assignments   221
Notes   222

C h a p t e r 1 0

Investigating Health Care 223

The Medical Profession   225
Medical Licensure, Discipline and Privacy   226
Government Inspections of Medical Facilities   227
Insurance Claims and Fraud   230
Case Study: Investigating Licensed and Unlicensed
   Medical Professionals   232

Reporter as Ombudsman   241
Chapter Recap   243
Class Assignments   243
Notes   247

C h a p t e r   1 1

Investigating Businesses   249

Document-Based Investigations of Privately Held
   Companies   250
Case Study: Sports Equals Big Business   251
Document-Based Investigations of Publicly Held
   Companies   255
Original Surveys   258
Case Study: Survey: Auto Mechanics, Routine Checkup   259
Case Study: Survey: Speeding and Tailgating Trucks   265
Chapter Recap   271
Class Assignments   271
Notes   272

C h a p t e r   1 2

Special Topics and Tricks of the Trade   273

Religion   273
Nepotism   275
Labor   277
Money   277
Schools   278
Case Study: School Food: The Lowest Bid   279
Back-Pocket Documents   282
How Not to Do It   287
Chapter Recap   290
Class Assignments   291
Notes   291

Appendix 1: Freedom of Information Act   293

Appendix 2: Law that Makes Financial
   Information of a Tax-Exempt Organization
   Public   311

Appendix 3: How TV, Newspaper and
   Internet Writing Styles Differ   319

Web Sites and Readings to Investigate   325
Glossary   329
Index   331

Tables and Figures

Tables

Table 1.1	Ideas to Examine	16
Table 1.2	Deciding the Approach	18
Table 2.1	Selected Documents	25
Table 10.1	Nursing Home Spreadsheet	245
Table 10.2	Sorting Nursing Home Findings	246
Appendix Table	Auto Repair Story	320

Figures

Figure 2.1	Freedom of Information Act, sample request letter 1	31
Figure 2.2	Freedom of Information Act, sample request letter 2	32
Figure 2.3	Freedom of Information Act, sample request letter 3	33
Figure 2.4	Provo City Corporation, proposed budget, fiscal year 2004–2005	40

Figure 2.5   Provo City Corporation, statement of
activities, fiscal year 2004–2005   41

Figure 3.1   Middleton, budget and actual schedules   69

Figure 5.1   Detroit Fire Department dispatcher log,
page 1   111

Figure 5.2   Detroit Fire Department dispatcher log,
page 2   112

Figure 7.1   Wahoo Middle Manager Club annual
financial report, page 1   162

Figure 7.2   Wahoo Middle Manager Club annual
financial report, page 2   163

Figure 7.3   Charting an investigative idea   169

Figure 8.1   Sample deed   189

Figure 8.2   Sample deed, exhibit A   190

Figure 8.3   Sample declaration of value   191

Figure 9.1   Typical e-mail scam   209

Figure 9.2   Direct sales advertisement   214

Figure 11.1   Letter requesting comment   254

Figure 12.1   Freedom of Information Act request
letter, river port pilot review board   276

Figure 12.2   Sample Uniform Commercial Code
(UCC) financing statement   285

Preface

I STARTED MY JOURNALISM CAREER as a news announcer at a small radio station, where I would rip the wire association news summaries off the teletype and read them into a microphone. After a while it seemed the news was going into my eyes and out of my mouth without pausing in brain matter. Wanting more from journalism than that, I volunteered for duties in the radio station mobile unit. This led me to where news was made. I might be at the mill gate interviewing strikers or at the county fair talking to the owner of the best sow. I grew closer to the news when I became a print journalist, but even then I felt like a mere observer. I discovered that I would have to be an investigative reporter to satisfy my quest for finding and reporting the news. In this role I could investigate and then report on my own findings; I could help by revealing wrongdoing.

The same desire that pushed me toward investigative reporting led me to the classroom. I wanted to tell others what I learned and devised an investigative reporting course that I could teach while I worked the craft. As investigative reporting became more important to journalism and as technology changed how we report and investigate, my students wanted workable instructions for the twenty-first century. I believe *Investigative Journalism: Proven Strategies for Reporting the Story* fulfills that need. It is designed to work within a full fifteen-week course. It is also a vital companion to a text for public-affairs reporting to help reporters investigate the inner workings of government. It is a necessary supplement to in-depth or feature writing courses because it underscores the value of good and thorough investigative research. And it is crucial to computer-assisted reporting classes because it illuminates the usefulness of technology.

Now more than in years past, vast amounts of information—city records and financial disclosures of charities and campaign contributions, for example—are easy to obtain with a few clicks of a computer mouse. While information available online may seem inexhaustible, reporters also need to know *if* there is a story. They must learn ways to generate story ideas and choose subjects to investigate, and they must uncover and sift through information and data to get the job done. Reporters must learn how to dip into this mother lode of information for extensive surveys or quick checks of facts. They need to know what information to trust and how to use it.

Organization

As a concise and practical how-to guide, *Investigative Journalism* will get you started on the road to being a successful journalist. The book is organized by broad topics—subjects of most investigative reports such as government, elections and campaigns, not-for-profit companies, charities, big business, private business, licensed professionals and consumer fraud.

In each chapter, you will be introduced to the chapter topic with real-life stories and investigations, plus plenty of examples and discussion. Once the discussion is started, several strategies and methods used by practicing reporters for uncovering key documents, interviewing subjects, tracking down information and checking for accuracy are provided.

Case studies follow and bring to life an investigative reporter's day-to-day work. The case studies in this textbook are based on true-to-life experiences of real reporters. Some, like the auto repair and medical insurance investigations, are detailed reconstructions of real investigative reports. Names and places have been changed to protect reporters, their sources and the confidential information revealed to the author. Other cases are composites, but widely applicable to the bureaucratic entanglements, the loosely run local government or possibly the medical insurance fraud found in countless cities and towns on which you will report in your first job.

Concluding each chapter are a chapter summary and class assignments and exercises. Because this book takes a hands-on approach to learning investigative reporting, the exercises are short of completing a full-blown investigation. As a student, you are not yet positioned to complete a publishable investigation of the nature described in the textbook. You can launch plans for real investigations and "break stories," however, and this text shows you how.

Key Features

To get you in the mind-set of an investigative reporter, *Investigative Journalism* uses a unique case-study method to teach you what investigative reporting is, why it is important and the basics of its practice. The case studies are marked by periodic junctures of reflective questions to systematically guide you through the narrative. This device mimics the mental path a reporter travels while gathering information and working on a story.

For instance, the case study in chapter 1 covers such topics as working with a tipster, protecting a reporter's beat, investigating during an election campaign, finding and using campaign disclosures, and simultaneous rebuttals. At the end of each case history is a "memoranda" section that sums up that case's major lessons (e.g., "reporters can protect the identities of tipsters by not knowing their names and confirming their information from documents or other sources they can quote," or "campaign contributions and government payrolls are public record").

While you may never learn much about the personal lives of our case study protagonists, you will quickly understand why these reporters succeed professionally. They are loyal to their readers and work long and hard hours in dedication to their causes. They resist taking shortcuts or stepping over the line but will take chances. They never lack ingenuity. Although they stay calm and polite when confronting the worst of local rascals, there is a sense of outrage seething not far beneath the surface.

Along with tools and strategies to use in investigative reports, you will come away with eight basic concepts crucial to your success as a reporter. You will learn how to

- recognize a social problem worthy of investigation;
- appreciate the legal and ethical constraints on public officials that will enable you to uncover wrongdoing;
- understand the legal and ethical constraints on reporters;
- find public records and know how to use them;
- recognize the special problems of dealing with private records;
- provide balance and fairness to an investigative story;
- respect and value the importance of accuracy; and
- present a story in a manner so that it receives the attention it deserves.

Having utilized the tools of investigative reporting myself, I am satisfied that I have been able to work in the realm of the highest level of news gathering and reporting. I believe investigative reporting to be part art and part science. A beginning reporter can learn the *science* by honing investigative research methods and putting those practices into reporting and writing. It may take more experience and on-the-job training to learn the *art* of investigative reporting, but with a solid foundation of the skills required, a student or beginning reporter is well on his or her way to becoming a topnotch investigative reporter.

Acknowledgments

This textbook is the product of many talented staffers at CQ Press. It was my good fortune to work with Kristine Enderle, whose high professional standards, knowledge, hard work, enthusiasm and friendly guidance made this project possible; Mary Marik, whose dedication to accuracy places her among the best of editors; and Anne Stewart, whose talent for perfection put in the final touches.

I also appreciated and incorporated the overview and suggestions of foremost academic and professional craftspeople: Ira H. Chinoy, University of Maryland; David E. Sumner, Ball Sate University; and Mary M. Tolan, Northern Arizona University.

I owe thanks for the support of Ron Yates, dean, and Walt Harrington, journalism department head, of the College of Communications at the University of Illinois at Urbana-Champaign; and to my wife and family, especially my grandson, Chris Galocy, who helped in many ways.

C h a p t e r   1

The Investigative Reporter

INVESTIGATIVE JOURNALISM HAS IT ROOTS in good literature. Two hundred years ago, what could be called investigative journalism was mostly in the form of popular fiction. When Charles Dickens told of the travails of "Oliver Twist," he was speaking out against child labor practices; and when he wrote about Scrooge in "A Christmas Carol," it was more than a Christmas story. Dickens was exposing loan sharking and the need for a minimum wage law for the unfortunate Bob Cratchit. With "Les Miserables," Victor Hugo took on the judicial system. In the early 20th century, Upton Sinclair wrote of scandalous conditions in the meat packing industry in "The Jungle." Such true-to-life "fiction" gave people an insight into social problems through a vehicle that was acceptable.

Reporters actively pursued investigative stories in the 1920s. Investigative journalists grew to be thought of as independent overseers of government—the watchdogs of society who provided another layer of public confidence in their system of government. After all, freedom of the press was high in the esteem of the Founders, and investigative reporters exercised that freedom to the fullest.

Such reporters branded a unique kind of journalism in which the reporter is not limited to reporting on those matters before public agencies; instead investigative journalists develop their own information through investigative research, conduct their own investigations and then report on their findings. Because of those functions, they carry a heavy load of responsibility to make sure their reports are accurate, meaningful and fair. In this chapter, you will learn how investigative reporters work, from the initial story idea to publication, and the tools reporters have to get the job done.

What Is Investigative Journalism?

Tracking the winners of the Pulitzer Prize through the years shows that the awarding judges most often favored investigative reports that exposed wrongdoing over coverage of breaking news or explanatory feature writing. In 1921, a memorable investigative report by the *Boston Post* won one of the first Pulitzer Prizes in the "public service" journalism category. The Post's report exposed the financial schemes of Charles Ponzi when it detailed his trick of paying investors with money from new investors and claiming it was profit from their investments with him. Those *Boston Post* revelations led to Ponzi's conviction for mail fraud. Two reporters with the *Chicago Daily News* won a Pulitzer Prize in the "reporting" category in 1925 for helping police solve the notorious murder committed in Chicago by Nathan Leopold and Richard Loeb.

Throughout the 1930s and 1940s, investigative reporters developed many stories of local political corruption, but they also wrote of social problems like slum conditions, inadequate medical facilities and unsafe motor vehicles. In the 1950s, news stories by George Thiem of the *Chicago Daily News* and Roy J. Harris of the *St. Louis Post-Dispatch* won a Pulitzer Prize for public service for their simultaneous individual work that surprisingly targeted the journalism community by showing that 37 newspaper reporters and editors were on the Illinois state payroll.

Pulitzer Prizes show that investigative reporters continue to perform their special kind of journalism. More recently, in 2003, Pulitzer Prizes went to the *Boston Globe* for its reporting of sexual abuse in the Roman Catholic Church and to *The New York Times* for stories of the abuse of mentally ill adults in state-regulated homes.

By looking closely at the winners of such prestigious journalism awards, a student can find a common definition of investigative reporting. While the criteria for best investigative stories may not be explicitly stated or might change over time, selection committee judges award published reports that

- reveal information that someone is trying to hide or that otherwise would not have been known,
- are a matter of importance to the public well-being,
- are the work product of the reporter rather than a leak from a government agency investigation,

- expose a waste of tax money caused by mismanagement or corruption in government, dangerous conditions posing safety hazards or fraudulent conduct in the private sector that preys on the consumer.

Newspaper readers, radio and television audiences and people who get their news from the Internet have grown to accept investigative reporting as a public service. They may see the investigative reporter as a recourse when other efforts fail to correct a wrong. But investigative reporting is also a business. A revealing book may be written to examine an issue or event thoroughly, and the reward is sales of copies. A magazine article may contain investigative reporting of such interest that sales of the particular issue will soar. A television station may broadcast an investigative series at a time that it is being judged by audience rating services, and it will draw viewers and enable the station to boost commercial rates. A Web site may draw more hits from Internet surfers and be recognized as a medium for more advertisers.

More indirectly, a newspaper, broadcast station or Web site may publish investigative stories so that it will be thought of as an advocate of the taxpayer and consumer. It is the overall hope of media owners that investigative stories will forge a closer bond between them and the readers and viewers and therefore will foster a long-term relationship, loyalty and a strong base for dissemination.

Other investigative reporting might be carried out with more specific and perhaps selfish purposes. A segment of the media that espouses a certain cause may seek to expose those who dispute that cause. The publishers of an investigative story might promote a certain political party and seek to discredit their opponents.

A dedicated investigative reporter does the job because of a belief in the job's importance. The work provides the reporter a constant challenge and affirmation of being on the side of truth and fairness. The reporter knows that a job well done will result in public approval.

Investigative reporters often are the last hope of those who want to correct a wrong.

Investigative Reporters: Who Are They?

Investigative reporters may work for newspapers, magazines, webmasters or television stations. Or they might be employed by a multimedia company that calls upon them to investigate and report for a combination of print and broadcast media. They may be independent freelancers who sell individual stories to magazines or book publishers, or they can go online with their own Web sites to tell their stories. Also, some enterprising reporters use investigative techniques in their day-to-day reporting.

Investigative reporters, employed by the major media, work under close supervision of editors; however, as a defined group they are without formal rules. They are not licensed and often not treated differently from any other reporters in a newsroom. They do not carry special privileges and must work within the law. They do not flock together, but, like birds migrating, they seem to share a common instinct about what to do when a tip to a big story is pushed under the door. They acknowledge each other's good work, but they do not impose controls on each other. They have accepted high standards of conduct and a basic code of honor that is unwritten.

Investigative reporters who carry that title are full-time employees of the larger newspapers and television stations, and after years of successful performance they have earned their employers' confidence. The investigative reporters at the larger media newsrooms will be found working on the important stories, those that carry newspaper editors' hopes for a contest win or those the TV station has slated for periods in which viewer numbers are counted. Also, when a major news story breaks, the reporting staff will gather around the center desk in a newsroom and turn to the investigative reporter for guidance in pursuing aspects of the story.

In this book, we will examine some top stories to learn how they were gathered and presented. Investigative reporters for the major media have years of journalism experience, and when they become accomplished investigative reporters they seldom return to general assignment reporting. But this is not a closed membership. Any reporter for any of the media is expected to be capable of conducting the in-depth research necessary to produce an investigative report.

Reporters who work for newspapers with smaller circulations now are employing more investigative techniques because of more easily accessible information available online. A reporter in a first job will make a favorable impression as a completely equipped reporter if that reporter can demonstrate the abilities and mind-set that are accorded investigative reporters. In small and medium-sized newsrooms, where ad hoc teams of reporters may be impaneled to pursue the most important stories, the beginning reporter with knowledge of investigative research methods and who uses proven investigative practices in reporting and writing will be chosen to be among them.

Even when it is acknowledged that investigative reporters are essential to a quality newspaper or television news operation, the investigative reporter often has to struggle to get adequate space for a story. Newspapers have become smaller in size and lesser in content, to make them easier to hold and to cut costs. A proper telling of a newspaper's investigation could absorb the news column space that would otherwise contain other important stories. A large investigation—of problems at an airport, for example—may not be of interest to everyone because many seldom go to the airport. Thus, if such a story is displayed day after day with pictures and charts, some readers will feel that it is swallowing up space in their newspaper. Those readers may be irritated and driven away. Reporters and editors have adjusted to this possibility, and they keep investigative stories tightly edited and to the point.

Television investigative reports are also trimmed for fast-paced viewing because of time constraints. Every investigative report, no matter how important, must compete for airtime with all the news of the world, the weather and sports. The need for brevity has placed in demand the hard-hitting, one-shot, exclusive follow-up to a breaking news story, and investigative reporters must possess the skills to deliver it.

Online publishing can be an aid to newspaper and TV reporters. Newspapers and TV stations usually have Web sites, and reporters can make good use of them by posting the details of the investigation that did not make it into print or into a broadcast and inviting interested readers to click on the Web site for the full story and more.

Legal Issues: Investigative Reporters and the Law

An investigative reporter must have a commonsense knowledge of basic law. A successful reporter knows both the laws that restrict the gathering of information and those that can help. With the exception of some scattered state laws that protect news sources, U.S. law does not provide a reporter with an exemption from criminal and civil laws that affect everyone. Among the criminal laws that might be violated in the careless pursuit of information are those related to trespass, theft, extortion and bribery. Civil laws involve libel, invasion of privacy and fraud. Laws that better enable an investigative reporter to gather the facts include federal and state freedom of information acts, open-meetings laws, public licensing, campaign disclosure regulations and laws that create state offices like the clerk of the courts and the recorder of deeds.

Tools of Investigative Reporting

Investigative reporters are not only apart from other reporters in experience and mind-set, they are also expected to have skills that others may not have cultivated. They have the ability to find and use documents, whether

5

private or public records. They have adopted the special use of interviews, surveys and surveillance as tools of the trade. Over the years, they have been able to add the tape recorder, the videotape, the computer database and the spreadsheet to their arsenal of working aids.

The tape recorder may be used in interviews to reassure the interviewee of being quoted correctly. The videotape has become important for recreating an incident. Steve Berry, when reporting for the *Los Angeles Times*, went from door to door in a neighborhood where a man with a gun was shot and killed by police on February 14, 1994. Knowing how common it was for people to have video cameras, he was asking whether anyone had taped the incident. Yes, someone had, and the videotape showed the shooting was not as necessary as the police had claimed. Use of a database for otherwise unmanageable information allows the reporter to find facts and match them in minutes rather than in the hours previously needed. The spreadsheet organizes the information for quick retrieval.

One axiom among investigative reporters that is not likely to be challenged is that there are more stories to be done than there are time and reporters to do them. By carefully considering a proposed story idea, the reporter can be assured of working on problems or questions that are among the top concerns of the public and that the project idea can be reasonably fulfilled. No reporter wants to get bogged down in dead-end stories that waste valuable time. Investigative reporters are an inquisitive lot, but they are also skeptical, so they will take time to do preliminary research before they launch into an investigation. Their story ideas come from a variety of places, but they most often come from tipsters, follow-ups to a breaking story, observations from a colleague, consumer complaints and shared experiences.

Following a Tip

Information or ideas for an investigative story may come from a person who has a complaint and has specific knowledge of threats to the public welfare. This tipster may be a public or private employee who wishes to remain anonymous but yet provide an investigative reporter with the idea for a story by alleging some wrongdoing. Often tipsters are labeled "disgruntled" because they have a long-term dissatisfaction with the performance of others. A tip-off to a story might come in an anonymous letter or from a secret meeting in a parking garage, as was the choice of one of the most famous of all tipsters, Mark Felt (aka Deep Throat) of the Watergate investigation.

A successful investigative reporter will know how to check out the tip without identifying the source or even indicating that a source exists beyond the public records that are cited in the investigative story. This strategy protects the tipster from disclosure and protects the reporter from publishing unsubstantiated allegations. Reporters recognize the importance of tipsters and will take every step necessary to protect the identities of those who wish to remain anonymous.

The reporter will move quickly to either substantiate the information from the source or rule it out. If the tipster says that the license of a prominent physician has been revoked, for example, the reporter will go to the state agency that administers medical licenses and find all the public records pertaining to the doctor's license to see whether any action has been taken against the license by the hearing board. The reporter will certainly not want to quote the tipster even as an anonymous source. The story will be based on the documents.

Example 1. A former janitor, who was recently fired from a hospital job, reports that tonsils of entire families on welfare are routinely removed on the same day. An investigative reporter will check with medical experts to learn whether tonsillitis is contagious and whether it is proper practice to have them removed on the same day. Upon learning that tonsillitis is not contagious and tonsillectomies are not without risk, the reporter will check state records of payouts to the hospital for public assistance recipients to learn whether such procedures are being performed and find out the compensation of the medical practitioners.

Example 2. The sheriff requires all new employees to make a contribution of $2,500 to his political fund, disgruntled sheriff's deputies confide to a reporter. The reporter checks the sheriff's payroll and matches the names to the list of campaign contributors on file in the county clerk's office.

Example 3. Plumbing work in all the municipal buildings is being done by a corporation owned secretly by the mayor, according to a defeated candidate for mayor. The reporter learns which company got the contract by reading the minutes of the city council meeting and then runs that company name through the corporation division of the state-level office of the secretary of state to identify officers.

Following Up on a Breaking Story

Sometimes stories are spawned by an incident such as a school bus accident, a fatal fire, or a breakdown of public services. Often, while the general assignment reporter goes to the scene of a breaking story and reports on the circumstances as would the police officer first arriving at the scene of an incident, the investigative reporter—much like a police detective—looks for the hidden story that may be the next-day follow-up in the newspaper or on TV. An investigative reporter may pursue the many questions presented by the breaking story.

In the most familiar of these reports, *Washington Post* reporters Bob Woodward and Carl Bernstein were following up on a breaking story. In June 1972, Democratic National Committee offices in the Watergate office building were burglarized. Woodward and Bernstein relentlessly sought an answer to the question of who was responsible until the facts exposed a White House cover-up and led to the resignation of President Richard Nixon in 1974.

Example 1. A fire burns down the stables at the racetrack. The general assignment reporter will want to know the cause of the fire, the number of horses lost, the dollar amount of damage and whether any firemen were injured. The investigative reporter will want to know when the most recent building inspection was carried out and whether any citations remained uncorrected.

Example 2. A truck crashes through the front entrance of a restaurant. The general assignment reporter is gathering reports of the dead and injured while the investigative reporter is requesting the driving record of the trucker.

Example 3. The school board is unable to meet its payroll because the computer system breaks down repeatedly. The initial newspaper article will focus on the hardships experienced by school employees who miss a paycheck. An investigative reporter may look further into the story and will want to know who got the contract for the computer system and how it performs in comparison with the systems in other school districts.

Looking for Subjects for Planned Projects

Sometimes the editorial body of the newspaper or broadcast station suggests, "It's about time we looked at _____"—such questions as where the tollway money is being spent, the safety hazards in public buildings or nepotism in the city workforce. Such a suggestion spawns the planned project. It may best be a subject that is a hot current issue with the public. One way to learn of a timely concern that deserves a plan of attack by an investigative reporter is to check the letters and e-mails to the editor or the complaints to the newspaper's consumer columnist. An investigative reporter who specializes in writing about consumer problems may plan a project because of the actual number of complaints or questions about a current problem that readers have encountered.

In a landmark investigation by the *Chicago Sun-Times* in 1978, the reporters convinced their editors to have the newspaper buy a bar, keep the ownership secret and then operate the bar; they wanted to learn how many times they would be solicited for bribes when they opened for business. The series of stories that resulted was nationally acclaimed for the ingenuity of the journalists. There had been no breaking story; neither did the reporters have to be told by a tipster about what was happening. They merely decided it was about time somebody exposed shakedowns. Their project was carefully planned and executed.

Example 1. Readers may complain about auto repair mechanics. As car owners, they may tell of feeling threatened when they bring their cars into a repair garage and are placed at the mercy of a mechanic. The investigative reporter could respond by setting up a survey of auto repair shops: a driver would drop off for repairs a car that an expert has certified needs no repair. The reporter might get a story about which shops charge for unnecessary repairs.

Example 2. There may be some public concern expressed about the quality of patient care in nursing homes. A reporter will get inspection reports and then tour the facilities to see whether the violations cited in the reports are corrected. Some nursing homes may have hazards that are not corrected even when warnings are issued. How well are they inspected?

Example 3. Complaints may tell of Internet scams. Investigative reporters will attempt to trace the perpetrators of the schemes and expose their operations.

Example 4. A well-intentioned government loan program may have gone awry. Citizens may complain about mismanagement of programs for disaster relief, scholarships or housing, and the complaints may lead to an investigative series by a reporter. Program overseers will learn of the problems from media reports and could be encouraged to take corrective action.

Investigating Observations of Colleagues

A reporter may have an investigative idea from working a beat such as the courthouse beat and will tell the editors about it. The beat reporter cannot investigate this perceived corruption without losing valuable news sources within the group of people who regularly provide information. The sources themselves could turn out to be the target of the investigation or possibly be offended by the story. The beat reporter may explain the situation to an editor, who may then assign an investigative reporter to work on a project that may turn out to be a series of articles in the newspaper or reports on the nightly TV news.

In 1986 the *Philadelphia Inquirer* began a series of stories about connections between judges and lawyers. The reporter assigned to cover the courts, Fredric Tulsky, worked alongside two investigative reporters, H. G. Bissinger and Daniel Biddle, in a two-year investigation. For their series, "Disorder in the Court," which revealed transgressions of justice in the Philadelphia court system and led to federal and state investigations, Biddle, Bissinger and Tulsky won the Pulitzer Prize for investigative reporting in 1987.

Reporting on a Shared Experience

A story idea may come from an experience the reporter and the general public have shared—being tailgated by a truck, having water back up into a basement or getting the runaround during a call to city hall. It could be that a question arises during a discussion: "Why does the transit system have to raise fares again?" At the *Chicago Tribune*, a weeklong series of stories about denial of services or overcharging in minority neighborhoods was initiated when a reporter mentioned to an editor that people in those communities were calling it the "black tax." That phrase grew into an award-winning series that examined costs and availability of home loans, home improvement loans and auto and property insurance.

Example 1. A local service club raises money for its charitable works by sponsoring an annual street carnival. The reporter, among others, often wonders how big of a slice of the proceeds goes to the traveling carnival and how much is left over for the charities. The reporter may start by locating the charitable trust's financial reports filed with the state or its IRS form 990 to learn the amounts taken in and expended for charity.

Example 2. A reporter's elementary school child says the food is bad at school and fights take place in the schoolyard every day. The reporter asks other parents about it, and they say their children make the same complaints. It seems to be outside the realm of investigative reporting, or is it not?

A Public Document Denied*

Bob Wright covered his police beat thoroughly. He understood the law and respected the police officers in the departments he covered. In return they rewarded him with accurate accounts of police law enforcement activities. They thought of him first when they had a good story.

The police chiefs and the elected sheriff, in contrast, tended to give out only information that made the performance of their offices look good, and they suppressed incidents with a negative aspect. Police officers were told to get their commander's approval before releasing a story to reporters.

When a police officer shot himself in the foot during a demonstration of how to handle a firearm, Wright chose not to tell the story. Wright believed he made only a small concession when he passed over the story in return for continued amicable relations with the police contacts on his beat.

What do you think?

Is it correct to suppress the story about the police officer shooting himself in the foot?

Yes: It was not an important story.
No: Reporters should not take it on themselves to ignore a story.

Two weeks before the local elections, two young officers in the sheriff's department came to Wright secretly and told him that the sheriff was requiring them to do political work on behalf of his candidacy for reelection. They had also heard that all new personnel hired by the sheriff were forced to donate $2,500 each to the sheriff's campaign fund to get on the sheriff's public payroll. Also, the sheriff was placing new hires on the roster as part-time, hourly auxiliary officers who, the sheriff said, were to be called up in an emergency. The real purpose was to get the campaign contributions; in return, the tipsters told Wright, each auxiliary officer would get a badge that could be shown during any police traffic stop as well as permission to carry a gun.

Wright faced a dilemma. He would have to give up his beat if he wrote such a story.

---

*The cases are based on real investigative stories, but the names and places have been changed to protect reporters, their sources and the secrets they have. Some are actual stories told in a step-by-step reconstruction and others are composites.

Were the sheriff's officers acting improperly by breaking department rules?

Yes: They should not break the rule about contacting the press no matter how they might justify it. If they think it is okay to break that rule, they might as well break them all. Law enforcement officials should be models for everyone and adhere strictly to the rules.

No: The allegation against the sheriff is more serious than breaking a department rule, and the officers are bound by their duty to the public to come forward. Whistleblower laws in most states protect government employees from retribution when they report misdeeds of their superiors.

Is it worth sacrificing a productive police beat to cover one story?

Yes: Every reporter has a duty to the public to report the facts and expose wrongdoing. If Wright does not report the story, he will become a part of the corruption. How could he continue to work with the sheriff and write favorable stories when he knows the sheriff is abusing the people's trust?

No: Not only will Wright be shut out of the sheriff's office, but others who trusted Wright to espouse their cause will regard him with suspicion. He will have lost the value that his readership depends on to get accurate police stories.

Wright had an alternative. He decided he should take his problem to his editor. The metropolitan editor was responsible for gathering and editing for publication all the news that originated in the city and suburbs. She assigned stories to reporters and judged the importance of news events. She recognized the importance of the story about the employee contributions. The sheriff was generally thought to be a reformer and had run for office on a platform of taking politics out of government. The local election was approaching so the editor knew that she would have to be careful in handling the story because it could be a fabrication by the sheriff's political opponents. She therefore assigned her best investigative reporter, Charles R. Miller, to do the story. Wright was relieved that he could go back to his beat, knowing he had done his duty.

Wright wanted to set up a meeting between Miller and the tipsters who had brought him the story, but they were reluctant to deal with someone they did not know for fear that he would identify them in his stories. But Miller was an experienced reporter who could put a source at ease. "Tell them I don't even need to know their names. We can deal anonymously on the phone. Then, if I was forced to testify about my sources, I could truthfully say that I did not know." The two sources were impressed. All Miller wanted from them was their guidance. He would prove the story with public documents, Miller explained, and it would not be known that he had an inside source.

Is it unfair to pursue a story about a candidate running for public office if it could swing the election?

Yes: The newspaper should not involve itself in political races. Most of the stories leaked to reporters during campaigns are exaggerations or flat-out untruths designed to break in the media close to the day of balloting so that an opponent does not have time to make a proper rebuttal. Even if the story is true, if the newspaper prints it and swings the election, the winning candidate might be worse for the job than the candidate the newspaper exposed.

No: The public needs to know every bit of information about a candidate in order to make an informed choice. The newspaper could write of corruption by the other candidate as well, and as long as it does not use an investigative story to twist the facts or withhold derogatory information about either candidate it is doing a proper job that the readers expect.

Miller had not made an idle promise to the anonymous sources. He knew that he could prove the story with public documents. The story could be pulled together with two important documents: the sheriff's campaign disclosure form and the office payroll.

The campaign reports were open for all to see upon request at the county clerk's office. They had to be filed every six months. They contained the names of donors, the amounts of their contributions and the dates of the contributions. They also showed the amounts spent on the campaign and to whom they were paid. In addition, a balance of money coming in and money going out was shown. Every candidate had to file one such report. Miller had no trouble getting it immediately.

The sheriff had a large staff. Not only did the sheriff's department provide a trained police department, the duties of the department included taking care of the county buildings by providing janitors and yard workers. The sheriff had teams to serve court papers and execute evictions. The sheriff ran the jail. The office payroll under state law was obviously in the public record. But the sheriff would not release it, citing a provision in the state statute that said that information could be withheld if it endangered the life of a person. The sheriff said that the lives of all sheriff's employees would be put in danger if they were identified. The idea was laughable, but the mirth subsided when the state attorney general confirmed to Miller that the sheriff had the right to use discretion to determine who was or was not in danger. In the sheriff's opinion, even office clerks and administrators would be in mortal jeopardy if their names were published.

Miller knew the law. He believed the sheriff was misbehaving and stretching a well-intended law to cover up corrupt practices. Miller knew that his recourse was the courts, so he contacted the newspaper's in-house attorney and asked for help. The newspaper's attorney was sympathetic and agreed that the sheriff was out of line, but she urged Miller to not be too hasty about filing a lawsuit. Litigation is costly and justice is often slow. Even a swift court order could be appealed. By the time the newspaper could muster its legal staff, the election would be over.

Should a legal route be pursued, even if this means missing the story before the election?

Yes: The reporter would eventually get the story and could use the court decision as an example for others who might try to circumvent the law as did the sheriff.

No: Miller has an obligation to his readers to go ahead with the story even if he has to rely only on the campaign report and anonymous sources.

Miller pursued the story without the payroll documents. He found that the top managers in the department had their names on the doors of their offices, and some had parking spaces reserved with signs that displayed their names. Police officers signed their names on traffic tickets they issued, and they were listed as witnesses on court agendas. While talking to his unidentified sources, Miller learned that when they were first sworn in as deputies they had to take an oath at the county clerk's office. Miller made a quick trip to the clerk's office and found the list of new officers in a log kept by the clerk under mandate of the law. The names of the new auxiliary officers and the dates of their swearing in appeared on the sheets, recorded officially with their signatures. The list showed that 41 new badges were listed for the auxiliary police, and the campaign reports showed without exception that during the month their hiring took place each had paid $2,500. The records showed that the sheriff received a $102,500 windfall for the campaign!

Ready to write the story?

Yes: There is no disputing the facts that Miller has obtained from public records. They speak for themselves. The election is days away. He should write and the newspaper should publish the story immediately.

No: Documents are the mainstay of investigative reporters, but they do not tell the full story. Miller will have to move quickly, but he will want to contact as many of the auxiliary police officers as possible to get their reaction. He must also talk to the sheriff and allow a fair chance to reply.

Miller knows that readers of his newspaper, *The Middleton Daily News*, expect balanced reporting. In investigative stories, the newspaper will drive home a point with a strong argument but always give the target of the investigation a fair chance to reply. A fair chance means a simultaneous rebuttal in the same story that makes or implies the allegations, not in a next-day story. Although persons explaining or denying actions attributed to them may not always receive equal space in the story, reporters and editors are expected to give them enough space for their best arguments. An ambush interview in which the subject is approached on the street and surprised with questions is seldom productive. An ideal situation is when the reporter and the target of the investigation can sit down together and go over all the facts the reporter is planning to write. Such a meeting avoids mistakes that the reporter may have made. The reporter may believe the sheriff's brother-in-law is on the county payroll, for example, when it is a different person with the same name. Experienced investigative reporters know that can happen.

The sheriff did not agree to such an interview and instead issued a statement through the department's public relations spokesperson that there had been no wrongdoing, all campaign contributions were voluntary and the auxiliary police were an asset to the community. Miller had failed to show that the money was extorted, but showing that each contributor paid the same amount cast question on the sheriff's version. The sheriff's refusal to release the office payroll was noted in the story and caused such an outcry on the day before the election that the sheriff finally yielded to public pressure and allowed its release. By then, other media were on the story, and Miller and other reporters started running down leads from the payroll. They found a unit of elevator operators although the elevators were automatic. The so-called elevator operators were doing political work. Office staff in high-level law enforcement positions included relatives of the sheriff with no experience in law enforcement. The news undermined the candidacy of the sheriff, and the voters voted in a new sheriff.

Case Memorandum

- A reporter can break an investigative story and protect beat sources by turning it over to an investigative reporter.
- Reporters can protect the identity of tipsters by not knowing their names if the information is confirmed elsewhere.

- Campaign contributions and government payrolls are public records.
- If a public record is withheld, other ways can often be found to get the information without suing.
- A reporter must always seek an interview with the target of an investigation.

Choosing a Subject for an Investigative Report

Some story ideas might seems promising at the beginning, but after closer examination they could be found wanting. A successful investigative reporter learns to spot good stories, but there are guidelines that can help.

Exercise, Part 1: Choosing a Story

Consider the decision facing the producer of the news on a local TV station. The ratings period is coming up, and the newscasts need an investigative story that will draw viewers. An exciting investigative story will reflect well in the ratings. Here are the choices that the producer is considering. Choose the best story idea.

TABLE 1.1   Ideas to Examine

NO.	STORY IDEA	ANGLE OR FOCUS
1	Lawyers soliciting clients in the courthouse hallway	It is a violation of attorney ethics for lawyers to approach people and suggest they hire them, but in the county courthouse it is openly practiced.
2	Food inspectors skipping inspections	A source complains that food inspectors are so overloaded with work that they often have to miss a few stops and mark them down as okay.
3	High cost of shoes	Why are shoes so expensive?
4	Allegations of embezzlement from a union pension fund	The union is the largest in the broadcast coverage area.
5	Unsafe delivery trucks at a local dairy company	Company drivers have told of mechanical problems that could be safety hazards.

Story 1. Solicitation by lawyers. If you chose this idea, you would have a story for sure. Observation could be followed with camera shots on public property, persons solicited in the hallways would agree to interviews, documents could be found in court records to show which of those lawyers got the most business. The state licensing board would have to at least order an inquiry, generating many follow-up stories. But let us reconsider. What real harm are the lawyers causing? Are the viewers going to be outraged? Are the lawyers perhaps breaking a rule within the legal profession—a rule that protects lawyers from having their clients stolen—that shows no element of consumer abuse? We could make a lot of noise with this one, but the viewers will only yawn. Try a better story before your competition beats you to it.

Story 2. Food inspections. You may be on to something here. Food is inspected to protect the public from food poisoning and the spread of disease. Skipping an inspection is like asking a person to step off the curb into the street without looking and hope there is no traffic. The culprits may not be the inspectors but the system that is not working. A viewer will want to watch the broadcast after hearing during the day: "Tonight at ten on Channel One, Shocking revelations! Is your restaurant food safe?" We can follow food inspectors; get their reports, which are public records; and go into restaurants and see violations ourselves. But what if the inspectors are not skipping the inspections? We are still in good shape because from our observation and the inspection reports we will have a report on sanitation in restaurants. We will have to drop the shocking part, but viewers will want to know which restaurants are cited the most. Now go back and look at the other choices and see whether you agree this is best.

Story 3. Shoes. We have a subject here that affects just about everyone. Shoes can be expensive. But wait a minute. We already know that, so what's the story? Maybe the shoes are manufactured by child labor in a Southeast Asian country. Okay, but how is the local TV station going to have the time, knowledge and money to find such a place? The sad truth is that substandard working conditions make shoes cheaper. Shoes may be expensive, but the prices are subject to a competitive market and consumers have a wide range of choices. We have no allegations of price fixing, hidden cost or misrepresentation. The price of shoes is not among consumers' major concerns; it is not the mortgage or heating bill. There would not be a follow-up story and little would be accomplished by a report on the price of shoes. Look for something that is a step or two above this one.

Story 4. Union embezzlement. Embezzlement from the union pension fund is a serious criminal matter. Such an investigation is probably beyond the scope of subject matter able to be investigated. Although no one limits what a reporter can investigate, a criminal financial investigation is best accomplished by government investigative agencies and the courts. If those government agencies fail to act, however, journalists can be quick to expose their inaction. This story would be weak, though, because the reporter would have to refrain from making any criminal accusation about a person who is not convicted. Yes, there might be a story here, but it is not the type that will work for the local TV producer. It may be an insignificant amount of money, and the losses may be insured so the story would not directly affect the viewers, even union members. You can feel good about choosing this, but for practical purposes try another.

Story 5. Dairy truck. Can you imagine a truck driver at the local dairy standing before a local-news microphone for three nights straight, complaining about mushy brakes? This story has an important safety factor, but it has very limited impact. The threat to the public is obscure, and the story presents a temptation by the reporter to exaggerate. The only way such a story might be significant enough for the TV news is if the company has a horrendous accident record. The story could be done, but a reporter and a producer should be able to find something better. Go back to the choices and see whether you can upgrade your idea.

Exercise, Part 2: Examining the Food Inspection Story Idea

Which method is best to get the story? Select the best.

TABLE 1.2 **Deciding the Approach**

NO.	METHOD	WHY?
1	Surveillance: Get an undercover job as a food inspector	TV viewers like the excitement of undercover reporting.
2	Document research: File a Freedom of Information Act request for all inspection reports	Stories could highlight the worst violators.
3	Survey: Choose a random sample of restaurants and inspect them yourself	Photo possibilities would be abundant.
4	Interviews: Talk to employees and former employees	What stories they could tell!
5	Document research: Review published stories and court cases involving restaurants	Earlier stories and cases state the situation in black and white.

Method 1. Surveillance. Getting an undercover job is almost always unproductive. Many news organizations consider this method unethical, and in the story suggested here it would be illegal to falsify one's background to get a government job. Food inspectors have special training, and if the reporter was not trained, disastrous consequences would be possible. What if, out of ignorance, the reporter-inspector allowed utensils to be cleaned at a lesser degree of heat than is sanitary and scores of restaurant patrons got sick? What if an undercover reporter-ambulance attendant had no training and a patient died? If the reporter wanted a job in the kitchen of a restaurant, the idea might be viewed differently, but that limits the story to only a few restaurants. Better to choose another method of getting the story.

Method 2. Document research. Describing inspection reports from restaurants will make a quick story, but it will not be investigative reporting. It will report on someone else's investigation. How can we be sure others' reports are correct? Investigative reporters are supposed to check on the work of government agencies, not blindly support them. Also, it is possible that violations described in the reports have been corrected or that the ownership of the restaurant has been changed. It is a good idea to get the reports, but a proper story will take more work. Try another approach.

Method 3. Survey. If the sample is truly at random and manageable, this may a productive approach. It might call for a computer program to create a random sample, but simply drawing names of 40 restaurants out of a hat that contains the names of 500 would serve as well. Inspection reports on the 40 should be a true sample, and the reports could be bolstered by tours of the restaurants to see whether they have corrected the problems. However, this method will not show that food inspectors are skipping inspections. It will take more effort to find the story that needs to be told.

Method 4. Interview. Former employees would be able to tell us colorful stories of poor sanitation in the restaurants where they worked, and they would not hesitate to go on camera with their stories. The question we are faced with is whether we want to turn over our investigation to them. Can they be trusted to refrain from exaggeration? They may have been fired and thus fit the mold of "disgruntled former employees." If we rely on this plan, we will have to be in a position to defend ourselves from criticism of unfairness. It would be proper to interview employees and former employees but only to support facts we have already learned elsewhere.

Method 5. Document research. Court case files may have allegations of injury from food poisoning. We do not want to omit that from our investigation, so it is wise to check them, pull the case files and find the persons alleging injury. That person may have a story that can be documented, but the reporter must keep in mind that the plaintiff's claim in a lawsuit is merely an allegation. It would be unfair to base an investigation on such claims alone. A suit would have to be settled with a clear admission that the defendant restaurant did wrong. Use of lawsuits will be examined in a future lesson.

Exercise Summary

Because there will probably not be one best method, we may find it best to use a combination of the ideas. We can get our random sample of inspection reports, follow up with undercover observation rather than employment, talk to former employees to make sure we have touched all the bases and look for court cases. We can organize this information on a sortable electronic spreadsheet that would show patterns of noncompliance and then pull up all the violations of a particular kind to show which restaurants had the most violations in several areas important to food safety. A reduced version of this spreadsheet could go online for public reference.

Chapter Recap

Does it matter whether a mayor has approved a secret contract with the city for his private business? If a charity announces it is raising funds for a certain cause and spends the money otherwise, who needs to know? What if child care centers have poorly trained workers and their buildings are unsafe? Investigative reporters write such stories. An investigation does not require that a law has been broken, only that the possibility of wrongdoing exists.

Class Assignments

1. Bring to the next class an example of an investigative story published recently. If you wish, you could tape the TV report of an investigation and play it. Be ready to discuss which elements make it an investigative story by asking these questions:

- Why is this story investigative compared with, for example, a story about an escapee from a county jail being apprehended by police officers?
- Does the investigative reporter give the target of the investigation a fair opportunity to state what happened from the target's point of view? Show exactly where in the story it was placed.
- Does the reporter or writer or producer point to a key document?
- Do graphics and pictures accompany the story? Do they aid the reader or viewer by providing more understanding or do they merely repeat the facts in the story?
- Who among the public will be most interested in this story? Will many people be affected by it? Who might get a copy and pass it around?
- Is there a follow-up to this story? Are many questions unanswered?
- Are the newspaper reports overwritten, with harsh headline words; are TV stories reported in inappropriate shrill or frantic tones?
- Can you determine where the reporter got the information for the story? Was it in following up on a breaking story, from a tipster or a project idea?

2. Bring to the next class a written one-paragraph original idea for an investigative story. Make sure the proposal meets the requirements: that it is about something someone has made an effort to hide, that it is important to the public welfare and that it is to be the product of the reporter rather than the result of a government investigation. Also, the idea you conceive should be reasonable within the constraints of time and space. It should be neither too large nor too small. You will not want to suggest a story as big as the causes of drug addiction or as small as how somebody conned you into buying an ugly Christmas tree. Be prepared to defend your idea.

C h a p t e r   2

How to Investigate and Pitch a Story

INVESTIGATIVE REPORTERS DUFF WILSON AND DAVID HEATH of *The Seattle Times* had an informant on the record, but they needed to document all that he had told them for a March 11-15, 2001, series of reports on the deaths of people who were tested with experimental drugs.[1]

Many participants in the study had not been told clearly of the real risks, Wilson said. People were also not told about possible financial conflicts of interest. *The Times* reported that three doctors carrying out the experiments held stock in the drug companies providing the drugs to be tested.

"The story had all three strong elements of financial conflicts, bad medicine and patients misinformed," he said.

Wilson and Heath started with a Freedom of Information Act request to both the federal and state governments for all paperwork involving the claims of the informant. These were documents that concerned the experiment protocol and a federal investigation. When the reporters received the records, the names of the patients were deleted because medical records are private. Wilson described the reporters' tasks:

"We had to piece together who these people were. It was hard to find them, since many died fifteen-twenty years ago. Through a lot of labor-intensive skip tracing, we found some of these people and explained what we were looking at, and next of kin would authorize release of their medical records. For instance, we knew one of them was named Becky Wright. She had maybe lived in Alabama, at some point. So, we looked up all the Wrights in Alabama until

23

we found somebody who knew of her or her husband. We used death certificates. We looked up databases and found who died of leukemia in Seattle during a certain time."

They skip traced the surviving spouses by following forwarding addresses provided to the U.S. Postal Service, used people-finding searches on the Internet, and interviewed the relatives who could be found.

The reporters examined some 10,000 pages of documents from federal, state and medical sources and interviewed dozens of people, including medical experts, patients and their families.

When the stories ran, Mike Fancher, the executive editor of *The Seattle Times*, wrote: "We hope our stories help inform the policy discussions around how clinical trials are conducted, and how patients are protected from possible conflicts between medical and financial interests."

The Seattle Times investigation illustrates the importance of the tool most closely associated with investigative reporters: the document. In this chapter, you'll learn about different types of documents, how to find such documents and how to use them to investigate. All this together will then lead to how to promote and pitch a story to your editor.

Using Documents

A document is information that is preserved. The information may or may not be preserved on paper. If it is recorded on electronic tape or disk or stored in a computer, it is considered a document under the definitions of most state laws that provide public access to government records. When the information is on record, we use in this text the label "document." With the overall use of public and private records and published accounts, we say that we are going to "document" our facts to prove our argument.

The material that sustains the document does not matter. The document could be written in stone—like a tombstone or the cornerstone of a building. It could be a dental chart or a flag. The contents are the document. They relate happenings. Photographs store and convey information but are treated separately from documents in journalism.

Documents include more than public records. They also include private documents and published accounts. Laws address the availability of public records. Documents that are private include medical records, contracts between private persons or businesses, personal letters and bank statements. A journalist may publish such private information only with the permission of the owner.

Published papers contain information that has been revealed to the public but is owned by private persons who hold a copyright. They include

TABLE 2.1 Selected Documents

PUBLISHED INFORMATION	PUBLIC RECORDS		PRIVATE PAPERS
	OPERATIONAL	DISCLOSURE	
Biographies	Minutes of meetings	Licenses	Personal letters
Trade magazines	Budgets	Lawsuits	Bank statements
News releases	Contracts	Inspection reports	School papers
Scientific articles	Payrolls	Political contributions	Medical records
	Elections	Corporate filings with the Securities and Exchange Commission	

nonfiction books such as biographies, corporation news releases, and advertising and scientific papers. Information can be used when attributed under copyright rules.

Public records are owned by the public and laws define which of them is available to be viewed and reproduced and under what circumstances. They are divided here into two groups for easier study (see Table 2.1).

Disclosure Documents

People come to federal, state and municipal governments with requests. They may want to record the ownership of property, open a bar, become a medical practitioner, settle a dispute with a neighbor or license a dog. Governments accommodate citizens in these and other ways. In exchange, citizens give up some of their privacy when they deal with governments. In these examples, they are required to complete forms with specific information about the property and the owners in land transactions, affirm that they do not have felony convictions in liquor license applications, show their medical training to get a medical license, go to court and state allegations against a neighbor under oath, and declare ownership of an animal in the municipal clerk's office.

The same laws that provide these services also may mandate that the public office that administers the laws make them available to the public under certain conditions. Well versed in those laws, the investigative reporter knows what can be retrieved immediately and from which office. The county clerk and the state secretary of state carry much of the responsibility for keeping and providing public disclosure records, but the clerk of the courts, the election commission, the recorder of deeds and the county assessor share that load. They often employ the Internet to deliver the records. Federal agencies like the Federal Election Commission and the Securities and Exchange Commission require the disclosing party to file electronically so they can place the reports directly online.

Operational Documents

Cities, counties, states, the federal government and taxing districts that run the schools operate very much like private businesses. They have employees and contracts, they pay bills and they buy and sell property. They deliver such services as garbage pickup, street repair and police and fire protection. As stockholders elect officers to run their businesses, the public elects the officials responsible for conducting government business. Private businesses gain income by selling products and services to people, and governments get money by taxing the people they serve. All of this public business generates documents—budgets, annual reports of expenditures, payrolls, election returns, bidding processes for contracts, minutes of official meetings. These are operational rather than disclosure documents because they detail the inner workings of the government rather than regulate private business.

The public is provided access to these documents through state and federal laws. There are some limitations, but if the activity involves the expenditure of public money, records of it are almost always available. Operational records of each special local governmental unit—from the mosquito abatement district to the regional transportation authority—are in the trust of a clerk who records the minutes of meetings and a treasurer who keeps a tally of expenditures. Legislated rules mandate that records be provided to the public during business hours in their offices. Also, much of the information from public records is placed by the administering agencies onto the Internet, where it is accessible to the fingertips of the reporter through a computer terminal at any time of the day or night on any day of the week. If the agency does not put information on the Internet, the newspaper may get an electronic copy or printout of a database from an agency, keep it in the newsroom and update it from time to time so that it can be accessible during weekends. One example of this kind of document is the state payroll.

Document Review

Review each of the following documents. Is it a disclosure document or operational document? (A discussion of the classification of each document follows this numbered list.)

1. Annual financial report of school district
2. Campaign contributions report
3. Public payroll
4. Economic disclosure statement of elected official
5. Building inspector report
6. Divorce case file
7. State legislator's voting record
8. Minutes of the school board meeting
9. Budget of school district

1. Operational document. Accounting for the expenditure of tax money (in this case, school district finances) is a responsibility of officials in their operation of the schools. This information is usually required to be published and therefore would not require a request under a Freedom of Information Act (FOIA).

2. Disclosure document. A political campaign is not a part of running the government. It has to be kept separate, but the candidates must disclose the source of the contributions received and show how the money was spent. Local candidates file with the county clerk, statewide candidates with the state board of elections and presidential and congressional candidates with the Federal Election Commission. Local, state and federal laws allow the public immediate access to this information. No FOIA request is needed.

3. Operational document. To operate government offices and conduct projects, people have to be hired and compensated with tax money. A list of employees and how much they are paid may require an FOIA request, or state statutes may establish that they are open records available without an FOIA request. Reporters get payroll records from the offices of the financial controllers for the agencies of their interest.

4. Disclosure document. Laws require some public officials to file financial disclosure statements, showing that their own private holdings have not benefited from their actions in public office. The laws are separate from the FOIA and may impose severe penalties for fraudulent reports. These statements of economic disclosure are found in the administrative offices of the government agency where the official is employed.

5. Disclosure document. The owner of property where the public is invited or the owner of a large number of multiple residences must disclose to the government that the premises are in compliance with safety rules.

Building-inspector reports are easily attained by reporters, and no FOIA application should be needed.

6. Disclosure document. Divorce cases seem quite personal, but they are court cases nonetheless. No FOIA request is needed to request divorce court proceedings or any other records that have been filed in open court.

7. Operational document. Is the legislator voting for the issues that the legislator claims to support? State legislators' voting records are public records, and no FOIA is needed to request these documents. They are usually published by the clerks of the legislatures. Voting records of the local member of Congress are published by the Office of the Clerk of the House of Representatives and the Secretary of the Senate.

8. Operational document. Minutes of school board meetings are public records. A reporter may want to check on how the large portion of the local tax dollar budgeted to run the schools is spent, and open-meeting laws provide access. Therefore no FOIA action is needed to request the minutes. Records are maintained by the school district clerk and often can be found online at the Web site maintained by the local school board.

9. Operational document. Again, the budget of the school district is open for inspection. This should not be confused with the annual report. The budget states how the schools plan to spend the money, and the annual report reveals how the money was actually spent. Is the budget being followed or being ignored quietly? No FOIA is needed to get this information.

Gaining Access to Public Documents

Every state and the federal government follow specific laws about which documents are available and when they can be seen. The broadest law is the Freedom of Information Act. This federal law and similar state laws require that a government office make its operational documents open to the public. Some of the operational documents, like minutes of meetings and budgets, are readily available without a FOIA request, but the others may require a letter to the agency in possession of the documents.

It is important to remember that federal and state FOIAs were created to give the public access to the government's operational records, not to disclosure documents, which are covered by other specific laws. A reporter should not be required to adhere to the rules of a FOIA to get, for example, a report of lobbyist activities when there is a state law requiring it to be on file. Campaign contributions are deemed public by election laws, court records by the laws of administration of the judicial branch of government, state license disciplinary hearing records by another state law. Even some operational records are not covered by the state FOIAs because they are openly available. Reporters gain access to minutes of board meetings because of open-meeting legislation, and they can get the records of state lawmakers because of legislative rules.

Why have two levels of FOIAs? Could a reporter use the federal FOIA to demand public records from state and local offices? No, that is not the way the law reads. The federal FOIA has power only over the records of the executive branch of the federal government. For further information about the federal Freedom of Information Act, see excerpts in Appendix 1.

A citizen must use the state act to get local records. If a specific local FOIA is challenged, the federal courts may eventually hear the case after it has been heard first by many lower-level courts. Thus, it is the federal courts and their interpretation of a state's local laws, not the federal FOIA, that can determine the fate of a local FOIA request.

The state FOIA, for example, prevailed under a 2004 Michigan Court of Appeals decision that upheld a lower court ruling that the sheriff's department had to release records of an internal affairs investigation.[2] The ruling was in response to a rather unpleasant event, to express it as politely as possible. In May 2002, Grand Rapids police netted two police officers among 18 men caught in a solicitation-for-prostitution, undercover sting. Sixteen of the men were arrested and charged, and they spent the night in jail. The other two, a county sheriff's deputy and a state trooper, were released without charges.

A call came to the news desk of the *Grand Rapids Press*, tipping the paper about the incident. Reporters were able to get the story from the records of the Grand Rapids police, but their source told them that the two officers had also had previous contacts with prostitutes. The reporters made a request under the FOIA for internal investigation records, but their request was denied by the sheriff, who cited two FOIA exemptions: invasion of privacy of an individual's personal life and personnel records of an officer. The appellate judges decided the news story was not an insignificant oddity-in-the-news item because it addressed the question of whether law enforcement officers were involving themselves with criminals.

The court determined that the disclosure was in line with "the state's policy of providing full and complete information regarding the affairs of government" and opened the records.

A FOIA request should be put in writing either by filling out a form at the government agency in possession of the records requested or by writing a letter. An FOIA letter must be simple and direct, and it should

- provide enough information so that the government information officer is mandated to provide certain documents without further explanation,
- be narrow enough and not so demanding that it would cause burdensome work that would interfere with the daily duties of the government office and
- state specifically that the request is provided for under the FOIA.

Note that an FOIA letter need never plead the case or explain its purpose.

Good and bad sample FOIA letters are shown in Figures 2.1 through 2.3.

Searching Databases for Previous Stories

Investigative reporters check past articles on everyone they plan to write about. The reporter needs to know whether the information has already been reported because it would be a waste of time to go over the same ground twice. The reporter also may get leads for the investigation. If the person of interest has been sued in an unrelated matter, for example, the reporter will get the court case and attempt to talk to the other parties in the suit.

Reporters still refer to this practice as "pulling the clips" when they search the newspaper database archives. Before the 1980s, librarians at a newspaper would clip out stories from the previous day's paper, circle all the proper names and stick them in small envelopes with the key word on it. Thus, an envelope called "Middleman" would contain all the mentions in the newspaper of anyone named Middleman for maybe the preceding 50 years. The reporter would then sort through the clippings and find the person named Middleman whom he was researching.

Today only the delivery system has changed. Newspapers maintain archives online. Daily stories are stashed in electronic envelopes to be pulled out. The reporter can search by key names or terms and can pull up all related articles. You can easily look for the person whom you are researching.

A freelance writer or student who does not have access to newspaper clips or Internet newspaper archives is able to get the same information from major newspapers at a public library. Most libraries have indexes of back issues of *The New York Times* bound in annual volumes that list names of persons and the subject matter presented in the year's articles. Articles of interest can then be pulled up from files of microfilm on the library shelves. Larger libraries and campus libraries have other major newspapers such as the *Washington Post, Chicago Tribune* and *Los Angeles Times,*

Figure 2.1 Freedom of Information Act, sample request letter 1

Letter 1

> This request is sure to be rejected; no appeal would overturn the rejection because of the voluminous records requested in a short period of time.

Information Officer
Bureau of Sewers
Garfield Metropolitan Sanitary District
Garfield City Hall
Garfield City, Oregon

Attention: Mr. Vogel

I am requesting access to all records of the Bureau of Sewers for the previous five years. It is your responsibility to provide these documents and to have them copied for me and available 10 days from this date, at 1 p.m. in your office.

This information is for a very important story for The Garfield Record-Citizen, and the FOIA law requires that you give them to me. Please respond as requested.

Lloyd Smithson
Reporter
The Garfield Record-Citizen

> The writer implies that he is to be treated differently under the law because he is a reporter.

> Setting the time and place is, in addition to being rude, unreasonable and demanding. The reporter is being adversarial, and he misquotes the law.

Figure 2.2 Freedom of Information Act, sample request letter 2

The letter does not state it is a FOIA request and is not directed to any individual. It goes to "City Hall" although the other letters show the project was an operation of a separate government unit, a sanitary district. There is no telephone number for easy contact with the reporter, but chances are he will not be hearing from the recipient, and his competitor will get the story.

Letter 2

To Whom It May Concern
Garfield City Hall

I am a reporter for the Daily Post, and I am planning a story about the extra pay-ments that were made to the contractor who did the work on the Kennedy Avenue sewer extension. This cost overrun is believed to be significant, and it is a matter of seri-ous concern to taxpayers.

Please do everything you can to get the correct documents and deliver them to me at the Post. If you are not permitted by law to do this, you could remain anonymous and meet me at the central filtration plant near the main flushing drain at midnight Sunday. As a responsible journalist, I am sworn to keep confidential my sources.

Most sincerely,

The reporter tips off the subject of his investigation.

Elliot Cramer
Reporter
Garfield Daily Post

It is unprofessional to suggest a public official should steal a document.

Figure 2.3 Freedom of Information Act, sample request letter 3

Letter 3

This is a request under the state Freedom
of Information Act

> The requestor cited the law and directed the request to the responsible person.

Mr. Arthur Vogel
Information Officer
Bureau of Sewers
Garfield Metropolitan Sanitary District
Garfield City, Oregon

Dear Mr. Vogel:

I am requesting access to all records
involved in the construction of the Kennedy
Avenue extension of the main sewer line
completed in 2005. Although this request is
not limited to the following documents,
I would like to see and copy: bid specifications, bids received, contracts, work
orders, work sheets, payments, expense
vouchers, correspondence and interdepartmental memos involving the project.

Please let me know when I may view these
documents and whether there is more information I need to provide.

> The requesting reporter makes a reasonable request in a reasonable tone and without stating why the documents are wanted.

Yours truly,
Roland Richards
Reporter
The Garfield Daily Times
(555) 555-5555
RLRich@GDTimes.com

> Request is specific and workable.

accompanied by indexes. Local libraries often have archives of smaller local newspapers, too. The Library of Congress in Washington, D.C., has hundreds of newspaper files and indexes.

Case Study

Mayor Mixes Public and Private Business*

Lori Benton, a reporter for the *Buchanan Record-Journal* sometimes went on what she called "forays" or visits to public agencies whenever she had time in her busy schedule. She might stop at the state office building, the county courthouse, the federal building and city hall. Her purpose was not to say hello but to glean as much information as she could from public files. She would especially be on the alert for recent filings of civil lawsuits, campaign disclosure reports and economic disclosure statements. In such public documents she had found many a surprising story, stories that had been overlooked by other reporters because they were able to cover only the big lawsuits and give only superficial attention to documents such as the voluminous campaign reports. Economic disclosure statements were usually checked only if a question came up about a public official. These documents were available on request at counters in the clerk's office or by using public access computer terminals to search databases of documents such as land records and court cases.

Once when she was checking the court cases, Benton found the pending divorce case of the city purchasing agent. It had been reported that this official was under federal investigation for accepting payoffs. The purchasing agent's estranged wife wanted to divide the marital assets, and she listed $1 million in cash in a bank deposit box. The *Record-Journal* ran the story and was able to name the bank and even the box number to show readers that the newspaper was not speculating. This story was also news to the federal investigators, who seized the contents of the box after they read the newspaper.

Probate court cases had also turned up stories for Benton. When the brother of the highway commissioner died, his probate court case

*The cases are based on real investigative stories, but the names and places have been changed to protect reporters, their sources and the secrets they have. Some are actual stories told in a step-by-step reconstruction and others are composites.

file, which listed all his possessions, showed he had been in a partnership with his brother in a hidden land trust that bought hundreds of acres of land at a proposed highway interchange.

When the *Record-Journal* published these stories, the paper did not always reveal its sources. The story might say, "it was learned," of the land holdings or the bank deposit box. That would send other media into a spin trying to find out the source. If the competitors were not able to confirm it and did not pirate the story, they had to write for attribution, "The *Record-Journal* reported. . . ."

Benton calls economic disclosure statements "ethics statements." She found that they generally revealed little. They had to be filled out each year by candidates for public office, elected officials and top-level managers. They contained a series of declarations about whether the public official had a conflict in different areas. But one line item was a little different: It required that the official list the addresses of any properties sold during the year in which the official realized a gain of more than $5,000. Benton noted that the mayor had listed two addresses in a nearby city. She then got the disclosure statement for the three previous years and found five more properties sold. All were outside the city of Buchanan, so it appeared to not be a conflict of interest for the mayor of Buchanan.

Is it fair and ethical for the Record-Journal *to withhold the source of information for a story when it is a public document?*

Yes: Nowhere in any journalism code of ethics is it stated that a news article has to state its origin. Reporters are supposed to protect their human sources, so why not their document sources? A competitor should not find it easy to steal a story from another.

No: The newspaper is not only withholding information from its competitors but from the public as well. The news belongs to everyone, and journalists have a duty to provide it to all; they should not be trying to embarrass their competitors with selfish scoops.

Benton was already in the county building, so she went to the assessor's office and found the property identification number (PIN) for two of the addresses. Then she checked the land sale database for those numbers in the office of the recorder of deeds across the hall. There she found a series of transactions involving a numerical land trust. The purchase of the properties coincided with the years of sales on the mayor's disclosure statement. All of the parcels were resold after about six months and showed inordinate profit. Could someone be bribing the mayor by selling him properties below the market price to be resold for as much as three times the purchase price?

Benton found the names of the sellers and saw they were individuals who appeared to have no connection with each other. In addition, each had owned the parcels of land for many years. Benton knew that looking at a real estate transaction on paper would not necessarily show whether it was a single family home, an office building or a vacant lot.

She took a drive to nearby St. Williams and viewed each of the addresses. They were single-family homes, well maintained, in clean and comfortable neighborhoods. They could not have been built in the previous year, so they must have been renovated. Benton could find nothing wrong with the mayor fixing up houses in another town.

What should the reporter do next? Confront the mayor?

Yes: The mayor may have a simple explanation about what the transactions mean. Why waste time barking up trees on this one? There seems to be nothing improper here. Anybody should be able to buy and sell real estate for profit.

No: There are many public records to be checked before going to the mayor. Pardon the expression, but Benton smells a rat here. Her gut feeling is that something is wrong and she should keep digging.

The next morning, Benton picked up the phone on the first ring. It was the friendly voice of Danielle Thomas, the mayor's public information spokesperson, who said: "Lori, I hear you pulled the mayor's disclosure statements." When Thomas had been a reporter at the *Record-Journal*, she was assigned to cover the mayor's first election campaign. When he won, she joined the city as a member of his staff at a much higher salary than she had received at the newspaper. Benton detected an immediate personality change: No longer was Thomas interested in disseminating news; instead she wanted to control it.

"Just routine, Danielle. You know that's what those ethics statements are there for."

"I can't recall anyone pulling an ethics statement for no reason when I was at the paper," Thomas rejoined.

"We are trying to do a better job."

"Well, you can tell me what it's about. I'll help you on the story."

"I will let you know if there is going to be a story," Benton promised.

If the mayor is going to be fixing up houses, he has to get a building permit, Benton surmised. Many cities have building permits archived in their Web sites. St. Williams, however, had not offered such a convenience. She drove back to St. Williams, stood in line in the city building department and got copies of the applications. Benton already knew that it is the application for the permit, not the permit that is issued to the applicant, that contains the most important information. The recent application forms showed that substantial rehab work was done on the houses after the mayor bought them.

Then Benton thought it might be worthwhile to get the permits for the mayor's own home, which she noticed had also undergone some renovation. She got in line at the Buchanan building department in city hall and filled out a slip with her name on it and waited to be called when the copies were ready. A few minutes after submitting the request, a man came out from a back office and asked for Benton. "I'm afraid I can't help you today. All information for the press has to come through the press information office," he said.

"I don't want any special information, only a copy of an application for a building permit, like other people in line here."

"It doesn't matter. I have my orders."

"The city code gives access to these records to everyone. Reporters are not excluded. Reporters are people."

"You'll have to talk to Danielle Thomas, and she is gone for the day."

Benton got Thomas on the phone the next morning. It was obvious she had alerted city hall employees to contact her if Benton made any requests.

"Of course you can have all the documents relating to the mayor's home. It was a misunderstanding. Don't go writing some editorial about it," Thomas said. "I have them for you in an envelope. Come over anytime and pick them up. I am sure you will find nothing amiss. I think we should talk about this and clear up any questions. You know how the opposition political party likes to start rumors."

"Thanks. I'll get back to you," Benton replied.

By this time, though, Benton didn't need to hurry to get the documents because she had asked a copy clerk to stand in line that morning on his way into work to pick up the same reports.

Benton studied the reports and found that Jerry Middleman was listed as the contractor for all the mayor's properties. She was not familiar with the name, so she pulled the clips of back issues of the *Record-Journal* from a database and found several recent clips. She found that Middleman was Buchanan's building commissioner. She knew it was the same person for sure when she saw that the address listed on the documents was city hall and the telephone number was the same as the building department. Then Benton saw that the electrical work was done by the chief of the electric bureau and the plumbing by the chief plumbing inspector. She saw from the real estate documents that the city attorney represented the mayor in the purchase and sale. It appeared that the mayor was using the free labor of city employees for his private enterprises.

Benton started contacting the city officials who had done the work, and none but the city attorney would say anything. They all referred her to Thomas. The attorney said he was not paid for the legal work but that he had done it willingly to help the mayor. The investigation was stalled. She suspected that Thomas might have reached the workers ahead of her and told them what to say.

An interview with the mayor was next on Benton's schedule, but he would speak only through Thomas and he asked for questions to be submitted in writing.

Is there enough information to go to the mayor for an explanation?

Yes: She has all she is going to get. She may not have discovered an indictable crime committed by the mayor, but he has made an effort to hide his transactions; also, a person in his office should not be secretive. Although all the questions have not been answered, it still is an interesting story.

No: The mayor has done nothing wrong, and any further pursuit of his private transactions is an obvious vendetta by Benton, who is jealous of Thomas because Thomas has a better-paying job than she does. The public disdains investigations that overreach.

Should questions be submitted in writing?

Yes: It is ideal for both sides to put the questions and answers in writing because each can take the proper time to structure them so there is no misunderstanding. The mayor will not be able to say he was misquoted.

No: Benton needs to be able to follow up with other questions when an answer is incomplete or brings out new lines of questioning to pursue. It would be too inviting for the mayor to evade the point of the question if he took time to write it. Also, Benton needs real, live, spoken quotes from the mayor to put in the newspaper, not a formal statement.

As a compromise of sort, Benton wrote a summary of all the information she had and sent it to the mayor with a request for an interview. That way she could say that she had given him a chance to respond and explain his actions. The mayor declined the interview, and Thomas issued a brief response stating that the mayor had always been interested in improving property in the area and did it as a hobby.

An investigator for the county prosecutor confided in Benton that he had looked into the transactions and could find no violations of state law. The *Record-Journal* ran the story, stressing the profit the mayor had made and the fact that the work was done by city employees. Readers responded with calls for the resignation of the mayor, but their interest waned and the mayor continued in office. Benton realized that this was just the first skirmish in a long-term battle with city hall.

Case Memorandum

- Government spokespersons can be helpful only to a degree.
- A FOIA letter must be carefully written.
- Many public offices have computer terminals to facilitate public access to their files.
- Documents can be quoted in the same way as people can be quoted.
- Courts have ruled that the public interest outweighs privacy.

Rubbing Two Documents Together

Investigative reporters use documents to check out the validity of allegations by tipsters and to research subject matter for long-term projects. But also they uncover important stories by exploring and matching documents. For instance, a reporter may examine the annual budget and the annual financial report of the city. The budget is a document drawn up after much discussion in public hearings and is a plan of how to spend the tax money. The annual report shows how the money was actually spent and is usually quietly accepted by the board or council and filed away. The investigative reporter will want answers to many questions.

Does the city spend the money the way it was budgeted? Did the money allocated for new police cars end up in the mayor's wife's beautification program, which is upgrading the mayor's own neighborhood?

In preparation for this book in 2007, we punched up the search words "city budget, council," and "financial report" on an advanced Internet search engine. We wanted to find out whether the idea of comparing the budget with the actual expenditures was easily done. This is one of the URLs that came up: http://www.provo.org/finance.rpt_main.html. It connected us with the budget for Provo, Utah.

The budget reflects a pleasant city with a population of 111,714 in 2005. The city offers recreation and culture, and Provo is the home of Brigham Young University. Scanning through the budget, we discover that the city has a municipal golf course that is expected to make a little money for the city treasury. At least, that is what the figures in the Provo proposed city budget (see Figure 2.4) show:

Revenues: $858,000
Expenditures: $848,454
Fund Balance: $9,546

Citizens might study the budget and believe that the golf course was paying its way, although with a small amount in relation to a $147 million budget. But the budget would tell them only what was projected. The annual report, published more than a year later, would deliver the sad truth. The golf course that year was a big loser (see Figure 2.5):

Revenues: $755,211
Expenditures: $1,085,625
Loss: $330,414

Payment records in the finance office would show details of the costs. The city had to bring the golf course up to par by sending it $116,476 that year and another $192,186 the next.

When money was transferred to a special fund like the one created for the golf course, it was shown in the budget for that fund as revenue, which can give a most favorable look to an unfavorable situation. An example in the Provo budget is the Arts Council. The numbers in the budget show revenues of $154,966 and expenditures of $162,000. That is not so bad. Arts centers are not expected to be revenue producers. But $132,966 in tax money has gone from taxpayer pockets to prop up the Arts Council, and it is listed with the revenue. Actually, the adjusted figures show that the Arts Council only has $28,224 income with which to pay out its $161,966.

Budget people apply the same formula to tax-supported operations as they do to income-producing corporations. The commonsense conclu-

Figure 2.4 Provo City Corporation, proposed budget, fiscal year 2004–2005

ATTACHMENT A
PROVO CITY CORPORATION PROPOSED BUDGET
FISCAL YEAR 2004 - 2005

FUND	BEGINNING FUND BALANCE	REVENUES	TRANSFERS IN	EXPENDITURES	TRANSFERS OUT	CONTRIBUTION TO (APPROPRIATION OF) FUND BALANCE	ENDING FUND BALANCE
ENTERPRISE FUNDS							
AIRPORT	120,413	268,600	0	268,109	491	0	120,413
ENERGY	16,266,982	48,744,039	203,642	43,130,027	6,254,805	(437,150)	15,829,832
GOLF COURSE	0	858,000	0	848,454	0	9,546	9,546
SANITATION	682,896	2,816,312	0	2,451,215	280,065	85,032	767,928
TELECOMMUNICATIONS	309,938	21,992,571	27,839	2,279,450	19,737,161	3,799	313,737
WASTEWATER	2,419,898	4,890,327	0	3,104,367	1,719,556	66,405	2,486,303
WATER	235,448	5,912,153	223,553	5,374,377	719,226	42,103	277,551
TOTAL	20,035,575	85,482,002	455,034	57,455,998	28,711,304	(230,266)	19,805,308

Source: Provo City Finance Department, http://www.provo.org/files/finance/purch/budget/fy05.pdf

sion—if the taxpayers have to pay it, then it is a loss—does not seem to matter to the numbers people. City financial people have only to overbudget for the departments in the general fund, declare that they have saved the taxpayers that money and then send it to another fund and call it revenue.

Another example is in bigger numbers. Provo runs the cable TV system as well as the golf course, water and electric utilities. The proposed budget shows expected revenues of $21,992,571 million for the cable system and expenditures of $2,279,450 (see Figure 2.4).

In reality and in real money, however, the annual report (called "Statement of Activities"; see Figure 2.5) shows only $770,780 of income (charges for services) and $3,310,102 in expenses.

Comparing the proposed budget with the annual report can reveal discrepancies like this one.

We did not find the Provo officials deliberately misleading. They followed a common practice, and they appear to have complied with Utah state law. Also, the daily newspaper did an admirable job of keeping up with the budget, but it showed no interest in checking back to scrutinize the actual expenditures.

Residents also got no hint from the proposed budget that they would be paying $12,403 for the cost of lunches for city officials in the year that ended on June 30, 2005. We found these items in the list of "previous expenditures" in the budget for the year ending June 30, 2007. Also absent

Figure 2.5 Provo City Corporation, statement of activities, fiscal year 2004–2005

PROVO CITY CORPORATION
Statement of Activities
For the fiscal year ended June 30, 2005

Functions/Programs	Expenses	Program Revenues — Charges for Services	Program Revenues — Operating Grants and Contributions	Program Revenues — Capital Grants and Contributions	Net (expense) Revenue and Changes in Net Assets — Primary Government — Governmental Activities	Net (expense) Revenue and Changes in Net Assets — Primary Government — Business-type Activities	Total
Governmental activities:							
General government	$12,812,803	$2,456,372	$2,500,721	$0	($7,855,710)	$0	($7,855,710)
Public safety	19,656,764	2,433,901	423,296	0	(16,799,567)	0	(16,799,567)
Public services	6,500,531	75	0	4,340,299	(2,160,157)	0	(2,160,157)
Community revitalization	5,088,706	439,530	6,372,957	0	1,723,781	0	1,723,781
Culture and recreation	9,495,980	1,377,716	168,526	0	(7,949,738)	0	(7,949,738)
Interest on long-term debt	1,504,963	0	0	0	(1,504,963)	0	(1,504,963)
Total govermental activities	55,059,747	6,707,594	9,465,500	4,340,299	(34,546,354)	0	(34,546,354)
Business-type activites:							
Golf course	1,085,625	755,211	0	0	0	(330,414)	(330,414)
Water	5,589,083	5,241,448	0	263,190	0	(84,445)	(84,445)
Sewer	4,217,370	4,686,423	0	249,779	0	718,832	718,832
Energy	41,452,688	44,661,470	0	102,149	0	3,310,931	3,310,931
Airport	1,010,936	152,908	0	1,372,016	0	513,988	513,988
Sanitation	2,655,833	2,889,022	0	0	0	233,189	233,189
Storm drain	1,442,114	1,667,645	0	0	0	225,531	225,531
Telecommunications	3,310,102	770,780	0	0	0	(2,539,322)	(2,539,322)
Total business-type activities	60,763,751	60,824,907	0	1,987,134	0	2,048,290	2,048,290
Total primary government	$115,823,498	$67,532,501	$9,465,500	$6,327,433	(34,546,354)	2,048,290	(32,498,064)

Source: Provo City Finance Department, http://www.provo.org/downloads/finance/cafr05final.pdf

from the proposed budget was $6,176 for "employee appreciation." Other items were also overspent. The city paid out $46,088 for books, subscriptions and membership, which was $4,588 more than budgeted. The Christmas decoration budget of $16,160 was overspent by $2,555, and the city paid $26,945 for a parade float that was budgeted for $22,442.

A parade float? Yes. In Utah municipalities participate in parades but few residents know that it is their money that is being paraded around. Some other expenses stretched the definition of city services. The city paid $3,000 for the Miss Provo contest, and $13,000 to support the a festival called Winterfest. Another $15,540 went for Christmas gifts for employees.

The Christmas gifts were $20 checks for each of more than 700 city employees and the amount has not changed for at least 20 years, according to Denise Roy, city accounting manager. The expenditures are listed under the category of "nondepartmental," which totals $675,713. Although she could not recall each expenditure, she said the funds were for unexpected needs. All of them are accounted for in vouchers that are available for public viewing, Roy said.

Getting Attribution

When a reporter locates a public document that is important to the story, the next step is to find both the persons who created it and those who are the subject of the documents; they can verify its contents and expand upon the information in the document. Often the writer is deceased or refuses an interview. The document then has to stand on its own.

Information from documents is attributed in much the same manner as information from interviews. Instead of writing, "Mayor Smith said in an interview with the *News*," the reporter writes "according to minutes of the city council meeting of March 21." Note the attributions in the following news story.

> West Eaglewood Mayor Clyde Homer and his wife, Floringa, are officers of the privately owned Triple Dip Construction Company, according to Secretary of State corporation records.
>
> Triple Dip got the bid to rebuild the village sewer system, and Homer voted to grant the contract, minutes of the city council meeting reveal.
>
> A public official is prohibited from voting on a contract in which he has a financial interest, the state conflict of interest law states.

Promoting a Story Idea

A successful reporter instinctively reacts to the mere suggestion of an important story and, although there are many stories and too little time, will want to chase it down by learning more. Editors know the limits of space and time and must choose the most important story ideas and advise the reporter on how to proceed. The reporter, then, is placed in a situation of having to make the equivalent of a sales pitch for the story idea to the editor by presenting an argument for its suitability, importance and practical execution.

This can sound crass. The idea of having to persuade the editor to run a story might seem unnecessary; the story should stand on its own strengths, one might argue. Even if it is a really important story, though, the reporter might not be skilled enough in communicating this to the editor, and the good story never sees print or broadcast.

It is no secret that print reporters have to know how to talk, and broadcast reporters have to know how to write. A print reporter spends the day talking on the phone, interviewing people, setting up interviews, chasing down documents and, finally, telling it all to editors. A broadcast reporter has to write down everything that will be said on the news because on-camera reporters do not ad lib the news. Thus, a reporter must be prepared to go to verbal battle, studying the merits of the story and presenting them in an organized manner. Three broad concerns—suitability, importance and practical execution—about a story must be met.

Suitability

Will the audience or readership find the story important enough to respond? Suitability refers to the interest in the subject matter by the readers or viewers. Is the audience for the story young or mature? If the story is about the threat to the sponge industry in Greece, will it have any impact in Denver? It may be important and interesting to some, but it is not the most suitable for a local publication.

Importance

A local college fraternity needs a new refrigerator and members are washing cars to raise money to purchase one. It may be closer to home than Greece, but it is a yawner on the importance scale. Importance generally refers in this usage to the number of people who are significantly affected. It does not matter to the reader or the viewer that money is being raised for and by a fraternity, and there is no original idea that makes it newsworthy.

43

Practical Execution

Let's say it is suggested that we determine the percentage of people in a metropolitan area who have been abused as children. It is of local importance, but can it be done? Practicality is merely determining whether the degree of difficulty has surpassed reasonable expectations that the proposed idea will be completed. To find the percentage of abused persons, we would have to get a response from everyone or, alternatively, make a large, at-random sample. Would people be honest about it? What some people see as abuse, others would not. It would not be practical within the limitations of time.

Winning Support for an Idea

Having passed the hurdles and being convinced that the story is suitable for the audience, important and can be done in the parameters of a newspaper story or TV feature, the reporter sets out to sell the idea. One proven method is to outline the story proposal in brief form, using a set format. For example, the story idea outlined below came about because of several instances in which private security guards got in trouble on the job. This treatment of the subject is adapted from a 1985 CBS investigation in Chicago. Security guards had shot people, stolen from the places they were supposed to protect and neglected their jobs. A reporter could create this outline:

```
TO: Editor
FROM: Reporter

RE: Story Outline: Armed and Dangerous

Subject: Untrained security guards endanger public
safety.
Scope: We will research the qualifications of securi-
ty guards who are licensed to carry guns and show
instances of them attacking people and stealing from
their employers and yet continuing to work in sensi-
tive jobs because of a lack of state supervision. (In
this state, security guards are licensed as a profes-
sion, and we should be able to pull the license of a
serious violator.)
Need: Because of increased security fears, companies
are hiring more private security guards. People do not
```

realize that many of them have criminal felony records. We will show that people's lives are in danger because of the serious problem of lack of training and criminal intent.

Methods: This story can be documented by drawing together all the complaints to government agencies and contacting the complainants. We also can get an electronic list from the state of all licensed security guards, search for and pull out those in our metropolitan area and run those names through the criminal court case lists of defendants.

Sources: We will check the names of security companies in the Yellow Pages, make a list, and run the names through the county court clerk's index of civil suits. We expect to find many civil lawsuits involving the guards who are employees of these companies. We will contact attorneys for the plaintiffs and ask them to let us talk to their clients. They may have some information about the guards and companies. (In this state, discovery is public record only if it is entered into the court record.)

We will find national experts in the field of private security who can tell us what other states do to train and monitor security guards. We will contact spokespersons for those agencies in other states and get more details.

Presentation: This can be a three-part series, starting with the overview on Sunday of everything we found, which would include the names of the felons and the crimes they committed. The second-day story would be the lack of training. The third day would be gun incidents.

Follow-up: There will probably be a move for new legislation to require security guards to have state clearance to show employers they have no criminal history.

This format for a memorandum organizes the thinking about a particular story idea; it is used throughout this book with the case studies. It is possible that its use is the reason for the success of the fictional reporters. Editors will look at the memo and recognize the proposal represents an important story, much in need of being told and that—most of all—the reporter knows how to do it. How can they say no?

The idea behind the choice of words for the title of the investigation is to draw attention to the outline in a form the press and TV news have adopted. Each story should have a logo that will appear with the story in print or that frames what goes on the screen. It separates the story from the other news items and says it is special. By giving a name to the outline, the reporter shows that the idea has been well considered.

The subject section of the outline expands on the title and gives a straight and simple explanation of the story. It is said that if the story cannot be explained in fewer than eight words, it cannot be told. Here, we did it with six words. The editor reading this knows immediately what statement this story is going to make.

The scope section explains what the story is going to include and the limitations of the story: It is about the lack of regulation of security guards. It is not an essay about whether industry should hire security guards or whether guards should be able to carry guns.

The need section begins the argument for the story. It answers the question of why we should we do this story before that question is asked. It is not enough to say, "I don't know but it seemed like a good idea." There must be a need for this story, and in this outline, it is obvious that the answer is that public safety is jeopardized. Even if the need is obvious, it must be stated in strong persuasive language. Editors and publishers are pledged to respond to the public need and believe it is their calling to correct problems. If they did not, they would be in some other business.

The need section may also have some reference to the timeliness of this story. Any recent shooting or other tragic event involving a security guard should be pointed out. Statistics are always impressive. We have none in this example, but if the memorandum were about the safety of school buses, we might include some data about the number of deaths and injuries from school buses.

Methods describes the game plan. What is the best approach to this story? Is it a survey, a series of interviews or a documents story?

The big question is answered in the sources paragraphs, which should include an exhaustive list of all the documentation the reporter expects to find and an assessment of all of the leads that might come from those documents. This important section shows whether the reporter knows how to develop the story. At this point, the reporter takes a little latitude and speculates what might be found and to what it might lead.

The presentation section will explain how the story will be told. If it is for a newspaper, how many days will be needed and what will the subject of each day be? Usually the first day will have a report some call an "umbrella" story, which will summarize the entire investigation and then tell of the most shocking or meaningful example in the investigative argument. In the following days, the newspaper will cover different aspects and details of the story.

This story could be presented on TV, as was the similar 1985 CBS report, aired at a time when television attempted few investigations. The 1985 report was advanced in thoroughness and technique for its day and was a winner of a Peabody Award, a national honor for television similar to the Pulitzer Prize for newspapers.

In the presentation section, both print and broadcast reporters will suggest ideas for pictures and graphics.

The follow-up is an assessment of what realistically could happen upon successful completion of the presentation. No editor wants an investigative story that suddenly ends and is not heard from again. Will laws be introduced or amended, will officials announce crackdowns in enforcement, will wrongful operators cease their wrongful practices? What do we want to happen?

How Not to Do It

Chip Shotten was a reporter who winged it through his career by writing stories with overstated leads, heated prose and minimal substance. For the most part, the stories were cheap shots at lower-level government workers, facts were twisted and the officials were made to look foolish when given the opportunity to explain.

One day he got a tip that an alderman was having an improper relationship with an intern in his office, so Shotten demanded the expense account records of the alderman from the city controller. He hoped to show that the alderman used government funds to wine and dine the young lady.

"Who says I have to give you those records?" the controller said. He remembered a bad experience with Shotten in the past and wanted to give him a hard time.

"The Freedom of Information Act says you've got to turn over those records," Shotten replied.

"You mean this law states that I, Barry Parker, city controller of Buchanan, has to give you those records. Now where does it say that?"

"You know what I mean. It doesn't say that, specifically, but it requires that you turn over those records."

"What does it say? Tell me." A small group of Parker's staff overheard the conversation as it grew louder. "Have you got a copy?"

"I don't carry one around. Everybody knows what the Freedom of Information Act says."

"You don't! When was this law passed?"

"Congress passed this law many years ago and keeps updating it."

"Oh! The Congress of the United States decided how little Barry Parker in Buchanan should run his office? The Congress can only create federal laws. Their FOIA is for federal records." People began snickering and Shotten became flushed. "I don't have to give you copies of my records until you apply in the proper manner."

Shotten fled to the elevator, shouting, "You're wrong. You are not going to get away with this." As the elevator door closed he heard a ripple of laughter from the controller's office.

Of course, the controller was correct. The state had its own FOIA, but long before it was passed, financial records of the alderman's office were public through other state laws. After all, the alderman's office spent taxpayer money. Those records showed that the alderman had indeed spent tax money improperly by occupying a honeymoon suite with the intern at a ski resort in Idaho.

While Shotten stormed about, Lori Benton quietly obtained the necessary information immediately and beat him to the story.

Chapter Recap

In this chapter, we have seen that public documents are not in hiding. They are in the open, protected by law and almost asking to be put on a copy machine. Documents are the bricks in the wall that will support the mural that is the investigative story. It is seldom a pretty picture, but there is some beauty in its truth. The story must be well constructed to withstand the attacks of those who have reason to hide the truth. In the next chapter, we will study further about how to meet that challenge.

Class Assignments

1. Bring in a sample of an investigative report initiated by good document and report research. How did the reporter get results? Where and how did the reporter uncover the evidence?
2. Try a side-by-side analysis of building inspection reports and campaign reports to see whether violators who make political contributions later get approved.

3. See what comes up when we compare the budgets of several school districts. Are funds going to academic programs rather than activities considered less important? How are funds used?
4. Combine the campaign report of the governor with a list of state contractors; check whether the contractors make large contributions to the governor's political fund.

Notes

1. Duff Wilson and David Heath, "Uninformed Consent: What Patients at the 'Hutch' Weren't Told About the Experiments in Which They Died," *Seattle Times*, March 11-15, 2001. http://seattletimes.nwsource.com/uninformed_consent/.
2. Herald Company, Inc. d/b/a Grand Rapids Press, and Tribune Television Holdings, Inc., d/b/a WXMI-TV Fox 17 v. Kent County Sheriff's Department and Michigan State Police, Michigan Appellate Court, No. 243400; Kent Circuit Court LC No. 02-005767 CZ. http://courtofappeals.mijud.net/DOCUMENTS/OPINIONS/FINAL/COA/20040302_C243400_90_33O.243400.OPN.COA.PDF.

C h a p t e r   3

Investigating a Person, Place or Entity

DURING THE 1987 PULITZER PRIZE-WINNING investigation of the Chicago City Council by the *Chicago Tribune,* the reporters researched the financial situation of a young, newly elected council member both before and after he entered into government service.[1] One document anchored the financial investigation. It was his divorce court file. During his divorce proceedings, which occurred before he was elected, the council member settled for only a modest house and a nine-year-old used car. But before he had completed his first elected term, he appeared to be the epitome of entrepreneurial success. He shared ownership of real estate developments in partnership with developers who had business before the city council, and his law practice had risen from obscurity. A series of articles in the *Tribune* examined the many ways a council member could use public office for enrichment. The series of stories about the young council member was called "An Alderman Who Earned While He Learned."

Many important investigative stories are written about political issues and social problems. But as the story develops, a target of an investigation—a person, place or thing—may emerge. The person may be a private individual or a public official. The place may be, for example, a dangerous intersection. The thing could be a business entity such as a corporation. No subject has ever been off-limits to an investigative reporter. Investigative reporters have more range of choice than public prosecutors because subjects may include perceived wrongs that are not illegal.

Investigating a Private Person

The reasons to scrutinize a private person—one who has not sought public office or is not a government employee—are varied, but that person could have come into the public eye because of an appointment to an important position, a serious criminal or civil complaint or generally anything that might propel one into the news. Chances are the subject has left a trail of public records that can be followed without breaching privacy. In such a search for information, one item of interest leads to another, and the reporter can go with this flow. Usually, for a start, a search of people-finder features of computer services and of search engines like Google will turn up a few facts about the subject's activities and possibly a short biography if the person was appointed to a position or has made public appearances. Also, publications like the Martindale-Hubbell directory of attorneys or "Who's Who in America" might contain a biography of the subject.

In Carl Bernstein and Bob Woodward's book, "All the President's Men," about the Watergate investigation as well as in the movie based on the book, much is made of how the reporters learned that Everett Howard Hunt, whose name and phone number were found in the address book of one of the Watergate burglars, was a consultant for the White House. Woodward is shown making numerous phone calls to sources, including Deep Throat, to confirm the connection. His efforts were successful, but one published document shows that Hunt was not at all the highly secretive operative hidden in the White House, as he was portrayed in the book and movie. We found that he proudly listed himself in the 1972–1973 edition of "Who's Who in America 1972–73," as a consultant to the President, and gave his address as the White House.

But not all person searches are that easy. A more private person outside of government presents a more difficult challenge. The investigative reporter has means to chase down the facts. Each document chase may take a different direction. Knowledge of what is available leads the way, but also the reporter can walk on previously trod paths.

Name Trace

A search can start with as little as a name and perhaps where the subject of interest works. The first step is often a broad search of phone directories, driver's license databases and voter databases. To begin, a reporter might start with a computer search on www.whitepages.com, which lists phone subscribers and their addresses. But only people with listed phones will turn up here. If the state allows a search of driver's license information, one can pull up the names of everyone with the same name, get an address and date of birth for each and then eliminate those persons who cannot be the subject of the investigation. They are dropped from the list if they do not live in the area of the state where the subject of the investigation is known to work or are not within the age range the reporter knows the subjects to be.

Some states will not provide driver's license information, but the same information can be found from electronic poll sheets of registered voters from the election board in each of the counties on the list of named persons. Voting records will not reveal how a person voted, but they will show when and where that person voted; thus, they can be used to track residency. The voter registration will also provide the names of everyone else who votes from that same address. If a candidate for public office never voted in private life and is running for public office, it is a something a voter might like to know. A voting record will show in which primaries the registered voter cast a vote, and so it might call for a declaration of party preference. In private life was a candidate loyal to a party different from the party the candidate now claims to be representing?

Date-of-Birth Records

A researcher might try the county clerk's office to check birth records. Voter records or driver's license databases cannot tell in which state or county the subject was born, but one can guess. If successful, the searching reporter will learn the parents' names and can start running searches of databases on them. Some states consider birth records private. A reporter would then run the name through civil and criminal court dockets, which show an age and address. The reporter hopes by that time to be successful in zeroing in on the right person. If not, more public records can be used.

Property Records

Having an address will provide an opportunity to check property records in the office of the recorder of deeds at the county building. Mortgages and liens against property are filed there; also the name of a spouse might be on documents. By searching the records electronically from public access computer terminals in the county offices, the reporter might find other properties owned by the subject or spouse.

Licenses

Is this person a licensed professional: a medical doctor, a real estate broker, barber, exterminator, surveyor, appraiser, insurance agent or horse trainer?

These are only a few of the professions licensed by the states. State licensing agencies vary from state to state, and states may also license more than one professional group. In the medical field, for example, states not only license medical doctors but also pharmacists, psychologists, chiropractors, nurses and ambulance attendants. The professional conduct of lawyers and stock brokers is overseen by the states.

An investigative reporter will learn the profession of a person without many problems because professionals make their positions known in order to do business. Then the reporter will locate the state agency that licenses that profession and find information in its public file. A search of the main Web site of any state will provide a list of agencies to click on. Searches within that Web site with a description of a profession, such as "registered nurse," would lead the reporter to the agencies that can issue and revoke a license. Alternatively, the reporter could go to a search engine like Google. If interested in the license of a registered nurse in California, the reporter would type in the key words "California, state, licensing, nurses" and would be taken to the correct Web site.

If the subject is doing business as a professional who is presumably licensed but that person is found to be not licensed, the reporter has a story at the outset—all from the government source. But the real purpose of checking the state for the license is to gather information about the subject of the investigation. The reporter will want to find when the license was first issued, what the limitations of the license are, whether the license shows the university where the subject received the required degree, and whether any action was taken on complaints filed against the professional person. The reporter might also find an address that would help decide whether this growing file of information is a file about one person or several people with the same name.

Yearbooks

A university will confirm little more than the degree a student earned and the year of graduation, but the school library or the alumni office will have yearbooks. The yearbook of the subject's graduating class might have some interesting items about the student and most certainly will have a picture. Aha! There may be a familiar face. The reporter may now have the parents' names and may get a current address by running database searches. The current address may be where the subject lived during high school. We can approximate the year of graduation and get access to that yearbook. As a starting place for a biographer, a yearbook provides names of classmates who can be contacted for interviews.

Political Activity

The reporter can also find out whether the person is politically active by checking campaign contributors. They are searchable online by donor name. On federal forms, the contributor has to declare an address and profession.

Published Works

If the person is a prominent professional, the reporter will check for articles published by or about the subject of the search. Such information is available online in search engines and databases such as Google and LexisNexis. Even a not-so-prominent person may have been the subject of published reports.

Court Records

The reporter will check civil court records for lawsuits involving the name of the subject or the names of any businesses owned by the subject. Is the subject of the investigation single, married, divorced or remarried? Divorce records can be found in the county court clerk's office. They are lawsuits and are therefore public records. They are revealing when financial information is declared before dividing the property. It is possible that a judge may have sealed this part of the case upon the request of the parties to the divorce, but most people do not think to make such a request. Even when sealed, a reporter can request that a sealed court document be unsealed and hope to get lucky.

Filing a probate court case could be called "cashing in the chips" because a person's estate is tallied soon after death. The subject of the reporter's investigation might be deceased, but the subject is more likely to be a living person. If so, the parents' probate records filed in the county court clerk's office can be sought. They will provide information about relatives and inherited property.

A person with a criminal conviction may have a prison record that is public and kept by the state department of corrections, as the prison system is called in most states. Such records are likely to be online on the state corrections department Web site.

Tax cases and bankruptcies are filed in federal courts, and the dockets and filings are electronic and easily retrieved. A personal bankruptcy will list all the assets and debts of the person filing, and that information will give the reporter a handle on business associates of the bankrupt person. If the target of the investigation is involved in a corporation in bankruptcy, the file will list the business partners as well as persons or companies owed or owing money to the bankrupt corporation.

Death Records and Obituaries

In this chain of documents, the reporter may want to go online and electronically search the Social Security Administration's Death Master File for the parents' or grandparents' names. The names, locations and dates of death of persons who were recipients of Social Security payments are immediately available. With that information, a newspaper obituary can be located from the local newspaper archives, almost certainly online, and that information can be added to what is found in the probate case. Not all estates go to probate, but few deaths will be without obituaries. The obit will contain the names and locations of brothers and sisters and biographical information about the deceased.

Business Holdings

The state secretary of state supervises a corporation division that requires every corporation doing business in the state to file an annual report of officers. In many states, the officers' names can be inserted into a database in the office or online, and the reporter can learn immediately of any corporation in which the subject is an officer.

With this sweep of documents and interviews made possible through those documents, a reporter has some certainty of having identified the person of interest and that all relevant documents involve that person and not a "same name."

The story can go forward if the reporter interviews that person, tells the person about the information that has been gathered and then receives confirmation of the validity of the information. If this does not happen, the reporter will be reluctant to use the information. Subjects in the public arena, whether appointed or candidates for public office, generate a lot of documentation that is much easier to get.

Investigating a Public Official

Public officials leave voluminous public records. First of all, they leave the same documents as any private person before they run for office or are appointed to public office. Then they leave records of both private actions and government actions while in office.

Following the career of an elected public official starts with the candidate's first campaign for office.

Petitions

The candidate will file a petition to get on the ballot; this is a public record filed with the election board. It will show the names of supporters of the candidacy and offer some insight into the identity of associates' and campaign workers. It may answer the question, "Who is backing this guy?"

Campaign Documents

Campaign committees, lists of contributors and expenditures are found in the clerk's office, at the Federal Election Commission and at the equivalent state election offices. Campaign documents best indicate the scope of a candidate's backing from people who are serious enough as supporters to put their money on the line.

Financial Disclosure

Political candidates are not required to reveal their private Internal Revenue Service form 1040 filings. Often the public is confused about this because candidates will appear in public and offer their tax information. They are doing so to challenge their opponents to do the same, but not because it is required. Both President Bill Clinton and President George H. W. Bush revealed their tax information. Federal election rules, however, do require a financial disclosure filing by candidates. Ross Perot, a third-party presidential candidate in 1992 and 1996, had to disclose where he had invested his billions of dollars. It showed the flamboyant celebrity businessman to be a rather conservative investor who had the bulk of his investments in tax-free municipal bonds.

Official Documents

If the candidate is elected, the number of documents escalates. Now there will be a payroll for staff members, an expense account, and a voting record. Any letter or memo sent will be archived. In public meetings, utterances of every subject, word-by-word, might be recorded into the record. Public utterances are under the control of the official clerks who provide them in compliance with open-meetings laws. The officeholder's expenses as government operational records may require a FOIA request to the financial officer, who may be called the treasurer or controller, or they may be published. They reveal the specific activities of the official, and the reporter can determine whether the officeholder is pursing the agenda promised during the election campaign or is perhaps being driven by the size of campaign contributions received from special interest groups.

Investigating a Business Entity

Along the way, the reporter attempts to identify businesses in which the subject of the investigation may be involved. The next step is to learn more about those businesses. A business entity is a recognized legal means of doing business. It is a structure that comes in different forms. It could be a corporation or a partnership, something that is created on paper. The entities may be for profit or not for profit. They are owned by people, but they are independent of people because they can be passed from one person to the next.

Not-for-Profit Organizations

Not-for-profit organizations are privately owned, but their charters state that they are not out to make a profit. They have a purpose other than making a profit; they claim the purpose is the welfare of the people. Their domain includes health care facilities, day care centers, membership organizations, schools and senior citizen associations. Churches are not included and are exempt from disclosure.

The not-for-profit status is by choice, not by government order or by definition of purpose. Therefore, not all schools are not-for-profit. Some others are government operated and others are for-profit. There are government-run hospitals such as state, county or Veterans Administration hospitals, for-profits, and not-for-profits. Those organizations that have received not-for-profit status from the IRS and have cited their status on their state incorporation papers must file an IRS form 990 to disclose on the public record that they did not take any profits from their operation. The 990 forms are as inclusive as the private forms filed by individual taxpayers. They show the revenue and expenses, including officer salaries. They are available from the not-for-profits themselves and from the IRS. See the law for not-for-profit financial disclosure in Appendix 2 in this textbook.

Charities are not-for-profits that declare a special charitable purpose—for example, the American Cancer Society and the United Way—and they must file charitable-purpose annual reports with the states in addition to the federal IRS 990 disclosure forms. The state forms require financial information to show how much money went toward the proper charitable purpose. Many of these reports are accessible from Web sites of state attorneys general.

For-Profit Businesses

There are various legal ways to organize for-profit businesses. They can be single-owner businesses, professional corporations, paper corporations, partnerships, privately held businesses or publicly traded corporations.

Personal. A professional person might have a corporation that was created to handle that person's individual business and that involves no one else. The professional has separated business from personal affairs for clarification of tax obligations. Because the professional is responsible for the conduct of the business, in the eyes of the reporter there is little difference between the single-owner corporation and the individual. But an investigative reporter will want to check whether such a corporation exists because any lawsuits and permits could be in the name of the professional corporation and not the person.

When a private person is also a business entity, a declaration to that effect must be filed with the county clerk. This is usually called the assumed-name record. If Joe opens a hot dog stand and calls it Joe's Hot Dog Stand, he will reveal his full name in the assumed-name declaration. It will help the lawyer who might want to file a lawsuit to be able to cite Joe Joseph, doing business as Joe's Hot Dog Stand in San Mesa; and it helps the reporter who needs to know the name of the person who furnished the hot dogs for the political rally.

Paper. Some corporations are loosely called "paper corporations." That designation seems to have a bad connotation, but it can be as legal an entity as any other. A paper corporation will have all its proper papers in order, but it is created to be an intermediary between other corporations or to have one specific function. All this is on paper, but the corporation need not have an office, property or employees. The negative connotation has arisen because a person, such as a public official, may create such a corporation for the purpose of becoming a hidden middleman in a public contract in order to siphon off money without performing any service. The officers of every corporation, however, are listed with a state's secretary of state corporation division.

Partnership. If people want to work together, they may form a partnership without incorporating. Their business is nobody's but their own, but they can be examined by reporters who look for licenses, public contracts and lawsuits. A partnership can be a simple 50-50 division of the profits and responsibilities.

Another partnership structure is more formal. Called the limited partnership or the limited liability corporation, it has a general partner who operates the business and investors who do not have to be revealed and do not have to accept any responsibility for actions of the partnership. So, for example, if the county commissioner had a stake as a limited partner in a corporation that wrecked a landmark building to erect a glue factory, it would make a dandy news story but the commissioner could rightfully argue that it was out of his control. If that same partnership got a county contract that the commissioner voted on, the commissioner would be in big trouble because of the profits from the interest in the partnership.

Private. Some corporations are not much different from partnerships because they are owned by a group of people who, although they hold stock, do not list the stock with any stock exchange or make public solicitations for its sale. They might operate a nightclub, own a waste-hauling business or a sports team, or develop subdivisions. Their businesses are important to the community, and they can be investigated by seeking out court cases, licenses, public contracts and published reports. An investigative reporter can use the tried-and-true reporting techniques to flush out the particulars about a private corporation and will run corporation name searches in databases in the same places.

Publicly traded. Big companies whose stock is traded on a stock exchange will provide detailed corporate financial information to the U.S. Securities and Exchange Commission (SEC), whose reports are online. Like campaign disclosure reports, SEC filings are made electronically by the company submitting them. In addition, certain industries are regulated by state and federal agencies: the airlines by the Federal Aviation Administration, the insurance companies by the states, broadcasters by the Federal Communications Commission, factories by the Environmental Protection Agency, truckers by the Department of Transportation and banking by the Federal Deposit Insurance Corporation. The reporter can match the company with the agency and find what is available.

Okay, so there might be nothing to indicate improper conduct or a secret agenda so far in the paper trail left by the subject of the investigation. But the reporter might have found something in the chain of documents that is of interest. Perhaps the person built a vacation home on the nest of an endangered turtle species while touting the importance of conservation. An investigative reporter has the instincts to know whether this would make an interesting story.

Investigating a Place

A location in itself—a dangerous intersection, a waste dump, the location of a planned airport or a bridge that might be on the verge of collapse— may be cause for investigation. If there is cause to believe a bridge is unsafe, the reporter might be able to consult experts or use special equipment to learn the condition of the bridge or tunnel or other structure.

The condition of a waste dump and the story of how it got that way may be found by combing local government permit records that could be filed with the city, state or federal environmental protection agencies. Independent labs might carry out studies of possible tainting of nearby land, water and vegetation. Has the dump spread beyond the boundaries authorized for it? EPA records can be searched for information about the limitations of the license to dump and for reports from inspections and complaints. Then simple observation coupled with careful map study could answer the question of whether the dump has spread illegally. An aerial photo from the Internet might both prove and illustrate the investigation.

Do newspaper readers or television viewers realize that the street corner where they cross every day has been the site of two fatal pedestrian accidents within the last year? An investigative reporter can tell them after surveying police accident reports. Perhaps a reporter might reconstruct an accident by diagramming the intersection or chart the repetition of accidents in a story. Details of the accidents can show whether they are similar and whether the cause is an obscured sign or street marking. Once again, an aerial photo could be downloaded from the Internet and the exact places where the accidents occurred could be superimposed on the photo.

The land for a new airport is likely to be owned by private persons. Land records from the recorder's office can be studied to find out the owners. An aerial photo again? Photos can be purchased for a reasonable cost—no one needs to go up in an airplane—and they can be used to pinpoint the parcels of land and identify the owners.

The story ideas we have mentioned show that there is no shortage of targets to investigate, of reasons to investigate or of actions to investigate. Although there are too few investigative reporters to discover all wrongdoing, they are not lacking in desire and commitment. And they are brazen enough to think they can do it all.

Ethics: Written and Unwritten Rules

Good common sense and fairness in journalism can be called ethics. Investigative journalists are often thought of as the loose cannons of the trade, but they have as broad a code of ethics as some regulated professions. Although the only government oversight of investigative reporters is whether they commit acts that might fall outside the law, the publications they work for and the reporters themselves have created written or broadly understood rules of behavior.

The most often cited written form is the code of ethics advocated by the Society of Professional Journalists (SPJ). It advises against deliberate distortion, staged news events, conflicts of interest, pandering to "lurid curiosity" and unnecessary intrusion into a person's privacy. The rules are voluntary, but successful, well-respected investigative journalists adhere to them. You will find the full text of the code at the SPJ Web site at www.spj.org/ethicscode.asp.

The SPJ suggestions should be adopted as a cornerstone for conduct by every journalist, but they are not enforced. What are enforceable are the newsroom policies that every reporter must know and follow. These are the house rules, similar to but more inclusive than the professional society rules. Following are some examples that a reporter must display or adhere to:

- Certification. Plagiarism or stealing another writer's work by calling it one's own will not be tolerated. The reporter must identify all writings as original or cite the author under copyright constraints.
- Identification. Reporters should identify themselves when talking to a person whom they intend to quote. However, they may request routine information available to the general public without declaring they are reporting for a newspaper. For example, a reporter can take a copy of demands from a picket who is handing out flyers on the street or can stand in line to get a sample election ballot.
- Truth. Photos of news events must never be staged. Photos may be trimmed down to give a more succinct representation, but such cropping should not change the message conveyed. Quotations from interviews should not be altered even to conceal poor grammar. The reporter-writer has the option of paraphrasing the spoken words to avoid such embarrassment.
- Honesty. Reporters should be aware that monetary awards for favorable stories may be seen by business and professional associations as opportunities for back-door payoffs to influence reporters to slant the content of stories. Gifts may not be received as a reward for publishing a story. Reporters will not allow government officials or private persons who are subjects of a story to pick up the tab for wining and dining, or even for

lunch. Likewise, the investigative reporter will not pay for information. Sources have been known to enhance their information to attract higher fees.

- Responsibility. Reporters must not make veiled threats or flaunt their positions by hinting of an unfavorable story if a contact does not comply. They must not use their positions to avoid a responsibility, such as paying parking tickets.
- Independence. Investigative reporters must not become tools of government investigators or private attorneys who seek to use their findings in prosecutions or litigation.
- Confirmation. Reports and data found on the Internet must be confirmed.
- Balance. All efforts must be made to contact a person named in an investigative report in order to enable that person to comment or to correct misinformation. Such people must be given an opportunity to explain a differing view to give the story balance. Investigative reporters should strive for a sit-down interview in which the interviewee is given adequate notice to prepare and is not subjected to an ambush interview.

This list borrowed heavily from the rules of *The Northwest Indiana Times*. These rules are "shop rules." Each publication or broadcast outlet has similar working agreements. The rules have evolved with the practice of journalism, and investigative reporters adhere to them because they advance the craft.

Case Study

Waste in City Government*

During his regular rounds as an investigative reporter, Charles Miller often saw city workers in Middleton loafing on the job. The only time they seemed to keep busy was when an election was approaching. Citizens usually disregarded the lackluster performance of city employees or made jokes about it. Newspapers and TV news

*The cases are based on real investigative stories, but the names and places have been changed to protect reporters, their sources and the secrets they have. Some are actual stories told in a step-by-step reconstruction and others are composites.

from time to time caught workers sleeping on the job or absent from their work assignments; they might run a brief story and the workers would face discipline, such as a suspension for a few days. Reporters in the newspaper city room joked that the occasional suspensions were with full pay, but no one ever checked.

One afternoon, Miller was crossing the Main Street bridge, which had decorative light poles spaced along the railings. He noticed a city work crew and stopped to watch. He found five workers with one task: to replace a light bulb. One worker was at the top of a ladder and had unfastened the globe that contained the bulb. A second worker was halfway down the ladder; he received the bulb that was handed to him. Two workers were holding the ladder at the base, and the fifth was seated in the driver's seat of a city truck, reading a horse-racing publication.

Miller told an editor about what he had seen.

"That's pretty funny," said the editor. "Five men to change a light. Too bad we don't have pictures."

Miller suggested an investigative project that would show the extent of the waste in dollars instead of with a one-shot picture caption.

"But that's an old story. We've done a lot of stories about the city wasting money. And everybody knows city workers loaf on the job," the editor said.

?

Should the newspaper spend any time and give any space to a story about city workers loafing?

Yes: If the newspaper backs off on stories critical of city hall, who else can inform people? An opposition mayoral candidate might use citizen complaints during an election campaign, but people distrust such rhetoric even if a candidate has the facts. This investigation is basic to local government and could be more meaningful than any other investigation of government operations.

No: People will recognize that this is an old story, and everyone in the Middleton area already knows it. Wrapping it in fancy graphics and cute pictures is not going to improve the content.

Miller had not lived in Middleton for as long as the editor or most of the other reporters. He could not as easily accept the status quo that they seemed to accommodate. He began to observe other incidents of city workers going about their municipal chores. Soon after the scene on the bridge, he saw a single worker on a short ladder that was propped against a stop sign. The man held a spray bottle of soap and a rag and was cleaning the face of the sign while another man was sitting in the driver's seat of a city truck nearby. The worker moved slowly, but he was not loafing, and after he cleaned the first sign, he took the ladder to a one-way-street sign and cleaned it as well.

Miller approached the man and told him he was a reporter for the *Daily News* and that he was curious about the purpose of the city worker's job and about why the other city employee sat nearby and offered no help.

"We have to keep the signs clean or people would have accidents," the sign washer said. "We're specialists. I don't drive the truck, and the driver doesn't wash signs. It's the union, I think."

Miller made a point to go to the municipal garage in the early mornings to follow city trucks as the crews left on their work assignments. Many were street-sign washers, and their duties included washing no-parking signs.

When he was walking to the county court building one day after a heavy rainfall, Miller was splashed with water from a taxi that was driven through standing water in the street. At first, he was outraged at the taxi driver, but then he realized it was unavoidable. The water was standing at the curb where the traffic had to pass. He wondered whom he could blame for this unpleasant experience, which he was confident he shared with many readers of the *Daily News*. He knew also that someone had to be responsible for allowing the water to flood the streets instead of running down the sewers. He called the department of streets and sanitation and asked.

He was transferred to the division of sewers.

"Do you want to make a complaint?" a clerk there asked.

"Maybe. I want to know whether the sewers are regularly cleaned so that water doesn't stand in the streets."

"It sounds like a complaint to me. You will have to come down to the sewer division and fill out a request form. Then an inspector will come out and report back. We always respond to complaints, but we have a heavy caseload and it may take some time."

It seemed to Miller that city hall was creating work: there was a question of whether it was necessary to wash traffic signs, and the idea of an inspector coming out to write up a report and file it with the sewer division seemed like an extra layer of bureaucracy. Miller sought answers from a former member of the city council who was voted out of office after opposing some of the mayor's programs. The former member had also complained that the city was overstaffed with unnecessary politically active workers.

"You would think the people in my district would have supported me when I went after waste in city government," the ousted council member told Miller. "But as soon as I went on the attack, the mayor started withholding services from my district. The streets were not cleaned, the streetlight bulbs were not replaced, the potholes were not repaired, and even the garbage collection was cut back and garbage was overflowing before it was hauled away. There was nothing I could do about it, and the voters blamed me."

"But why does the mayor want to run an inefficient, wasteful government?" Miller asked.

"Come on, now. You ought to be able to figure that out. The bottom line is jobs. That's how a political machine works. The mayor creates jobs, and the workers are indebted to the mayor. It's called patronage. Every election they turn out the vote for the mayor, and the mayor's political machine gets stronger and stronger. They take control of the state government and have influence in Washington."

Do you rate highly the quality of the comments of the defeated council member?

Yes: The former member of the council is relating a personal experience. The former member is a responsible, professional person whom Miller consulted. The former council member did not contact the newspaper to vent anger over political losses.

No: It is sour grapes from a loser. There is little in the way of facts; instead it is conjecture and opinion. The former council member has offered no proof that the mayor was behind the withholding of municipal services in the district.

Miller did some quick research. He got a copy of the city budget and its annual financial reports. The operations of government were separated into categories, and aspects of the department's performance were detailed. It showed how many tons of garbage were picked up and the total cost of garbage pickup. Different activities of the city, like maintaining the streets, putting up traffic signs, reading water meters, and cleaning the sewers, were listed along with the results. Miller then checked these figures against data from other major cities and found that Middleton's costs were higher than the rest; in fact, Middleton sometimes spent twice as much for the services than other cities did.

While he was checking other cities' budgets online, he called administrators in those cities to ask about details of their operations and to make sure he was reading their reports correctly. He did not want to give away his story, but he had to keep up their interest by mentioning the five men on a light bulb.

"Ha, ha! That really didn't happen did it?" an assistant superintendent of streets in a major coastal city asked. "People like to make up stories like that. It really takes two men—a driver of a crane truck and one man in a high-lift bucket—to go down the street and change all the bulbs."

"Change them all? You wait until all the street lights on a street are burned out before you change them?" Miller questioned.

"No, we couldn't get away with that. The bulbs have a life expectancy of about two years. When the time is up, we go through a neighborhood and change them all at once. Why, we would go crazy racing around the city changing a bulb every time one burned out. We would never catch up. The cost would be outrageous compared with the few days or weeks more we might get out of a light bulb."

Miller knew, though, that Middleton was doing exactly that—it was changing bulbs one by one when each burned out!

Each time Miller talked with administrators of operations in other cities, he asked about the cost of washing street signs. He wanted to put a price on the job he saw the city worker doing. None could find a breakout of such a cost. Finally, one department head in a large Midwestern city told him: "Nobody washes street signs. They are laminated and we just let the good old prairie wind and rain blow in and wash them off."

Miller then surveyed all the major cities in the country and found none that washed street signs.

Is it okay to accept everything as true when talking with out-of-town officials?

Yes: They have no reason to falsify their information. Besides, Miller has their city financial reports, and they are merely explaining or confirming the numbers.

No: All government officials should be treated with equal skepticism. They are as likely as the Middleton department heads to misrepresent or exaggerate. If they have provided erroneous information, Middleton officials will use it to discredit the story.

Miller decided to lay it all out in a pitch to his editors. He had devised an outline—he liked to call it a "prospectus"—that argued the merits of the newspaper doing a complete investigation. This is what he submitted to the metropolitan editor:

```
TO: Metropolitan Editor
FROM: Charles Miller

RE: Story Outline: City Waste

Subject: The waste of taxpayer money caused by over-
staffing of city departments with workers who provide
unnecessary functions.
Need: The city has created so many unnecessary jobs
that residents often pay twice as much as other cities
of the same size for the same services. Residents have
```

been accepting this practice as standard, and they need to be told that it is costly to them.

Scope: This would not be another routine newspaper story about workers loafing on the job. Many of the workers believe they are serving a purpose when actually they are not needed. The investigation would probe into the reasons for this waste: it would learn whether these jobs are going to relatives of elected officials, their campaign contributors or political workers. I will limit the project to street and sanitation functions, which have large payrolls.

Methods: I will try to put an actual dollar amount on each function and make comparisons with other cities around the country. I will carefully examine the geographical differences among cities and eliminate any disparities. It is obvious, for example, that snow removal costs are higher in Minneapolis than in Dallas.

Sources: I will obtain copies of the city budget, annual report and payroll, and also obtain the budgets and annual reports of other major cities that post them online. The payroll will require a state FOIA request, but it has been well-established that it is public record. Campaign contributions are online or available immediately in the county clerk's office.

Presentation: This investigation would result in a series of stories that could have as many as five parts. It would be a natural for pictures and graphics. We could get pictures of the light-bulb crew and the sign washers. Graphics such as bar charts would compare the cost of operations in each city.

When the metropolitan editor read the memo, he was impressed with the idea and proposed it to the managing editor. It was difficult to sell the managing editor on any idea that took up a lot of space in the paper as well as reporting time, but Miller's memo provided a clear and concise plan. It showed the editors that he was proposing a definite idea that was doable, and, most of all, it showed that Miller knew how to do it. Miller got the go-ahead but with some reservations.

"We don't want some long stories with a whole lot of dollar figures in them. Readers are turned off by numbers in the millions," his editor said.

Miller had the solution: he would use the small number instead of the large one. He started with the Middleton budget (Figure 3.1) where he found the expenditures of one fund—for streets and traffic.

Figure 3.1 Middleton, budget and actual schedules

Budget and Actual Schedules

H-10

TRANSPORTATION FUND
SCHEDULE OF EXPENDITURES AND OTHER FINANCING USES
ON A BUDGETARY BASIS (NON-GAAP) COMPARED TO BUDGET
For the Year Ended December 31, 2004
(In Thousands)

	2004 Budget Original	2004 Budget Final	Actual Expenditures	Outstanding Encumbrances	Unexpended Balances Appropriations Continuing	Lapsed
EXPENDITURES						
Street Maintenance	$ 19,993	$ 19,993	$ 17,878	$ 22	$ 480	$ 1,614
Structure Management	8,787	9,224	4,783	43	4,272	126
Traffic Management	23,565	23,911	20,313	196	1,420	1,982
Traffic and Street Use Management	8,201	8,201	6,673	-	-	1,528
Neighborhood Traffic Services	1,071	1,046	573	-	336	137
Capital Projects Management	55,412	55,734	23,514	49	32,111	59
Policy, Planning, and Major Development	20,897	21,502	8,175	110	13,064	153
Urban Forestry	2,296	2,257	2,091	-	-	166
Resource Management	7,293	7,647	7,140	-	414	93
Department Management	3,304	3,281	2,486	2	-	792
General Expenses	13,318	11,939	8,848	-	3,000	91
Total Expenditures	164,137	164,734	102,474	423	55,096	6,741
OTHER FINANCING USES						
Transfers Out	-	840	840	-	-	-
Fund Totals	$ 164,137	$ 165,574	$ 103,314	$ 423	$ 55,096	$ 6,741

The budgeted amount of each listed operation is in the first column to the left. The first line shows that street maintenance was allocated $19,993,000 (he noted the figures in the chart are in thousands, so he added three zeros) when the budget was first proposed, and the second column shows that it was unchanged when the budget was approved by the city council. In the third column, he saw that only $17,878,000 was spent. From the statistical section of the same document (not shown here), he learned that the Middleton street division maintains 3,938 miles (5,280 feet per mile) of streets. He quickly calculated that it costs Middleton an average of 90 cents to maintain 100 feet of street.

He also learned, from data posted by Central City, that during the same year Central City spent $10,229,254 to maintain approximately 3,250 miles of streets. This works out to 59 cents to maintain 100 feet.

But Miller had to be careful. The cities had to be similar in climate and geography before his comparisons would work. Would Baltimore, with older pavement and hilly terrain, be comparable with flatter, newer Kansas City? The statistics from other cities were merely an indication that something was amiss. But when Miller learned that comparable cities had two-member work teams while Middleton had four-member teams producing the same amount of work, his concerns vanished.

Miller found that Middleton employed so many sewer workers that extra seats had to be installed on their trucks. They were observed cleaning sewers with hand shovels when other cities used high-pressure flushing equipment installed on trucks.

In addition, two other reporters who were assigned to Miller's project uncovered at least $100 million in wasted tax dollars.

Miller and another reporter called on the street commissioner, Mel Roberts. His office was surprisingly ornate. A huge picture of the mayor hung on the wall behind his desk, and city and U.S. flags flanked the desk. The conversation was relaxed, and the two reporters took turns asking questions and writing down the answers.

Miller asked why there were so many workers in the sewer division that he needed to add seats to the trucks.

"If we didn't add seats, then we'd have to get more trucks. It was economically wise," Roberts replied.

"But are the workers necessary?"

"The mayor wants the city to have the best public services possible. He is in favor of a heavy concentration of workforce assigned to the streets and sewers," Roberts countered.

"In other cities, vacuum trucks are used to flush out the sewers instead of using individual workers to shovel," Miller suggested. "It costs more than twice as much to clean one mile of sewers here than in any other major city. In Philadelphia—"

"Philadelphia? What do you know about the sewers in Philadelphia? They might be smaller than our sewers," Roberts interrupted.

"Well, in Atlanta—"

"Atlanta? Have you ever been to Atlanta in the summer?" Roberts shot back. "They can't have workers out in the heat and are forced to use other equipment. I am afraid you have been getting bad information."

"We got copies of the city budgets from these cities and compared the cost of operations," Miller said. At that moment Roberts leaned back in his chair and folded his arms across his chest. Miller knew body language and read the gesture as a defensive move. Roberts was digging in for a difficult defense.

"I can tell you, the mayor demands a day's work for a day's pay," Roberts said. The reporters listed their facts, and Roberts offered an explanation for each, often calling in an assistant to explain the operations that he was not sure about. Roberts was relatively young for a department head, and he had moved up in rank after the mayor was elected for his first term. Few people in city hall knew that he was the son of the mayor's law partner.

Miller drafted a lead for the first day's story:

"Flanked by flags of our city and our nation, Mel Roberts sits beneath a picture of the mayor and presides over a multimillion-dollar empire of city workers."

Miller was rather proud of his lead and was shocked when his editor sent the lead back with an e-mail message, "SO WHAT!" The editor wrote that the story needed a factual lead rather than a lead that backed into the story.

Miller responded with: "Taxpayers in Middleton often spend twice as much or more than other cities for the same municipal services, a study by the *Daily News* shows."

When the stories ran day after day on the front page of the newspaper, people started watching in their neighborhoods for overstaffed city crews. Television news picked up the stories, and the city officials who were interviewed scoffed at the numbers published by the *Daily News*. "People need jobs," the mayor said in a television interview. "What's wrong with giving people jobs?"

Chesterfield Smith III, the highly respected publisher of the *Daily News*, was always called "Old Man" in the newsroom although he was not even near retirement age. His stature was unquestioned, and newsroom staff referred to him with respect and awe.

The Old Man kept a close watch over his newspaper and sometimes even wrote an editorial. For Miller's story, he responded to the mayor in an editorial. He said that he agreed that people should have jobs, but those jobs should be productive. While eight men were being driven around in city trucks, the parks and alleys were unclean and the sewers clogged, he wrote. These workers should be properly trained to use modern and efficient equipment. He suggested that the mayor was better at running a political organization than a modern city.

Still, the city took no action and would admit no wrongdoing. But a year later, when the new budget was drafted, the jobs of the sign washers and light-bulb changers were eliminated, and they were transferred to more productive jobs. Also, the sewer crews got modern equipment.

Miller had a feeling that his story was incomplete. He had shown the waste but not the underlying cause. His opportunity came from a tipster who was a clerk inside city hall. The clerk called and told him that the special jobs program of the federal government that subsidized the cities to create new jobs for the unemployed was being misused. Only those with political connections were hired. The tipster knew that every job recipient had a letter from a district alderman inside the application folder in the special city office that administered the federal jobs program.

Miller remembered that the mayor had gone on TV and announced the program. He had invited any person whose employment benefits had expired to call a special phone number to request a job application. Miller's source said at least 1,000 applications were received but were never opened. They were still in three mailbags in a back storage room at city hall.

The clerk provided Miller with the names of the persons who were placed in the jobs but did not have access to the files that were said to contain letters declaring political sponsorship from the employees' neighborhood councilman. Miller ran the names through the city payroll and found that the new workers were all city pothole fillers whose work was seasonal. At the end of their work season, they had to be laid off and rehired again when they were next needed. Payroll records indicated that the federal jobs money permitted them to be paid year-round although they did not qualify for the program. Their political loyalties qualified them.

Miller was in a quandary. He could

1. submit a FOIA request for the files,
2. go ahead with the story on the word of his reliable source,
3. reveal his information to federal investigators with whom he might cooperate or
4. forget about the files and contact the new employees and ask them how they got their jobs.

Which of Miller's choices is best?

1. Some personnel files in city hall would be covered by an FOIA request, but the city administrators would be able to remove any information from a file that was of a personal nature. The political patronage letters would no doubt be removed because they do not belong there and officially do not exist.

2. On the basis of his absolute confidence in the source, it would be possible to write a story telling of the letters. As with the FOIA request, however, when the story appeared the letters would be yanked.
3. It is always dangerous to work with a government investigative agency because such agencies must also be monitored by the press. Newspeople are reluctant to do so because they then feel like an arm of the establishment even though they merely share information.
4. If he goes to the workers, chances are they will immediately contact their superiors and the letters will be pulled. Even if the workers tell Miller about the letters, a newspaper story will cause the city to pull the rug out from under him by snatching the letters from the files and claiming there were none.

Miller decided that the federal investigator was his best refuge. The funding for the jobs program was supervised by the U.S. Department of Labor. A Labor Department officer was assigned to answer questions from the cities that were using the special funds. Miller told the federal officer what he knew and asked that the department look at the files in city hall and tell him whether the letters from the aldermen were there. The federal officer informed Miller that he could not reveal any information from the investigation even if it was a follow-up to a complaint such as this.

Surprised and disappointed, Miller slumped back in his chair. He had been reading the competing local newspaper and scanning all the local media Web sites with trepidation for fear that he would be scooped. (Although a reporter's ego is seriously wounded by becoming the victim of a competing scoop, perhaps a worse scenario is that the city would continue to get away with its improper hiring practices.) Now that he had reported the facts to the federal agent, he thought, most likely an investigation would be carried out and the news would be released on the Internet. He and the *Daily News* would not be credited.

But, then, the federal agent proposed an alternative: "I can't tell you if the letters are there, but I can tell you if there is no basis for your complaint. So, after I go over tomorrow and take a look at the files, you will get a call from me."

"You mean, if you tell me you can't talk about it, then the letters are there?"

"That's right. If I have nothing to report, then what you have told me is true," the Labor Department officer said. "If the letters are not there, I will tell you there is no basis for your complaint."

Miller had to sprint halfway across the newsroom the next after-noon when his phone rang. He breathlessly picked it up.

"Mr. Miller, I have nothing to report to you."

"What? Nothing to report?"

"That's right, Nothing to report."

The federal investigator's word that there was "nothing" meant something to Miller: a confirmation. Although the story was ready to go, everyone was a bit uneasy. If only they had a picture of the unopened letters in the mailbags in the back room. Miller recontact-ed his source, the clerk, and asked exactly where the bags were located. They met, and the clerk drew a floor plan of the city hall office: "Take two right turns from the front desk, and it's the door by the Pepsi machine." The clerk also told Miller precisely when people in that room would be gone for lunch.

At noon the next day, Miller and a photographer watched the lady who worked in the mailroom leave for lunch. Then they showed up at the front desk and Miller asked for her. "She's left. She won't be back for an hour."

"There was someone else I was supposed to see if she wasn't here," Miller said, dropping his briefcase on the desk and pulling out papers and rifling through them. The receptionist, witnessing such a disorganized person, watched in disgust.

Meanwhile, the photographer had drifted away. Minutes passed, and he came out from the back of the office and nodded in the affir-mative. "Let's go, Tony, I think we're probably on the wrong floor," Miller said loudly.

Although most readers were accustomed to stories of arrogance from city hall, when the story and the color photo of the job applica-tions overflowing the mailbags appeared on the front page of the *Daily News*, readers were properly shocked, as were high federal offi-cials. The federal government took away the administration of the jobs program from the city and gave it to the state, and deserving and needy people were hired for the jobs intended for them.

Was it wise to seek help from a government agency?

Yes: In a story of this importance, a reporter should seek help wherever it can be found. Miller's decision worked out perfectly. He got the story, and the wrong was corrected. After all, who can you trust if not federal investigators?

No: A reporter should not work with a government agent because the reporter might have to testify in court as an arm of the government. Also, the government agency might be covering up for the target of the reporter's investigation. Did someone say we can trust all federal investigators? Have they heard about the FBI and Watergate?

Memorandum

- Reporters have written and unwritten ethics.
- Private individuals leave a trail of public records.
- Elected officials may waste tax dollars by rewarding political workers with unnecessary jobs.
- Government budgets and annual reports may produce a wide range of investigative stories.
- Failure of a federal program may first be detected on the local level.
- Editors may not always be delighted with a writer's cherished prose.

Chapter Recap

Knowledge of the documents in this chapter will equip the investigative reporter with the ability to start an investigation or to learn enough to decide no investigation is warranted. But there is more. In recent years, investigative reporters have been joined at their desks by a friendly giant: the Internet. The Internet provides assistance in more ways than one, or two, or three. In the next chapter, we will explore the depth of the resources of the Internet.

Class Assignments

1. Can you improve on Miller's lead for the city waste story? It seems like the editor's decision was a matter of personal choice.
2. Get the budget and annual financial report from your city. Copies might be kept by the public library or might have been placed on the Internet. Find cities of comparable size and get their online budget information. Compare selected operations. Reduce the big numbers to smaller numbers (per piece and per job), as explained in this chapter.

Notes

1. Ann Marie Lipinski, William Gaines and Dean Baquet, "An Alderman Who Earned While He Learned," *Chicago Tribune*, October 7, 1987.

C h a p t e r   *4*

Using the Internet During Investigations

In April 2000, a California newspaper, *The Orange County Register*, was chasing a tip that body organs donated to not-for-profit organizations were being sold to companies that used them to make cosmetics.[1] People who designated on their driver's licenses that they were willing, in case of sudden death, to have their "organs and tissue" transplanted to persons in need might actually have given their approval for one of those not-for-profit firms to sell their body tissue to for-profit firms, which would use that tissue to make cosmetic products. Few donors realized that "tissue" meant the remainder of the body without the organs. The *Register* produced a thorough investigation about every aspect of the handling of body tissue and took care to make sure all parties to the debate were given an opportunity to be heard. As a result, the largest tissue bank stopped supplying tissue to a maker of cosmetic products.

Ron Campbell, an investigative reporter at the *Register*, wasted no time in closing out his investigation because he learned that his competition was also contacting his sources. Campbell had the financial reports of some of the not-for-profit organizations—the form 990s that are available from the IRS. (A copy of the IRS 990 disclosure law is Appendix 2 in the back of this textbook.) The forms showed that certain for-profit companies were paying for the tissue and the dollar amounts of the purchases. But how could Campbell find out what the private companies were doing with the tissue?

The Internet had the answer. The for-profit companies were small but were selling stock to the public; thus they had to file financial reports with the U.S. Securities and Exchange Commission. These reports were required to be in electronic form so that they could be placed online. Working from his desk, Campbell was able to pull up the SEC's Web site at www.sec.gov and search for the names of the companies. In less than a minute, he had the reports on his computer screen. One line on the forms told it best. In answer to the question of whether there could be an occurrence that would cause the value of the stock to drop, an official of one company wrote that it would be an adverse event if people found out what the company was doing.

Campbell then learned the names of the products the company made and ran them through a full search of the Internet. He flushed out many advertisements for cosmetic surgeons who told how they used the very same products from the companies to remove wrinkles and patch up scars. "For my part, it was the first time I used the Internet extensively in an investigation," Campbell said. The key Internet sources were the SEC's EDGAR database on its Web site for corporate filings and the FDA site, www.fda.gov, which listed recalls of tissues suspected of being tainted. Information from the IRS 990s came from a Web site called Guidestar, at www.guidestar.org, which offers a searchable database.

Where to Look Online

Online computer databases can provide public disclosure and government operational records for government offices from the White House and Congress to the small local municipal districts. Even an application for a building permit for a new garage in a residential neighborhood in some cities can be found on the Internet. The Internet provides quality information via Web sites of newspaper and broadcast companies, universities and associations of professionals. It also has much drivel of the kind that used to come to the newspaper as lengthy diatribes in letters to the editor; such writings are without fact but replete with fancy.

A simple code will guide reporters to the reliable Web sites they can best use. At the end of the address of the Internet site—after the dot—the reporter will find the defining terms. The most common are .gov, .org, .edu and .com.

.gov—Official Government Web Sites

Web addresses ending in .gov are official government information Web sites. These have the highest level of accuracy because they deliver the same official government information that a visitor to the government office would receive. One must be aware that they also aggrandize the current officeholders and usually spout the current official line. Web sites are supposed to stop short of advocating reelection for those in government because such advocacy would be a violation of election laws. Information on dot-govs is usually free of charge because taxpayers have already funded the Web site.

So far in this text, we have shown the utility of several dot-govs. In the Provo, Utah, story, we downloaded budgets and financial reports from Provo's official Web site. Cities, counties, states and school districts across the country have Web sites and use them to provide information quickly to the public; this is cheaper than maintaining a staff of clerks in a government office to hand out the information. Agencies of the federal government have official Web sites, and some of the sites are very useful to reporters.

www.ftc.gov. The Federal Trade Commission is very media-oriented. One of its missions is to educate the public about consumer protection issues. Its Web site has a wealth of information about such topics as identity theft, Internet commerce, credit, automobile sales and telemarketing. The FTC may sue a person whom it believes to be treating consumers unfairly, but usually the FTC will issue a cease-and-desist order and work out an agreement with that person to stop doing what the commission charges is improper. Those agreements are listed online in the media section of the Web site.

www.fbi.gov. Actual FBI reports are scanned into this Web site. They are mostly historic, like the shooting of 1930s bank robber John Dillinger, initial reports of the Watergate break-in, and the attempted assassination of presidential candidate George Wallace. It is beneficial to journalism for reporters to consult these files when they write stories that refer to historic events. Reporters for newspapers in those years would not have had the advantage of access to the reports and may have gotten the story wrong; thus, it's not always best to use a published report from an old newspaper. Information about current investigations will not be found at www.fbi.gov, but news releases are there.

www.usda.gov. A reporter does not have to be in the Farm Belt to find cause to explore the U.S. Department of Agriculture (USDA) Web site. It lists the recall of food products by name of manufacturer, and it provides consumer education about dieting. Investigative reporters who specialize in consumer issues may be more likely to visit the site than other reporters.

The USDA runs the National School Lunch Program, and a reporter who wants to see whether the local school lunch is up to par can visit the Web site to learn of the standards USDA sets.

www.hhs.gov. The Department of Health and Human Services includes the National Institutes of Health and is an important source for reporters working on medical investigations. It can help them translate scientific terms into understandable common usage. The NIH Web site provides information ranging from simple health tips to all clinical tests registered with NIH.

www.dot.gov. Do not let the "dot" confuse you. It stands for Department of Transportation, and it regulates those big things that have wheels. DOT enforces rules for the transportation companies and educates the public concerning railways, highways, trucks and school buses. It posts online detailed accident investigations.

www.faa.gov. The Federal Aviation Administration is also a regulator of transportation. Its Web site provides a very convenient registry of airplanes and their owners. It is searchable by name of owner, serial number and make and model of aircraft. Most useful is the state and county index. The reporter does not need to know anything about the owner or the aircraft but can get a list of all the aircraft registered as home-based in a specific county. If the reporter is profiling an important local person, the list will show whether that person owns an airplane.

www.ssa.gov. Individual Social Security records, including Social Security numbers, are private. But when a recipient dies, information is placed on the Web. The Social Security death database—the Death Master File at www.ntis.gov/products/ssa-dmf.asp—contains a listing of all persons who died who were receiving Social Security benefits. The file includes the Social Security number, name, date of birth, date of death, state or country of residence, ZIP code of last residence, and ZIP code where final lump-sum payment was sent. A fee is connected with this service; the fee is explained on the Web site.

www.fec.gov. All of the campaign reports from federal elections are on the Federal Election Commission site; in addition, the FEC posts complaints and the findings of the commission about those complaints. The documents are detailed even if there is no violation of election law, as in the following example concerning the candidacy of Senator John Kerry in the 2004 presidential election.

The complaint filed with the FEC alleged that the Kerry campaign committee may have accepted, and the senator's spouse Teresa Heinz Kerry may have made, an unreported and excessive contribution "to the extent (Mrs. Kerry's) property rights in the Kerry family home or any other jointly held property were pledged as collateral for any or all of the secured loans received by the Committee."

Several questions were raised in the complaint as to whether a loan from the Mellon Trust, a bank, constituted an excessive or prohibited contribution and whether the loan was accurately reported. The FEC found cause to investigate but found no violation:

> "Information obtained from the respondents established that Senator Kerry did not borrow in excess of his share of the collateral property; that the Mellon Trust loan was a standard loan product offered to a number of other customers during the relevant time period, and the committee's reporting of the loan in most respects accurately reflected the flow of funds from the bank to Senator Kerry and from Senator Kerry to the committee."

The FEC decided to take no further action against the committee and Mellon Trust and found no reason to believe Teresa Heinz Kerry violated the law. The FEC closed the file.

The FEC did not stop there with its disclosure. It posted the documents from the investigation of the complaint and provided this instruction for the Web visitor: "Enter number 5421 under case number in the Enforcement Query System. The records are also available in the FEC's Public Records Office at 999 E St. NW, in Washington D.C."

www.fedstats.gov. Reporters have complained that no one believes their stories until they are backed with solid government data. The fedstats.gov Web site provides numbers on a wide range of issues and can be cited to show the seriousness of a problem. It provides numbers reflecting on education, agriculture, employment, health, safety and crime.

www.gao.gov. The Government Accountability Office (GAO) is an independent agency that answers requests from Congress. Its Web site lists its investigative reports, which cover an array of topics. GAO reports are important to the investigative reporter, but the publications rarely name specific persons or companies. A reporter may want to get the full story by requesting the notes of the GAO investigator; for that, filing an FOIA request is necessary.

www.sec.gov. For-profit companies that sell stock across at least one state line must file financial information with the U.S. Securities and Exchange Commission (SEC), which regulates both the sales of securities and the exchanges that facilitate the sales. Corporations that qualify have to file electronically, and the SEC conveys this information straight from the companies. Reports the companies file with the SEC are signed by corporation officials. Investigative reporters can pull up these reports on computer terminals. The companies are of course not filing these reports for the convenience of investigative reporters; the purpose of the filings is to conform with federal law about informing stockholders or potential stockholders of their financial situation. The investigative reporters working for *The Orange County Register* took advantage of this when they put together their report about the sale of body tissue.

Any financial activity of any company that must register with the SEC must be reported individually and in a timely manner. Large corporations often file many documents; the most comprehensive is the annual report, which is filed on form 10-K.

Even though every government agency sets out specific standards for reporting the required facts, reporters must consider the information offered on fedstats.gov as part of the official version of the truth. Those filing the reports may bend the truth to reflect well on their cause. The fire chief may want to play down the losses from fires to make the fire department look good, and the police chief could downgrade the classification of a crime to make the police department appear to be doing a good job of combating crime. It is an important step in an investigation to look over the fedstats Web site for statistics on the subject being investigated.

.org—Not-for-Profit Organization Web Sites

Web site addresses ending in .org are Web sites of not-for-profit organizations. Some dot-orgs are as reliable as the dot-govs. A dot-org can be a business like a hospital that is owned by a not-for-profit company, an association such as the Association of Trial Lawyers of America, and a charity like the American Red Cross. The quality of the information found on such Web sites depends on the reliability of the organization.

One especially handy Web site is www.opensecrets.org, run by the Center for Responsive Politics. It posts the campaign records the same as the Federal Election Commission, but on opensecrets.org they are interpreted and more easily navigated.

Also, associations for government officials have Web sites. These are membership organizations. The National Association of Insurance Commissioners, for example, is designed to keep state insurance commissioners informed of the laws and the ideas and programs involving the insurance industry in all the states. There are associations of sheriffs, coroners, city managers, county clerks, judges, police and fire chiefs and prison wardens. A reporter who in the past could get valuable information from their magazines now can get it from their Web sites.

Membership organizations have annual conferences or seminars or both, and local administrators who are members of their group organizations will want to attend and bill the cost to the taxpayers. A reporter doing a local waste-in-government story will want to check with the local government finance office for the expenditures for the trip and see whether the administrator has made a report to the staff or the public on what was learned at the meeting.

A similar category of dot-orgs are the membership organizations for professionals. There may be more than one for a single profession because they serve opposing factions of those professionals. There are associations for both trial lawyers and defense lawyers, for instance. Membership associations for people who have an interest in sports or hobbies can also be found on the Internet. Let's say we are working on a story about people being approached to contribute to a fund to provide bulletproof vests for police officers. A legitimate organization of police chiefs could be helpful. Professional organizations do not provide much statistical information, but they can put a reporter in contact with an expert in the professional field who is quotable.

Some special interest groups take diverse stands on issues. The reporter who is working on a story that involves such an issue will want to find these groups on the Internet and contact each one. For example, the National Abortion Federation (NAF), a professional association for abortion practitioners, is at www.prochoice.org, and Planned Parenthood offers health information about abortion at www.plannedparenthood.org. The National Right to Life Committee, an organization with opposing views, is at www.nrlc.org/.

.edu—Educational Institution Web Sites

An educational institution Web site ends with .edu. Universities, secondary schools and elementary schools carry this designation. Universities may have central Web sites for all functions, but they spawn separate Web sites for the expertise of individual professors or projects with no tie-in to the university administration. Reporters in need of an expert opinion may find knowledgeable people at a university.

Local public schools have Web sites and place the school calendar and lunch menus on them. They may place agendas of school board meetings online and even include the minutes.

.com—Commercial Web Sites

These are for businesses, and they include newspaper and broadcast Web sites. Anybody can set up a commercial Web site, so a reporter must be wary of the quality of the information. The site must be checked to establish who has control over the information in the site. If it is a Web site of a known and respected publication, it can rate high in reliability. Most valuable are newspaper archives. For the examination of the Provo, Utah, city budget in Chapter 2, we used the archives of the *Provo Daily Herald* and the *Deseret Morning News* (Salt Lake City, Utah) to learn what had been written on the subject.

Surfing the Net

Whoever came up with the word "surfing" for exploring the content of the Internet must have envisioned riding information from wave to wave. Endless waves of important and frivolous facts crest and break across the computer screen of a true Internet surfer. An investigative reporter will want to know everything about the subject of an investigation and will go along for the ride.

A good starter is through a list of data servers like the one offered by Duff Wilson, the reporter for *The Seattle Times* who produced the investigation of clinical trials described earlier. From his Web site, Reporter's Desktop, we can glean a summary of Web sites important to reporters. He finds that of first importance to a surfer are the data server Web sites with super search engines. Google emerged in the first decade of the century as the leader, but Reporter's Desktop lists others—Dogpile, Ask Jeeves, and Alltheweb—and they have information that Google may not.

Let's search for a name on each of the Web sites. Why not Duff Wilson? When searching in a data service, the advanced search is the most advantageous. If we put the two words Duff and Wilson in the primary search slot, we get every item that mentions the words Duff and Wilson. The number of returns is staggering: 1.48 million, by one count. But it we put "Duff Wilson" in the "exact phrase" slot we get only mentions of people named Duff Wilson; this came up with 635. This led to a biography that told us that Wilson left *The Seattle Times* in 2004 for *The New York Times*. We learned that he wrote a book called "Fateful Harvest," which explored the issue of whether toxic-laced fertilizers make food unsafe.

If a surfer is interested in getting information about Vice President Richard Cheney's hunting accident, the key words have to be placed differently. Some of the stories may call him Dick Cheney and others call him

Richard. So we put the phrase "hunting accident" in the exact line, and in the line for "at least one" we place Dick and Richard. In the "all" line we place "Cheney" and "vice president" so we don't get the wrong Cheney.

To illustrate how to find a person who shares a name with many others or with a celebrity, we searched for any mention of an attorney Michael J. Fox in Seattle. We got 28 million hits when we put his name in the basic search slot. But when we placed his full name in the "exact phrase" slot, "Seattle" and "attorney" in the "all" slot, and in the "without" slot the words "movie," "actor" and "Parkinson," it eliminated all the references to Michael J. Fox the movie actor who has Parkinson's disease. This left a manageable number of references to all the other Michael Foxes in Seattle. We got 680 hits and found that attorney Michael J. Fox is a judge in Seattle.

Next we try http://alltheweb.com, which promises 11,000 hits on "Duff Wilson." Among those hits are a few we did not catch on Google. This search engine locates a story from the magazine "Editor & Publisher" reporting that a judge has ruled that Wilson does not have to turn over notes about his interviews of former research patients to lawyers for the research center.

Published: April 08, 2002

SEATTLE (AP) A federal judge has ruled that *The Seattle Times* does not have to turn over documents sought by the Fred Hutchinson Cancer Research Center in its defense against several lawsuits.

U.S. District Judge Robert Lasnik ruled that by providing information to relatives of patients who died in a leukemia trial in the 1980s, reporter Duff Wilson and the newspaper had not overstepped the "bounds of journalism," as argued by Hutchinson.

Lasnik said journalists generally can't be forced to disclose information gathered while reporting news stories.

Alltheweb.com had the "Editor & Publisher" article but Google did not, although it had a story about the ruling from *The Seattle Times.*

Next, we tried http://dogpile.com, which has a search engine characterized as a puppy that is prompted to "fetch" the information. Dogpile chased down only 68 hits, and there was nothing we did not know from Google and Alltheweb.

Finally, we asked the faithful butler of the data services, Ask Jeeves (www.ask.com/), to tell us about Duff Wilson. Jeeves served us with 177 items but none that Google did not have. Google was the overwhelming best performer in our little survey, but it seems worthwhile to check others in case something falls through the cracks.

Following are highlights from the Wilson list of documentation sources that have not been previously mentioned in this text:

- Wikipedia. This is an online encyclopedia, at www.wikipedia. org, that lists a limitless number of subjects and persons in the news. It provides a quotable summary of definitions and expla- nations.
- DoctorFinder. This is a service of the American Medical Assoc- iation, at http://webapps.ama-assn.org/doctorfinder/home.html? 2701824260. Specialties and education are cited in the listings.
- The Right-to-Know Network. This site, at www.rtknet.org, is concerned with environmental issues. It was started in 1989 in support of the Emergency Planning and Community Right to Know Act (EPCRA), which mandated public access to the Toxic Release Inventory. It is a service of Ombwatch, www. ombwatch.org, an organization that fights for more open records in all aspects of government.
- BRB Publications, Inc. BRB Publications (www.brbpub.com) provides a free resource center that is described as a compre- hensive and searchable list of free public record sites along with additional tools to locate sources for civil records, crimi- nal records, driving records, real estate records, public record vendors, record retrievers, legislation and more. It also lists some services that may charge fees.

Attribution

Even when using a top-of-the-line Web site, reporters will want to confirm the information and will try to reach the author of the material. Information then can be attributed to that person. Because there is always a possibility of fraudulent identity, even in e-mails sent, it is wise to find the author before printing Internet information. Such caution is similar to the newspaper policy of contacting the writers of letters to the editor to make sure that the signatures are not hoaxes.

Information from the Internet should never carry the attribution, "according to the Internet." That would be as inappropriate as attributing information to the public library because the book that contained the information came from the library. Throughout the examples and case studies in this textbook, mention is made of the resources on the Internet. Internet entries that mention a specific person can also be used to locate people and provide background on that person.

Although it is a little complicated, a true attribution might say, "according to information revealed by Company XYZ to the SEC and then placed on the SEC Web site . . ."

E-Mail

E-mail is a side issue of the Internet. It is private conversation, but it gives a reporter one more way to find and communicate with the target of an investigation. Often the response to a reporter's question is attributed to an e-mail from the individual.

The Internet Audience and Bloggers

Nigel Jaquiss of the Oregon weekly, *Willamette Week*, for his Pulitzer Prize-winning story in 2005 made use of the Internet in still another way. He wrote the story, which was about an ex-governor's sexual relationship with a 14-year-old girl, but the story received little attention from the big media. Instead, Internet bloggers picked it up and made it an issue. Then other newspapers ran with the story. Jaquiss said he believes that the Internet gave him the break he needed to circulate his story.

Jaquiss' experience illustrates the power of the new journalism of the Internet. Many voices can be heard that otherwise would not be. Independent Web sites are programmed to be received by geographically separated persons with similar interests or are specifically designed for the home folk in the smallest of communities. Just as local radio stations have for many years reported the births and deaths and public affairs of communities of as few as 10,000 residents, a local Web site or e-mail newsletter can provide a needed news source in a town. The costs are low compared with a newspaper or radio station, and the site can receive some support from advertisers.

Unlike the local broadcast station, which is limited in range and number of competitors by the FCC because its signal would interfere with other stations' signals, the local Web site is a model of independent journalism. Bloggers have their say on Web sites. The newsletter is not delivered to the door; it is delivered beyond the door because an interested person can have each issue e-mailed to home and office computers.

A typical expanded newsletter with all those facets is produced in Ypsilanti, Michigan, a city (pronounced IP-suh-LAN-tee) of 22,000 between Ann Arbor and Detroit. Some of the newsletter content could be considered investigative because it would not have been known if it were not for the enterprise and knowledge of the reporter-editor, Steve Pierce, who has run the Web site, called All Things Ypsilanti, since 2002.[2] One example of Pierce's investigative credentials occurred in December 2006 when a third attempt by the city to get a developer for a public project failed. Pierce wrote:

87

The current financing plan, which now includes over $40 million in taxpayer funding, depended on the project being completed in five (5) years in order to pay back the money already borrowed. The City had already refinanced the city's Water Street bond debt of $13.1 million. The refinance, completed earlier this year, jumped the interest rate by almost 2% more than the original rate. Worse, because the Water Street project was stalled with no units being built, Council had to roll three years worth of payments into the new debt to give the project time to be built.

In effect, the Council refinanced the credit card, and negotiated a deal whereby there would be no payments for three years, but at a cost. The refinance scheme added $2.1 million in new debt. Add in the payments to [the] developer the city fired in 2004 and the money owed by Ypsilanti City taxpayers was over $16 million.

The facts are there, and, if not convinced, the visitor to the Web site can see and hear the videotape of the city council meeting. In an e-mail interview, Pierce commented:

"We have some 2,000 (free-of-charge) subscribers to our e-mail newsletter. We are getting a 40% confirmed readership, [which] means that we can confirm that 42% are opening the e-mail newsletter. We know there is more because we can't track all the e-mails. But we know this is a solid number, not an estimate. Of the e-mails that are being opened, 42 to 48% of the readers are clicking through to read the full story on our Web site. That is extraordinary. The industry says 8 to 18% click-through rate is very good.

"The online videos have also been extraordinary as well. Just one video was viewed by over 18,000 world wide.

"Just by doing the videos in Ypsilanti has now encouraged the County Commission to do the same. Tonight we are video taping our first school board meeting and this week we got our first paid advertising and another advertiser has committed to a one-year media buy. It is very rewarding and exciting."

Case Study

Military Guns Sold on the Internet*

Nicholas Strong, *Tri-Cities Star* police reporter, learned that a street-gang-style, drive-by shooter who killed two teenagers had used

*The cases are based on real investigative stories, but the names and places have been changed to protect reporters, their sources and the secrets they have. Some are actual stories told in a step-by-step reconstruction and others are composites.

a military rifle, an M1 carbine of World War II vintage. This fact was only one part of a tragic story, and it was easy to overlook it. Three other teens were under arrest at the time the story broke, and because their lawyers had prevented them from talking to the press before they went to court, Strong—on deadline—could not pin down much more for his story than the names of the dead, the injured, and those arrested. That meant the details of the shooting and even the motive were left to rumor and speculation.

A year later, another shooting took place in which a similar weapon was used. It was an armed robbery, and a store clerk was shot. Bill Talbot, an enterprising investigative reporter for the *Star*, had questions about the two shootings. He found that a year after the teenagers were shot, he could get information more readily. He wanted to find how military rifles meant for the battlefield could end up in the hands of gang members in the Tri-Cities.

Talbot called the criminal prosecutor who, at first, said he could not discuss the case, but Talbot explained he wanted to know only about the gun.

The prosecutor said, "Now, Bill, that case is on appeal, and the gun is a vital piece of evidence. I'm not about to talk about it, but I'll tell you, there are plenty of those weapons around. People call them rifles but they are assault weapons. They are rapid-fire, clip-fed weapons, same as a mounted machine gun but made to be carried by a soldier who is assaulting the enemy. I have seen many of them around. Why, when I was in private practice, I took one for my legal fee. Don't tell anyone about that."

"But I thought assault weapons were illegal."

"There are federal laws that prohibit manufacturing or importing assault weapons, but no law says you can't keep one or sell it. There can't be a law that says you have to destroy the guns or the government would be confiscating private property. Assault weapons can be sold at gun shows, and they don't even have a record of the sale," the prosecutor said.

Talbot was surprised by the prosecutor's comments. Because Talbot had been thinking of a story about how many people had these weapons illegally, he at first thought that it meant there was no story. Then he realized that, because he had been ignorant of the law and surprised by it, the readers must also in the same manner be misinformed and would be concerned as much as he. There were unanswered questions: How many military guns are in private hands? How did they get there?

Sources like the prosecutor were important, but Talbot thought also of his other source with vast knowledge: the Internet.

He punched up a search engine and put in the word "guns." He got a list of 147 million items on his computer screen. The first six on the list were Web sites for the sale of guns, and assault weapons were among the guns offered. There was no way he could read all the material the Internet offered under the search word "guns." If he worked a 12-hour day and read each item for 10 seconds, he could read them all in 101 years. But he did his best to surf the Internet list.

He found Web sites for gun manufacturers, instructions on the use of guns, different and numerous Web sites for hunters of squirrels and rabbits, lobbyist groups both for and against stricter gun control laws, guns used in crimes, and what piqued his interest the most: military guns. Along the way, he had discarded useless writings that were no more than opinions of people who had no firsthand information. He learned a lot by reading major Web sites of recognized organizations and governments.

But none of the information was directed toward the question of how military guns get back on the streets. Talbot was pleased that the subject matter had not been overly written because it would make his story more important.

Talbot then did his own fact gathering with the search engines. He wanted examples of shootings similar to the gang-style shootings in the Tri-Cities. He used the advanced search and put in the phrases "military rifle," "military weapon," "army gun," "M1 rifle" and "assault weapon" as they might appear in a newspaper story. Then, to narrow his search, he put in the words "shooting," "killing," "murder" and "deaths." In a matter of seconds, he had available hundreds of stories than fit the category. It would not take 101 years to trim them down to about 200 stories of shooting incidents published in newspapers across the country. Talbot had the luxury of choosing those he thought important to tell the story, and he selected those stories with multiple deaths or unwarranted violence. By careful pruning, he had his list down to 10 stories that needed more checking.

Talbot had a long talk with an army public relations spokesperson. The military was no longer allowing any weapons to leave its possession, and soldiers had not taken their guns home with them since the Civil War, the spokesperson said. But there were several ways they could be getting into civilian hands. Some foreign countries allied with the United States were provided with those weapons during the Cold War years, and the weapons are unaccounted for. The spokesperson reminded Talbot that military weapons have been stolen. Also, some weapons are not authentic military weapons; they are copies. But they are often reported by police as military weapons when they are in fact military-style weapons.

"We destroy every weapon that becomes obsolete," the army spokesperson asserted.

Talbot outlined the story he planned to gather:

TO: Metropolitan Editor
FROM: Bill Talbot

RE: Story Outline: Arming the Killers

Subject: How military weapons fall into the hands of individuals who may use them in crimes.
Scope: We can trace the ownership of military assault rifles to see how they got from the military to the crime scene. We can detail crimes like the gang shooting here in the Tri-Cities and show people the real impact of this problem.
Need: People are unaware of the weaknesses in gun laws that allow rapid-fire weapons to be owned, bought and sold. The story about military guns will educate them and send a message to the legislature.
Methods: Once a weapon has left the possession of the military, it is untraceable. Buyers and sellers do not have to reveal their private transactions. But we can get some military history of the rifle from the serial number, and we can find out where the killer got the weapon. We will have to explain to the readers the missing links in the chain.
Sources: We will talk to the army officers in charge of destruction of weapons to get the official version. Then we will confront the officers with the overwhelming number of shooting incidents we have found in which the shooter used weapons that the army should have destroyed. We will get in-depth information, emotional reactions and analysis of each of the shootings we want to profile.
Presentation: This story could run as a series of four or five days, each with a main story about what we find and a large sidebar about the victims of the shootings. There could be pictures of the guns, the victims and anything we can find about the army destroying weapons.

The idea aroused the editors to action. They wanted to go big on the story and give it full national scope. They decided that the story needed more than one reporter, so they assigned Michelle Jacobs, a new reporter they had hired from San Mesa, to work with Talbot. She would concentrate on the color and background of the shootings story while Talbot gathered the main story about the overall problem, including the laws.

Talbot set up an interview with Maj. John Tyner at the Army's Central Regional Ordnance Depot. Tyner was in charge of the destruction of hundreds of thousands of assault rifles from the Vietnam War.

"Why are you destroying them? Is something wrong with them?"

"There's nothing wrong with them when it comes to killing," the major said. "It's just that we got new weapons that can kill more."

Tyner said that the entire government issue was ruled obsolete and was being chopped up, rifle by rifle, in a metal-crushing machine, and was rendered into scrap metal and sold as waste for the value of the metal chippings. Tyner put forth the same theory: that weapons on the street had come by the route of foreign armies or that they were from a grand theft of weapons from an arsenal that had occurred about 10 years before. Talbot suggested that he be allowed to go to the army post in a nearby state where the rifle chopping was being done and see for himself and get pictures.

"You'll find we are very thorough, and not one weapon has slipped out of our hands," Major Tyner promised.

Jacobs, meanwhile, was talking to the participants in the street shooting and learning of a different and unexpected scenario. Almost one year earlier, two teenagers had been shot and killed as they stood outside of a closed convenience store at about 2 a.m. A third was seriously wounded. Two of three occupants in a passing car from where the shots were fired were held accountable for the murders. The *Star* had run a story but had little more than the names and location of the shooting. Nobody carried stories of the court case because the sad truth is that Tri-Cities residents were accustomed to, and pretty much ignored, stories about gang violence.

Jacobs located the criminal court records. One boy had been identified and admitted to pulling the trigger of the M1. He pleaded not guilty, and at trial the other two testified against him. The court file of one of the witnesses who threw himself onto the mercy of the court was revealing. Andy Daniels was about to be sentenced, and letters supporting his character packed the file. He was described as a serious but only moderately successful high school student, a wide receiver on the varsity football team, and a well-liked kid in the neighborhood: not at all like a gang member, Jacobs concluded. Jacobs wanted to learn more. Because the shooter, Milt Christopher, had appealed his conviction, a copy of the transcript of the trial was in the folder. As a witness to the shooting, Daniels told his story, which went like this:

He had graduated from high school a week before, and his mother rented a car for him for the weekend as a graduation present. It was an emerald-colored Chrysler convertible, and he used it to drive his girlfriend to the beach that Saturday afternoon. When he returned, he parked it in the front driveway of his home. The striking look of the rental car caused neighbors to stop by to ask how Daniels had come into such good fortune. Two friends from school, Milt Christopher and Ray Pasadena, dropped by and showed him the M1 rifle they had.

There had been fights at school recently, and they said they got it for protection. They would like to try it out and to be able to shoot with it from a convertible would be perfect. Daniels yielded and drove them to an abandoned factory area where they shot at billboards. They were surprised at the power and rapid fire. Daniels returned home. Late that warm evening the two friends with the gun came back and asked for a cool-off ride. They drove the expressway system with the CD player blaring. Pasadena sat with the gun in the back seat while Daniels drove and Christopher sat in the front passenger seat. The gun was fully loaded with a clip of bullets.

It was about 2 a.m. when they drove back to their homes, but as they drove by the neighborhood convenience store, they saw three people standing in the adjoining, darkened parking lot.

The one survivor of the shooting testified to his view from the parking lot. He said he had been "hanging out" with another boy and two girls; then his cousin got off work and the group was in need of a third girl to round out the party. One of the girls said she had a friend who could meet them at the convenience store at 2 a.m., so the boys went there and waited. They were standing in the parking lot when an emerald-green convertible drove by with three young men inside. Who tossed the first barb is in dispute, but jeering was almost the guaranteed outcome because of the attractive car.

Daniels said they drove by and Christopher said, "Let's go back and kick their asses." Daniels drove around the block and approached the parking lot again. "Hand me the gun, I'll give them a scare," Christopher said, and Pasadena handed him the gun. Christopher rested it on the open window ledge.

One of the boys in the parking lot approached the car and said in what Christopher later described as a mocking tone, "What are you going to do, shoot us?"

With his finger already on the trigger, Christopher squeezed and in two seconds fired off five rounds, killing two of the boys and hitting a third in the stomach. Shocked, Daniels drove away. Christopher was in shock, too. "Oh, no, it can't be," he cried out.

The survivor of the shooting crawled to the door of the first house next to the store. The occupants had been awakened, and they called the police. The survivor was able to describe the car but not the people in it. It was not difficult for the police to make the arrests. All they had to do was ask people in the neighborhood whether they had seen an emerald-green convertible. They found Daniels, and he told them what happened. Further research into the case by Jacobs showed that Christopher and Pasadena had stolen the gun by breaking into the home of a gun collector. Christopher was sentenced to life in prison, and Daniels got 10 years.

Jacobs interviewed both Christopher and Daniels in prison. Christopher told Jacobs he became enraged when he believed the youth was mocking him and, in a moment of anger, pulled the trigger. Daniels gave the story an added twist. He did not know until the trial whom they had shot. Then he learned that the shooting victims were friends he had played ball with, but it was too dark to recognize them.

Daniels said, "If it hadn't been for the gun, we would have gotten out to fight and would have recognized them and said, 'what's up?' "

Jacobs was excited about her discovery that the shooting was not an unexplained, violent street-gang encounter. Instead, she saw that the fault lay in the availability of such a weapon. She told Talbot.

"We can't get away with saying the gun did it. You know what they say, 'guns don't kill people, people do.' But here is a situation where Daniels was completely innocent of the crime and his life is ruined," Jacobs argued.

"Are you kidding? He drove a guy with a loaded assault weapon to fight with three unarmed kids! What you are trying to do is make heroes out of the killers. They are not the victims. The dead boys and their families are."

Jacobs was taken aback by the criticism. She had also talked to the families of the shooting victims, and she believed it was a tragedy, but it was not, in reality, the kind of a story one always reads. She believed she had something different.

?

Is it wise for a newspaper to include aspects that show concern for the convicted murderers?

Yes: Murderers are shown in literature to have remorse for their crimes. Like Lady Macbeth. Good reporting can show all the aspects of an incident, and a good writer can weave an interesting narrative by telling all sides of a story, from the points of view of all participants.

No: Investigative stories have to point out wrongdoing and not make excuses for it. We have a story here about military guns in the hands of very dangerous people. This is not some social question about how some murderer got a bad break. Lady Macbeth could not wash her hands of her crime, and neither can these guys.

Should a newspaper print the expression, "kick their asses"?

Yes: Let's be realistic. We are quoting from the sworn testimony of three people who used those exact words. We can't change the wording, and the idea of writing "kick their a----" is laughable. It is important to the story, and it has to stay in.

No: It is not necessary to be explicit in a news story. It could be paraphrased. Instead of the phrase, we could merely write that one of them suggested they go back and engage the others in a fight. To say any more is excessive and a shallow attempt to be shocking.

One morning during the course of the gun investigation was to be memorable. Reporters arriving at work that day received the unexpected news that the *Star* had been sold to a huge media conglomerate. Some stockholders who had been supporting the publisher had deserted him in the face of the newspaper's shrinking profits, and they voted for the sale.

The media giant that swallowed the *Tri-Cities Star* had an infamous reputation for putting profits ahead of good journalism. The company worked its staff hard and carried no dead weight. The bottom line in the report to stockholders was said to be the company's goal. Employees who had reported for so many years on other people's adversities did not know how to cope with their own sudden misfortune.

Within a matter of weeks, top editors had resigned and new people were in place. Talbot and Jacobs, pretending that nothing had happened, hunkered down and kept at work on their story.

Talbot was chasing down the guns story and got a break. Gun manufacturing was small compared with the business of major industries, and competition among gun manufacturers was bitter. Gun makers, in interviews with Talbot, told stories on one another. One said that a competitor was bidding up the price of scrap steel from crunched-up guns. This gun maker believed that his competitor was piecing the guns back together. He told Talbot that the bidding information was easy to find. It was on the Internet.

Talbot found that auctions of surplus items from the military could be found on the Internet at a site called www.dof.gov. Talbot located the bids for the scrap metal from the ground-up rifles and saw that gun makers were the only parties interested in the scrap. The scrap metal from old guns was at times selling at 10 times the price of other similar scrap metal.

Talbot and Jacobs discussed how to proceed. They had to get inside the factory where a boxcar full of gun scraps had recently been sent from the crusher. It was an amazing story if true. The Defense

Department officials who were in charge of the bidding and the army officers who had to get rid of the guns had no knowledge of where the surplus they were selling was going. Talbot and Jacobs needed to get inside a gun maker's operation. They discussed the possibilities:

- They could pose as prospective gun buyers and be given a tour, but that would be as deceitful as an undercover job and would take a lot of preparation.
- They could go to the parking lot of the factory and write down the license plates of workers and call on them in their homes, but that would be met with resistance and the company bosses would hear of it.
- They could go through the waste dumpster, take out all the paperwork and see whether it contained revealing information. In most states, it has been established in law that material placed in a dumpster on public property is "abandoned property" and free for anyone to take. Reporters are known to have searched the garbage of J. Edgar Hoover, long-time FBI chief; Henry Kissinger, the former secretary of state; and Dr. Jack Kevorkian, advocate of assisted suicide. Police investigators are known to have gone through discarded waste without a search warrant.

The waste search seemed to be the only plausible approach, but there was no guarantee they would find anything. Talbot decided to call the head of the company and interview him—get the official version—the same as he had done with other companies. After identifying himself, Talbot asked the company head why the company had bid on scrap metal from the Defense Department and paid such a high price. The answer stunned Talbot to the degree than he was at a loss for words: the company was piecing the parts back together to make assault weapons out of them, but the company claimed the buyers were small foreign countries.

The weapons had been broken up in such large pieces, the executive said, that out of thousands of rifles destroyed, hundreds could be rebuilt from undamaged parts. People were working in the factory putting them together. The company believed it was doing nothing wrong because it was not creating new weapons or importing them; instead, it was reassembling existing guns. The company head commented that he had heard from other company owners that Talbot was investigating the process and that he had been awaiting his call. The company was in favor of the newspaper investigation because it hoped the federal government would stop the practice of selling the scrap. The reason was selfish: the company had a warehouse filled with millions of dollars worth of guns, and it wanted to be the only company with such weapons to sell.

Talbot and Jacobs were invited into the factory and warehouse and were permitted to take pictures. Only rarely does a company want to be exposed.

Talbot felt the investigation was lacking something. He and Jacobs had not been able to trace the weapons used in street crimes to the rebuilt weapons or to any other such origins because of the lack of regulation and registration. So the impact of being able to say that a gun used in a crime had a particular history was lost.

Talbot thought it might be a good idea to buy an assault weapon on the Internet to show people how easy it is. He liked such showmanship, but the editors had quashed some similar ideas in the past. When he was gathering information for a story about redlining—the practice of racial discrimination that denies services to persons living in minority neighborhoods—he suggested that reporters have a house moved from an African-American community to a white community.

His plan was to have company representatives come out and make estimates for the cost of roof repair and auto and homeowner insurance premiums and also learn the interest rate on home improvement loans in the minority neighborhood. The house would then be moved by a professional house mover to a vacant lot in the all-white neighborhood. The same agents would be called and asked to provide estimates in the new neighborhood. The editors saw the plan as not only risky because the house could be damaged in the move but also they worried that the differences in rates might not be significant enough to make a good story. They labeled the plan a stunt. The same information could be found elsewhere, they said. In the end, Talbot was able to find comparable homes in white and black neighborhoods, and he got his story.

But buying a gun on the Internet was a different matter. How else can one illustrate the availability of assault weapons on the Internet other than by buying one, the reporters reasoned. So they bought an M1 rifle similar to the weapon used at the convenience store shooting.

For this story, then, they used the Internet in three ways: to locate the shooting stories they needed, to document sales by the government, and to actively carry out an Internet transaction.

Jacobs was finding more and more stories about military guns and was not always taking a hard line against the shooters. Her stories were thoroughly researched and revealed the suffering of the shooters as well as the persons shot and their families. Talbot predicted the idea of telling people the murderers had suffered, too, was sure to be dismissed rapidly by an editor; and Talbot wondered whether the new editors valued investigative reporting. Talbot and Jacobs met with the new national editor, who had been an assistant to the conglomerate national editor in their big newspaper in Coastal City.

"The story is excellent. It is the type of story the other papers can pick up on," the national editor said. "I like the broad strokes you two take with the story—not advocating regulation or restriction but dealing with an issue by presenting the facts. Getting inside the brain of the shooter is brilliant. There is one thing that worries me. I don't think we should say, "kick their asses." It is a low-class remark, and we want a high-class paper. Both Jacobs and Talbot argued for using the raw language, saying it would be wrong to leave it out and stilted to use dash marks instead of the words.

"Okay, we leave it in, but let's hope we don't catch a lot of heat for it," the new editor said. "We know that everyone here is apprehensive about what the new owners want. The word is, we only care about the bottom line. Well, there is no disputing that the bottom line is vital because there is much financial pressure on newspapers now. Readership is down and costs are up. But the way to get readers is to present them with unique and timely stories like the series you have here. We don't care about carrying a political agenda with our stories or taking sides in an issue. All we want is a newspaper that delivers the facts in a fair and balanced way."

Talbot and Jacobs decided they would be able to work with the new ownership after all.

Memorandum

- Newspapers regularly watch their competitor's Web sites and try to catch up with them on breaking stories.
- Companies are required to list significant operating problems and lawsuits in their filings with the SEC.
- New revelations may result from going back over a news story that was underreported at the time.

Chapter Recap

Although the field of documentation, organization and accessibility has become more fertile because of the Internet, spreadsheets and databases, the result is not a lesser burden for the investigative reporter. The reporter's work might be even more difficult because the reporter has much more information to check, interpret and crunch down to newspaper article size. Good reporting from such documentation can prevent what sometimes used to happen: investigations driven by self-serving leaks from special interest groups. It has become imperative that the reporter accepts the Internet as a working partner and be familiar with all that it offers. Although we rely on government agencies to provide information that helps an investigation, we also must investigate those agencies to see whether they are doing their mandated jobs. The next chapter explores how to do that with agencies that are entrusted with the public safety.

Class Assignments

1. Go to the SEC filings on the Internet (www.sec.gov). Find five companies that are large employers in your local area, read their filings, and then write a report about the problems they anticipate. You can come up with a list of those companies by surfing the Internet and plugging in the name of the city and the word "industries." The company problems you find may be ones that the companies are reluctant to publicize. In fact, your report could be upgraded to the level of an important local story that you could offer to a local newspaper or broadcast station. You would have to contact spokespersons or officials of the companies for comments and write it in journalistic style.

2. Go to a search engine on the Internet and find organizations that have interests on opposing sides of a social question of your choice. For example, you may want to investigate prisons. Can you find an organization that works for prison inmates' rights? Can you find one that represents corrections professionals? Make a list of 10 subjects for investigation, and find Web sites with opposing positions on each.

3. Can you design an important investigation that could be carried out using only the Internet? One example is an analysis of the sources of campaign funds for the local member of congress. You would find this on the FEC Web site, www.fec.gov. Also, the Small Business Administration (SBA) at www.sba.gov has success stories about people who received SBA loans, prospered and paid them back. The SBA public relations office does not turn out stories about people who failed. Search the SBA cite for audits of defaults, and scan for defaults in your community. Then go to the local court clerk's office and look for lawsuits involving those companies. You can also check U.S. bankruptcy filings online at www.uscourts.gov/bankruptcycourts.html. You will also want to talk to the officers of the defaulting company to find why their business failed.

Notes

1. Mark Katches, William Heisel and Ronald Campbell, "The Body Brokers," *The Orange County Register*, April 16-20, 2000, www.ocregister.com/features/body/.
2. All Things Ypsilanti, info@ypsinews.com.

C h a p t e r   5

Investigating Those Who Guard the Public

IN 2001, AUSTIN (TEXAS) AMERICAN-STATESMAN REPORTERS Jeff Nesmith and Ralph K. M. Haurwitz found a far-out-of-sight danger and a government agency that was unable to control it properly.[1] The reporters learned that for decades an agency of the state Department of Transportation—the Office of Pipeline Safety—did not know the exact location of some of the pipelines or even whether pipes existed. Nesmith and Haurwitz dug deeper and found even more: unreported spills, inconsistent record keeping and loss of life. They discovered a pipeline regulatory system that did little to enforce the law and thus essentially protected the interests of the industry. Nesmith and Haurwitz called their story "Pipelines: The Invisible Danger" and led off their series with these words:

> "Out of sight and unnoticed, America's sprawling oil and natural gas pipelines are leaking oil on the scale of a ruptured supertanker. They are fouling the environment and causing fires and explosions that have killed more than 200 people and injured more than 1,000 in the past decade."

Using a strong lead to open their story, the reporters packed a punch by comparing the pipelines with a supertanker spilling oil. The report was not slowed by numbers in the takeoff; instead it created a startling image of the dangers underground and put the story in a context everyone understood. The *Austin American-Statesman* series brought many calls for reform. Thus, investigative reporters such as Nesmith and Haurwitz work to help ensure the safety of the public by checking on the performance of government agencies that were created to protect people from physical harm.

101

Local police and fire departments play an important role in the front lines of life and property protection. Many other government agencies also regulate industry and enforce safety rules to help citizens feel safe and secure. Some lobbying groups complain of too much regulation. Meanwhile, the agencies amass reams of documents that help an investigative reporter assess their performances. Reporters often find huge gaps in the system.

In this chapter you will learn which local, state and federal agencies protect the public and how to find and report about those that are failing to do the job. Many of the agencies are familiar because we examined some of them in Chapter 4, which was about access to information on the Internet. In Chapter 4 we were looking at the agencies to learn what official information we could glean from them to help us in investigations. Here we are looking at the agencies to see whether they are fulfilling their purposes.

Issues of Safety

Investigative stories are often of great interest to readers if they cover topics that concern average people, every day, as they go about their daily routines. Safety issues concern everyone, and investigative reporters find revelations about them are in demand.

Buildings and Structures

Local building inspectors are public safety officials who have the power to issue citations that could close down a business or condemn an unsafe property just as food inspectors can close a restaurant. The investigative reporter can conduct an inspection as well, exposing dangerous conditions such as fire escapes that are chained shut or blocked by furniture. Such reports have high visual impact and show that the inspectors do not always find the dangers, or even if they do, those unsafe conditions have not been corrected because there is no follow-up.

Cities and states have building departments. They must approve new construction to make sure it meets all the standards set by law. They also are called upon to remove hazards in existing buildings. They do not usually enter a private home to inspect, but state law provides various reasons for inspections. A business that invites the public in or has employees and an apartment building of a certain number of units would probably qualify under the law for inspection. Building inspectors are responsible for checking on elevators and carnival rides, and those inspections reports will be on file along with reports on theaters and sports complexes.

Local statutes may require that local government officials carry out inspections within a certain time period. Inspectors' work sheets are public record and in most places will be released after a written request. The local inspector may be reluctant to close down the football stadium when the local team is on a winning streak, but the reporter will be concerned about loose roofing and shaky handrails. And the reporter also can note the rigged-up electric systems around the food concession booths, where electric cords dangle or stretch across walkways. All the reporter needs do is look.

One special area for an investigation of the work of building inspectors is the access to restrooms in public places. States have laws that set rules for public restrooms. Wisconsin statutes, for example, demand that in an amusement facility where the public congregates, "the owner of a facility shall equip and maintain restrooms with a sufficient number of permanent or temporary toilets to ensure that women have a speed of access that equals men." [2] A reporter can complain if the ballpark does not comply and learn how long it takes inspectors to act.

Such investigative findings call for an answer as to the causes of the oversight. Are the public safety officials understaffed and overworked, or corrupt or lazy? We might follow them around for a day.

Transportation

Traffic experts in the local street departments mark the lanes and repair and replace the traffic signs. The purpose is safety. The public often complains that markings fade at such places as crosswalks, and their absence causes accidents. Once again, the reporter has a visual story, this time from the lack of markings. If a stop sign is knocked down, does the policeman on the beat notify the street department? And does the street department take immediate action to replace it? Maybe not, because the police officers may not have regular rounds but only respond to calls.

The investigative reporter will learn of the sign being down when a bad traffic accident is the result. Then the reporter will talk to residents in the neighborhood who may know how long the sign has been down and will file an FOIA request with the police and street departments for any records of it having been reported. Does it seem like too small of an investigation? Not if it is a matter of life or death.

Likewise, the reporter will follow up accident reports to learn whether the accident was caused by an obstruction such as high weeds. It could be that the accident was caused by a pothole that local drivers had reported weeks before.

Federal regulations require that school bus drivers walk around their buses each morning and check them for any problems before taking them out on the road. They must check the tires, the electrical system and mirrors. Do they really do it? Who is checking on them? Do they never miss a morning? Am I supposed to believe that they never miss a morning inspection in a deserted parking lot when the sun is not yet up? An investigative reporter could observe.

Are the conditions that caused a fatal bus accident in another state present in similar circumstances in the reporter's coverage area? And should they have been corrected by the street department? For example, in an accident in another state, a bus jumped the curb and smashed into a sheltered sidewalk bus stop, and several people who were waiting in the shelter are killed. A U.S. Department of Transportation report obtained off the Internet cites the fact that there had not been any protection between the shelter and street traffic. The reporter will observe whether such a hazard exists on local streets and will write about it to warn the public and local officials.

Environment

State and federal environmental protection agencies protect citizens from unclean air and water. A reporter could enlist the aid of a private laboratory to test water or air samples and learn whether the inspectors are reporting all contamination. The reporter could dip a cup into the local river, take the water sample to a lab and pay for an analysis. The sample would be taken from the river upstream as it enters the reporter's local area. Then, if a problem is found, the reporter will want to contact university public relations offices for names of experts who accept requests for interviews. They will most likely offer their thoughts about what caused the contamination. The reporter will be a big hero in town after exposing the fact that an industry far upstream is polluting the local water and is being forced to stop.

Workplace

The Occupational Safety and Health Administration within the U.S. Department of Labor works to remove safety hazards in the workplace. OSHA's findings make an interesting survey that is placed in detail online. Is OSHA finding all the hazards and following up to see whether they are corrected? One way for a reporter to find out is to go to the local files of claims under workers' compensation laws. "Workers' comp" is a federal program that provides workers with payments for any injuries at work, and it protects employers from inordinate damages in lawsuits. The records are public and are indexed according to states. A reporter must find the agency that administers the program, run names of employers through the database and learn who had the best and worst accident records. Did OSHA inspect and find or not find hazardous conditions that caused these claims? Reporters are not satisfied with writing about what the local or federal inspectors saw; they will try to learn whether the dangerous safety conditions have been corrected, which can sometimes be seen from the public entrances and passageways.

Medicine

The Food and Drug Administration (FDA) controls the marketing of pharmaceuticals and the production and importation of food. After an official announcement of spoiled food, a reporter might ask how much of the spoiled food ordered off shelves was located. The agency provides such information on the Internet.

A story alleging FDA errors won a Pulitzer Prize in 2001 for David Willman of the *Los Angeles Times*.[3] He showed with statistics and reports from the FDA and interviews with experts that too many dangerous drugs were being approved with too little testing. Telling this highly technical and scientific story was a challenge that this reporter met. It deserves a close look for content, organization and style:

> "For most of its history, the United States Food and Drug Administration approved new prescription medicines at a grudging pace, paying daily homage to the physician's creed, 'First do no harm.' "

This investigative story opens with a traditional, familiar narrative. It tells the reader "Once upon a time . . ."

> "Then in the early 1990s, the demand for AIDS drugs changed the political climate."

Immediately one can feel an ill wind blowing. Change is in the air, and the reader is set to hear some bad news. Tell us what happened next!

> "Congress told the FDA to work closely with pharmaceutical firms in getting new medicines to market more swiftly. President Clinton urged FDA leaders to trust industry 'as partners, not adversaries.' The FDA achieved its goals, but now the human cost is becoming clear."

The reader has the background in three short paragraphs and is now ready for the full impact. The "nut graph" goes here, and the writer must summarize the story as briefly as possible.

> "Seven drugs approved since 1993 have been withdrawn after reports of deaths and severe side effects. A two-year *Los Angeles Times* investigation has found that the FDA approved each of those drugs while disregarding danger signs of

blunt warnings from its own specialists. Then, after receiving reports of significant harm to patients, the agency was slow to seek withdrawals."

At this point, the reader knows what the story is about and will read on
if the promised story is meaningful. A series of informative paragraphs
follows:

"According to 'adverse events' reports filed with the FDA, the seven drugs
were cited as suspects in 1,002 deaths. Because the deaths are reported by doctors, hospitals and others on a voluntary basis, the true number of fatalities
could be far higher, according to epidemiologists."

Another defender of the public from accident and disease is the
local health department. Local and state health departments regularly
inspect nursing homes and hospitals to check whether they are maintaining high standards. A reporter can get these reports, many from the
Internet, and then see whether the complaints of hazardous facilities
have been corrected.

Officials of the Chicago Board of Health and the Illinois Public Health
Department were embarrassed to be found lacking in 1975 when the
Chicago Tribune sent a reporter undercover as a janitor at a hospital. The
reporter learned that the owner, a surgeon, was performing unnecessary
surgery, overbilling Medicaid, and running an unsanitary surgery room.
The stories that resulted were an example of how to find a problem in a
nationwide program by investigating it on a local level, but the stories were
perhaps not a good example of how to gather information.

The reporter, William Gaines, author of this text, worked on a series
of stories that won a Pulitzer Prize in 1976,[4] and he testified about his experiences to the U.S. Senate Special Committee on Aging.[5]

The hospital that was the focus of the stories was dangerously understaffed and poorly maintained. Doctors used its surgery facilities to rack up
payments for surgery that experts said was unnecessary—for example, the
one-day removal of all the tonsils from all the members of a family of five.
The reporter told the senators of his discoveries.

Mr. Gaines: When the *Chicago Tribune* Task Force began an investigation of
hospital care, one hospital soon emerged as needing special scrutiny.

It was Von Solbrig hospital, an 83-bed facility in a white, middle-class neighborhood in Chicago. The hospital is unique in Chicago because it is the only
general hospital in the city that has profit making as its expressed purpose.

Its founder and sole owner is Dr. Charles von Solbrig, who is also the
administrator, medical director, and chief surgeon. He controls every facet of
the hospital operation. He conducts surgery without fear of criticism of any
hospital board that he does not control.

The Board of Health of the City of Chicago, which is empowered to
enforce state regulations on the licensing of hospitals, would make routine

inspections, carrying a checklist of possible sanitary violations. The fire department inspectors would check fire extinguishers and doors and the like.

A hospital surveillance program set up many years ago in Illinois to monitor decisions in the use of public welfare money did not check on Von Solbrig Hospital. The hospital was judged too small for that.

Professional medical organizations would not be critical of doctors. We found that no doctor would go on the record as critical of another doctor. And when a lay person complained, doctors would say, "Who are you to criticize? You're not a doctor."

So I got a job as a janitor in Von Solbrig Hospital and I found that I didn't need to know anything about medicine to know that something was wrong. All I needed to do was count the staff in the surgery area, patient wards, and emergency room. I found that nurses were doing the job of doctors. Nurses' aides were doing the job of registered nurses, and I, as a janitor would do the job of orderly, aide, and nurse.

There was no doctor specifically assigned to the emergency room. On some days, the only physician available was the radiologist. There was no specialist in pediatrics or geriatrics available although patients ranged in age from infants to octogenarians. The short staffing of the surgery room was shocking.

Many times, the only doctor in the hospital would be in surgery, performing one operation after another. Assembly line operations were performed on children on public aid.

The recovery room would either be bypassed entirely or an untrained aide would be placed there to awaken a patient after surgery and remove him to his room.

One aide inside the surgery room was a 16-year-old high school student who volunteered to work in the hospital and was assigned to the surgery room within four days and without any training. His duties included counting sponges to see that none were left inside the patient.

Later, I would be called into the surgery room to help move patients off the table during a week when the high school boy was home with the measles. It didn't matter that moments before I was called into the surgery room, I was mopping floors or unloading a truck in the parking lot and wearing my dirty janitor outfit.

Every day, between janitor jobs, I would help lift elderly patients. One elderly Medicaid patient was in a cast, and an aide, the teenage volunteer and I struggled to lift her in and out of the bed as she cried out in pain. None of us had any training in handling patients, and the hospital had no mechanical lifts. . . .

Senator Moss: On these family surgeries of five children, did you talk with members of the family, the mothers and the father of any of those?

Mr. Gaines. Yes, we did; we talked with as many as we could find.

Senator Moss: And was this on the recommendation of the doctor, that all of this occurred, or how did they get five of them in a row?

Mr. Gaines: Well, the symptoms for tonsillitis are sore throat, loss of hearing and high fever, and we found that when a child was brought in by his

107

mother into the clinic he might just have had a sore throat, he might not have had the other symptoms, and that the other member of the family did not have those same symptoms, but the mother was asked to bring in the other members of the family, and have them examined, and then the diagnosis would be tonsillitis for the entire family.

The mothers who brought their children in felt that the doctor was concerned, because he asked them to bring in their other children.

It seemed to them he was doing his job, and they would trust him when they brought them in, and although the governing authorities did not find out about these mass tonsillectomies, when I first started at the hospital, I found out that even janitors there were aware that something was wrong. . . .

Senator Percy: How many others were on the maintenance staff?

Mr. Gaines: There were no more than five fulltime employees, including myself. There was one shift of maintenance workers on the day shift. There were no maintenance workers at night or overnight.

Senator Percy: Did the other people on the maintenance staff have the same kind of experiences that you did, or were you an exception rather than the rule?

Mr. Gaines: I saw other janitors called to assist with the patients. Sometimes they took two janitors to lift a patient, that we were called together to help with the patients.

Senator Percy: Did anyone check your references before you were hired?

Mr. Gaines: No, they did not. . . .

Senator Percy: In the period you worked at Von Solbrig, did you see any evidence of monitoring of conditions at the facility by state officials?

Mr. Gaines: I was not there at any time when an inspection was conducted, but I learned that since I left, that there was an inspection.

Senator Percy: But while you were there, you saw no evidence of inspection procedures?

Mr. Gaines: No, I did not.

Senator Percy: Would it be apparent to an inspector walking in [that] there were flagrant violations of minimum standards that should be corrected?

Mr. Gaines: I think by a head count of the nurses and the aides, checking what positions they were assigned to, and the inspector could walk in at any time, and interview these people, and check their qualifications, as they worked and find this out, but it would not be a matter of just coming and seeing them, I would not think, because it did take me quite a while myself to find out who was doing what, because in this particular hospital, no one wore name tags, and there was no uniform to designate who had what job.

Senator Percy: Finally, do you have any reason to, or did you come to any conclusion as to why these conditions could exist, when we had investigations 4 years ago revealing the laxity in inspections by city and State officials? Why is it that a facility like this had to be discovered by you when there are inspectors paid for by departments funded for that very purpose?

Mr. Gaines: I think they did not have enough experience to find out what happens. They have certain lists, and those are the things they would check. . . .

Senator Percy: There is a picture, and I am sorry that we cannot put pictures in the record but there is a picture of the staff directory in the lobby of the Von Solbrig Hospital. Very imposing, staff doctors, and names of them, how many names roughly are on that list?

Mr. Gaines: There are 50 names on that list.

Senator Percy: And how many of them actually could be located by you, that actually worked at the hospital?

Mr. Gaines: Eighteen persons. They were not staff doctors, but at one time, they had a patient there, and considered themselves associated in some way at the hospital.

Senator Percy: Were all of the doctors listed on that list alive?

Mr. Gaines: No. Several were dead. Some had never brought a patient to the hospital.

Senator Percy: Do you suppose they were still voting in Cook County? I will not ask for an answer to that.

So that there was an apparent deception here, or at least the listing had fallen out of date certainly. . . . Mr. Chairman, I would request that when our hearings are available and printed, in printed form, that copies be sent to appropriate law enforcement officials, the attorney general of the State of Illinois, the state's attorney in Cook County, and wherever in whatever county we might have testimony. . . .

Government agencies had overlooked rather than overseen this hospital and other medical facilities about which the *Chicago Tribune* wrote. The conditions at the hospital were widely discussed in the medical profession, and the fire department stopped taking emergency cases there, but the local inspectors took no action. These conditions are what had caused the *Tribune* to employ the once acceptable practice of a reporter secretly gathering information through misrepresentation although very little such undercover reporting is done by journalists. It is considered unethical, dangerous and a nightmare for media attorneys.

Could this report on Von Solbrig Hospital have been done without the infiltration of the target of the investigation? To a degree it could have. If a reporter was doing a complete study of the workings of the hospital, bills to the state for public aid recipients would have been found and examined, and it could have become apparent that inordinate numbers of tonsillectomies were being performed and that patients had much longer stays than their diagnoses required. The names of the doctors who were missing from the roster were displayed in the hospital lobby and could have been checked by anyone dropping in. Of course, the impact of the story would have suffered without the excitement of a first-person account, but critics would say that the story should stand on its own merits and not be hyped by an undercover adventure.

Fire Protection

The Detroit fire department was found by *The Detroit News* to be poorly equipped and thinly staffed and unable to do a proper job. Investigative reporter Melvin Claxton joined with Charles Hurt in 2000 to show that rampant negligence and mismanagement in the fire department had led to 20 deaths in four years.[6] Claxton, winner of a Pulitzer Prize at a Virgin Islands newspaper in 1994, said he finds it best to focus on three areas of investigation when he deals with a large organization such as the fire department:

Personnel training. How are personnel trained? Are there enough firefighters (in this case)?

Equipment. How is equipment maintained?

Management decisions. Where does the department spend its money?

"One interesting thing about fires is that people never blame the fire department," Claxton said. The reporters could find no lawsuit against the fire department blaming it for a death. Working with sources in the Detroit firefighters' union, Claxton and Hurt learned of internal dispatcher records that had not been included among routine records kept by the department and dispatcher broadcast tapes. The broadcast tapes revealed this plea: "I'm at the scene, my ladder doesn't work. I can't rescue people."

This dispatcher log, accessed through an FOIA request, reveals a litany of daily problems (see Figures 5.1 and 5.2).

The training program had no burn tower on which to practice, so firefighters had to practice with make-believe fires. Stations did not have the required four men on a truck, and firehouse cooks had to go out on calls. In one incident, six children died in a fire when unqualified engineers could not operate a pump.

Claxton and Hurt used a vignette lead for their series of stories, stories that were about as dramatic and tragic as the written word can tell.

"For 25-year-old Norfessa Shannon, it was an act of sheer desperation. With a fire raging down the hall and black smoke billowing into her living room, she smashed the heavy glass of her eighth-floor window with her bare hands and tore away the screen. Shannon heaved her 7-year-old daughter onto the ledge and pleaded with her to jump if she wanted to live.

"Then, screaming for someone to catch her baby, she let her child go. On the ground 80 feet below, anxious neighbors waited with blankets pulled taut to catch the little girl.

"Nearby, a fire truck with a 100-foot ladder designed to rescue people from multi-story buildings sat in the driveway of the 188-unit Pallister

Figure 5.1 Detroit Fire Department dispatcher log, page 1

Detroit Fire Department
COMMUNICATIONS DIVISION

TO: Fire Commissioner   DATE: __October 31, 1999__

The following companies were placed out of service during the past twenty-four (24) hours, from 0001
hours through 2400 hours on ____October 30, 1999____

COMPANY	REASON	TIME OUT	TIME IN
E22X	RIG WON'T START	0220	0256
E22X	RIG WON'T START	0300	1429
E/4X	R/S FIAT	0846	1026
E52	AIR LEAK	1013	1034
C03	R/S WOR	1052	1119
E5	RS-MDT	1139	1241
E38	WOR	1335	1608
* E05	missed run	1334	1340 *
E49	BROKE DOWN	2220	

Sr. Fire Dispatcher
Abner Garrett

Shift Supervisor

Source: Melvin Claxton and Charles Hurt, Freedom of Information Act request, 2000

Plaisance Apartments on Detroit's west side. It had been there for more than
five minutes, firefighters and witnesses agree.

But the truck, the first sent to the April 1 fire, couldn't help in the rescue
effort. Its ladder didn't work.

Figure 5.2 Detroit Fire Department dispatcher log, page 2

Detroit Fire Department
COMMUNICATIONS DIVISION

TO: Fire Commissioner   DATE: November 17, 1999

The following companies were placed out of service during the past twenty-four (24) hours, from 0001

hours through 2400 hours on ___November 16, 1999___

COMPANY		REASON	TIME OUT	TIME IN
L08		AIR LEAK	0728	0926 ✓
L25		MANPOWER	0751	0755 ✓
TAC 2	1	MANPOWER	0751	
E54	2	NOR	0752	1820 ✓
E17	3	NOR	0757	1551 ✓
E10	4	P,M	0804	1702 ✓
C04		R/S	0822	1643 —
E58		REPLACE LINE	0828	0953 ✓
505		WOR	1012	1208 —
E40		ENGRAVE LINE	1101	1209 ✓
S01		R.S-Repairs	1324	1643 ✓
L30		W.O.B. @ R/S	1500	1602 ✓
L19		R/S WOR	1655	1908 ✓

Sr. Fire Dispatcher
Abner Garrett

Shift Supervisor

Source: Melvin Claxton and Charles Hurt, Freedom of Information Act request, 2000

Case Study

The Firehouse*

People in Buchanan were proud of their fire department, and Chief Phillips was known to take every opportunity to boast of its number one rating. Firefighters were town heroes, pictured carrying children out of burning buildings and taking part in civic activities with a marching band that performed on holidays. No one dared criticize the fire department.

Residents who had gone through Buchanan schools nurtured fond memories of the fifth grade class tour of a firehouse, during which they got to sit in the fire truck and ring the bell. Although Chief Phillips was in his 70s, there was no talk of replacing him even after the canning factory burned to the ground.

Lori Benton, investigative reporter for the *Buchanan Record-Journal*, did not report on the canning factory fire when it was a breaking story. That task was performed well by two general assignment reporters. But the next day she started looking for the causes of the fire and checking on the performance of the fire department. She found Chief Phillips in front of the main fire station ending an on-camera interview to a TV reporter. The chief was dressed in his fully festooned uniform, and he wore a fire helmet that looked like it belonged in a museum. She asked why the fire had gone out of control.

"It was a sudden oxygeneration event," he said. "It was completely out of control when we got the call."

"I would like to hear the tapes of the 9-1-1 calls that came in," Benton said.

"Certainly, and as soon as we transcribe them, we will get them to you. I am familiar with the state law, and I am eager to help the public to be informed," he said. "By the way, you might mention in your story that we offer home safety and fire prevention instruction at the library every second Tuesday of the month."

Benton wanted to learn how long it took from the first call until the fire department got to the factory. If she gets the information from the 9-1-1 calls, she will know when the first call came in but not when the trucks arrived. She needs the tapes and the log of the dispatcher. That should provide the information about the arrival of the trucks.

---

*The cases are based on real investigative stories, but the names and places have been changed to protect reporters, their sources and the secrets they have. Some are actual stories told in a step-by-step reconstruction and others are composites.

"The dispatcher tapes?" Chief Phillips asked. "Yes, I guess that is covered by the state open records act."

"And chief, we want the tapes, not a transcript," Benton commented. "Electronic recordings are considered to be documents under state law." Benton remembered the 18 1/2 minutes of the Nixon Watergate tapes that were "accidentally" erased.

"Yes, well, I can assure you we responded to the call immediately. We are a number one rated fire department. We are not slackers."

The police department had received the 9-1-1 calls, and Benton got them within a few days of her request. While she was at the police station, Police Chief Roscoe cornered her and asked what was going on with her interest in the fire. Did she have some inside information about the possibility of arson?

She really did not have more than a routine question of whether the firefighters performed well, but she teased the chief with the idea that the firefighters were somehow remiss.

"That's not news. The fire department is always slow. I've seen a whole row of houses burn while they are trying to untangle their hoses. Now, this is off the record. I don't want you quoting me. They've got a new truck, but nobody knows how to operate it. The only time they are in a hurry is when there is a bomb scare. They try to get to the bomb before my bomb squad gets there. If we get there first, our technician goes into the building quietly and dismantles the bomb, but if they arrive ahead of us they bring a big vat on wheels that is like a cement mixer with an opening at the top. They zap the suspected bomb with a freeze gun and carry it out to the street and throw it in the vat. Meanwhile, a crowd has gathered, and if that bomb were real and it exploded, the concussion would kill people nearby and would shatter buildings for blocks around."

Benton had not thought before that the fire department was actually dangerous.

"They have an arson investigation team but they have no power to make an arrest. They turn over their findings to us, but my officers are more capable of investigating for arson than they are, so we don't want their help," Chief Roscoe confided.

"Well, they have a number one national rating," Benton mentioned.

"You had better check on that. I don't see how anybody could rate them other than the lowest," Chief Roscoe continued. "Remember, I'm off the record."

Benton visited a firehouse when the chief was away giving a lecture on civic responsibility at the American National Convention of Fire Fighting Chiefs on Padre Island. She introduced herself and said she was interested in doing an in-depth story about the fire department. The firefighters and their captain exchanged quick glances.

"All contact with the media has to be through Chief Phillips," the captain said.

"I just want to know that everything is okay with the fire department. Chief Phillips is such a nice fellow, but he is hard to pin down," Benton tested.

"Look, we'd like to talk to you, but that's the rule. Chief Phillips seems like a nice old man, but he's got a mean streak when it comes to breaking the rules about the media."

Two days later, an envelope arrived downstairs at the newspaper reception desk; the address was a short one: Lori Benton. Inside were work orders for fire department equipment, personnel assignment records and interdepartmental memos. The documents showed that the firefighters were not assigned to the duties for which they were carried on the roster. The designated duty was penciled out and the true function of the person was written in.

Benton saw that several of the firefighters listed as fire safety inspectors were actually serving as drivers for the chief, the mayor and some of the mayor's staff. Benton had been told that the members of the marching band performed on "off duty" time. The documents showed that band members requested time off even for practice sessions to the degree that they never showed up for work. Chief Phillips promoted the idea of fitness, and everyone in the department was allowed access to a commercial health club; the documents showed they were assigned to the health club. The consequences were apparent. The firehouses were understaffed, and a count revealed fewer than half of the firefighters were present for a fire call. Benton was finally getting to the facts.

Should the investigation proceed with the information found in the documents?

Yes: Benton has official documents that are public. She cannot testify firsthand about where they originated, but she has enough confidence to believe they are authentic. It is an important story that cannot be assembled otherwise.

No: The documents may be authentic, but they need to be checked. She can prove easily enough whether they are factual; all she has to do is go observe the firefighters.

Benton watched and took pictures of firefighters chauffeuring officials and hanging out at the health club during duty times. To document the band members, she showed up at their place of duty and counted the firefighters going out on a fire call without them. She got pictures.

Benton surmised that if the organization that rated fire departments knew the truth Buchanan would be at the bottom, not the top.

She contacted a spokesperson for an organization that rates fire departments in an effort to keep them up to high standards on behalf of the insurance industry.

"I can't give you information about individual departments. We give out the ratings, and the fire departments decide whether they want to publicize them. Ratings are based on the availability of water, of personnel and of equipment."

"We had a big fire in a canning factory here, and the firefighters couldn't handle it. Does something like that factor into the ratings?"

"We don't observe fires. If there is a well-trained and -equipped department, they are going to succeed."

"I was told that this fire was a rapid oxygeneration," Benton told him.

"You mean oxygenation," he corrected.

"Is that what it is? What does it mean?" Benton asked.

"It only means it is a fire," he said. "That is the technical term for a fire. A fire or burning is a persistent chemical reaction between a combustible substance and oxygen. Or it can be called the rapid oxygenation of a material."

"But isn't it a fire that can't be controlled?"

"It's any fire. Whoever you've been talking to doesn't know the first thing about fires."

Benton saw that the *Record-Journal* had quoted Chief Phillips in the past as excusing a fire loss as a "rapid oxygeneration."

?

Should Chief Phillips' erroneous quote be used?

Yes: We don't care whether it's embarrassing to the chief or not, a quote is a quote and should never be doctored.

No: There is no need to drag the chief's malapropisms into the story. The quote can be paraphrased; for example, "The chief said the fire had too rapid a start for them to be able to contain it."

Later, the dispatcher tapes from the time of the canning factory fire were made available to Benton at the clerk's office, and she was able to take notes. She was stunned when she heard the driver of the new fire engine that Chief Phillips had bought call in desperately to say that he was not able to get the new high-rise equipment through the underpass of the Buchanan and Vancouver Railroad at Main Street. He said he had to take Blackoak Boulevard to the old bridge, which he decided was too shaky to attempt with the weight of the equipment. His transmission made it clear that the entire industrial area on the Southwest Side was unprotected by the new equipment. The driver had to turn back to the firehouse.

Chief Phillips had taken great pride in the purchase of the new fire truck, commenting that it was the best in the state and far better than anything his archrival, Chief Blount, had at San Mesa.

The tapes also showed how long it took the firefighters to respond. Fewer than half were on duty because the band had performed at the annual Founders Day festival the night before, and they had to be called from their homes.

Is the story ready to be written and published?

Yes: Benton now has enough to go with. If she holds up on the story for any reason, she will contribute to the danger facing Buchanan residents.

No: Benton should not chance an overreaction by the public. Besides, Buchanan residents got along without the new engine before it was purchased, and the firefighters responded as quickly as they could.

Benton did not have to agonize over a decision for long. That very night, a fire broke out in the paper clip factory. She went to a firehouse and found that the firefighters did not try to take out the new truck because the engineers knew they could not drive it to the fire. Hundreds of wire-bending machines were destroyed and, although no one could get an accurate count, it was obvious that millions of paper clips melted down from the intense heat.

Benton wrote a detailed story. The city council held hearings, and Chief Phillips admitted that he bought the new equipment to fulfill requirements to obtain a number one rating, although he knew it was not functional for parts of the city. The marching band and the bomb squad were disbanded, and firefighters were required to be at their designated posts. A new firehouse was built on the far side of the railroad tracks, and it was named for Chief Phillips.

Memorandum

- Government inspectors often do an inadequate job.
- A fire department can have good public relations but poor performance.
- A law does not always work as it was intended.
- A government agency may not get complaints although misapplication of rules is rampant.
- Repeated complaints about an enforcement agency may spawn an investigative project.

Children

The Federal Trade Commission (FTC) at www.ftc.gov protects the public from dangerous products such as toys that might harm a child. A reporter might check local emergency rooms for incidents of injuries to a child from a dangerous toy that was overlooked by the federal enforcement agency. The schools are supposed to provide a safe haven in which children can be educated, but the shootings at Columbine High School in Colorado and other school shootings have caused concern and have led to increased security from primary- through college-level schools. Investigative reporters have produced stories showing that the schools are not fulfilling the promise of tighter security. They ask who is responsible.

Karen Hensel, investigative reporter for WISH-TV in Indianapolis, found serious threats to child safety in Indianapolis-area schools. In her November 2003 reports,[7] Hensel showed that middle and high school teachers literally turned their backs on ever-present schoolyard bullies who openly attacked classmates, causing them serious injuries and making them afraid of going to school. The Channel 8 investigative team was surprised to find, Hensel said, that school officials did not have to report bully incidents to the state department of education, and so it was impossible to tell how often such attacks occurred. One school official told the reporters that he did not report the incidents because it would appear the school did not have control of the pupils. WISH-TV used its Web site to gather citizen comments, and the story, which was originally scheduled for two nights, was swept along with follow-ups until it resulted in the enactment of an anti-bullying law two years later.

The WISH-TV report was done in a traditional TV investigative format. The station promoted it throughout the day and planned for a two-part series. It is no coincidence that it was broadcast during a ratings period. Each report started and ended with Hensel in the broadcast studio at the anchor desk. She was dressed in the popular attire for women news reporters—a blazer-style business suit—and she was introduced by the news anchor. The report is special, viewers can see, because it is set apart from the news of the day by a logo displayed over Hensel's shoulder with the words "Bullied: Silent Tears, TEAM 8." The logo was carried throughout the investigative report, from night to night, to give the series of reports added continuity.

Hensel documented the story with interviews of parents, children and school officials, but the most convincing evidence turned out to be action pictures taken from hidden cameras. Because of legal and ethical issues, the hidden cameras were placed outside the school property in public areas, and parents granted permission before children were interviewed.

Source: WISH-TV, 24-Hour News 8 I-Team Investigative Unit

The hidden-camera aspect of the story was introduced on the first evening as an audience teaser for the second night's report. Hensel led the audience on with, "We took hidden cameras to recess." The cameras did not reveal severe beatings, but fists flew, scuffles ensued, and boys and girls were knocked to the ground while the cameras rolled. At the same time the cameras showed teachers, unconcerned, taking their recess away from the pupils.

The cameras revealed more. Hensel stressed the element of the story that showed social exclusion of some children by their classmates. This ostracizing showed up on the videotapes as children were repelled, sometimes pushed away, when they attempted to join a group. It was a problem, she said, that needed to be addressed by parents and teachers.

Hensel often reported from a school corridor when the halls were empty. TV producers like to have their reporters at the scene of the story because their presence adds realism to the story.

The overall caution about identifying children makes the thoroughness of Hensel's TV report suffer, but Hensel was able to get a photo of a child in Connecticut who died from a school beating. The story did not rely heavily on documents, but knowing that viewers find comfort in the display

Source: WISH-TV, 24-Hour News 8 I-Team Investigative Unit

of printed documents, the reporter used examples of written statements of children. The words were highlighted on the screen as they were spoken by Hensel.

Television reports have an advantage over print because they can show emotion much better than it can be described. Interviews with parents were an important element of the story.

Indiana parents responded with demands to the schools for protection. To many adults, it brought back unpleasant memories of bullying during their school days. The WISH-TV Web site became "bully central," where people could report bully attacks, and those complaints could be passed along to the schools or the police. Politicians promised action.

"It was a problem that everyone knew existed but no one had documented," Hensel said. Although it turned out to be an important report, Hensel found the idea a hard sell with the editors. "I pitched the story for more than a year before they let me do it," she said.

Although an investigative project for TV, like the WISH-TV series about bullies, will seldom show lengthy interviews, interviewing techniques are employed nonetheless. There is a distinct approach to TV interviews that we will examine and then contrast with print media interviewing.

Source: WISH-TV, 24-Hour News 8 I-Team Investigative Unit

The Investigative Interview

Arranging, conducting and then writing about an interview are skills learned by every successful reporter. Investigative reporters need to be good interviewers: well-prepared, concise in questioning, and devoted listeners with all the attributes of a girl scout or boy scout. They also have to develop some special investigative interviewing techniques.

Television Interviews

A viewer watching a TV investigation expects to hear from other people as well as the reporter in order to be convinced of the investigative conclusion. The battle is half won if the producer-reporter finds an interviewee who both looks knowledgeable and is knowledgeable. In TV journalism, the person being interviewed is, in effect, speaking directly to the viewer and must carry the load of winning the argument. Much effort goes into preparing and filming an interviewee, whether that person is touted as an expert or has been a victim of the wrongdoing that is exposed. The process is laborious and time consuming, and the product is likely to be a five-

121

second sound bite. Time is precious for the TV producer-reporter who is presenting an investigative piece, so the interviewee has very little time to make a point. An editor must extract a quick but meaningful quote from hour-long conversations, and the remainder of the interview will end up on the infamous cutting-room floor.

Television investigations are quite open. The reporter will tell how the investigation was conducted, and the viewer—behind the lens of the camera—will follow along. In an interview, the camera will shoot over the shoulder of the reporter to get the viewer "on the side" of the reporter. If the reporter knocks on a door and asks for an interview, and the potential interviewee slams the door in the reporter's face, the door is also being slammed in the face of the viewer who was in effect right behind the reporter.

One closely held secret not shared with the viewer is that a nameless, faceless producer is at the side of the on-the-air reporter, and together they create the investigative piece. They are partners, receiving about the same pay in a local station and sharing the responsibility. In many smaller TV markets, one person carries the camera, sets up the interviews, conducts them and edits the tape. But in those stations that have ongoing investigations, it is the producer who sets up the interviews, guides the interviewee and primes the reporter with the questions to ask. The producer may even rehearse the interviewee by playing the role of the reporter.

But the reporter is no phony. The reporter must be well-versed in the subject matter investigated to be properly enthusiastic when on the air. In the early days of radio, some announcer booths had signs that urged, "If you can't be sincere, force yourself." On-the-air investigative reporters will not need to subscribe to such a motto. They will present people in their interviews who are sincere and will not hold back their emotions. Television has the advantage over print of being the medium in which a person can tell the world, one-on-one, of a personal suffering.

Print Interviews

The print reporter, rightfully jealous of the TV reporter for the emotional advantage of television, must convey ideas and emotions in cold type. That calls for special skills. The print reporter may also work in a partnership or team, and one partner may be especially good at interviewing. Another can be the writer and a third the documents-research person. During an investigation, the reporters conduct many interviews: first to get the official version from someone close to the subject of the investigation, then to get at the truth, and finally to confront the target of the investigation. For all of the interviews, certain approaches have been perfected.

Interviewer as friend. The interviewer is relaxed and personable. The interviewer does not march into a room with a briefcase stuffed with papers and place it on the desk, causing it to become a barrier between the two participants. Instead, the interviewer enters in a friendly manner and doesn't forget to comment on the excellent view from the office window or praise the frightful lamp shade.

The reporter will carry on a conversation with the interviewee and will not work from a list of questions. At the end, though, having touched all the bases, the reporter may want to pull out from a pocket a summary of the questions and scan them to make sure all were covered in the interview. The reporter will hope the leave-taking is as friendly as the arrival, but it will not matter much if that hope is not realized.

Good guy–bad guy. Police detectives are known to employ this scheme. One of the questioners is harsh and accusatory. The other pretends to be shocked at the conduct of the fellow reporter and sides with the target. The end that the reporters want is for the target to bond with the nice guy and confess wrongdoing.

Let the statement stand. When a statement is made, it is accepted without argument. When President Nixon said, "I'm not a crook," nobody said, "Yes, you are." The statement had to stand without contradiction for the time being. But if it is a factual error, such as when a Watergate burglar said he was out of the country the week of the burglary, the reporter must then show the bank deposit slip from a bank in Florida (found in the files of the district attorney) that showed that he signed a receipt in that bank that week. He would be asked to explain or clarify his claim.

Just the facts. It is especially important in an adversarial interview (even though it might not have started out as adversarial) that the reporters get the facts right the first time because there will probably not be an opportunity to return and ask questions about the answers. If two reporters are conducting the interview, they will take turns writing notes while the other is asking questions. The reporters must get it right by asking for more complete answers or, if they do not understand the answer, asking that it be repeated and clarified.

A dramatized example of that is a scene in the movie "All the President's Men" from the book by Woodward and Bernstein. It shows some good, and ageless, reporting techniques. When Kenneth Dahlberg, a Nixon campaign official, told Woodward on the phone that he gave a check to "Stans" that ended up in the bank account of a Watergate burglar, Woodward asked, "Maurice Stans?" Dahlberg replied, "Yes." Woodward did not stop there. "Head of finance for Nixon?" he asked. Dahlberg confirmed. It was a proper portrayal of how a reporter should pursue questioning to make it certain. He wanted to be sure it was the Stans he knew of. Interviewees are not usually riled by being asked to repeat their answers; in fact, they may be flattered at having their words treated as so valuable that they are being carefully conveyed.

Follow-Up Questions

Investigative reporters prefer in-person interviews over written responses when they confront subjects of their investigations because the reporters want to ask probing follow-up questions. By the time of an interview the reporter should be familiar enough with the story to have a detailed knowledge of the subject along with an ability to detect a half answer on the spot. Many responses are predictable, and the reporter can decide in advance what to reply if the subject comes up with a standard answer.

What is the best response if the target of an investigation makes any of these possible replies in a close-out interview?

"I don't have any financial involvement in that company. The stock is in my wife's name."

1. But you put it there to hide the ownership.
2. Oh, I'm sorry. I didn't know that. I will be sure to clarify that in our story.
3. Do you and your wife file a joint tax return?
4. I knew that. I just wanted to see whether you would confirm it.

Number 3 works best. The reporter asked a simple question. If the stock is in the name of the wife and they file a joint return, the subject of the interview would share the profits. The subject could reply that tax returns are a private matter, but that reply would appear to be withholding information, and that isn't helpful to the subject of the interview. With comeback number 3, the reporter has moved the interview along and taken control.

Number 1 is confrontational and accusatory for no purpose. The subject is likely to say no, and then what does the reporter say? Yes, you did? Reply number 1 offers the reporter no support because it was an undocumented conclusion, a mere opinion.

Number 2 is complete surrender. The reporter indicates that the newspaper will go along with any rationale the subject may come up with and, in effect, promises the subject editorial control. Attorneys would say that the reporter has entered into an oral contract that must be fulfilled.

Number 4 is both weak and brash. It is unwise for the reporter to reveal a motive for a line of questioning and to be chortling about having fooled the interviewee. An interview is not a game of one-upmanship; it is an opportunity for the subject of the interview to explain personal actions.

Subjects of interviews by investigative reporters often try to challenge the reporter by asking:

"Who told you that?"

1. This information is from the public record. It is not hearsay.
2. That's none of your business. I am not being grilled. It is you who has to answer questions.
3. If you tell me how much you made off the deal, I will tell you my source.
4. I don't have to tell you. Reporters are supposed to protect their sources.

Number 1 is the commonsense comeback. Let's hope the reporter has the documentation. Such a response gives the interviewee notice that the investigation is on a high level and that personal actions will be difficult to hide or deny. Another reply could be, "I never base a story on uncorroborated allegations."

Number 2 is impolite and might lead to disaster if the interviewee gets up and walks out. In that case, the story would be only partially told and could be incorrect. The reporter cannot be a hothead and ruin an interview that has taken some doing to set up.

Number 3 is out of line because the reporter is supposed to have the facts going into the interview and would never want to make such a deal. No reporter would ever sell out a source in such a manner.

Number 4 is a toned-down version of number 2, and it is still a bad policy. The reporter does not want to become a direct adversary of the person interviewed.

Sometimes the person being interviewed tries to postpone an answer:

"I can't answer that. I will have to confer with my attorney. I will get back to you in, let's say, about a week."

1. Okay.
2. I will have to write that story without your comment. My deadline is immediate.
3. No way. This is not an arrest where you have the right to an attorney.
4. I refuse to talk to a lawyer.

Number 2 appears to be the best approach. The reporter conveys a sense of urgency and, without threatening the subject with a bad write-up, also conveys a mild threat that hangs in the air, unspoken. The subject is made to understand that there is one chance to state the case. Any lawyer is likely to tell any client not to talk to the press because lawyers usually warn clients not to make themselves legally vulnerable. Lawyers, however, often do not consider the public's negative response.

Number 1 is obviously wrong. The reporter has given up the control of the interview. The subject cannot be given an open-ended time to reply. Investigative stories have a way of coming apart or becoming too complex as more and more information is inserted and time is given for new material to be generated.

Number 3 shows the reporter preaching to the subject and being unnecessarily belligerent. The interviewee has the right to be treated fairly.

Number 4 is needlessly confrontational. If the lawyer is present for the interview and represents the person being interviewed, a reporter should have no reason to reject the lawyer's comments.

How Not to Do It

Chip Shotten, the freewheeling reporter who seemed to take the low road in all of his reporting, thought he might get some kind of a shocker from out in Ridgewood, where people were complaining about the smell coming from the county-run slush pond that bordered their community. He called Philo Johnson, a county board member who was one of his secret tipsters and who had provided embarrassing tidbits about other board members' private lives, and suggested that Johnson tour the slush pond and expose the conditions there. Shotten had been having a hard time getting his stories through the editors and into the paper because of the many mistakes he made in the past. He thought that by using the board member as a tool, he could write almost anything and put the words in his mouth.

Shotten drove the board member out to the unpleasant place where the matter from raw sewage that is drained off is processed. It was in an ugly, swampy area of high weeds and muddy ruts for roadways. They approached the entrance and found that a gate had been left open. Driving into the property, they found a group of workers, and Johnson shouted at them to make sure the front gate was closed and locked at all times. Then he gave Shotten a long lecture about his concern for the safety of children. Shotten took copious notes. Johnson decried everything he saw in the sewage treatment facility, and Shotten had his story.

They started to return to the city, but the front gate was locked and the workers were gone. They were trapped in the slush pond. Fortunately, Shotten had his cell phone and gave it to Johnson to call his office. It took three hours to find the person who had the key and could come and let them out.

Johnson was worried. He had been made to look stupid in the presence of a reporter. He mumbled, "This is not part of your story, is it?"

"Well, it's pretty funny being locked in the slush pond."

"Look, I don't think it's really that funny," Johnson said, pressing $90 (a 50 and two 20s) into Shotten's hand.

Shotten was faced with a decision. He had several alternatives.

1. Take the money and do not write any story.
2. Take the money and write a favorable story, omitting the part about the gate.
3. Do not take the money but write the story as Johnson wants it.
4. Do not take the money and write a story making a joke of Johnson.
5. Do not take the money and write a story of Johnson's attempt to bribe a reporter.
6. Take the money and write a story about the bribe.
7. None of the above.

It should be obvious that the reporter cannot take money, so the choices are down to 3, 4, 5 and 7:

3. Shotten could in a friendly manner refuse the money but assure Johnson that he will not mention the gate incident or the bribe attempt. Everyone will be happy, and Shotten can continue to get gossip from Johnson.
4. It is really funny that Johnson told the workers to keep the gate locked and then was locked in, and it should be told. The bribe attempt and the self-serving story about Johnson cleaning up the sludge pond should be dropped.
5. It is an outrage that Johnson would offer a bribe to a reporter, and it is an indication that he is a corrupt public official. If Shotten had learned of another reporter being offered a bribe, he would probably be all over it. He has to write about it or he is guilty of concealing a crime.
7. He could drop the whole story, write nothing about any of it and get legitimate, uncontrived stories.

We will not know what decision Shotten made. He may have changed his ways and decided to reform his poor journalistic conduct, or it may have been Shotten who was seen at the racetrack that night betting $90 on the daily double.

Chapter Recap

We have seen in this chapter how inspectors, investigators and enforcers may fall short of performing the vital services that protect the public and how reporters can look over their shoulders and set them straight. The stories that improve the performance of the protectors may be of the greatest value—they are about matters of life and death—but the immense area of administering justice is not far behind. The United States is a unique nation, driven by its Constitution and the amendments. We will examine in the next chapter how investigative reporters help make the system work.

Class Assignments

1. Form a team of students in the class and make an inspection tour of all of the campus buildings, looking for obvious problems. Get pictures. Go on the Internet and get aerial shots of the campus buildings. Find out whether the school or the municipality in which the campus is located is responsible for fire and building safety. Invite the chief inspector (the fire chief, fire prevention chief or building commissioner) to come to the classroom and talk about the safety department's operations and accomplishments. Show your findings and quiz the chief about each finding as if it were a news conference. Is the result a story worth writing and publishing?

2. Go to the Web site of the legislature of your state by typing into a search service the name of the state and either "general assembly" or "legislature." You will find a complete searchable set of state laws that before the Internet came into use could be found only in voluminous tomes on the shelves of law libraries. Find and interpret a law that helps reporters. A hint or two: laws that provide access to public records help reporters, as do laws that protect sources. Write a report that summarizes the law, and quote the law. Your report should then answer the question of how this law helps reporters.

Notes

1. Jeff Nesmith and Ralph K. M. Haurwitz, "Pipelines: The Invisible Danger," *Austin-American Statesman,* July 22-29, 2001, www.statesman.com/specialreports/content/specialreports/pipelines/index.html.
2. "Safety and Buildings Division Links to Codes Topics," http://commerce. wi.gov/sb/SB-DivCodes.html.
3. David Willman, "How a New Policy Led to Seven Deadly Drugs," *Los Angeles Times,* December 20, 2000, www.pulitzer.org/year/2001/investigative-reporting/works/willman1.html.
4. William Gaines, "Filth and Neglect Bared at Von Solbrig Hospital," *Chicago Tribune,* September 7, 1975; "William Gaines, 'Janitor' Helps with Patients," *Chicago Tribune,* September 7, 1975.
5. "Medicare and Medicaid Frauds. Part 1—Joint Hearing before the Senate Subcommittee on Long-Term Care and the Senate Subcommittee on Health of the Elderly, 94th Congress, 1st Session, September 26, 1975," NCJ 061554, U.S. Department of Justice, National Criminal Justice Reference Service, Washington, D.C., www.ncjrs.gov/app/publications/Abstract.aspx?id=61554.
6. Melvin Claxton and Charles Hurt, "Out of Service," *The Detroit News,* November 5-8, 2000, http://detnews.com/specialreports/2000/firedept/.
7. Karen Hensel, "Bullied," 24-Hour News 8 I-Team Investigative Unit, WISH-TV, www.wishtv.com.

Chapter 6

Examining the Police and the Courts

IN 2002, *THE DETROIT NEWS* LEARNED that the Detroit police department had a poor record of capturing fugitives. The reason for this was that the department wasn't trying very hard. The reporters who were wondering about this—Melvin Claxton, Ronald Hansen and Norman Sinclair—were able to find the fugitives merely by looking in the phone book, at voter records or by going to their homes.[1] One felonious fugitive was at home at the address on the warrant for his arrest for attempted murder, but there was no indication that police had ever come looking for him. He went about working at his landscaping business, which was listed in the phone book; and one time his home alarm sounded and police came to see whether he was okay.

After a diligent six-month investigation, the reporters wrote:

> "Some fugitives have used their ill-gotten freedom as a license to kill. They represent the ultimate danger posed by fugitives. And they demonstrate how criminals graduate to far deadlier crime when police fail to catch them. In the past three years, at least 50 people have been charged or convicted of murders committed while they were fugitives. In just about every case, there is little indication that police went hunting for them before the killings."

The police, courts and prisons are the agencies that guarantee justice, and each has spawned many an investigative story.

In this chapter you'll learn how to keep a check on the fast-moving, vital and yet often flawed justice system.

The Police

The first encounter a citizen has with the justice system may be with the individual police officer who makes immediate decisions under pressure and with danger present. The investigative reporter wants to know whether the right persons have been selected for the job. The police officer must be honest, fair, capable and psychologically prepared. The investigative reporter will expose conduct that indicates otherwise. The reporter will also evaluate police department budgets, crime statistics and investigations. Additional questions often seek investigative answers:

How political is the police department?

Are promotions based on political or family ties?

If the department has a test for promotions, is it fair?

Is there a fund-raising arm that runs a club for police officers?

Does the police organization outside the department give breaks such as overlooking minor violations for those citizens and merchants who kick in donations?

Are police officers adequately trained or are they only given a badge and a gun and sent out on the street?

Do police officers have second jobs that might interfere with their performance?

Are crime statistics doctored by the police chief to make the department look more productive?

The trick of doctoring local crime statistics is achieved by understating unsolved crimes and overstating those that have been solved. One game the police play on the statisticians goes like this: The police tow a car off the street. When the owner comes in to the police station to retrieve it, the owner's request goes on the record as a stolen car. Then, when the police find it in their lot, it is recorded as a stolen car recovered. Crime reported and crime solved!

Investigations from within most police departments are thin on documents. Any investigator needs guidance from sources inside the department to know where to find any telling documents, and much rests on the testimony of witnesses. The reporter is likely to face the obstacle of a challenge when filing an FOIA but will try anyway, exercising the philosophy that all government records are open records until proven otherwise.

Evaluating Police Action and Investigations

Traffic enforcement is vulnerable to ongoing police corruption. If residents routinely clip a $20 bill to their driver's licenses in case of a traffic stop, it is obvious the police are regarded with little respect. Such an assumption is difficult to report because a reporter should never commit the crime of bribery by attempting to bribe a public official, even for the purpose of writing about it. However, if it is known that there is a notorious speed trap where police officers are routinely shaking down motorists, a news organization might have a reporter stopped in such a speed zone to see whether a bribe is solicited.

The transaction could be filmed or taped, depending on provisions of local law. In some states it is illegal to record a conversation without the consent of all persons involved. A news organization might choose to confer with a state or federal enforcement agency to get its permission or at least provide the agency with knowledge of the purpose before launching such an elaborate plan.

Perhaps the police are not taking payoffs but are bending the law to favor some people over others. If a leading citizen—a banker, for example—has much too much to drink and is weaving his way home in his car, he might be escorted home by a local police officer, who has his mortgage with the bank, and then taken to his door where his wife is asked to put him to bed. The same police officer viewing another driver—a young person, a member of a minority, or an out-of-towner—apparently under the influence of intoxicants might take that person directly to jail without "passing go."

Such misconduct is ingrained in local law enforcement and also has a high scale of difficulty in the proof. If no arrest takes place, no documentation exists other than police radio calls. A check of the log of police calls might be revealing, but even more revealing would be a statistical approach in which all arrests in a particular period are compared with other departments or the national average.

In university towns, students believe they are treated unfairly compared with permanent residents. The police also have been found to use profiling, including racial and ethnic identification, in the belief that matching common characteristics or a particular composite profile of persons committing certain crimes against other people could then be used to predict who might be more likely to commit a crime. In the past, police might refer to such a profile to cast suspicion on a person with similar characteristics. Profiling has been discredited and discouraged throughout the country because of the vigilance of reporters and civil rights groups.

Using Police Crime Investigative Documents

Investigative reporters complain that police give out little information. There is general agreement that the incident report that tells when a call came in to the 9-1-1 system and what was found when police arrived—like where the body lay—is a public record. The reporter might be able to get those incident reports, but any follow-up investigative reports prior to an arrest will not be made public. Such reports may be opened later in the court file, but that doesn't happen until the documents are filed with the court.

When a reporter gets such a report, care must be taken to not accept everything as fact that is reported to the police. People who are interviewed want to be helpful in most cases, and with little or no evidence they will speculate about who might have committed a crime. Wild charges by neighbors and witnesses are found in local police and FBI reports. Traffic accident reports are usually available to all who request them, but in some locations even those reports are withheld. Reporters have learned to live with such customs by getting information from the county prosecutor or from court records.

While there is a high level of difficulty in getting reports on crimes investigated by the police, there is even a greater level of difficulty in getting information from the police about their own problems. Law enforcement officials are very protective of internal memos that might show errors or improper conduct by their own officers.

Assessing Police on the Street

The first step in the criminal process is the act of stopping a person. The stop and subsequent arrest is signaled when police read the legal rights to the detained person. The police-citizen encounter can be routine or can turn ugly. If it turns for the worst, police are put to the test of using some force short of unnecessary violence. At times, they flunk the test.

The 1991 videotape of the arrest and beating of Rodney King gave television news the pivotal story that awakened the public to the reality of police brutality. Before that, investigative reporters wrote about brutality, but those stories were sometimes read with skepticism by the citizenry.

One way to tell of the prevalence of brutality in a law enforcement group is to circumvent the police department and go to outside for documents. That way, any attempt by the police department to hide the facts is thwarted. The *Chicago Tribune* in a 1991 story did not wait to get official police reports, which might have contained numerous deletions.

Instead, *Tribune* reporters David Jackson and William Gaines, the author of this text, took refuge in the court system when they were denied Chicago police reports of complaints records and disciplinary actions against police officers. The victims of the alleged police attacks sued, and the names of certain police officers came up again and again on the civil court dockets in the local and federal courts. The reporters found in the court files additional reports of other incidents involving the same officers; these reports had been turned over to attorneys during the legal discovery process. The reporters found that the city had made multimillion-dollar settlements to the complainants over police behavior, but the police officers were still on the job.

Much of the information in the *Tribune* story was attributed to the internal memos the attorneys had been able to get from the police files. Competing reporters who failed to get the reports asked Jackson and Gaines whether they had a source in the police department. Jackson and Gaines had no comment.

Working with the Police

Reporters will, at times, find it proper to work with police officials, such as when they arrange the surrender of a felon, find witnesses, or locate clues that would be helpful in investigations. But such an arrangement does not always work well.

A metropolitan suburban newspaper once undertook an ambitious investigation by working with the police departments in its area, but this unusual arrangement meant trouble. (It would be unfair to name the newspaper or the reporters here because the ownership and staff have changed.)

The project started when a reporter learned of an impending roundup of alleged gang members on drug charges. The police were planning to make undercover buys of street drugs, then later make simultaneous arrests. The reporter suggested that the reporters might ride along with the police and view the preparations for the arrests and be able to write about it in advance, with colorful, first-person accounts. The story would be published only after the arrests. The fact that gang activities were prevalent in the suburbs, not only in the inner city, seemed to be an important story worthy of special coverage and front-page display.

Reporters went with the police but actually were kept far away from the undercover drug buys the officers were making. But the reporters did have one advantage: they had been given the names of those targeted for arrest, with the provision that they would not publish any names until arrests were made. The reporters quietly went about gathering background information on those to be arrested and awaited the arrests.

They were surprised to find on the list the name of a well-known high school football star of the graduating class of two years before. The thought of a football hero who was also a popular class officer turning to crime was an unexpected twist that the reporters expected to highlight or emphasize in their story. The reporters gathered all the background they could but were not able to contact the football player, who was out of town at college, because of their promise of silence to the police. But they were able to get a picture from the high school yearbook.

The raid took place, and the reporters and editors, under pressure of competition from metropolitan newspapers and local television news, rushed the story into the paper. The filed a story about young people gone wrong, and the reporters named the football player as a prime example.

But to the reporter's shock and dismay, they had named the wrong person. The person arrested had the same name as the football player, who was away at college when the buy and arrest took place. The newspaper ran an immediate correction.

The reporters said their picture of the football player was the same as the one the police had, and that meant that they had confirmation from a public agency that their identification was correct. A libel suit resulted.

How did the reporters go wrong? Did they libel the student?

> The reporters meant no wrong. They were fair and open-minded. A libel suit should not be won by the football player because of an inadvertent error.
> The investigation was ill-conceived from the start. Reporters crossed the line between police reporting and their own investigation when they gathered information from the yearbook. They then were ethically obligated to go to the subject of their investigation for his rebuttal, but they had already given away that necessary step when they entered into the agreement with the police.
> The reporters also wrote that the football player and all the others arrested in the sting operation had "gone wrong," in other words, were guilty of a crime, when in fact they had only been charged and not convicted.

The Courts

Daily newspapers usually have a reporter or two who specialize in the judiciary and have the courthouse as their beats. These reporters produce a sizable portion of the local news that appears each day in the paper. In addition, a senior reporter is often assigned to cover a high-profile trial from start to finish. Even within this traditional structure, there is room enough left for investigative stories.

The justice system, established in the U.S. Constitution, entitles everyone to a fair trial. From the conduct of the arresting officer to a decision of the U.S. Supreme Court, measures are taken to ensure that the entitlement is guaranteed. When it does not take place as it should, an investigative reporter can become the last hope of the wrongfully accused, the victim of brutality or the unjustly treated minority.

The road to justice can be bumpy.

In the legal process, proper bond may not be immediately set, denying an innocent person freedom. The arrested person may be kept overnight in a cold and filthy jail cell for a minor violation—even though innocent of a crime—without a opportunity to enter a plea before a judge. Known felons may be housed with persons accused of minor offenses, or misdemeanors.

A jail is a local facility run by the county and used to temporarily house persons who are charged with a crime and awaiting bond hearings. Also, jails can provide confinement for persons sentenced to short periods. The county is expected to run a safe, clean and secure jail. The reporter could inspect the jail and report on conditions. In some jurisdictions, the county board or grand jury periodically inspects the jail, and the reporter can get the results of those inspections and then observe whether the reports are no more than a cover-up.

The judge may be inexperienced in the law, inattentive, overworked, opinionated, biased or speak abusively to those who appear in court. A reporter or a team of reporters needs only sit in on court sessions to get a handle on a story about a judge, and this story would have the backup of the court reporter who transcribes every word of the proceeding. An unprofessional attitude leads to miscarriages of justice.

Reporters have revealed wrongful imprisonment, even of prisoners sentenced to death. They have taken long looks at prosecutors run amok and judges indifferent to prosecutorial excesses. But the defendant is not always the injured party in a flawed justice system. Criminals may be wrongfully exonerated by poor police work or loose court procedures. So much court procedure is open to the public that it is surprising to learn how much is hidden. But deals are made at the coffee shop across the street, and judges and attorneys have unspoken agreements. Judges are mainly elected or appointed from the ranks of the criminal prosecutors, and they seem to favor their former colleagues. Attorneys may have social or political ties among themselves.

Investigating the Selection of Jurors

Investigative reporters in Dallas and Pittsburgh are among those who have examined the racial makeup of juries. In 2002, Mark Houser of one of the Pittsburgh newspapers wrote: "The system that picks people for jury duty in Allegheny County consistently overlooks blacks and favors whites, a *Pittsburgh Tribune-Review* investigation has found."[2]

Although every ninth person in Allegheny County is black, only one in 20 is selected for juries, he reported.

How did the reporter know from court records that the jurors were black or white, as such information is not recorded on public documents? The key is in the second paragraph of the story: "People living in white neighborhoods are more than twice as likely to be called for jury service as residents of black neighborhoods. . . ." The reporter had noted the jurors' addresses and was able to chart them as living in a racially separated community. The reporter did not actually know the color of each individual's skin.

Steve McGonigle, veteran award-winning reporter for the *Dallas Morning News,* reported on two of his jury investigations, which were 20 years apart. In 1985, racial inequality in Dallas juries was rampant, and reform was undertaken because of his work. Returning to the subject in 2005, McGonigle found racial imbalance still prevalent.

McGonigle said the 2005 story took a year to research and write because the courts, which are not covered under the Freedom of Information Act, had tightened control of the information and caused a series of court appearances by the newspaper's attorneys.

The reporter's key findings were printed in a box on the front page on the first day of the series of stories: "Dallas County prosecutors excluded black jurors at more than twice the rate they rejected whites."

Sound familiar? Two newspapers, three years, more than 1,000 miles apart and using different research methods had come to the same basic conclusion.

In Dallas, McGonigle and his reporting team—Holly Becka, Jennifer LaFluer, and Tim Wyatt—uncovered a secret database known only to the prosecutors. It rated prospective jurors.

Judging Judges

One of the earlier milestones in the investigation of courts was the 1986 Pulitzer Prize-winning *Philadelphia Inquirer* report of the close association of judges and attorneys. The reporters, Fredric Tulsky, H. G. Bissinger and Daniel R. Biddle, used a computer database to match times and places in order to show that attorneys who made campaign contributions and even managed the judge's reelection campaign were appearing in court before those very same judges. The reporters were able to write: "The records show the candidates for judgeships in Philadelphia routinely accept donations from lawyers and then allow those lawyers to try cases in front of them a short time later." Tulsky had done a story about overbilling by court-appointed lawyers and found that one lawyer who had charged the county for more than $200,000 in one year must have worked 32-hour days.

Using Court Files, Records and Documentation

If one person sues another, the case enters the court system as a civil case and is assigned a civil case number. But if state law enforcement officials go to court and file a suit against a person for violating a specific law and endangering the public, it is designated a criminal case. Separate branches of the courts are established to deal with criminal cases and civil cases; an exception to having separate courts sometimes occurs in small counties, but even then the civil and criminal procedures are different. Access to court information—whether civil or criminal—is handled in the same office: the clerk of the courts. The clerk of the courts is usually elected and is not to be confused with the county clerk or the judge's court clerk. The clerk of the courts is mandated by law to provide information about court cases.

Some newspapers may print the criminal court docket every day, irritating a resident who is charged with drunkenness or taking part in a family fight. The resident must understand that, for the benefit of the public, there can be no secret arrests. Criminal charges are open and defendants' names are indexed to be searchable. An investigative reporter always checks the criminal court files to see whether any persons connected with a current investigative story has an arrest record. Sometimes, criminal court files of one person will contain what police call "a rap sheet"—a list of previous arrests and convictions. Rap sheets are not meant for public dissemination because they may not be correct, may be missing some crucial information or confuse two people with the same name. But a rap sheet gives the reporter clues about where to find other possible criminal case files.

Most criminal matters are handled in the county courts, but some criminal cases—for violations of federal laws like tax fraud and racketeering—are the responsibility of the federal court clerk's office.

Facts and not-so-facts are found in court case files. A wealth of charges and countercharges are written up, stuffed into folders, and are sitting on shelves in the county court clerk's office. They are there to facilitate the judicial process, and they also have an important role to play for an investigative reporter. Important stories that would otherwise not be known by the public lie in the civil court case files, awaiting discovery and interpretation by an investigative reporter. But the facts must be separated from the not-so-facts.

Not-so-facts may or may not be true. They are the allegations of a person who feels aggrieved and goes to the courts for satisfaction. In writing up the complaint, the lawyers pile it on. But the sworn statement of an individual found in a case file is the highest level of truth. If only reporters could demand such truths from people they interview, with the penalty for lying to a reporter as serious as perjury. That will never happen, but next best is for a reporter to get a sworn statement out of a public file.

A reporter enters the awesome legal world by arriving at the courthouse with a name or names of persons or businesses to be investigated. Somehow, by asking directions or looking at the directory on the wall, the reporter finds the office of the clerk of the courts. In this office, computer terminals will be available to the public. In small jurisdictions, an employee of the office often wants to operate the terminal, but in most places members of the public can use the computers independently. No one (neither a reporter nor anyone else) needs to show identification in order to get a case file. The clerk's office will be busy with many legal researchers and litigants requesting files, and reporters fit in among them.

State laws require the office to keep an index of all court cases, filed by both plaintiff and defendant. In the past, the offices kept index books, but with the advent of the computer age, the clerk offers a search engine with designations for plaintiff or defendant.

The reporter fills in the names of entities to be investigated and receives a list of all the court cases involving that name. Case numbers are also included. In most computerized court clerk systems, that number can then be placed into a search engine to call up the complaint and other important documents involving the case. If that convenience is not available, the reporter can take the case number to a clerk and get the file.

The file has no order or index. The reporter will have to figure out the sequence of filing and read the more important aspects of the case. First the reporter will shuffle through the documents and find the complaint that started the lawsuit.

The following example works us through the paperwork and records in a case, in this instance it is the case of Cat v. Aspidistras.

Complaint.   A citizen has gone to the courts claiming to have been wronged by another person or a business. In this instance, a neighbor's cat ran into the yard of the complainant and destroyed a patch of rare aspidistras.

Answer to the complaint.   The neighbor makes a written response, denies wrongdoing and states that she is not the owner of the cat. It is a stray cat that she often feeds. She makes a countercomplaint, alleging that the plaintiff has left a fence unrepaired and that caused animals to enter her property.

Interrogatories.   This is lawyer jargon. This fifteen-letter word is simply a way of saying "questions." The parties in a suit send each other a list of questions. When did the owner acquire the cat? How large is the cat? What is the breed of the cat?

Answers to interrogatories. The parties answer the questions in written form, or they object to the question and set it aside for future argument. The questions for the most part are routine; for example, the injured party in a lawsuit is asked the extent of the injuries, what medical care has been required and the number of days of work missed. It is helpful for a reporter to read this because it may also contain the full name, address and date of birth of the questioned person. If so, the reporter can make sure this person is identical with the person of interest and is not a same name that the computer found. In the cat case, the civil defendant has denied ownership of the cat and, therefore, states that she has no information about the breed of the cat. The defendant fires off additional questions, asking the value of the bed of aspidistras and requesting a list of all people or animals with access to the flower bed.

Motions. Attorneys for the defendant may move to have the case dismissed, arguing that cats are unlicensed by the city and that no ownership can be attributed to the client merely because she feeds the cat. The attorney will probably cite some court decisions in favor of this argument and file a written request that a judge can use when ruling. The judge may or may not dismiss the case at this point; if it is not dismissed, it is set for trial.

Up to this point the case has been debated on paper, and the paper is in the file. The problems of defining the ownership of the cat are not what the reporter came for. That is a side issue. The reporter is interested in the lady who feeds the cat because the reporter believes she is one of many "ghost payrollers" in the city sewer department. A city hall source told the reporter that she is a political worker who appears on the public payroll as a health department inspector, but she never comes to work—an allegation of "ghost payrolling," when a person draws a salary without performing a service. Reporters have even found persons ghost payrolling on more than one payroll at the same time. The reporter sifting through the cat lawsuit file is hoping to find some information in that file that will help to determine whether it is true. After setting aside the arguments about the ownership of the cat, the reporter comes upon the most valuable documentation in the discovery.

Discovery. Each side asks the other for certain documents and may arrange for a deposition. The idea of a deposition is to obtain testimony under oath in advance of a trial. The opposite parties in the litigation can then know what their chances are if they go to trial. This encourages

141

an out-of-court settlement, which makes the judge very happy. The deposition, meanwhile, given in the presence of attorneys for both sides, can make the search worthwhile for a reporter. Perhaps the suspected ghost payroller describes her occupation as a full-time restaurant manager and shows no government job. The reporter has a clue that she is hiding such employment. That will not be enough proof to go with a story. It will be necessary to confront her and her government supervisor with the allegation.

Disposition. The spelling of "disposition" is so similar to "deposition" that it could be confusing. The disposition is how the original case was closed off and removed from the court docket. It may be that the two litigants have settled their dispute and informed the judge. The judge breathes a sigh of relief. The case is then closed with no further debate or written record other than it was dismissed by agreement. The cat owner has agreed to replace the flower bed and mend the fence without admitting responsibility, and the plaintiff has agreed to take no further action against her. But if no settlement is reached, the case will go to trial, a judge or jury will reach a decision and the appeals process will begin.

Appeals. If a reporter is looking for information from a case that has gone to trial, there may be a transcript of the trial or portions of it that the reporter can get. If the cat case goes to trial, all the parties involved will have a chance to testify, they will be cross-examined and their testimony will be recorded by a court stenographer. Afterward, the losing party is going to be unhappy and may file an appeal with a higher court. When the losing party files an appeal, the appeal court will require a transcript of the testimony, to be provided by the appealing party. It will be in a public file and the reporter will have another opportunity to try to resolve the ghost-payroll accusation by looking for further evidence in the file. If the information the reporter has obliquely sought is in sworn testimony, the reporter will have information from the highest level of reliability.

What of the cat case? If it goes to appeals court, it could be a landmark case about ownership of a cat. If the case has not been covered by the press, the investigative reporter will want to alert the newspaper's editors, who might assign a reporter to work up an interesting feature.

Off limits. Little is held back in a court case, and everything introduced in evidence is most certainly public. But the list of exclusions of court records is actually quite imposing. We sought the help of the Vermont Supreme Court for a summary list of items that are excluded from the public record:

The public shall not have access to records on file with the probate court in connection with an adoption proceeding, records of sterilization proceedings, records of a grand jury and any indictment of a grand jury, records of the family court in juvenile proceedings, records of the court in mental health and mental retardation proceedings.

Also the privacy of citizens is protected by an exclusion of a pre-sentence investigation report, records produced or created in connection with discovery, and a deposition, unless used by a party at trial or in connection with a request for action by the court, which would place it in a court file.

Also excluded are records of financial information furnished to the court in connection with an application for an attorney at public expense, records representing judicial work product, including notes, memoranda, research results, or drafts prepared by a judge or prepared by other court personnel on behalf of a judge, and used in the process of preparing a decision or order.

Any federal, state or local income tax return, unless admitted into evidence is off limits, so are records of the issuance of a search warrant, until the date of the return of the warrant, unless sealed by order of the court. Records containing a Social Security number of any person may not be used until the Social Security number has been redacted from the copy of the record provided to the public.

Checking on Prisons

A prison is a place of confinement for felons sentenced to terms as long as life. Prisons are run by the state and are usually optimistically called "correctional facilities" with the hope that they rehabilitate criminals. Prisons may be poorly run and in need of investigation. Guards have been known to smuggle drugs into prisons. Inmates may be either abused or pampered. States provide Internet access to information about prison inmates; these records can be searched by name and prisoners' online files will show their crimes and lengths of sentences.

Judging at the Curbside

Parking meters, in use by most communities, rank in the nuisance group of public concerns. Questions arise, however: Are the meters a source of revenue for the municipality, or does it cost the local government more to purchase, repair, replace, collect and count quarters, and chase down people who do not pay tickets than the government earns? The answer should be in the jurisdiction's annual financial report. Another question for reporters is how aggressively the city pursues the collection of parking tickets. Some newspapers print the names of persons with unpaid tickets. The investigative reporter can take the idea a step further and try to learn whether certain groups or individuals are allowed to ignore tickets. Let us hope journalists are not among these groups!

Case Study

A Look Behind the Judicial Robe*

Judge Long was a local hero in Middleton County. He was known for his long, harsh sentences for drug dealers and child molesters. He often refused to set bond for out-of-town people even on a relatively minor charge, like writing a bad check. His courtroom decorum was serious and cold.

A former prosecutor, Judge Long often openly showed disdain for public defense attorneys who appeared before his court. But he was likely to tolerate the conduct of the prosecutors even when they misstated the facts or the law to juries. His tough reputation got him reelected, and he had been on the bench for as long as most court followers could remember. His decisions were reported in the newspaper without question, although he never had time to talk to the media.

Charles Miller, a skilled investigative reporter for the *Middleton Daily News,* learned that Rex Arsenic, an infamous local drug dealer, was arrested in a county not far from Middleton. Miller was surprised. He recalled that Arsenic had been convicted about a year before on drug charges and was sentenced by Judge Long. It seemed unlikely Arsenic would be eligible for parole. Miller pulled up the story from the newspaper database and saw that Judge Long had sentenced Arsenic to 12 consecutive terms of 100 years as a habitual offender.

Then Miller went to the courthouse to visit the office of the clerk of the courts and look up the case records on Arsenic. Some case information was available online, such as the docket that listed the charges, dates of appearances and acts of the court, but Miller wanted to make sure he got everything in the file rather than only what was fed electronically to the clerk's Web site. Miller knew that the court records were public because the state law that created the office of the clerk provided that the clerk make available all court records for access by the public on weekdays from 9 a.m. until 5 p.m. Miller did

*The cases are based on real investigative stories, but the names and places have been changed to protect reporters, their sources and the secrets they have. Some are actual stories told in a step-by-step reconstruction and others are composites.

not have to check in with anyone. He stood in line at the public access terminals in the office, put Arsenic's name in the search box in the computer and pulled up the case number. He took the number to a counter and gave it to a clerk, who retrieved the file for him.

Miller found in the file an order from the state appellate court that overturned the Arsenic conviction. Miller looked for a story in the *Middleton Daily News* but could find none. Apparently the appeals court was not routinely checked by the newspaper's court reporter, and the appeals court did not send out news releases stating its findings. The state Supreme Court, which tackled the interpretation of state laws, was covered by reporters; but it was the appeals court that handled the day-to-day questions of whether a judge was right or wrong, and it did its work pretty much out of the public eye.

Perhaps the appeals court should be investigated for allowing a dangerous criminal to go free, Miller mused.

Should the state appeals court be investigated?

Yes: The justices of the state appeals court always seem to be letting convicted criminals go free or get a new trial at a cost to the taxpayer. They will often overturn a jury finding, which represents the will of the people. They are powerful public officials but little is known about them. An investigation would be well-received by the public.

No: An investigation is not necessary merely because a reporter does not agree with the judgments of a court, or even if the public does not agree. There is no evidence here of any wrongdoing by the high court; only one decision that seems to be wrong. It is not very likely that the justices on the appellate panel would be so corrupt that they were conspiring to align themselves with criminal elements. Miller knows nothing about the courts; he has no knowledge of legal terminology, and he is likely to get it all wrong and embarrass the newspaper.

Miller probed on, knowing he did not have to declare an investigation of any person or group, but he could investigate a happening. He would investigate the incident of Arsenic's case and decide who was responsible. He talked to both prosecutors and defense attorneys. Prosecutors said the appeals justices were soft on criminals. Defense attorneys said judges were pals of the prosecutors. They were talking off the record.

Judges had to run for election, so their campaign funds disclosure reports were filed with the state election board, Miller knew. Also, judges had to file a more detailed economic disclosure statement than most other public officials; these were filed with the state Supreme Court. Miller looked at Judge Long's statement as well as the statement of other judges in the county court system. He found campaign contributions from attorneys who appeared before the judge; apparently there was no rule against it. Some attorneys had even helped organize his election campaign.

Much more was available to Miller, who kept a close watch on government Web sites. He discovered that every decision of judges that had been appealed was on view on the state Supreme Court Web site, and these included appellate court rulings. Miller was able to read detailed reports of the lower court decisions, including citations of statements made, comparable issues in other cases, and a determination by the justices whether to reverse the decision and order a new trial or affirm the decision of the lower court judge.

Miller discovered that Judge Long was the most reversed judge in the county, and the appellate court had overturned 39 of his rulings in fewer than three years. Then Miller expanded his research and found that Judge Long was the most reversed judge in the state; the next-highest judge had only eight reversals. Some of Judge Long's reversals showed a lack of knowledge of the law, a bias, or a careless error that he stubbornly refused to correct.

In one example, a man from a neighboring state who was charged with writing bad checks appeared before Judge Long and requested that a bond of $50,000 to guarantee his appearance in court be reduced. After hearing some testimony about the man's request, the judge "interrupted the proceedings" and stated the defendant would be held without the right to post money to guarantee his appearance in court. It was the third known instance in which the judge erroneously ordered a defendant entitled to put up a bond to be held without being allowed that right, the appeals court wrote.

In another instance, Judge Long set aside the life-in-prison sentence recommended by the jury and issued a death sentence instead. The higher court overturned the death sentence and sent the case back to the judge, but he issued a death sentence again, contrary to the jury's recommendations. There was nothing the higher court could do because the trial court judge had the right under law to reject a jury's recommendation. Finally, three years later, the state law was changed so that a judge did not have that power in a death sentence. The higher court was then able to change the sentence to 100 years.

Another time, the jury's finding was thrown out by the higher court because Judge Long removed a juror after deliberations had started. The appeals court noted that Judge Long had only the word of the jury foreman that a holdout juror was not considering the evidence. A portion of the trial transcript stated:

The Court: . . . the trial court may exercise its discretion and replace any juror who is experiencing a great deal of anxiety.

Attorney for the defendant: Judge, could we bring that juror in to see if that is true?

The Court: No, I'm not going to do that.

The higher court judges lectured in their reversal of the subsequent conviction that because Judge Long did not interview the juror whose conduct was at issue, the record is not as developed as is required for a juror to be removed once deliberations have begun.

"The record before us reflects that the juror reached a different conclusion than the other jurors based on his own life experiences." The appeals court quoted a state Supreme Court statement that a failure to agree, however unreasonable, is a ground for mistrial.

In another reversal, the higher court reminded Judge Long that a criminal defendant has a fundamental constitutional right to exercise the privilege against self-incrimination without adverse inference or comment at trial. The prosecutor in her closing remarks to the jury said:

"He takes the Fifth Amendment. You take the Fifth Amendment when you've got something to be concerned about. Incriminating yourself. Fifth Amendment. My constitutional right not to incriminate myself. That's what that means. So in order for that to apply, you have to have done something to incriminate yourself."

The defense counsel objected to the statement, but Judge Long overruled his objection.

The judge was again reversed when he ordered a man to serve two consecutive prison terms although the prosecutor, defense lawyer and the judge himself had agreed to concurrent terms.

When the appeals court in a state finds a judge has abused the discretion of the court, it means that his decision has no basis in law and is indefensible. In one appellate case, Judge Long was cited for an abuse of discretion nine times.

In another of Judge Long's cases reversed by the higher court, the justices wrote that "it is manifest injustice" to hold a defendant liable on a judgment simply because a clerk failed to make proper docket entries. Judge Long was responsible for such an act, the higher court justices concluded.

An attorney had submitted a jury demand and an argument against a complaint and had filed them on time with a clerk, documents cited by the appeals court showed. But the clerk made the docket entry (an official register of court case actions) for only the jury demand. A computer generated an order of dismissal for failure to appear, causing Judge Long to grant a $300,000 judgment in favor of the other party.

Of course, the losing side objected and showed documentation that it had responded in time. But Judge Long said he would set aside the judgment only if the defendant established a meritorious defense, which meant the defendant had to show good reason for not filing, when, in fact, the defendant did file. When the defendant responded in writing that he had filed, Judge Long rejected his answer and stated again that he had shown no good cause for failure to respond. Miller realized that he would have to explain to the readers that Judge Long was either not paying attention or deliberately and stubbornly breaching the law.

The default judgment stood for three years before the wheels of justice slowly turned and the appeals court reversed it.

The appellate court also advised Judge Long that when a police officer gets an anonymous complaint that a "white male, wearing blue jeans, a white shirt and a blue visor" is trying doorknobs, the police officer is not entitled to stop and search any white male wearing blue jeans, a white shirt and a blue visor. Judge Long had ruled that the "anonymous tip was sufficient to justify an investigatory stop."

The higher court countered that, although the tipster had provided information that a crime of attempted trespass or burglary was being committed, the officer was unable to verify any of the allegations of a criminal offense, only that a man who fit the description provided by the tipster was walking down the street.

"The officer's failure to confirm the reliability of the tip makes the man's detention and the discovery of contraband illegal," the higher court ruled. That was the reversal that freed Arsenic. Not only was the evidence obtained incorrectly, but the rules that placed Arsenic among habitual criminals were incorrect and the sentences of the judge were beyond the limits of the state statutes.

Miller saw that Middleton's favorite judge was grossly incompetent and his incorrect legal decisions could cost the taxpayers the price of retrials or let criminals go free. Also, the judge's acceptance of misdirected police work caused the police officers to become sloppy in their duties. It seemed that the judge's poor performance was the most important thing about the judge.

Miller tried to schedule an interview with the judge but could not get past his clerk. He had to try to catch the judge in the courtroom and explain his story. He confronted the judge as he stepped away from the bench. At first, Judge Long did not seem to hear Miller call out his name, but on the third call of "Judge Long!" the judge turned and looked at him vacantly. "I'm Charles Miller of the *Daily News*. I want to talk to you about . . ."

"I can't talk about cases," the judge said abruptly.

"I want to talk about you."

"I'm not interested," he said hardly breaking stride. Miller followed him to the door of his chambers. "It's about all the reversals of your decisions by the appeals court. You have more than any judge in the state."

"Aren't you the reporter who wrote those stories claiming there was brutality committed by some of our hard-working police officers? They put their lives on the line every day to protect our citizens, and you wrote that they were wrong to use physical force on some of these thugs I see in my courtroom. Yes, I've been reversed a few times, but that is because the appeals court justices are sitting up there in the state capital and have no idea of what is going on in this city. Gangs rove the streets, and drug dealers and hardened criminals will never change. And the appeals court says I should be protecting their constitutional rights!"

"But, Judge, haven't you sworn to protect everyone's constitutional rights?"

Judge Long snorted derisively, glared in his most severe judicial manner, strode stiffly into his chambers and slammed the door.

Miller wrote the full story of Judge Long's reversals, setting aside the part about the attorneys' campaign work for further investigation before publishing. The response was not enthusiastic. Miller and the newspaper received bitter e-mail messages, and the local radio and TV talk shows weighed in heavily in favor of Judge Long. They accused Miller, the *Daily News,* and even the appeals court of being soft on crime. Public indignation toward the newspaper and Miller was overwhelming. The editor of the *Daily News* stopped by Miller's desk to congratulate him on a job well done, and he brought good news: "The Old Man is backing you."

Newsroom staff called Chesterfield Smith III, the third-generation owner and publisher of the *Middleton Daily News,* the "Old Man"; they never used his name. His word was hallowed. They perceived the backing of the Old Man as the ultimate security, but Miller was worried. The Old Man often wrote stinging editorials, and they did not always agree with his investigative reports. When Miller in one story revealed improper conduct in the insurance industry, and the story quoted people calling for more regulation, the Old Man wrote an editorial stating that there was enough regulation and that current laws should be enforced.

Two days after the Judge Long story was published, an editorial appeared on the front page of the *Daily News.* It was an all-out trouncing of Judge Long, the prosecutors and the people of the city. The words flowed as if the writer had spilled it all out in one sweep of the keyboard. The construction was flawless, and it vibrated with urgency. There was no doubt who wrote the unsigned paragraphs. It was the Old Man's newspaper. He begged forgiveness from the Founders on behalf of the citizens for allowing the local justice system to have fallen in the control of such men as Judge Long, whose career he described as arrogant self-aggrandizement and propagation of incompetence. The Old Man reminded the people that injustice for one person was injustice for all. He wrote with an editorial "we" that resounded with the understanding that it came from all journalists everywhere as the guardians of a free society.

The editorial reversed public response. Judge Long took a sudden leave of absence to spend more time with his grandchildren and then soon returned to the private practice of criminal law, defending some of the very felons he claimed to have despised.

?

Should a newspaper or investigative reporter publish an opinion?

Yes: The significance of news stories, especially investigative stories, needs forthright interpretation by the media. As long as it is labeled as such and kept separate from the news columns, it can explain and provide guidance. The editorial is the cornerstone of a free press.

No: It is the duty of newspaper publishers to provide accurate information about current happenings. An editorial writer has gone far beyond that calling with an endorsement of a candidate for public office, alignment with a party in a legal matter, or support of civic issues. Just because the right to free speech exists, a journalist does not have to be telling people what is good for them.

Memorandum

- If a journalist reports on a government investigation and adds to the government's information with the reporter's own investigation, the story reaches a higher level of responsibility by the reporter.
- Court files can provide important information from sworn testimony, but allegations in complaints cannot be relied upon as fact.
- Editorials in newspapers are separate from news and investigations and must be labeled as such.

Chapter Recap

Monitoring those who protect the public and administer justice and safety is enough to keep an army of investigative reporters busy throughout their careers. But investigative reporters are put to a further test of persistence by the acts of private businesses, whether they are for-profit enterprises or not. In the next chapter, we will look closely at the organizations that say they are not out to make a profit, that they are only being charitable.

Class Assignments

1. First choose a topic. Then go to your county courthouse to the office of the clerk of the courts and look up a series of lawsuits that would help you with an investigative story on that subject. For example, you might suggest a story about the safety of school buses. Some schools own their own buses but most hire a company to provide the buses and hire the drivers. Get a list of companies from the phone book or state licensing agency and pull recent court cases in which they are either the plaintiff or the defendant. You will find they are being sued as a result of accidents, and you may find interesting leads. If you were working on such an investigation for publication, you would pursue the story by getting accident reports, driving records, inspection reports, and contracts with the schools they serve.

2. Pull up the Web site in your state for the agency that runs the prisons. You can get it by clicking on the Corrections Connection, at www.corrections.com/links/viewlinks.asp?Cat=20. You could also find it by entering the name of the state and the word "prisons" into an online searching service. By putting "Texas prisons" into a Google search, we arrived at the Texas Department of Criminal Justice and entered the site. There we found "general information" and "offender information," where we found this list of databases:

Federal Bureau of Prisons (contains online inmate locator)
  www.bop.gov/
Other State Department of Corrections
  www.tdcj.state.tx.us/links/links-states-doc.htm

County Jails/Courts (the following Web site is a compiled list of
Texas counties with possible links to sheriff and court offices)
www.county.org/counties/txcounties.asp
City Jails (and other Texas law enforcement agencies)
www.tdcj.state.tx.us/links/links-lawenforc-tx.htm
Sex Offender Database (features include search by ZIP code—
run by Texas Department of Public Safety)
http://records.txdps.state.tx.us/soSearch/default.cfm
Sex Offender Registration Mapping Utility
http://216.140.183.80/SOMAP/somapSearch.cfm?reset=true
Texas Conviction Database (for criminal histories—run by Texas
Department of Public Safety)
http://records.txdps.state.tx.us/
Links to offender search engines & public records—(not supported nor endorsed by TDCJ)
www.ancestorhunt.com/prison_search.htm
www.corrections.com/links/viewlinks.asp?Cat=20

Click on Texas Conviction Database. You will see the name of the prison
inmate, the location of the arrest, the nature of the arrest and the length
of the sentence. Pull out the locations of your choice and put the sentences
of the inmates with the same crimes, such as armed robbery, into a spreadsheet. Investigate the consistency of the courts by comparing the sentences.
If one court stands out as extremely high or low, learn the facts about the
crimes from local newspaper accounts, summaries of appealed cases and
criminal arrest records. Did 16 inmates from one county get a sentence of
five years while another inmate got 10 years? Did the inmate who got 10
years have a tougher judge? Write your findings.

Notes

1. Melvin Claxton, Ronald Hansen and Norman Sinclair, "Fugitives Murder
    While on the Loose," *The Detroit News*, December 8, 2002.
2. Mark Houser, "A Jury of Peers?" *Pittsburgh Sunday Tribune-Review*, July 21, 2002.

C h a p t e r 7

Investigating Charities, Nonprofit Organizations and Foundations

---

Aɴ ᴀɴᴏɴʏᴍᴏᴜs ᴄᴀʟʟ sᴛᴀʀᴛᴇᴅ ᴀɴ ɪɴᴠᴇsᴛɪɢᴀᴛɪᴏɴ into one of the most shocking misuses of charity money in recent memory. A switchboard operator at the *New York Daily News* answered a call from a tenant who complained about poor conditions in an apartment building. The tip was passed along to reporter Heidi Evans, who became especially interested when she learned the building was owned by Hale House, a nationally known shelter for women and children in Harlem.[1] She learned that Hale House had been given two city apartment buildings and $6 million in grants to rehabilitate them for the use of recovering drug-addicted mothers and their children. Instead, those apartments, owned by Hale House, had been rented to highly paid professionals.

Evans was joined by reporter David Saltonstall, and the two reporters pursued the investigation for six months. Starting April 1, 2001, they broke story after story. They wrote that out of $8.4 million dollars raised only $60,000 went to support 18 children in the care of Hale House.

New York state law prohibits officers or directors from accepting loans from organizations they oversee, but the president of Hale House borrowed money from the charity for other purposes and gave it to her husband's private musical production company to stage a Broadway play, the *Daily News* reported. The show, "Faith Journey," based on the life of Dr. Martin Luther King Jr., failed. Only two people attended the closing performance.

The *Daily News,* a tabloid-style newspaper given to headlines that occupy most of each day's front page, ran these headlines on four of their front pages:

Hale of a Mess!
Hale Storm!
Hale's $1.3 in Piggy Bank
Curtains! [for the story about the Broadway flop]

The stories in the *Daily News* got immediate action. The New York attorney general indicted the director and her husband on 72 counts, charging them with the theft of more than $1 million. In a deal, the couple pled guilty to one felony charge, and they are banned for life from charity work.

Not-for-profit organizations are privately owned, but they have an arrangement with the Internal Revenue Service. They do not have to pay taxes if they show they do not intend to make a profit and can report each year that they do not. They comply by filing with the IRS a form number 990, which is open to public inspection. (See Appendix 2).

Some of these not-for-profits are charities that also solicit money from the public. Those special businesses that raise money for charitable purposes not only disclose their financial status with the IRS, but they must also file reports with the states. An organization that has people shaking cans outside the supermarket entrance and specifies that it is raising money for seeing-eye dogs most likely would have to file reports. State laws vary, but they are similar in purpose. Some require that the financial filings be made electronically; these filings are readily available on the Internet.

Regulating Nonprofit Organizations

The laws are structured so that persons who are solicited for money to support charitable causes have some guarantee that their money is going to that cause. Very small special-purpose fundraising, like a few thousand dollars to help a family that is flooded or burned out of its home, would not require a report. If the wrong person got that money, it would be serious fraud; but there is usually a threshold of from $5,000 to $25,000 of annual revenue collected before a fundraiser has to file with the state. Religious organizations are exempt from the federal not-for-profit disclosure law.

Journalists have discovered misspending and outright fraud and theft by organizations posing as charities. Even the most respected and important fundraisers have suffered scandals over the handling of money intended for charity. They sometimes pay themselves and their relatives inordinate salaries, enter into contracts between the charity and private companies from which they profit, or spend the money frivolously on ornate offices. Sometimes a local charity with inexperienced officers hires outside operators to raise funds or run games like bingo and then loses control of its money. A letter-writing or phone solicitation campaign by an outside solicitor could turn to false representation or exaggeration if not monitored.

The disclosure forms, administered in most states by the offices of attorneys general, provide the hardest information that a reporter can find in public records to reveal these problems. Although the forms are filled out by the charities and often are not reviewed by the staff of the state offices, they are the official statements of the responsible charities. It is at times to the advantage of a reporter to point out in a close-out interview: "But these are your figures. You reported how little went into the seeing-eye-dog program."

Boys Town, a home in Nebraska for otherwise homeless boys, was internationally known and praised because of the 1938 movie, "Boys Town." It became the number one tourist attraction in the Omaha area, and each year it sent out 33 million letters soliciting contributions. The *Sun* newspapers of Omaha revealed in 1972 that Boys Town did not need the money.[2] Not only did it have a net worth of $209 million, it also had annual income from interest on that money that was four times as large as what was needed to run the home.

In the investigative report, which won a Pulitzer Prize, the *Sun* wrote that it confronted the chief financial officer of Boys Town with figures from the institution's 1970 IRS report. When the CFO told them that was confidential information, the reporters corrected him and said it was public information.

"Yes, I know, but it is still confidential," the confused official said.

The story resulted in the resignations of board members and the installation of a new director.

In Naperville, Illinois, in November 2005, the *Sun* newspapers found a new wrinkle to charities investigations when they examined the program of charities that asked people to donate their used cars rather than trade them in for a new car. The charities had to file financial reports, but the transactions were handled by intermediaries who were private operators and who did not have to show their financial reports.

The reporters for the *Sun* joined with TV reporters for CBS in Chicago to tell the story. They wrote that no one monitors how private towing companies and salvage yards handle car donation money, and "no one is ensuring the donation money is getting to the charities." They reported that these middlemen between the car owners and the charities had short-changed 187 charities. A CBS reporter then testified about their findings at a state legislative hearing.

Case Study

Everybody Loves a Carnival*

The Wahoo Middle Managers Club was well respected in Buchanan, and for good reason. Members sold candy on street corners twice a year and held a big street carnival every summer—all for charity, they said. They proudly announced that the money they raised was for children's disease research and for scholarships for deserving students. There was a good feeling whenever the Wahoos were involved because they were friends and neighbors doing a good turn. But when Billy Richards fell off the Super Big Thrill ride at the carnival, people started asking questions.

Lori Benton, top investigative reporter for the *Buchanan Record-Journal* found herself trying to come up with the answers. She heard Billy's parents were considering litigation and were sure to file suit in the very litigious county. She called on them at their home and asked for permission to talk to Billy, a 12-year-old, but they referred her to their lawyer, Steve Baron. On her way out of the Richards' home, Benton saw Billy throwing a ball against the garage wall.

"You bet we're going to sue—you can print that. The boy is maimed for life. He was the victim of gross negligence of a criminal nature," Baron told her.

"But who will you sue?" Benton asked. "The carnival was in a city street, it was put on by the Wahoos, and the ride was owned by a traveling carnival company. Have you determined who is liable?"

"Hell, I don't have to do that, I'll just sue them all, and the ride manufacturer, too. Let them argue they're not responsible. I might add, I have a record of success in such litigation."

? ***Should an attempt be made to talk to Billy and perhaps determine his medical condition or whether he was "maimed for life"?***

Yes: To be a proper reporter one should talk to as many people as possible, and age does not matter. Benton was asked not to talk to

---

*The cases are based on real investigative stories, but the names and places have been changed to protect reporters, their sources and the secrets they have. Some are actual stories told in a step-by-step reconstruction and others are composites.

the child but did not state her agreement with this. The public has a right to know, and an ethical question should not be an excuse for not doing a story.

No: The reporter is inviting criticism and a possible lawsuit for breaching the security of a child's home, asking questions and publishing the answers. It is common sense to conclude that if she questioned the child she would have gone beyond the bounds of conduct expected of a reporter. Also, she would not be able to make a medical judgment by talking with him.

Should the report contain, word-for-word, what the lawyer says?

Yes: The lawyer is a competent person who knew he was talking to a reporter and could be quoted word for word. He saw Benton writing down what he said and even suggested she print it.

No: The lawyer is making allegations without fact. He has not filed the lawsuit, and if or when he does he might not make the same claims. His comment about winning such lawsuits is self-serving and has nothing to do with the story.

Benton found the president of the Wahoo club, Phil Scott, behind the counter of the local pharmacy he owned. She asked who was responsible for safety on the rides.

"Not us. Those rides belong to The Original Buffalo Buck Traveling Carny Show. They are the best people in the carny business. We contract with them."

"Who rates carnivals and decides who's best?"

"I don't know. It's in all their brochures. I'm only a nonsalaried, part-time club president. Last year it was Joe, the barber. We don't run carnivals. We have our own problems," Scott said.

"I would like a copy of your 990."

"My what?"

"Your IRS 990. It's a form a not-for-profit organization has to submit to the IRS every year with all its financial information. It's public record."

"I don't know anything about those things. We have an accountant who handles those matters, and it's all private."

Anticipating Scott's lack of knowledge about IRS form 990, Benton pulled a copy of the federal law from her jacket. "I have a copy of the law here, and it specifically states it must be open for public inspection."

"Well, la-de-da! What's a little girl like you know about the federal law? Somebody put you up to this, and I'll bet it was that money-grubbing lawyer. There's possible litigation in this matter, and I will instruct our accountant to give out no information."

"If you call the IRS, they'll tell you it's public."

"No way am I calling anybody. You know the Wahoos are revered in this community. If you write something bad about us, you'll be besmirching every businessperson in town. I don't have to remind you we are the advertisers for the newspaper. The things you have been writing have made your publisher very nervous. I ought to know. I provide his pills."

Should a derogatory story about the Wahoos and their president be written?

Yes: He obviously is wrong about his responsibilities as an organization president and wrong about the disclosure law. He is rude, condescending and a sexist in calling Benton a "little girl." He threatened her with reprisal. He deserves to be taken down a notch or two.

No: Benton has a right to deplore the treatment she received, but she should not let her personal feelings interfere with good journalism. She should have the full story before she decides what to write.

What about backing off the story because it may anger local advertisers?

Yes: Benton has to remember who is paying her salary. The newspaper has hired her to produce a high standard of journalism for the reader. Readers learn to trust the paper, which leads them to purchase it, read the articles and respond to the advertisements placed and paid for by local merchants. She is a part of the system she would be attacking. Instead of critical stories, she should be writing about local people's good deeds—the beautification program run by the local garden club, for example.

No: Advertisers are not donating money to the newspaper as a charitable act. They are buying ads because they get results. Merchants who discontinue ads in retribution suffer. How does the pharmacist expect anyone to show up for his day-after-Easter, hollow-chocolate-bunny sale if he does not place an ad. People who say they are canceling their newspaper subscriptions because of a story that is unpleasant for them seldom get around to it; and, if they do, they are likely to be seen secretly buying copies at the newsstand.

Benton knew that not only did the Wahoos have to file financial information with the IRS, but even more detailed information was required from them by the state. Every organization holding itself out to be raising money for charitable purposes has to file as a charitable trust with the state attorney general. Those reports were on file in the statehouse and could be viewed there or sent by mail after receipt of a reasonable charge for copies as provided by state law. Benton called the attorney general's office and learned that the reports were available; then she wrote a letter requesting them. Meanwhile, she had some time for surveillance.

She visited the carnival on its last day to observe how the operation worked. She saw that tickets were sold at several booths around the midway and were used for all purchases, including food and drink. The Original Buffalo Buck Traveling Carny Show could account for the money, control theft by workers, and ensure the Wahoos that they were getting their fair share.

The beer tent and the bingo game were side by side, and as the hours grew late, the crowd got loud and sloppy. Benton saw a group of young people laughing and drinking and wondered whether they were of legal age to drink. Police officers were out in force, and even Police Chief Roscoe was there in uniform.

"Hi, Lori, having fun?"

"I'm doing a story about the carnival. It seems to me there is underage drinking going on."

"Oh, I'm not so sure. We're not here to check IDs or spoil everyone's fun. We are security."

Just then there was a disturbance across the midway. A man was shouting, and a crowd had gathered. Chief Roscoe ran over and Benton followed. A man was yelling that the games were rigged, that one of the bowling pins that players had to knock down was weighted with lead and would not go down no matter how hard it was hit. He was challenging the carnival worker to show the crowd it could be done.

"Sir, you are causing a disturbance," Chief Roscoe said. "Move on."

The man protested, and Roscoe placed him under arrest.

"But, chief," Benton said, "what about the rigged game? This man may be right. I don't see how he's done anything wrong. What are you going to charge him with?"

"He created a disturbance. We'll think of something. Now, I know you are hell-bent on getting a story wherever you go, but this is just a friendly carnival game and it's all for charity. You'll find it's no different from what's done in any other town in America."

Benton decided to check on other towns. She looked at back issues of a carnival trade magazine for the traveling schedules of the larger carnival shows. Then she found the local newspapers from those towns on the Internet and learned who sponsored the carnivals. She called those places and asked them about their experiences with the carnival. All the sponsors' answers were similar: They were not entirely happy with the carnival, but they accepted that there would be problems. Finally, one church pastor in Wisconsin wanted to talk.

"We don't want them back next year. They were so demanding in their contract that there was hardly any profit for the church school. They controlled all the games and food and drink concessions and used our men's club liquor license to sell beer. They made us get volunteers for the ticket booths, to direct parking and to pay the police officers for security."

"You paid the police? The chief, too?"

"Of course. That's how they buy off the local police and get away with anything. We paid the city building and electrical inspectors. Put them on the payroll and called them technician advisers. We got so little out of it that we're going to do something different next year."

Benton suggested the carnival brought in about $100,000 in three days, and then she asked how much of that estimated amount the church received.

"Six-hundred-and-fifty dollars. And more than $200,000 was brought in."

"You got only $650 after people paid $200,000 for charity?"

"It was better than nothing."

Is a story developing that is of importance and worthy of an investigative story?

Yes: Someone is hiding the facts from the public, and the welfare of the public is at stake. It often happens that an investigative reporter starts out following up on a breaking story, and it turns out that a much bigger story is discovered. Benton is surprised and concerned at what she has learned and believes her readers will be also.

No: Benton has gone way off the track. She was supposed to be doing a story about why Billy Richards fell off the carnival ride, and now she is involving herself in everybody's business. No law was broken. Nobody in Buchanan is complaining. She is looking for trouble to make a name for herself.

When the financial statements came from the attorney general's office, Benton knew what to look for. They showed income of $242,215 and expenditures of the identical amount. She had been told at the attorney general's office that "program services" meant the amount of money that was used to pay for the services that the charitable organization funded as its purpose to exist. She saw one of the items listed under program services was $28,000 for "specific assistance to individuals." She deduced it must be Wahoo's scholarships for deserving kids. The *Record-Journal* every year wrote a story from a Wahoo news release stating that it had granted four scholarships of $7,000 each, but it never listed names of the recipients. Also, under program services, Benton found listed a pool party for $5,278; an officer's ring,

$933; travel, $12,100; and conferences, $30,010. The only other item under program services was $872 for "grants and allocations."

Even though she had been prepared for the outrageously low number, she still was stunned to realize that $872 was all that was going for the children's hospital research that year.

She wished she could have gotten the statement of the church organization that was kicking out the carnival, but because it was a religious organization, it was exempt from filing both the attorney general's form and the IRS form 990.

Benton believed she needed a comparison but backed off the idea when it seemed there was nothing comparable.

She got the forms for the local Wahoos for the two preceding years and found the figures were much the same.

Should Benton go ahead with the story on the basis of the documentation she has?

Yes: She has the necessary document and can start writing. Documents do not lie and do not change their story. All she needs are a few examples from the state report because the story should not be too complicated.

No: Benton should not take at face value everything in a document without talking to the people who created the document or who are the subjects of the document.

Is it necessary to compare the reports of the Wahoo operations with the reports of other organizations in the state?

Yes: The reader needs to know whether the Wahoos are out of line in their operations, and Benton can show this by comparing the Wahoos with a properly run charity. If she does that, the investigative story will not imply that all charities are poorly run. Telling of a well-run charity will help the story because it will make the poorly run charity look all the worse.

No: There is really no comparison that the reporter can rely on. Circumstances are not similar in different clubs or in clubs in different cities. What if the "good" charity turns out to be as bad or worse as the Wahoos because it is falsifying its records? If Benton cannot spend as much time investigating the good charity as she has spent on the Wahoos, she should not make such a comparison.

Benton needed to know more about the Wahoos. She knew from her interview with Scott that Joe, the barber, was a member. She found him in the shop at closing time.

"Hi, I'm Lori Benton, a reporter for the *Record-Journal*. I'm doing a story about the Wahoos."

"Oh, that's nice," he said. "We do good work."

Figure 7.1 Wahoo Middle Manager Club annual financial report, page 1

Annual Financial Report of Charitable Organization

This form is to be completed by an organization which does **not** file an annual federal information return with the Internal Revenue Service.

Name of Organization	State registration number
WAHOO MIDDLE MANAGER CLUB	309323875
Address	Employer identification number (EIN)
111 CHESTER STREET	G2173337554
City, State, ZIP Code E-mail address	Exempt under IRC Section 501(c)
BUCHANAN EW 60634	

This report is for the year ended (Month/Day/Year): 6/30/06

Fair market value of assets at year end: 6/30/06

Part 1   Statement of Support, Revenue, Expenses, and Changes in Net Assets or Fund Balances

Support and Revenue

1 Contributions, gifts, grants, and similar amounts received	—
2 Government contributions and grants received	—
3 Program service revenue	—
4 Membership dues and assessments	—
5 Net gain or (loss) from the sale of assets other than inventory	—
6 Interest	213
7 Dividends	
8 Other investment income	
9 Other revenue	242,002
10 **Total revenue** (add lines 1 through 9)	242,215

Expenses

11 Program services (from Part 2, line 28, column B)	76,381
12 Management and general (from Part 2, line 28, column C)	16,225
13 Fundraising (from Part 2, line 28, column D)	149,609
14 **Total expenses** (add lines 11 through 13)	242,215

Net Assets/Fund Balances

15 Excess or (deficit) for the year (subtract line 14 from line 10)	—
16 Net assets or fund balances at beginning of year (from Part 3, line 29, column A)	—
17 Other changes in net assets or fund balances (attach explanation)	—
18 Net assets or fund balances at end of year (add lines 15 through 17)	—

"What do you do?"

"We raise money for charity—children's disease research. And we get scholarships for children."

Benton knew from experience that it would be best to not challenge the barber but to let him talk instead.

"How do you decide who gets the scholarship? Is it based on need or academic achievement?"

"It is based on the recommendation of members. Look, I'm about to close up. If you want more information, you'll have to get it from Phil."

Figure 7.2 Wahoo Middle Manager Club annual financial report, page 2

Page 2

Part 2   Statement of Functional Expenses

Expenses	(A) Total	(B) Program services	(C) Management and general	(D) Fundraising
1 Grants and allocations	872	872		
2 Specific assistance to individuals	28,000	28,000		
3 Benefits paid to or for members				
4 Compensation of officers, directors, etc.	8,400		8,400	
5 Other salaries and wages				
6 Pension plan contributions				
7 Other employee benefits				
8 Payroll taxes				
9 Professional fundraising fees	149,609			140,609
10 Accounting fees	5,200		5,200	
11 Legal fees				
12 Supplies				
13 Telephone	2,500		2,500	
14 Postage and shipping	125		125	
15 Occupancy				
16 Equipment rental and maintenance				
17 Printing and publications				
18 Travel	12,100	12,100		
19 Conferences, conventions, meetings	30,010	30,010		
20 Interest				
21 Depreciation, depletion, etc.				
22 Other expenses (itemize):				
23 pool party	5,278	5,278		
24 officer ring	933	933		
25				
26				
27				
28 **Total functional expenses** (add lines 1 through 27) (carry columns (B)-(D) totals to Part 1, lines 11-13)	242,215	76,381	16,225	149,609

"But did you know that only $872 went for children's disease research last year?"

"So? That's something!"

She noticed he was wearing a ring with a big "W" on it. "That's your officer's ring," she said, pointing it out. "Do all officers get rings?"

"I'm closing up. You'll have to ask your questions to Phil. He's the president now."

?

Was the ambush interview of Joe, the barber, fair?

Yes: She identified herself and was writing his comments in a notebook as they talked. She said truthfully that she was a reporter who was doing a story about the Wahoos. She need not say more about what kind of a story because she has not even gathered the information yet.

No: It was a typical ambush interview in which the interviewee had no time for familiarization with the facts. It is unfair for the reporter to imply that she is conducting a routine interview when she might make some serious accusations.

It was time for a close-out interview with Scott. Their first discussion had provided the official Wahoo version; now he would be given an opportunity to clarify any misunderstandings in connection with the state disclosure form and also comment about it. Benton now had a pretty good idea of what was going on. A large amount of the money for the carnival was going to the carnival operators, who paid off the police to have a free hand. The small group who controlled the Wahoos was spending the balance on travel and conventions and even had a pool party. They could be giving the scholarships to their own children. There was some documentation but not much detail. Scott's interview would be vital to the success of the story.

Her strategy was to let him know from the start of the interview that she had the documentation. Therefore, their time would not be wasted. She knew he might break off the interview when the questions got tough, so she had to nail down the important points.

"You told me you were not paid for your work. There is an item in the disclosure report of $8,400 for director's compensation."

"I said I received no salary; that money is for attending the monthly meeting," he said, proud of having made the distinction.

"Then there is quite a large item of $30,010 for conferences, conventions and meetings. What meetings are those?"

"We don't have a building or a place rented like some big charities, so we have luncheon meetings in the Holiday Inn. Members can bring their families, and it is an opportunity to discuss ideas for the club's charitable purpose."

The interview was going well, Scott believed. Benton was writing down what he said and was accepting his answers without argument.

"And the pool party?" she asked.

"Well, that's at my place, I'm sure you know. I know you have been asking around town and know about the pool party. The members work the carnival and sell candy. They deserve to have some fun."

Some fun, Benton thought, at the expense of medical research. But she only asked, "How does it cost $5,278?"

"It's a top-of-line catered affair for all the families. And I have to maintain the pool all year around, so I can declare those expenses."

"More than $12,000 for travel?"

"That's when we go to the big Wahoo Hoot, the national convention. Last year it was in Hawaii, and that's why travel costs were high."

"Couldn't they have it in Cleveland?"

"Ha, Ha! The Hoot would never be held in Cleveland!"

"Now these scholarships. They have been going to member's relatives."

Benton managed to speak the words in the same tone as her previous questions, but she was bluffing. She only guessed they were giving their own children the scholarships. She held her breath.

"There's nothing wrong with that," Scott countered. "We can give the scholarships to anyone we want, and just because we give them to our members' families doesn't mean they aren't deserving."

Benton got what she came for. From then on, it was merely writing down what Scott concluded and getting out the door.

"Obviously, you don't have a story here because nobody is complaining," Scott said in parting.

Benton must agonize over what she could write. She envisions a small group of local people enriching themselves with money paid by people who believe they are supporting a charity. She has the documents and now the confirmation she needs.

Is it time to write a story?

Yes: At some point in gathering information for a story, reporters or editors must decide whether they have the bulk of the story—not necessarily all, but enough to make a case. Then they must determine their time and effort to uncover more that might only be repetitious or "piling on." The time has come to go with the story.

No: Hold on now. No one else is going to get this story in the next day or two, so let's review it and make sure we have the facts straight. What about Billy Richards? Is he hurt or not? It may be that because building inspectors who inspect carnival rides have been put on the carnival payroll they passed over inspection of the rides, and it caused his injury.

Counterargument for Yes: Richards is not a part of the story. The idea that inspectors are to blame is hard to prove even if it is true. It would be a waste of time and would delay going ahead with an important story to go fishing around in this manner with a preconceived idea. The newspaper can report on the lawsuit if it goes to trial.

Benton decided to build her story on her most solid information, citing the large amount of income from the carnival and the small sum going for charity. The *Record-Journal* published a pie chart showing the gross income, slicing out the self-enriching payments and overhead and revealing the tiny sliver left for charity. The story started an investigation by the attorney general that turned up other questionable practices and resulted in the revocation of the local Wahoos charity license. The newspaper readership was appreciative. The Wahoos were not really the important business leaders of Buchanan after all; they were only a close-knit group of families that had taken over the local chapter of a respected organization. They controlled the board of directors and took turns serving as officers.

Judge Henry Wood threw out Billy Richards' damage suit. The boy had taken off his seat belt and was standing up and waving to the crowd when he fell, but when he did this, he was at the bottom of the wheel's cycle and his injuries were minimal.

Memorandum

- Solicitation for charitable purposes is regulated by the states, which make public the charities' financial information.
- Investigative reports have a symmetry that can usually be charted.
- An investigative reporter can often find a bigger story while following up on a breaking story.
- A close-out interview is an absolute necessity for fairness and accuracy, and it might also confirm or develop more information.
- Ambush interviews are avoided by investigative reporters unless they have no other way to inform the target of a story about allegations.
- Simple financial statements of receipts and expenditures can be explained in graphics in print and broadcast.
- Investigative reporters and editors must decide when to stop investigating and start writing.

Charting an Investigation Project

An investigative project by a reporter takes on a certain form that can be expressed in a flow chart. The project usually starts with an idea that could come from an editor, a tipster or a recent breaking story. This idea is placed at the top and center, and it has two branches. A column on the left shows the progression of the official version, labeled "Truth." The column on the right shows the unofficial version, labeled "What Really Happened." This sounds like a joke. The truth and what really happened are supposed to be the same. Should it not be true and false?

Not necessarily so. The official version, Truth, is often brought to us by persons who believe it to be the truth, but we find out it is not what really happened. Then, in a series of steps, we approach the information on two paths simultaneously. On the official side, we contact the person in charge of the program or most important to the subject, and we conduct a friendly, information-seeking interview. Then we gather as many official proclamations and news releases as we can find.

On the other side of the chart, we interview people affected by the subjects, seek out any and all documents, and observe people, places and things. We may find that the information we gathered from the real side does not agree with the official version. So we go back to the source of "Truth," confront the source with our findings, get comments and write a story that is marked on the chart at the bottom center as the final output.

Almost every top-notch, successful investigation follows this pattern. As an example, we will diagram an investigation of how a recently enacted state bingo licensing act is working.

A few years back and throughout the state, small, friendly bingo games were played in church basements. The prizes were small, and church members and mostly elderly neighbors played once a week as a pleasant diversion. The problem was that it was illegal. But what prosecutor would be foolish enough to arrest nice elderly church members and hope to be reelected? So the state legislators made bingo games legal for charities that followed regulations.

The idea at the top of the flow chart is that now, two years after the bingo licensing act became law, reporters should learn how well it is working.

The reporters call the public relations spokesperson of the state agency that licenses the games and request an interview with the administrator. The administrator tells them that each charity that wants to have a bingo game must register with the state and file an annual financial report. Each charity can have only one game per week, and the game can last for only two hours. A card cannot cost more than $1.00 and can be used for the entire game. The top prize can be no more than $500.

The administrator explains that inspectors are ready to respond to any complaint, but thus far there have been none.

It sounds like no story.

The reporters are given a copy of the law (which is also posted on the Internet) and a list of bingo licensees. The reporters have now completed the obligatory "Truth" side of the chart.

To find what is really happening, they study the list of licensees. It takes no great deduction to note that many of the charities list identical locations as the sites of their bingo games. Several clusters of charities set up games at four locations in the city. The reporters immediately tour the addresses and find they are big bingo parlors with neon marquees. Inside, each has a casino atmosphere, and liquor is served. Players have as many as 60 bingo cards spread out on tables in front of them. The games continue all evening, and one hall offers midnight bingo. People come by chartered buses from surrounding states.

The law was being circumvented because every two hours the bingo caller would announce that the next two hours were being sponsored at the hall by a different charity.

The reporters immediately requested files of the financial reports from the attorney general's Charitable Trust Division. The reporters surmised that it was the halls, not the charities, that were making the big money; and they quickly learned their supposition was true. The charities showed hundreds of thousand of dollars coming in and only a few thousand applied to any charitable purpose. The rest of the money was overhead paid to the hall operators for exaggerated prices for parking, food and employees. It appeared that some charities had been created solely for playing bingo at the hall.

The next step was to learn who ran these halls. Land records in the county were of no help because the buildings were rented. But the liquor licenses showed their names, and the reporters were able to find that some had gambling arrests in the past.

Now on the flow chart the reporters move from documents to surveillance. They interview the people affected. The reporters talk to the ministers and priests whom the law is supposed to help, and they find that the churches had to close down their games because they could not compete with the big halls.

The story, now that the reality side of the equation was complete, was ready to be closed out. Next the reporters would tell the administrator what they had learned, and the administrator would comment. It would all be drawn together at the bottom of the chart with a story describing the failure of the bingo licensing act in the state.

Here is an abbreviated chart that could be applied not only to the bingo story but also to almost any investigative project that starts out with an idea:

Figure 7.3 Charting an investigative idea

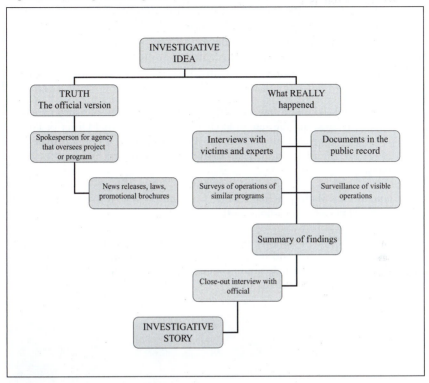

Chasing Telemarketer Complaints—How TV Presents Investigative Findings

Alan Cohn, investigative reporter for News Channel 8 in New Haven, Connecticut, is one of those investigative reporters who deliver every day. His taskmasters are the demands of the public and the constraints of time. His viewers may see him responding to a complaint of a troublesome tele-marketer and even challenging the U.S. Defense Department. His reports must move quickly, yet be understood.

Some of Cohn's investigative pieces are ground-zero budget items, involving no travel and no costly setups; yet they quickly tell of a problem, show how it was investigated and reach a conclusion. This 2006 report is an example.

One of his investigations was of a phone call, purportedly to collect money for the benefit of the Connecticut State Police. Cohn tracked down the call, talked to complainants and followed up with documentation. In a two-minute report, Cohn warned unsuspecting viewers that the money was not going to benefit the local police, as the caller had implied.

The TV story begins with a telephone, the sound of ringing and a hand reaching for the phone. The camera pulls back and a woman is shown answering the phone. We do not hear her; instead, we hear Cohn beginning his narration.

Cohn: News Channel 8 has learned that the Connecticut attorney general's office is investigating the statewide chapter of the Fraternal Order of Police. Specifically, Attorney General Richard Blumenthal says, the unfortunate and outrageous gimmicks the organization's fundraising arm is using to solicit money.

Cohn: Retired Madison schoolteacher Jeanemily Penta is just one of the countless shoreline residents who've gotten the calls.

Mrs. Penta: The young man on the other end of the phone said, "Hi, Mrs. Penta, how are you? And he said—I'm pretty sure he said—the Connecticut Police Foundations for donations, and right away I knew and said, "No, I'm sorry, I don't give on the phone."

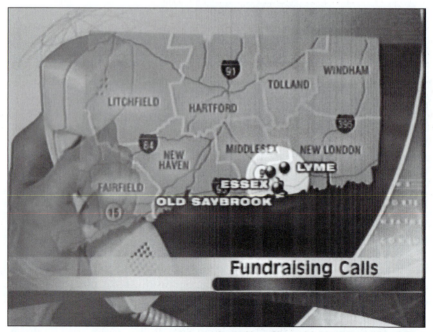

Source: News Channel 8, New Haven, Connecticut

Cohn: Other shoreline residents in Essex, Old Saybrook and Lyme have reported getting similar calls.

State Police Sgt. Thomas Heinssen: Some of the solicitations are quite aggressive. When victims questioned the caller, the caller responds by saying "How can you say, no, at a time like this when the police need your help." They're very pushy.

Cohn: Are any local police organizations legitimately soliciting money at this time?

State Police Sgt. Thomas Heinssen: I've checked with my union, the Connecticut State Police union and local unions along the shoreline, and at this time no police unions are soliciting money.

Source: News Channel 8, New Haven, Connecticut

Cohn: So what is the Connecticut Police Foundation? We've learned it's a fundraising arm of the statewide chapter of the Fraternal Order of Police. And we also learned that Attorney General Richard Blumenthal has opened an investigation into the organization's fundraising.

Source: News Channel 8, New Haven, Connecticut

Attorney General Richard Blumenthal: The reason for this investigation are very reliable reports that the paid solicitor is deceptively pitching for local police departments when in fact, none of the money helps those departments and people are misled into contributing.

Cohn: And, when people do contribute, the Fraternal Order of Police's own Web site acknowledges it keeps 18 cents out of every dollar raised.

Attorney General Richard Blumenthal: The main point is 82 cents out of every dollar goes to the paid solicitor, All Pro Tele-marketing based in New Jersey, and none of it goes to help anyone remotely connected to the State of Connecticut let alone someone associated with a local police department.

Cohn: The organization's statewide president denies its paid solicitors are using aggressive tactics.

The story has been told in two minutes. The reporter has made no accusations, only that the attorney general has stated he is opening an investigation. Cohn is dealing with a private organization and is using the organization's own information to challenge it.

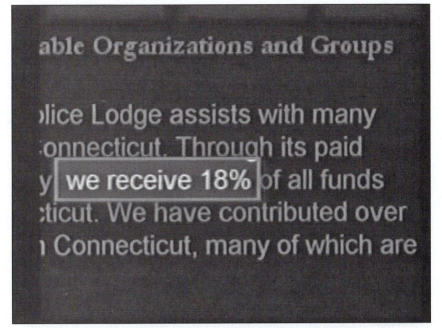

able Organizations and Groups

)lice Lodge assists with many
onnecticut. Through its paid
y we receive 18% of all funds
:ticut. We have contributed over
1 Connecticut, many of which are

Source: News Channel 8, New Haven, Connecticut

To make a stronger story, however, more information could have been supplied about what the FOP president said. The person to whom the president made the denial is not identified. It could have been in an arranged in-person interview, on the phone, in an ambush interview outside the FOP office or in an e-mail. Was the FOP president questioned about where the 82 cents went, and did the president refuse to tell?

Also, the victim of the call was really not a very strong example. Cohn probably should have tried to find someone who had been browbeaten by the caller and as a result gave an exorbitant amount of money and is only now learning the truth about the organization. These improvements could have taken Cohn considerable time, however, and the reporter and news management must weigh the worth of it all. Questions for discussion:

Was the opening telephone call scene improper because it was posed?

Yes: It is obvious that the phone ringing and the woman answering was staged and was not a call from the telemarketer in question because the reporters could not have been in her home when the telemarketers called. Journalists should never fake a shot no matter what the story.

173

No: Nobody said it was the telemarketer calling. It was only a picture of a woman talking on the phone, and we do not hear what she is saying. Stories would not get done if the camera crew had to wait in a private home for a telemarketer to call. In fact, a real call would have added nothing for the viewers because a phone conversation in Connecticut cannot be recorded without both parties agreeing.

Could Cohn and News Channel 8 have done a better job on the charity telemarketing story?

Yes: The story is important and should have been given more time on the air. It tells of a shared experience: Everyone who has a phone has received calls from telemarketers. More financial information on the FOP was available from public records in the attorney general's office. More people should have been portrayed getting calls. Also, the FOP Web site was available and must have had something that was positive about the organization. This could have been used to give the story some balance.

No: Anybody can find something else to add to an investigative report, but the reporter must always consider the time allowed for the broadcast. Another story just as important might be sacrificed. This is reality. The viewer does not need to know all the financial aspects of a story. Leave that to the newspapers.

The same reporter, Alan Cohn, during the same year confronted the U.S. Defense Department and Sikorsky Aircraft Company with allegations of poor inspections of the Black Hawk helicopter. This time, Cohn had whistleblowers—employees of Sikorsky or their contractors—who did not agree to be identified, so their faces were darkened on the screen and their voices were distorted. The words they spoke were superimposed.

Cohn backed up the anonymous allegations with documents that were shown.

Do the Sikorsky whistleblowers lose their credibility by being hidden?

Yes: It is of little value to hear the account of someone who will not go on the record. Whistleblowers are protected under the law, and these people should be sure enough of what they say to state it publicly.

No: If we did not allow sources to remain anonymous, it would be a great loss to journalism and law enforcement. It is courage enough for them to have gone to a reporter with their concerns. Besides, we are not taking their word for it. The reporter has demonstrated their charges with the additional use of documents.

Source: News Channel 8, New Haven, Connecticut

Chapter Recap

Charities have an important role in society. Thus, when a person who operates a charity abuses the role of protector of the donations for charitable purposes, suspicion is cast on all charities. A more balanced account of charities can be achieved by comparing properly run charities with those that are not and by highlighting some of the good work charities have done. Highlighting good charities does not hurt the story about a bad charity; in fact, it makes the bad charity look even worse.

In the next chapters, we will look at fraudulent land sales, insurance companies that use questionable sales tactics, unhealthy food in schools, and auto mechanics on the take—all while keeping in mind that the reader or viewer needs to be reminded that these examples of bad behavior should not be considered as standard for the industries.

Class Assignments

1. Search the Internet for the Web site of your state attorney general. You will find information about who has to file forms with the

office and copies of blank forms. If you are extremely lucky, your state will require electronic filing and put the reports online as the FEC and SEC—both federal agencies—do. Otherwise, you might simply get a list of recognized charities. If easy-to-get-at lists aren't available, contact the attorney general's office and ask whether a charity of your choosing has filed a report. If you are away from the state capital, you can order a file. Examine it and look for a story as Lori Benton did. Write a summary of what you found.

2. Write the top of the story that Benton should write about the Wahoos. The "top" is what an editor might ask of a reporter on deadline so that the editor can be knowledgeable enough about the story to plan for its prominence in the paper. This usually means a lead paragraph, a paragraph supporting the lead, a "nut" or summary paragraph, and two or three explanatory paragraphs. The best argument of the spokesperson for the target of the investigation should be high up in the story, and it should be reported fairly and accurately. Use exact quotations or paraphrase the persons interviewed. The story should be written with a straight news lead so that it is in the same style as other stories that might be on the same news page. The writing should be free of editorial comment and not overly wordy or punched up.

3. Chart an investigative story. Show how the official version (Truth) and the findings of the reporters (What Really Happened) are naturally separate by running them parallel in order down each side of the chart. You may have a favorite investigative report to chart, or you could use the case histories in the preceding chapters of this book. For example, the fire chief claimed the Buchanan fire department was the best when it could have been the worst. The Wahoo Middle Managers claimed their official purpose was charity when they really were lining their own pockets. The reporters learned both sides before producing each story. They combined their information and got the target's reaction. Very few stories do not fall into this kind of organization.

Notes

1. Heidi Evans and David Saltonstall, *New York Daily News,* April 1, 2, 18, 20, 21, and 29, 2001, and May 8, 2001.
2. "Boys Town, America's Wealthiest City?" *West Omaha Sun,* March 20, 1972.

Chapter 8

Investigating Government

N INETEEN REPORTERS AND RESEARCHERS worked together on *The Miami Herald's* 1998 investigation of the election of a mayor of Miami.[1] Their reporting led to a recount that overturned the election. They wrote:

> "You don't have to live in the city of Miami to vote there even though that's against the law. Dozens of voters cast ballots for Miami mayor and commissioners last November even though their homes are miles outside city limits, a two-month *Herald* investigation has found.
>
> "A Homestead janitor did it. So did a Miami Beach widow, a Kendall anti-porn activist and a high school teacher from Miramar—in Broward County. *The Herald,* after reviewing just 3 percent of the votes in the Nov. 4 election, has so far found 105 illegal votes for Miami's mayor and commissioners."

The Pulitzer Prize committee saw *The Miami Herald* story as another example of effective local investigative reporting of government issues and chose the project as the best in newspaper public service for 1999. The selection once again confirmed the importance of investigative reporting about local governments.

According to the U.S. Census Bureau, there are 83,000 separate units of government in the United States. Having a variety of governments, each with its own laws and procedures, allows ideas to be tested in one place before being adopted in another. This system allows more people to participate in government. But for an investigative reporter, this variety presents an ongoing challenge. The reporter reveals when government is not working well and so has to know its inner workings.

The reporter has to be familiar with each of the governments and must carry out research every time a story involves a unit of government. Abraham Lincoln is portrayed studying law by flickering firelight, but a 21st-century reporter can study laws by flickering computer screen. State laws are online and searchable. As each story develops, the reporter can insert the current topic of interest into the search engine and become an instant expert. The multilayered governmental system demands it.

Investigating Voting and Elections

The election process is often the first stop on a tour of trouble areas in governments. Who is qualified to run? Who is qualified to vote? How is residency determined? Are people given money or favors—$20 or a bottle of liquor—for voting? It may be that campaign contributors are promised government jobs that require virtually no work. Public employees have been known to campaign during work time; candidates play dirty tricks like sending anonymous letters. Public facilities—phones and copy machines—are sometimes used in campaigns. For only minor infractions police might detain or arrest workers who support opposition candidates.

Investigative reporters have a long-standing interest in keeping elections free of misconduct. In 1947, the *Atlanta Journal* wrote that the names of persons long dead or nonexistent had been certified as voting in a recent election.[2] Records of who voted were supposed to be written in ledgers in the order the voters appeared at the polling place; but at one precinct, *Journal* reporters found that 34 names appeared in alphabetical order. After the *Journal* story, in which the ledger page showing the names was printed, several people saw their names on the list and told the reporters they had not voted. The *Journal* used a handwriting expert who found the names written in the same handwriting. The reporters took pictures of tombstones of the deceased "voters."

Vote fraud is only the beginning of the corruption that will be found by investigative reporters this year and next in local government despite all the efforts of state and federal agencies to ferret it out and prosecute it themselves and despite the efforts of local officeholders to conceal it. Laws vary from state to state about almost everything in the statutes, including the age when a person is allowed to consume alcoholic beverages, how powerful legally purchased fireworks can be, and how much tax is placed on a gallon of gasoline. The investigative reporter must research the state laws.

Investigating Local Misbehavior

Investigative reporters on the local level, in the aggregate, are more likely than someone reporting from Washington to spot subversion of a federal program. If a jobs program for the unemployed is swiped for local political workers, or $1 houses for the homeless end up being deeded to public officials, or disaster-recovery loans fall into the wrong hands, a local media investigative reporter somewhere is likely to break the story. The local reporter is also the guardian of local tax dollars, which can be drained off in various schemes. What could go wrong? Property assessments could be unfair or inconsistent; large amounts of sales taxes or parking fines are not collected; money that was appropriated for community needs is spent on other projects, often frivolous ones; tax money is placed in a bank and receives little or no interest because the local government financial officer got a loan from that bank at little or no interest; the local government is a spendthrift and needs to borrow at high rates.

Departments are overstaffed (if the work is easy) or understaffed (if the work is difficult); nepotism—the hiring of relatives—is prevalent; agencies are top-heavy with supervisors at higher pay grades and too few workers; employee job descriptions do not tell what they actually do; resumes of top administrators can be fraudulent, especially if someone was fired from an earlier job.

Courts allow felons to go free on minimal bail bonds; prosecutors make deals because it's easier than prosecuting to the full extent of the law; no one checks whether sentences of community service are performed; police use excessive force, routinely excusing it by claiming the citizen had a gun or was acting strangely; members of regulatory boards are closely tied to the industries they are supposed to regulate.

Governments pay more than a customer in a store for a specific item because of the cost of the time to fill out paperwork for the purchase; contracts for outsourcing are granted for services that could be done by employees, thus, if things go wrong the government will have someone to blame; unnecessary and ornate furnishing are bought for executive offices; the bidding process is designed to favor certain suppliers who are friends or relatives of government officials.

Parks in rich or politically powerful neighborhoods are equipped and maintained better with the reasoning that residents there are more demanding; the council member's street is cleaned or plowed first; emergency response time of police and firefighters is slow; cracks and potholes in street pavement need fixing because street repair crews are slow; railroad crossings are poorly marked or obscured, a problem sometimes caused by overlapping jurisdictions not cooperating with each other; public assistance money is going to unqualified persons, for example, the relative of an elected official, after assets are transferred to hide their existence.

The good-ol'-boy relationship between judges and prosecutors lets them hang out together and share a few laughs in the judge's chambers; votes of legislators are in tune with those who make large campaign contributions; an official uses a public position to steer people to a personal private business—for example, a village president who owns a window business suggests to local contractors which window company to use.

Misbehavior of local officials gone wrong usually falls into three categories: conflict of interest, commingling of funds, and bribery-extortion.

Conflict of Interest

Conflicts of interest occur when an official profits from personal private enterprises that show a gain because of the official's government job. Such situations are improper whether or not any direct payment of money is made. For example, a manager of a government office who is in charge of buying computers might also be a computer salesperson who sells that office its computers. If the commission goes to the salesperson's spouse or children, it would still be a conflict of interest. Reporters' scrutiny is not limited to the level of conflict of interest the state law describes; any perceived conflict can be reported.

For example, corrupt officials might try to circumvent the bidding process. In 1971, the *Boston Globe* reported a series of stories about the bidding practices of the suburban city of Somerville.[3] The law required competitive bids for items that cost more than $1,000, but Somerville spent $4.3 million as it circumvented the bidding law by either declaring the work an emergency or splitting large projects into little pieces.

The *Globe* wrote that connections of blood, marriage or interlocking financial ties existed between the contractors who benefited and some public officials. The story was pieced together from city payment records in the city treasurer's office.

Commingling of Private and Public Funds

Some officials start treating their government offices as if they owned them, and they dip into government funds for all kinds of private matters, like taking a trip at taxpayers' expense and saying it was done for public purpose, using public employees to work on their private homes, and using public offices and office supplies to carry out a political campaign. Some of this commingling seems like small change, but the record shows that once an official starts crossing the line, that official tends to become bolder each day.

Bribery and Extortion

A police official will take a payoff from a motorist, and a building inspector will take a bribe from a shop owner. It happens. Bribery or extortion can occur on a larger scale when developers and zoning lawyers pay to have their way in city hall. These payoffs may be hidden in partnerships with the developer. Also, public officials may require a kickback of a percentage of the pay of a public employee assigned to them. These payoffs are unethical and illegal.

Reviewing Documents, FOIAs and Open Records Acts

To get information about government operations, a reporter uses the keys to the documents: open records acts and freedom of information acts.

The federal FOIA is reproduced in Appendix 1 of this book. When you read it, you will see that not all federal government records are covered. Only records of administrative agencies are included. That means Congress and the judiciary are not.

Also, information that endangers the national security will not be released. That causes debate over the interpretation of what is vital to national security. Plans for a new weapon in the Department of Defense certainly would not be included, but President Richard M. Nixon claimed that the release of any of his Oval Office tapes would compromise national security.

Information that requires that private trade information be released can be kept secret. Thus, if the government wants to buy soup for veterans' hospitals and this requires the recipe in the bid, it is a trade secret.

Information that violates the privacy of a person is exempt. Even if tax money paid for it, the medical care of a public official is not public.

Information that would reveal details of an ongoing investigation is also exempt from being released. But when does an investigation end? How long do Amelia Earhart and Jimmy Hoffa have to be missing before the case is closed?

State disclosure laws have similar exemptions. The laws are tested from time to time in the courts by government officials who either like to work secretly or mean well but truly do not want to invade privacy, compromise an investigation or compromise national security.

Courts usually look with disfavor at the excuses of public officials who claim documents are not public. An appeals court in Texas in 1995 affirmed a lower court decision against the city of Garland, Texas, and its manager for refusing to make public a memorandum that was discussed in a closed meeting.

In August 1993, Garland's city manager sought to remove the city director of finance. He prepared a draft memorandum concerning a possible resolution of the financial director's employment. The memorandum was considered at a closed executive session of the Garland city council attended by the Garland city attorney. Following this meeting, the city manager decided not to pursue the strategy outlined in the memorandum.

The *Dallas Morning News* sent Garland a letter requesting, under the Texas Open Records Act, "all written communications, including, but not limited to, memos concerning the finance director's termination as finance director and/or his assignment to new duties."

Garland declined the request on the basis that no documents existed that either constituted public information or were not exempt from disclosure. The *News* threatened to bring a lawsuit.

Garland tried to head off the *News* by filing a request for a declaration that the documents were not subject to disclosure under the act. In a closed court session, the city submitted to the court four documents, including the memorandum. Garland argued it was not a public record because it was not collected, assembled or maintained in connection with the transaction of official business, as defined in the state act.

The appeals court later wrote that the Texas Open Records Act provides public access to governmental documents, which must be made available to the public during normal business hours of the governmental body.

Garland maintained that the trial court erred by granting the *News'* motion for summary judgment because the *News* failed to prove as a matter of law that the memorandum contains "public information" subject to the act. According to the city's argument, the memorandum does not fit the legal definition of public information because "the document was not used to transact any official business."

The appeals court disagreed with the city and upheld the lower court's decision:

> "The undisputed summary judgment evidence shows that Garland's city manager drafted the memorandum in preparation for terminating . . . Garland's director of finance. . . . [He] took the memorandum to a city council executive session, distributed it to council members, and discussed it in connection with personnel issues. The council's discussion of the personnel problems Garland was experiencing was clearly 'the transaction of official business' of the city.
>
> "The policy underscoring the Act is that government is the servant of the people and each person is entitled to complete information about the official acts of public officials and employees, unless otherwise expressly provided by law."

Finding and Understanding Political Campaign Reports

Political campaign disclosure reports are among the most open and easily found of public documents. They also are the most telling. When a person decides to run for public office, it will cost money. In a small community election, the candidate may have some printing and postage costs for a campaign run from the candidate's home. In a countywide election, the candidate might rent a storefront, advertise in the local newspaper or on local radio stations and set up a Web site. A statewide candidate will advertise on TV, have a network of storefront offices and maybe hire full-time workers. Candidates for the U.S. Senate and the House of Representatives will stump the state or district and buy big-time TV ads.

Someone has to pay for this and the public wants to know who is picking up the tab so that citizens can judge whether the donors are getting favors in return. All financial activity on all levels must be disclosed. Even if all the money came from personal funds of the candidate, it has to be acknowledged on the form. Federal candidates must file with the Federal Election Commission, state candidates file with a state commission or board of elections and local candidates file with the county clerk. State election boards or secretaries of state have on file the disclosure reports for presidential primaries in their states.

The information is at the fingertips of reporters because most of the reports are online. Federal law specifically requires that federal campaign disclosure be posted on the Internet. Official reports are at www.fec.gov. A detailed and more searchable Web site is maintained by the Center for Responsive Politics at www.opensecrets.org.

Even though the reports are online, for some state-level campaigns only basic information might be posted. It is always better to get a paper copy of a report. After reporters have the reports, what do they look for?

Does the Candidate Follow the Rules?

State and federal laws impose limitations on contributions to candidates. Some donors may want to circumvent the limitations by making indirect contributions in the names of officials or employees. If those company employees are later reimbursed in some way, it would constitute a serious violation. Traditionally, the candidate is held responsible for such violations of the rules because the candidate is supposed to be sure of the source of the money before accepting it.

Why Do People Give Money?

If a reporter calls a donor who has given a large amount of money and asks why the donor contributed, the donor is likely to say it was because of admiration for the candidate, the candidate's good work and their agreement on the issues. A reporter may be a bit skeptical but has to accept the reply; however, the reporter might wonder why so many people give money for nothing in return—not even a tax deduction. Such musings could very well lead the reporter to look at contracts granted by the governmental body to which a candidate wins office. Were the contributors rewarded with contracts? It is a serious violation of the election laws if a candidate promises a person a contract or a job in return for a contribution.

Who Are the Candidate's Supporters?

When incumbents who are seeking reelection list their contributors, they often provide information that creates a profile of their associates. For instance, if the council member who heads the zoning committee receives a great deal of campaign money from zoning attorneys with downtown addresses rather than from the people in the neighborhood the council member represents, it would be worthwhile for the reporter to read the minutes of the zoning committee and sit in on some hearings to see whether those lawyers are getting breaks from the council member.

Also, if a council member in New Orleans is getting a large contribution from several people in Boston, the reporter goes on a hunt. Who are these people, and why would they contribute money to the campaign? They could be relatives, or they could be officials of a company in Boston that is seeking a zoning change for its property in New Orleans. If the zoning change would convert a residential property into property that could be legally used for a dance hall, neighbors are likely to oppose it. With whom does the council member side?

Likewise, when a lawmaker hears arguments on legislation that favors the medical profession and that same lawmaker receives large campaign contributions from medical practitioners or corporations in the medical field, a reporter could question whether individual citizens who oppose the matter will get a fair hearing.

How Is the Money Spent?

A campaign disclosure form is a financial statement similar to the report of a not-for-profit organization to the IRS or the report of a for-profit corporation to the SEC. The first page shows the amount of money held over from the previous reporting period, new contributions, the amount spent and also the balance to be carried over to the next report. Expenditures are itemized. It is worth a look to see whether money is going to relatives or to the candidate through some subterfuge. Also, it may be that much of the money is going to the central party of the political organization. For example, the community representative who gets heavy contributions from zoning lawyers might be understood to be merely a "fetcher" for the organization, among a network of fetchers. Such an arrangement propagates a political machine that could take elections away from the people.

Investigative stories about campaign contributions can be important. Contributions to President Richard M. Nixon's 1972 reelection committee were used to finance the burglars of the Watergate office complex; however, that money was donated to the campaign committee before today's federal campaign disclosure laws were in place.

Reviewing Minutes of Meetings

Minutes of board meetings may be the most detailed and official public documents that an investigative reporter has available. They reveal the business of the important decision makers in the community. They tell why laws were created, how money was received and about the important responsibility of spending taxpayer's money. Tapes of a public meeting are transcribed by a professional clerk who strives for accuracy and presents them to the board members for their approval; these minutes earn a top rank when it comes to documentation. Some public bodies have very detailed minutes, but others write only the bare essentials.

However, the professional clerk may have had a bad day, the board members may want to change a statement they made by claiming it was transcribed erroneously, or the clerk may be a part of a conspiracy to hide facts. That would be rare, but to indicate that official minutes are not always considered fact, the reporter will gain protection by attributing the information to the source—the minutes of the meeting, recognized as an official document.

Reporters for local newspapers cover board meetings regularly. Such coverage is an important chore of a local community newspaper because the news of local government activities provides local papers a way to compete for readership with the larger metropolitan daily papers. Local reporters cover not only the town or village board but also the county board and the school board; they also do their best to cover the boards of the fire, mosquito abatement, sanitary, library and park districts.

The most inexperienced reporters may attend such a meeting and then write about what transpired in the order that things happened: "The chairman of the Buchanan Rodent Control Board started the meeting at 8:02 and the first item on the agenda was . . ."

But readers are an impatient lot, and they are not about to read through every bit of minutiae to learn that at the end of the meeting the mayor announced she was resigning and relocating to Iceland. That should have been the news lead to the board meeting story. The reporter has to make decisions, and during a routine meeting might find the most important story to be: "The Buchanan village board last night approved changes in the construction plans for a new high school building." This news, important to residents, might have been buried in a list of other official actions.

Also, a reporter looks for other stories outside of the official actions that are discussed at the board meetings. Citizens come to the boards with their complaints about the police and fire departments, garbage pickups and happenings at the schools. Reporters often write feature stories (stories without an immediate need for publication) about people and their problems. People might come to a meeting and complain that a neighbor keeps bees. The reporter is interested and finds that the beekeeper is a longtime resident of the county's rural area and recently has become surrounded by new suburban homes. The reporter writes a feature story, using the beekeeper to show the problems of mixing city and country living.

The investigative reporter always wants to go a step further. So much goes on at board meetings that an investigative reporter should go to them all. But that cannot be done. Too many meetings; too little time! But there is time to read the minutes. Reading the minutes is a way for the reporter to stay on top of happenings and quickly get background whenever the scent of corruption perfumes the air.

There aren't enough reporters to have one permanently assigned to cover city water board meetings, so when John Bebow, an investigative reporter at the *Detroit News* in 2002, questioned why city water rates were being increased, he read minutes of water board meetings. They showed that companies, government agencies and individuals with delinquent bills as high as $250,000 circumvented their debts by installing their own devices—bought at a local hardware store—that overrode the shutoff of their water service.

Bebow might be called a one-man investigative team. He produces comprehensive newspaper stories as reporter and writer. He likes to stay away from FOIA requests, he says, and relies instead old-fashioned reporting, including getting reports from insiders.

Researching Property Ownership

Reporters are learning to use investigative reporting techniques in their daily assignments because the media have responded to public demand for better-quality reporting and the official records are so readily available on the Internet or in computer databases. Almost all reporters, who at one time would explore no further than what was told to them by officials, have waded into court files or campaign disclosure forms. But one mother lode of public records seems so formidable that few have dared seek it: it is the office of the county recorder of deeds, in some locations known as the land records office.

Why is it public? People record the ownership of their land because they want reassurance that it is their property and they are on record to have staked a claim. Others have their own reasons for wanting ownership documented. A bank or other lending institution wants to record the mortgage on that property because, in one sense, the institution is the true owner of that portion of the property that is the value of the balance of the mortgage. It's said the bank has a lien on the property. By requiring the owner to record the mortgage, the lender makes sure that the owner does not use that property as collateral for numerous loans that exceed the property's value.

The scope of the recorder's office is limited to real estate. If a person gets a loan on a car, it is registered with the title in the motor vehicle division of state government. If a loan is secured by a piece of machinery or other moveable property, it is registered with the Uniform Commercial Code agency of the state.

How can one be sure the real estate is properly identified? Land description is a relatively simple concept: lines on a map. Real estate salespeople are quick to point out that a person should acquire as much land as possible because "they are not making any more of it." So, with that possibility out of the way, the only purpose of the land records office is to describe boundaries of existing land and affix ownership within those boundaries.

In the 19th century, drawing the lines on the map was a snap. Townships were created by lines enclosing six square miles of land; this was divided into 36 squares; each was one mile long by one mile wide. Each square was given a number, and each contained 640 acres unless there was a natural boundary such as a seacoast. The 640 acres were then divided into four sections of 160 acres each. Then those sections were divided four ways into 40-acre sections. Because the United States was a farming economy at that time, it was not expected that any family could live on fewer than 40 acres. That meant that a piece of land could be described as the southwest quarter of the northeast quarter of section 22 in township 16. This made it easy to keep a ledger in the county office, describe the land accurately and write out the transfer of ownership.

The divisions worked well for awhile, but then people wanted ownership of fewer acres for a house in the city. That called for the creation of the familiar subdivision. A subdivision is not a social classification requiring patios, barbeque pits and cul-de-sacs; it is a simple description of the land. In a subdivision, ownership of property is shown by blocks and lots that are numbered.

What information is contained in the land records? The documents in the recorder's office show the succession of ownership. Ownership of the land goes from one person, the grantor, to another person, the grantee. (That is easy to remember because it is similar to the role of employer, who gives a job to an employee.) But then complications arise. In conversation, we say the bank gave us a mortgage, but the land records people do not see it that way. They record the property owner (or property purchaser) as giving the bank a percentage of their ownership, and the bank files a lien to be able to take it and sell it if the mortgage is not paid. It is all part of the concept of land records. The documents describe what is happening to the land, not to the owners.

What does a person have to do to get the records? The investigative reporter may want to know who owns land. It is the recorder's office that has the key. These offices usually have research rooms where computer terminals are available to the public to search the transactions, and microfilm of the documents is nearby in files. A researcher can get copies of the deeds and mortgages. These offices are busy places, and a reporter or student will fit in with the crowd and will not be questioned about the purpose of the research. Visitors to the offices are clerks of real estate brokers or investors who have sent them to file deeds or to look for opportunities to buy foreclosed property.

Many counties have placed all of the documents of this office online. Clark County, Nevada—where Las Vegas is located—was possibly the first to have not only the index but the actual documents available online. Clark County ownership records can be found by inserting a name into the search engine on the county Web site; records can also be found with the property index number (PIN), a number created to identify a taxed parcel of land. The PIN is good for finding the land in a computer search but not for researching all the transactions because one piece of property could have several tax parcel numbers.

What do the documents mean?

Of most importance to the reporter is the deed of conveyance, sale deed or warranty deed. This one document (it's called different things in different places) shows who bought and sold land, the date of the transaction, and the amount of money that exchanged hands. Figures 8.1 through 8.3 show an example of a deed pulled at random from the online database of the Clark County recorder. Because this is an actual deed pulled at

Figure 8.1 Sample deed

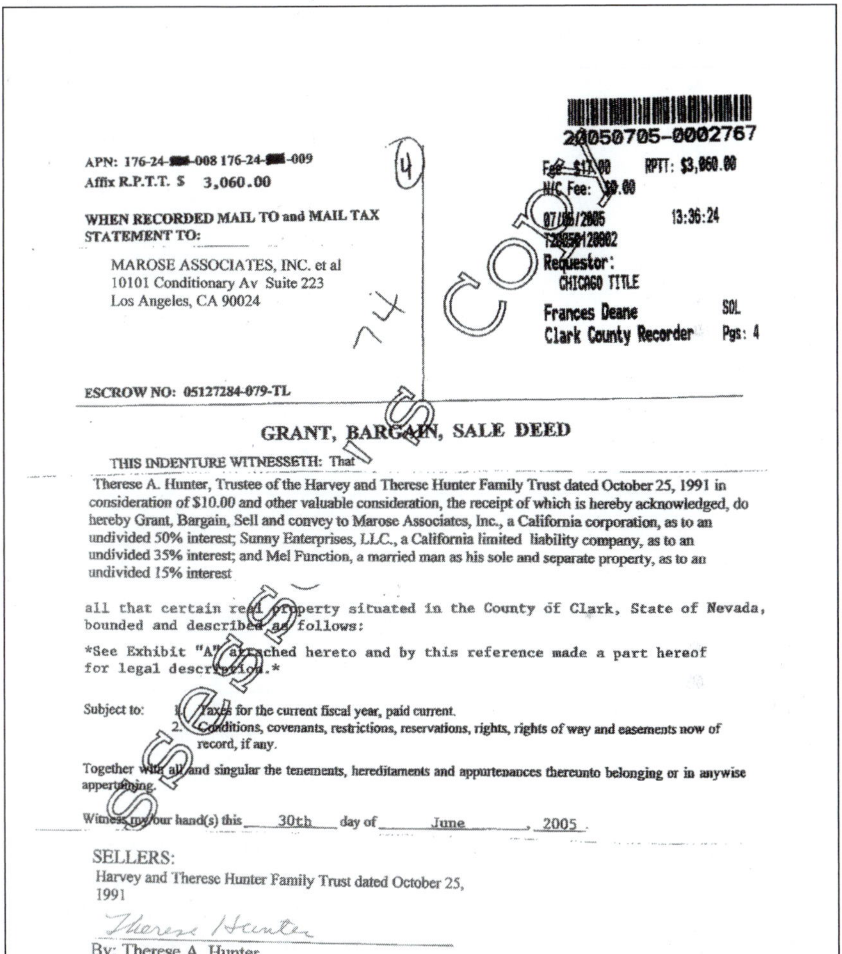

Source: Clark County, Nevada Recorder's Office Land Information, http://www.co.clark.nv.us/recorder/Land_Information.htm

Figure 8.2 Sample deed, exhibit A

Exhibit A

PARCEL I:

The East Half (E ½) of the Northeast Quarter (NE ¼) of the Northeast Quarter (NE ¼) of the Northwest Quarter (NW ¼) of the Northeast Quarter (NE ¼) of Section 24, Township 22 South, Range 60 East, M.D.B.&M., Clark County, Nevada.

PARCEL II:

The West Half (W ½) of the Northeast Quarter (NE ¼) of the Northeast Quarter (NE ¼) of the Northwest Quarter (NW ¼) of the Northeast Quarter (NE ¼) of Section 24, Township 22 South, Range 60 East, M.D.B.&M., Clark County, Nevada.

Source: Clark County, Nevada Recorder's Office Land Information,
http://www.co.clark.nv.us/recorder/Land_Information.htm

random from the files, the names have been changed and part of the tax numbers are deleted. The deed shows that a family trust has sold property to two corporate entities and an individual. The property is identified by the APN numbers at the top, left. Two tax parcel numbers were involved in the sale. There is no suggestion that the transaction on which this document is based shows any reason for investigation.

The document is dated, stamped with the hour received, a fee of $17 is charged and a Real Property Transfer Tax of $3,060 is assessed.

At first reading, it appears the sale was for a mere $10, but that is a technicality in the law that would cause embarrassment to a reporter who

Figure 8.3 Sample declaration of value

State of Nevada
Declaration of Value

1. Assessor's Parcel Number(s)
   a) 176-24-███-008
   b) 176-24-███-009
   c)
   d)

2. Type of Property:

   a) ☒ Vacant Land   b) ☐ Single Fam. Resi
   c) ☐ Condo/Twnhse   d) ☐ 2-4 Plex
   e) ☐ Apt. Bldg.   f) ☐ Comm'l/Ind'l
   g) ☐ Agricultural   h) ☐ Mobile Home
   i) ☐ Other _____

FOR RECORDER'S OPTIONAL USE ONLY
Documentation/Instrument #: _____
Book: _____ Page: _____
Date of Recording: _____
Notes: _____

3. Total Value/Sales Price of Property: $600,000.00

   Deed in Lieu of Foreclosure Only (value of property): (____)

   Transfer Tax Value: $600,000.00

   Real Property Transfer Tax Due: $ 3,060.00

4. **If Exemption Claimed:**

   a. Transfer Tax Exemption, per NRS 375.090, Section: _____

   b. Explain Reason for Exemption: ___

5. Partial Interest: Percentage being transferred: ___ %

   The undersigned declares and acknowledges, under penalty of perjury, pursuant to NRS 375.060 and NRS 375.110, that the information provided is correct to the best of their information and belief, and can be supported by documentation if called upon to substantiate the information provided herein. Furthermore, the parties agree that disallowance of any claimed exemption, or other determination of additional tax due, may result in a penalty of 10% of the tax due plus interest at 1% per month. **Pursuant to NRS 375.030, the Buyer and Seller shall be jointly and severally liable for any additional amount owed.**

   Signature ___ *Therese Hunter* ___   Capacity Grantor

   Signature _____   Capacity _____

SELLER (GRANTOR) INFORMATION	**BUYER (GRANTEE) INFORMATION**
(REQUIRED)	**(REQUIRED)**
Harvey and Therese Hunter Family Trust	Raoul Reitsma & Harry Monsoon
9707 Volstead St.	10101 Conditional Av Suite 223
Las Vegas	Los Angeles
NV 89139	CA 90024

   COMPANY/PERSON REQUESTING RECORDING (required if not seller or buyer)

   Print Name: Chicago Title   Escrow #:051██84-079
   Address 3980 Howard Hughes Parkway
   City/State/Zip: Las Vegas, NV 89109

   AN ADDITIONAL RECORDING FEE OF $1.00 WILL APPLY FOR EACH DECLARATION OF VALUE FORM PRESENTED TO CLARK COUNTY, EFFECTIVE JUNE 1, 2004.

   2767

Source: Clark County, Nevada Recorder's Office Land Information, http://www.co.clark.nv.us/recorder/Land_Information.htm

misconstrued it. Many years ago, it was required that at least $10 change hands before a land transaction could be valid. So, deeds needed to confirm that at least $10 had been spent, but it also states "and other valuable consideration."

Because this is in a trust, the trustee, a representative of the owners, is named as the person conveying the property; the trustee's name is shown. The names of the owners of the trust are not listed, and neither are the stockholders of the corporation and the partnership. The individual getting 5 percent is named. The date of the creation of the seller's trust is in 1991, so that is probably the date the seller bought the property. The reporter will research the files for that earlier transaction.

The declaration of value goes to the county assessor, who will adjust the property taxes on the basis of the recent sale price. The price is shown as $600,000 (Figure 8.3) for vacant land. The sale price is not shown in most county recorder's offices, but in the absence of a statement of a price, we could determine it from the tax charged. In this jurisdiction, at 50 cents per $1,000, we double the tax of $3,060 and multiply by 1,000. That indicates a price of $612,000. The $12,000 difference in the price here could be because the tax was figured on an amount that slightly exceeded $600,000. The reporter will probably want to write that the sale was for "at least" $600,000 and attribute it to the documents.

The names of the buyers (grantees), although not listed on the deed, are shown on the assessor sheet because they are to whom the property tax bill will be sent. Reporters have found that a party in a land transaction is sometimes careful to hide identity in the deed, but then openly list it with the assessor.

What next? Okay, we found the recorder's office, got the deed, and understand it. Why are investigative reporters interested in land transactions? In a case study in Chapter 2, we showed how Lori Benton used property records to learn of the mayor's purchase and resale of houses, and Thomas Dowling in Chapter 9 could have used these kinds of records to track the sellers of fraudulent retirement property. Also, rumors are common of government officials speculating in property that will be bought for public projects. If the courthouse is to be relocated to the suburbs, people will suspect that county board members own the land where it is going.

Such acts have taken place in the past and they are serious offenses in most states. But they are seldom actually carried out because the seller has to be revealed in a transaction with a governmental body, and the government can pay only the fair market price. So the insiders, who know in advance of the public where the new courts building will go, instead buy the land that surrounds the new courthouse. That land is going to increase in value because it will be in demand for the location of buildings for law offices. Speculation in such private sales transactions has no limit. A vigilant investigative reporter will reveal such official breaches of conduct although they might not be illegal.

Generally, a search of land records is on the reporter's list of records to check when investigating any person, place or thing. The next step after locating a deed is to run records of all the corporations mentioned, go to and view the location and, ultimately, talk to the parties involved.

Case Study

A Stolen Document*

Carol Santo worked a "vertical beat" for the *Alabama City Herald-Dispatch,* a large newspaper in the Gulf of Mexico area. Having a vertical beat meant she was assigned to report on the news from a single building—in this case the county building, which contained the offices of the board of commissioners, sheriff, assessor, treasurer, school superintendent, health department and recorder of deeds. In contrast, a horizontal beat cuts across many buildings in many places. The health reporter covered the county health department as well as the state and city boards of health; and the education reporter covered the county schools superintendent, the city schools and the state department of education.

Santo pushed herself to be productive and often went beyond the county building to get stories about the county. She checked campaign contributions of elected county officials and broke a few small stories. A reader saw her byline on one of these smaller stories and phoned Santo. When Santo answered, she heard the voice of a woman telling her that she had documents to show that County Commissioner Douglas J. Highberger was deeply involved in a complex scheme to siphon money out of all of the public works projects in the county in recent years. The caller wanted to meet with Santo, but she said she could not identify herself.

"You can drop your documents off at the desk downstairs at the *Herald-Dispatch.* You don't have to identify yourself," Santo told her.

"No, No. I want to give them to you to make sure no one else gets them."

*The cases are based on real investigative stories, but the names and places have been changed to protect reporters, their sources and the secrets they have. Some are actual stories told in a step-by-step reconstruction and others are composites.

"Have you taken this information to state or federal investigators?"

"There's not time for that," the woman caller said.

Santo knew that the caller was referring to the election that was two weeks away, and a federal or state investigation would probably take an entire year. It was obvious that the caller was aligned with the opposition party in the election. Just before elections reporters often experience an increase in the number of leads offered by sources. One candidate might learn something about another and would prefer that the scandal looked like it was generated by the media, not the opposition candidate's political camp.

"You will have to meet me somewhere," the caller said.

Santo had a rule she had imposed on herself. She would not expose herself to physical danger by meeting a strange person in an isolated location. This information sounded good, so she agreed to meet the informant at a very public place.

"Okay, I'll meet you at the west entrance to the train station at ten o'clock tomorrow morning," Santo said.

Santo kept the appointment and, at exactly 10:00, a man walked up to her, thrust a thick envelope into her hands and quickly walked away.

When Santo got back to the newspaper office she opened the envelope and was shocked to find that it was Commissioner Highberger's income tax returns for the past three years. They showed detailed information about a series of corporations controlled by the commissioner. Those enterprises were shown to have made enormous profits of hundreds of thousands of dollars each year. The tax schedules showed the names of some of his partners in the corporations. At first Santo had to suppress a shout of joy at the discovery, but then reality set in. How reliable was her information? From where did it come? How could she use it?

Can the information be used?

Yes: Santo knows her information is correct because it comes from a copy of an IRS form. She can go ahead and write the story and attribute it to reliable sources. What can the commissioner do about it? He can deny it, but if he sued for libel he would not prevail because to prove his case he would have to make public the tax forms.

No: In no way can she use the information. It comes from a private document. The document was stolen, and she has no right to use it. We know she did not steal it, but how can she explain having the information? She has in her possession stolen property that she intends to use for her own purposes. That is pure and simple theft.

Is this story too important to impose rules?

Yes: Santo did not steal a document; it was a copy someone made. She must go ahead with the story. How can she disregard the information she has learned in the same way as a jury is told to disregard the confession of a defendant? This is an issue of importance to the public, and the public has a right to know. Is she to go back to routine story coverage, knowing what she knows? She will be a party to the commissioner's crimes if she conceals what she knows.

No: Santo is under no obligation to report a crime she may suspect because she looked at the tax returns. In themselves, they do not show a crime has been committed; the documents are merely clues that need extensive research. And it does not matter that the document was passed over a copy machine. The value of the stolen property was the information, not the paper it was printed on. She will have to get the story elsewhere, using a traditional search of public documents.

If reporters do not follow up on leads, are those reporters breaching their duty to the public?

Yes: The people who gave her the documents are counting on her to do her job and report what she has learned. Her employer is also counting on her to beat the competition with stories. How can she turn her back on them? If she does not report the story, a competitor like Chip Shotten will take it and run recklessly with it. Knowing the commissioner is a crook, she can't very well continue attending board meetings and writing about him as if he were an honest public servant.

No: She will have to force herself.

Santo did first what is a matter of reflex for a reporter. She sought out every public document she could find on the subject.

According to the commissioner's form 1040 federal income tax return, he owned 15 percent of 10 limited liability corporations (LLCs). He was in one instance a limited partner in Heavy-Handed Asphalt LLC. That meant he had a share of the profits but had no responsibility for running the business; this arrangement protects him from being sued—and, in addition, protects him from prying eyes. The limited partners are considered by her state to be in the same category as stockholders, and they do not have to reveal themselves by filing with the office of the secretary of state or the office of land records.

Using the search engine for the state laws of her state, Santo checked the statutes online for the words "conflict of interest." She found that the law stated that no official—either elected or appointed—could have a financial interest in any contract voted on or approved by that specific official. It appeared the commissioner was in direct violation of the law.

Santo did not have all the facts, but it seemed implausible to her that the commissioner was a legitimate investor, employee or consultant for so many companies. His activities involved so many different types of businesses, and the companies were always those with which the county had contracts. The commissioner had no professional expertise in these areas. Before he was elected, he had worked as the top manager at the pet cemetery. It was more likely that the commissioner was secretly requiring a slice of the profits from companies that entered into contracts with the county, an arrangement that smacked of bribery—a criminal act. But that didn't matter to Santo at this point; she knew that if the town did business with these companies, the commissioner was violating conflict of interest statutes.

The next step for Santo was to get copies of the contracts with the county. Although these are without question public record, her request would tip off the county about what she was doing. Her request would be delayed until after the election, for sure. She knew of a better way: the minutes of the county board meetings! The state had an open meetings law that prescribed how a meeting was to be scheduled, what constituted a quorum, and under what circumstances a meeting could be closed. It also required that the clerk keep detailed notes of the meetings and that they be made available to any person during regular business hours. Many cities, school districts and counties now posted their minutes online, but Gulf County had never bothered.

Santo went to the county clerk's office, was given the minutes and started reading. It was a long read, but she learned that each of the companies listed on the commissioner's tax return did business with the county, and the commissioner had voted on the measures. She compared the dates of the votes with the dates of incorporation of the LLCs, which she located in the files of the state secretary of state. All were soon after the commissioner cast his favorable vote for each project. It appeared to Santo that the asphalt company and the other LLCs were set up as separate corporations for each county road repaving project. The commissioner did not own a share of the asphalt company; instead he was a partner with the company in the LLCs.

Santo also noticed in the minutes that the companies connected to the commissioner were not always the lowest bidders on county projects and that for the most recent contracts no one had bid against them. Now Santo knew for sure of the amount of corruption in the commissioner's office and could show the high prices the taxpayers were paying to line the pockets of the commissioner. But that knowledge didn't solve anything for Santo and actually made the situation worse because she still could not explain away the fact that she had gained improper access to the original information in the tax return.

She thought of every possible way to find the information elsewhere. How about the commissioner's account at the bank? The commissioner's bank recorded when checks were received from the corporations. She knew better than this, though. Banking information is private, and state law prohibits a person from even asking a bank employee for private information.

The clock was ticking. The election was near. Santo picked up the competition newspaper with trepidation. Would the other paper get lucky and get the story first? What of her sources? She did not even know who they were. A woman had called, but a man had given her the envelope. She had no way of identifying him. Was it a setup? Was the tax form a fraud that a political trickster had counterfeited? She in reality had no reason to place any value on the information.

Should the story be based on what has been uncovered to date?

Yes: She has confirmed that companies that are listed in the tax returns include the commissioner and have contracts with the city. She will have to attempt to talk to the commissioner, but even if he denies her allegations or makes no comment, she is solid with the story. She can write a lead that says: "Gulf County Commissioner Douglas J. Highberger has violated state law by illegally setting up corporations that received county contracts, the *Herald-Dispatch* has learned."

No: Be serious. The newspaper cannot go with such a lead to the story even if she had received her information properly. It says the commissioner is guilty. He has not been tried and convicted. There is only an allegation against him, and that allegation comes from the newspaper only. The lead sentence has the commissioner being guilty a second time by forming illegal corporations. There is nothing illegal about forming corporations. How the corporations are used is what is brought into question.

Also, we still don't know whether Santo is being set up by persons unknown who in fact want her to write her story with false information that would cause the commissioner to lose the election. The election would be over before the information could be shown to be false.

Santo's situation is similar to what happened to longtime CBS anchor Dan Rather and his team of investigators in the 2004 presidential election campaign.

Santo realized that she needed help. She had told no one of her story, not even her editor. She approached the metropolitan editor, with whom she conferred on all her stories. He took one look at it and escorted her to the top editor's office. The top editor listened to her story and said, "You've done a good job of chasing down the records, but you should have told us sooner. We could have had you work with an experienced reporter who would know what to do. The answer is simple."

It is obvious that Santo had missed an important step in investigative reporting. The editor said:

"You've got to contact the people in the partnership with the commissioner and get them to disclose the arrangement. Don't tell them about the tax return, and don't use any of that information in the paper unless they or the commissioner confirm it."

She made surprise phone calls. The companies were without media spokespersons and she was able to get through on the phone, but the answers she received were disappointing:

"I never talk to reporters."
"I have no comment."
"I don't know what you are talking about."

Then she found Asphalt Joe, a self-made millionaire who had risen from poverty by selling used tires and had built many local businesses. He was on his cell phone at his table at the Garden Path Country Club.

"The commissioner and me are on good terms," he said proudly. "He is a good partner."

"You and the commissioner are partners in the asphalt partnership, and he has 15 percent of the stock. Did he pay for that?"

"I don't keep track of those things anymore. The commissioner is like a consultant. He helps us in many ways with his knowledge of government. When we need things done, he knows how to do it."

Soon a county press spokesperson called Santo. One of the contractors Santo had called must have reported her call to the commissioner's office. "Now you know how it is at election time. People are desperate, and they will make all kinds of allegations," the spokesperson said.

Santo told the spokesperson that she had a contractor confirming details of a conflict of interest. Santo gave specifics. The spokesperson said that she would get back to her. An hour later, she called and said the commissioner would make a statement the next morning.

"But we need his comment now because we are going into the paper with the story." Santo was in control now. She had the story, and if she waited for the commissioner's statement, every one of her competitors would also have the story.

The spokesperson cautioned to not be in a hurry to run with the story because the commissioner would explain this "misunderstanding." But they needed some time to research the question.

The story ran, leading off with a summary paragraph and using the county spokesperson's comment that the commissioner would explain the "misunderstanding." Asphalt Joe was quoted, and the state law was mentioned. The story stopped short of concluding that the commissioner was guilty. It recounted all of the votes of the commissioner, and it detailed the bidding process on the Heavy-Handed Asphalt contract. Then the story explained the state law.

The next morning, the commissioner appeared before a crowd of media representatives. He read a statement, but he would not answer questions:

"In the heat of this election, a vicious allegation that bears no truth has been made against me and the county I love. We are all the victims of this kind of shabby journalism that would smear the integrity of the people of Gulf County. I want you to know that at no time was I a partner with any contractor when I voted to approve a contract for that person or corporation. I'm not a crook. Everything I have, I earned."

Asphalt Joe said he was misquoted and had only praised the commissioner for his good performance in office.

The TV stations that had not run the *Herald-Dispatch* story led the news with the commissioner's denial without mentioning the newspaper story. The *Herald-Dispatch* ran a story about the commissioner's denial and restated the information it had reported earlier. Santo understood what had happened. The commissioner was able to make his statement because he was not a partner at the time of the commissioners' vote on the contracts. His limited partnerships were created soon after each vote. She wished she had made that point clear in the story. She had mentioned the date of the incorporation far down in the story, but she had not stressed the idea that the timing of the business arrangement was an indication of a reward.

The commissioner was reelected. More than a year later a federal grand jury indicted him for tax fraud and bribery in connection with the scheme Santo had described. Santo switched beats with the city hall reporter and was accorded a high level of respect for her work on the commissioner story.

Did Santo do the right thing?

Yes: She got a jump on a story that warned the public of corruption by the commissioner. Her information was correct. She carefully avoided the possibility of being set up when she found Asphalt Joe and got him to confirm it. She did her job.

No: The public was confused by the story because it was hastily written and it left an escape route for the commissioner. The public has forgotten the commissioner's confusing story but remembers his allegation of shabby journalism, which was never rebutted by the newspaper.

Memorandum

- Minutes of meetings can be the most valuable yet most under-used document available to local reporters.
- Reporters need to look at the expenditures in a campaign disclosure form as well as the names of donors.
- Investigative reporters for local media are likely to detect flaws in a federal program before their colleagues in Washington.
- A conflict of interest by a public official may be important to report even if it is not illegal.

Chapter Recap

Every facet of government harbors potential malfeasance that the reporter must identify. Beat reporters often come up with investigative stories and need to use the skills of an investigator to pursue them. Another kind of specialist reporter is the consumer reporter who goes up against private business. In the next chapter, we will study how the public can be warned about consumer problems and how those problems can be exposed by using documents, interviews and surveillance and then adding surveys to the arsenal of defensive weapons.

Class Assignments

1. Find the online minutes of a local government body in your area. Then pull up the stories about recent board meetings from the Web site of the local newspaper. Compare the stories with the minutes. Are the stories complete? Did the newspaper reporter miss aspects of the meeting that are important? Did the board take any action that might bring government officials into question, as described in this chapter. For example, did the board grant a contract? Did questions arise about having city employees do the work instead? Was a new city manager hired? Did anyone check the new

manager's résumé? Using your most suspicious nature, list all the questions that could be pursued.

2. Go to the Web site of the Clark County, Nevada, recorder and find any interesting transaction. Detail the transaction in notes, and search for other transactions involving the same persons. If the transaction involves a corporation, look it up in the corporations database of the Nevada Secretary of State. Find a piece of property according to its legal description and bring up an online map. You might also want to "visit" the site by getting an aerial photograph off of the Internet. Be prepared to discuss your findings in class.

Notes

1. "Voters Crossed the Line in Miami," *The Miami Herald,* February 1, 1998.
2. George S. Goodwin, "Telfair Dead Were Voted," *Atlanta Journal,* March 2, 1947.
3. "Five Somerville Contractors Get $4.3 m in No-Bid City Work," *Boston Globe,* February 11, 1971.

Chapter 9

Reporting on Consumer Fraud

CONSUMER FRAUD STALKS ITS PREY every day. An elderly man received in the mail a bogus award notification, purportedly from the International Lotto Commission in Spain; it told him he had won $815,590. He went immediately to Spain, where he was told to meet the manager of the lottery's finance company at a local bank. He would receive his lottery check if he paid 5 percent of his winnings plus an additional $8,150 fee. He realized it was a scam and flew home.

Some elderly persons received phone calls from the "National Medical Office" and other official-sounding agencies that were not in any way connected with the government. The caller warned them that their Medicare cards were about to expire. To prevent this, seniors had to provide their bank account number so the so-called agency could quickly deduct a one-time fee ranging from $200 to $400.

Elderly members of minority communities responded to mailbox flyers offering loans for home repairs. They didn't realize the loans have interest rates of 19–21 percent. The contractor later convinced them to sign a form stating that work had been completed. The contractor then disappeared without performing the repairs. On the West Coast, an elderly woman reported that she was charged $900 to have her circuit breakers "cleaned."

The Defenders

Investigative reporters join with organizations and government agencies in exposing rackets, unfair sales tactics, misleading advertising, Internet fraud and fly-by-night repairs. Some investigative reporters specialize in exposing those and other consumer complaints. Their burden is great. The opposition is formidable—con artists are adept at their game—and readers find it difficult to believe that people can fall into a schemer's trap so easily.

Reporters who expose those who abuse consumers use some of the same techniques as reporters who expose wrongdoing in government, although the paper trail in consumer reporting is sparse. Reports by consumer reporters often make up for the lack of a clear paper trail by using expert opinion, laboratory tests and well-planned surveys.

Better Business Bureau

Better Business Bureau (BBB) sounds like a government agency because of the word "bureau." We know of the Federal Bureau of Investigation, the U.S. Weather Bureau and perhaps the Federal Bureau of Prisons, so the BBB sometimes is mistaken for a government agency.

The organization did not mean it that way when it organized at first. The BBB is a private, not-for-profit association funded by the memberships of businesspeople. It was formed in the 1920s as a group of local organizations that had as its purpose alerting the public about any bad apples among the business community. The name has become so ingrained in the public mind that it has not been changed. The BBB is likely to be the first refuge an abused consumer turns to, but all the BBB can do is help the person take action. It has no enforcement power.

The National Consumers League (NCL), www.nclnet.org, is a privately funded organization of consumers similar to the BBB. It provides an information center with an Internet Fraud Watch at a dedicated Web site, www.fraud.org. It also watches for fraudulent telemarketing, fraud against the elderly, counterfeit drugs and scams against businesses. According to it Web site, the league dates back to 1899 and was the result of merging a number of state consumer protection organizations. The Web site advises consumers about where to take their complaints, and, like the BBB, requires complainants to identify themselves but then keeps the information confidential.

For the investigative reporter, the BBB and the NCL are mother lodes of information that can place the proper focus and overview on the universal aspect of the consumer problem the reporter has found in the local area.

Legal Assistance Groups

Other charitable organizations that come to the rescue of beleaguered consumers are groups of attorneys who donate time to give free legal advice to persons who need help in civil matters, but not criminal defense. These organizations are local, and sometimes they are tied to a law school or a lawyers' association.

A reporter who is working on a consumer problem usually keeps in touch with local legal assistance groups to ask whether they can supply names of victims of consumer abuse who will go on the record with their stories. While working together with reporters on a subject of common interest, the legal groups can sometimes steer the reporters toward people filing civil suits that make the same complaints.

Congressional Offices

Members of Congress will do all they can to please their constituents, and helping them with a problem they might have with a federal agency is a way to show that they are doing more than just voting and caucusing.

Federal agencies give special attention to calls from offices of members of Congress, so if a constituent reports to the representative that a well is being polluted by a glue factory up the river, a congressional aide will alert the U.S. Environmental Protection Agency, which is likely to respond quickly.

Even a reporter far away from Capitol Hill may think of using a member of Congress as an important contact in Washington, but that might be unwise if the reporter is investigating an agency of government; it might appear to be politically motivated. Thus, a reporter will usually stick to working with members of Congress only on consumer fraud in the private sector. The member of Congress can then follow up the reporter's story with a news conference and announce intentions to introduce legislation to crack down on the defrauders.

Congress holds committee hearings on many national problems, and the testimony is published. The testimony and questioning can be lively as people tell of their experiences, and they serve as models for the story to be covered. Also, hearings are announced well in advance, and a reporter with knowledge of the subject matter to come can get the jump on the congressional investigators and report on the problem, making it almost a sure thing for the newspaper report to be discussed in the hearings. This provides a chance for a second round of stories for the reporter to write and another platform for consumer warnings.

Federal Government Agencies

In Chapter 5, about protecting the public, we studied the efforts of large federal agencies like the Federal Trade Commission to provide services. Other agencies also have specialized areas that provide help to consumers. The U.S. Department of Veterans Affairs knows about the problems of veterans, the U.S. Department of Justice may intercede in behalf of persons whose civil rights are violated, and the U.S. Department of Labor polices the pension funds.

State and Local Governments

Every state has an attorney general, the official who is the top lawyer for the state departments. We encountered the attorney general earlier, in Chapter 7, because the AG's office is organized so it has a charitable regulation function. The state AG also brings suit against fraudulent operations in the state and has enforcement powers to pull licenses. Most political officeholders understand the public relations benefit of this office because it translates into votes, and they will get into the consumer protection action. A large city may have a mayor's office of consumer protection, or something similar, or consumer protection might be a county function or part of a senior citizens' affairs office. These offices stand ready to supply information to reporters.

Advocacy Groups and Citizen Organizations

Professional organizations like associations of bankers or bill collectors or foot doctors, to name a few, are able to help consumer reporters who might be looking into abuse in their line of work. Bankers don't like fly-by-night mortgage lenders or credit card thieves; bill collectors are not about to condone any use of force or improper representation; and podiatrists do not want any of their practitioners employing their skills higher than the ankle.

These types of organizations have chief administrators who could become reliable allies. Reporters are of two minds about sources like these: Some would never trust an outsider with any knowledge of what they are investigating, while others gladly work with such sources. Each reporter has to decide whether such sources are worth the risk.

Small Claims Court

Metropolitan areas offer small-claims courts where persons can sue by going to the court clerk's office and filling out a form. Reporters will find that the files of the small-claims court are loaded with stories of frustrated consumers who could not get satisfaction elsewhere. They then get their day in court in a fashion similar to a daytime TV court program. These consumers are sometimes able to tell colorful stories that make good illustrations. A person upset enough to take a day off from work and go to court over a plumber's bill for $75 can be much more believable than a person suing for $1 million.

Fraud Schemes

Scam artists seek to obtain personal information (social security number, bank account number and credit card number) or money or both. And, according to the Council of Better Business Bureaus, unlike traditional burglars, scam artists are happy to find someone at home, particularly if that person is a senior citizen. Scam artists are very crafty, though, and they employ a variety of tactics to elicit information or otherwise rip someone off. Reporters can expose would-be scams by following up on suspicious e-mails, telemarketing pitches, repair businesses and shop owners.

E-Mail

Sometimes the subject lines hint at great wealth: Triple your income! Other times, they imply that a business stands ready to give you a great deal: We have four lenders competing to refinance your home! Frequently, the e-mail is disguised to appear to be from a legitimate financial institution: Please update your online banking records. Or it looks like it is from a government agency: Get tax refund on your Visa or MasterCard!

The National Consumers League gives these hints that a reporter should pass along to readers or viewers in reporting about Internet fraud:[1]

- Never pay to play. It's illegal for a company to require you to buy something or pay a fee in order to win or claim a prize.
- Buying something doesn't improve your chances of winning. It's illegal for a company to even suggest that your chances will be better if you make a purchase.
- Don't believe that you have to give the company money for taxes on your prize. It's up to you to declare your prize winnings when you file your income taxes.
- Be cautious about e-mails for contests and sweepstakes. Many unsolicited e-mails are fraudulent.
- Guard your credit card and bank account numbers. No legitimate sweepstakes company will ask for this information. Never

give your social security number to a sweepstakes operator unless you have carefully checked it out with the Better Business Bureau or your state or local consumer protection agency.

- Be on guard for imposters. Some con artists use company names that are identical or very similar to well-known, legitimate sweepstakes operators. Tell them that you'll get back to them and contact the real companies to ask if there is any connection.

- Be wary of offers to send you an "advance" on your "winnings." Some con artists use this ploy to build trust and get money from your bank. They send you a check for part of your "winnings," instructing you to deposit it and then wire payment to them for taxes, bonding, or some other phony purpose. The bank tells you the check has cleared because the normal time has passed to be notified that checks have bounced. After you wire the money, the check that you deposited finally bounces because it turned out to be an elaborate fake. Now the crooks have your payment, and you're left owing your bank the amount that you withdrew.

- Get all the details. Legitimate sweepstakes companies will tell you exactly how the contest works, including the odds of winning, the value of the prizes, the date that the contest ends, and how you can find out who won.

- Be especially cautious about foreign sweepstakes companies. Many fraudulent sweepstakes companies that target U.S. consumers are located in Canada or other countries, which makes it much more difficult for law enforcement agencies to pursue them.

The e-mail requests can seem urgent, like a dispatch received by a person who had never dealt with the bank mentioned (see Figure 9.1).

While these and other unsolicited e-mails might appear legitimate, the BBB knows otherwise. The BBB warns that con artists use emotional triggers when targeting unsuspecting consumers. Although such scammers sometimes use the latest technology tools to expand their pool of victims, most instances of identity fraud occur through traditional channels and are paper-based, not Internet-based.

On the Street

The fly-by-night repair person, known as a "chimney shaker," a fast talker who skips town with a deposit, literally works the street. These people tell

Figure 9.1 Typical e-mail scam

```
Dear Regions Bank Customer,

You have received this email because we have strong reasons
to believe that your Regions Bank account had been recently
compromised. In order to prevent any fraudulent activity
from occurring we are required to open an investigation
into this matter.

Per the User Agreement, Section 9, we may immediately issue
a warning, temporarily suspend, indefinitely suspend or
terminate your membership and refuse to provide our services
to you if we believe that your actions may cause financial
loss or legal liability for you, our users or us. We may
also take these actions if we are unable to verify or
authenticate any information you provide to us.

If your account information is not updated within the next
72 hours, then we will assume this account is fraudulent
and will be suspended. We apologize for this inconvenience,
but the purpose of this verification is to ensure that your
Regions Bank account has not been fraudulently used and to
combat fraud.

Please login into your account at this link, which is a SSL
secured connection:

https://www.regions.com/profile_verification/index.htm
<http://203.177.52.70/www.regions.com/EBanking/user&pass.html>

*Please remember that Regions Bank will never ask you for
your PIN.*

Regards,
Safeharbor Department
Regions Bank, Inc.
```

homeowners that they just happened to be in the neighborhood and saw their chimney was broken, then they will go on the roof and shake the chimney until it breaks. They have cars or trucks with impressive names and a phone number on the vehicle, but these are merely signs stamped in

209

plastic and held on the door with magnets. Tomorrow, they will have new names. These scam artists are very difficult to catch, and a reporter can only hope to warn people about the scam.

Telemarketers

Telemarketers are pests and may be dangerous to a person's financial health. They leave more tracks than chimney shakers because, although they are separate from the charities or companies they represent, the charities or companies can be held responsible for their actions.

Mail Fraud

Postal inspectors have always been serious about pursuing mail fraud. The mail defrauder advertises in publications and then does not deliver. Reporters can answer ads, learn as much as they can about what these people are selling and then warn consumers.

Unscrupulous Businesses

A defrauder may run a shop—an auto repair shop, for example—and do unnecessary work. A merchant can cheat customers by shorting them on products that are purchased by weight. For stories about these kinds of scams, reporters must set a trap: First have an expert find nothing is wrong with a car and then take the car in for an estimate for repair work, or document the true weight of something by having certified scales nearby to reweigh the purchase.

Reporters will learn of telemarketing abuse, chimney shakers, mail fraud and other scams from the experiences of readers or viewers who contact the media, from attorneys, from consumer advocates in government agencies and from privately funded consumer protection organizations. The reporter is then in a position to develop meaningful stories by zeroing in on and exposing repeat violators. A scam artist is likely to go from one scam to another, and, although the reporter cannot conclude guilt, the fact that the same person who is running a business opportunity seminar in Texas is under indictment for involvement in an investment scheme in Alabama and also selling worthless college diplomas in Virginia will be cause to warn the public.

Some journalists pose as a prospect for a fraudulent sales scheme to get the actual pitch word for word and then counter it with facts from consumer advocates or from a series of accounts of persons who say they were victimized. A team of reporters may set a trap by, for example, calling a suspected fraudulent roofer after several authorities have declared the roof sound and in no need of repair. The reporters will write it up if the roofer says otherwise. Such investigations are time-consuming but they serve the purpose of deterring other possible defrauders who will fear such public humiliation.

Survey and Undercover Investigations

Insurance companies may not be defrauding the public, but when they hire an army of salespeople and pay them more than policyholders receive in benefits, the story needs to be told.

The insurance industry is made up of private companies that are regulated by the government as a special category. Although some companies operate in all the states, the federal government does not regulate, make rules or examine the financial statements of insurance companies. Each state has a unit of government that takes on those responsibilities.

Investigative reporters will find detailed information about insurance company complaints, officers and assets in those state agencies. As revealing as those files can be, they are usually overlooked by reporters. Those who do look at the state financial reports feel overwhelmed by numbers and industry jargon.

Also, reporters often find a lack of enthusiasm for aggressive enforcement on the part of state insurance commissioners. In some states the regulators are so close to the insurance industry that questions arise whether the consumer is getting proper representation. State insurance commissioners are political appointees. With rare exceptions, they were executives of insurance companies who serve a term in the state office before they return to a better job in the industry. This is a good example of the problem in the relationship of industry and government, often called the "revolving door."

In 1978, the author of this text investigated health insurance companies by going undercover as a sales trainee and by studying the companies' state disclosure records. The story in the *Chicago Tribune* opened by setting the scene:[2]

> "The car bounced along a rutted dirt road in eastern Tennessee, lurching past primitive log cabins and wooden shanties set amid farmland and green valleys.
>
> "Harry Maddox, 55, crack salesman for Associated Doctors, Inc., an insurance company in Nashville, was out beating the bushes for elderly customers. Maddox was unaware that the "trainee" salesman beside him was actually a *Tribune* reporter, William Gaines.
>
> "The territory seemed unpromising. But the mountains of eastern Tennessee are filled with old people, many of them worried about health costs

211

and easily persuaded that they can buy protections for expenses not covered by Medicare, the government health insurance program for the elderly.

"Before the day ended, Maddox would sell a health insurance policy to an aged backwoodsman so poor that he had no need for it—he already had 100 percent coverage through Medicaid, the government insurance program for the indigent.

"I never say contract; I say it's an application," Maddox explained.

"The other day, I was back in the hills, and I went to this old woman's house and said, I'm here to enroll you. She said, Praise the Lord. . . . "

Gaines told a U.S. House of Representatives committee[3] that in the insurance industry the elderly are recognized as an easy sell and that some salespeople make them their specialty:

"I was able to experience a face-to-face encounter between elderly persons expressing their innermost fears and salesmen exploiting those fears. One agent told me he likes to employ salesmen of Medicare supplement insurance who are in their 40s because they are of the age of the children of the person over 65 and are therefore more likely to inspire trust.

"I got the job with Associated Doctors when I answered an ad in a Nashville Tennessee paper. It said, 'leads—leads—leads. Most leads over age 65. Over half the leads are wrap-ups.' I was invited to come and talk with Lewis "Buddy" Fortune, the sales manager for the office, on the east side of Nashville. He told me that health insurance for the elderly was the biggest thing going now and that's where the money is.

"I found out that what they were doing was saturating a particular rural area with a mail-out (mass mailing offering) for free place mats. . . . A salesman I worked with said he never gave out the place mats whether they asked for them or not, unless as a gift after they bought a policy. The pitch had nothing to do with the place mats and people I approached with the salesmen never quite understood how he got their names.

"The approach was usually, 'Dr. Garber sent me to talk to you about your Medicare.' Dr. Garber was an obstetrician who was the president of the insurance company until his death recently. If an elderly person asked how Dr. Garber heard about them, I heard salesmen tell them that perhaps their own doctor had told Dr. Garber about them. . . .

"The salesmen practically went from door-to-door, looking for homes that might contain an elderly person by spotting porch swings or potted plants. Buddy Fortune told me he found old people by looking in the phone book for old names, like Lulu and Ella, and then calling them and asking if they had their Medicare coverage explained to them. 'This is an enrollment period and we won't be back' was one of the lines they used."

Members of Congress also heard testimony (summarized here) from the *Tribune* reporter about his experience with other insurance salespeople who had a different approach to selling insurance to the elderly. Gaines drew on his experience with another sales team, which he joined after his report on Tennessee insurance sales practices. The new sales team sold policies for Pioneer Life of Illinois, based in Peoria, and Gaines learned that team members were identifying themselves to sales prospects as representatives of a senior citizens' organization. He found out that they got application cards from the senior club and followed them up with sales calls.

"It's the best possible presentation," one of the sales team members told Gaines. "I go in and I say I'm working with the senior citizens' association. I ask to see their policies, then I get rid of those and sign them up for ours. I signed one man and his wife for a $3,400-a-year premium. When I tell them I've got information direct from Medicare, that's when they start listening."

Another salesperson said old people are easy to sell because they are lonely and like having someone to talk with.

Gaines accompanied one of the salesmen on a sales call and reported that he told an elderly prospect, "I'm working with the senior citizens' association, and I have this member application you sent in," but that at no time did he represent himself as a salesman for an insurance company. The reporter told the members of Congress that at one point in the well-honed sales pitch, the salesman misstated that he represented a not-for-profit firm.

He did not identify himself as a Pioneer salesman; he talked about the association and then said: "We also have some health benefits. We have a plan that will pay 100 percent of the actual charges. There is no limit."

A Bloomington, Illinois, couple had a Metropolitan Life policy obtained through his employment for Caterpillar, Inc., formerly Caterpillar Tractor Company, in Peoria, but the sales agent convinced her she could use more coverage.

After leaving the house, the sales agent bragged that most salespeople would have given up when they found out the couple had Caterpillar because it is good insurance and the couple probably wouldn't need more insurance than that. But "he's been sick, and she's worried." He attributed the success to the sales presentation: "Did you see how well it worked? They don't know what's happening until we slam it to them, and then it's too late."

Members of the sales team were cautious in the wording that implied they were from Medicare because they could be found to be impersonating a federal official. By being among the salespeople, the reporter could learn that the salespeople wanted the purchasers to come to that incorrect conclusion.

The Lulus and Ellas of eastern Tennessee were unaware of the slim returns they faced with a policy from Associated Doctors. Gaines checked records in the Tennessee Insurance Department and found that only 32.2 cents of each dollar paid to Associated Doctors was paid in benefits the previous year. Pioneer Life returned only 37.1 percent. Some companies returned twice that much, and a person enrolled in a group plan with a major insurance company could expect to receive over 90 cents on his premium dollar.

Gaines then called on Associated Doctors assistant executive officer Thomas Campbell, identified himself as a *Tribune* reporter and asked about the firm's sales tactics.

Campbell said the company never had a complaint about any of its salesmen using unethical practices. A company spokesperson further said they did not misrepresent themselves and would not condone such practices by their sales force.

Case Study

The Deal of a Lifetime*

Figure 9.2 Direct sales advertisement

```
       DIRECT SALES
       Big Ticket Item
  We want only strong closers
  Experienced negative sales
     Leads – leads – leads
   Call today, Mr Mann
       709-881-7X45
```

The advertisement in the classified section of *The Ridgeland Register-News & Review* promised high payment for direct commission sales (Figure 9.2). The advertiser wanted strong closers who were experienced in the negative sales pitch.

*The cases are based on real investigative stories, but the names and places have been changed to protect reporters, their sources and the secrets they have. Some are actual stories told in a step-by-step reconstruction and others are composites.

The gaudy advertisement listed under "Help Wanted—Sales" caught the eye of Thomas Dowling, general assignment reporter for the same newspaper. He was curious because the ad gave no clue about what they were selling.

The ad invited a phone call to "Mr. Mann," so Dowling punched up the number and asked for Mann.

"Speaking," the voice at the other end established.

"I'd like to know more about the big-money sales job you advertised," Dowling said.

"You got experience? What have you sold?"

"I sold ads for my college newspaper," Dowling replied.

"Ads for a newspaper? That's not big-ticket sales! We're big operators. This is not your cup of tea."

"But what are you selling? Maybe I'd be good at it."

"Call me when you've got some experience." Click-Hummm.

Was the advertisement recruiting salespeople for some product that was so uncommon that it could not be revealed, or was it some sort of a scheme that was best left untold? Dowling thought of several places he could check to be updated on the latest consumer frauds—the Better Business Bureau and the state attorney general's office. First, he went on the Internet and scanned several Web sites. They showed that Internet frauds were overwhelming but that some old fashioned, never-die chain letters, Ponzi schemes, land sales, and franchise frauds still existed alongside the new, online schemes. Dowling called the AG's office and was directed to one of the attorneys in the consumer fraud division.

"What is a negative sales pitch?" Dowling asked.

"That is when the salesperson pretends the prospective buyer is not quite suited for the opportunity that is being offered, and the salesperson makes him qualify himself," the attorney explained. "Like, they keep asking, are you sure you can handle the responsibility? And the guy pretty soon is demanding they sell it to him. Actually, they would take anyone who has some money. It works with things like correspondence schools, franchises like vending routes and land sales. Nothing is illegal in it, but people should be warned. Try the newspaper ads for business opportunities."

Dowling scanned the ads and was surprised to find something so obvious it was amusing. He saw an ad for a new retirement community development in Arizona. "Prime location" and "wonderful living," the ad promised. "Available only for those who qualify," the ad cautioned. "Call Mr. Mann." It had the same phone number as the big-ticket salesman, Mr. Mann.

Once again Dowling punched up the number. Although Dowling recognized the same voice, Mr. Mann did not seem to recognize his.

"We want only responsible people, dedicated to making an idyllic community in the American way," Mann said, almost in a chant, as if he had said it many times before.

"That's me. I'm a solid American citizen, but I'm just looking for a good investment."

"How much have you got?"

"Ten thousand."

"Well, we don't usually deal in such small amounts. Have you got some family or friends who can come up with $50 thousand more?

"No, they're always borrowing from me."

"Is your credit good?"

"Yes."

"Do you have a job?"

"Yes."

"Okay, look, I think I can make an exception for you. We are having a dinner meeting for a few select persons Saturday night at seven in the convention center. Ask for me at the door."

Is this operation on the level?

Yes: The salesman is making sure only qualified people are involved in the venture. He has done nothing wrong. The reporter keeps pushing him. A good reporter should not be that doubting.

No: It smacks of fraud. Call it intuitive, but the reporter detects an air of deceit illustrated by the difference in the tone of the sales ad and the development ad.

There were more than a few select people at the dinner—it was more like 300—and Dowling did not have to ask for Mann to get in. Most of the diners were middle-aged or elderly. A pre-plated chicken dinner with a slice of apple pie was served, and Dowling got a chance to chat with the others. He learned that they had either responded to the ad, received an invitation by mail or received a surprise phone call. While the guests were consuming the pie, an emcee of sorts came out and gushed about the opportunity they were about to be offered.

The lights dimmed and a video with the sound on high was played on a giant screen. The room was filled with visions of a spectacular desert community with flowering plants and full sunsets. Happy people were going to church, playing tennis, and picking up children at school. In contrast, outside of the Ridgeland convention center that night the sky was a forlorn gray and a cold wind swept the parking lot.

Then Sweetwater Valley came on the screen. It was an architect's rendering of the community to be developed. There were homes and parks, golf courses on grassy expanses, wide paved streets and bike trails. One map showed the lots available. At the end of the video, the music soared and an American flag was shown flapping in the mild breeze. The narrator on the video spoke reverently of home ownership and the strength of unity in the American way.

The lights came up to a murmur of approval from the guests. The emcee explained that lots were being sold, but contracts had to be signed that night to be considered.

"Now we don't expect you to buy land without seeing it. We don't operate like that. You can sign the contract tonight, but you will see there is in large bold type—no small print in this contract—that you have no obligation and will get your down payment back if you don't like it for any reason after you have seen it. You have a full year to come out and see the land."

Dowling could see he would have a hard time convincing people there was anything amiss here.

He found a spokesperson for the attorney general in Arizona and asked about the promises of Sweetwater Valley and where it was located. The fellow laughed softly.

"So that's what they call it," he said. "That land has no water, not even electricity. Why, the closest shopping is 60 miles away in New Mexico."

"But they have designed a complete community," Dowling informed him.

"That's right—they designed it, but they didn't say they were going to build it. After the purchasers move in, if anyone actually tries to live there, the residents will have to put up the money to build the schools and parks and even pave the streets. That's the way people create towns. It is tough to get a judgment or conviction. If some con man sold you the Brooklyn Bridge and gave you a quitclaim deed, it would be difficult to prosecute because all the deed says is he is selling you any claim he has on the property. Legally, how can we say it was fraud when it is discovered he had none."

"Okay, but this operation has to be legit," Dowling argued in behalf of the developers. "Anybody can get their money back if they don't like it after they see it, and they have a whole year to decide."

"Few people will make the trip. A year goes by, and they don't travel to the site, and then they are locked in. They figure they don't need to come out here and see it because it's got to be okay or the company would not make that offer. Those who do come out are shocked by the remoteness, but that's when step two of the shell game starts. The company tells them their property is worth twice as much, and they show them recent sales contracts for similar lots in the project at more than twice the value. Then they will say they will give back the money they paid or they will list their property for sale at twice the price."

"Sounds like a good deal," Dowling prompted.

"But they have no buyers. The year expires while the company has the property listed. The sales contracts are fraudulent. They are selling the lots to each other. That's where they cross the line, and we can sue them. You can help by doing a story to make people aware of this and have them contact us if they had such an experience," the AG's spokesperson said. "We have several class action suits pending. You can pick them up online."

By looking up lawsuits from various states, Dowling researched the names of corporations and corporate officials involved in Sweetwater. It would have been a more complete and thorough investigation of the land fraud schemes if Dowling could have gone to Arizona for a week or so and looked up real estate transactions in the county land records offices to confirm the inside sales that the attorney general was claiming, but Dowling's editors were not warm to the idea of an expense account junket and said they were happy to keep the story on a more local level.

Dowling needed to get the story from the viewpoint of the local victims of the land sales. He located some from the Ridgeland area who had filed complaints with the Arizona AG by looking for them in the lists of parties in class action suits. Dowling then was faced with the chore of convincing people to go on the record in his story and even be pictured. Most families did not mind having their names on a lawsuit in a faraway state, but letting all their neighbors know they had been duped was another matter. Dowling had to use some of the very tactics that high-pressure salespeople use to win difficult sales commissions. Could he stoop so low?

When he got an elderly couple to agree to an interview, he convinced them to allow him and a photographer to come to their home that very night. Dowling and the photographer were invited inside, and Dowling headed for the kitchen table and waved the couple into a couple of kitchen chairs.

The interview was halfway there. Like any good salesman, Dowling visited them immediately after he contacted them. When he did this, he reduced the possibility that the interviewees would talk to friends, family or coworkers who would tell them not to do it because they would be sued. Dowling knew nobody could guarantee protection from a lawsuit, but he planned to explain—if he were pushed to do so—that a person is almost never sued for expressing an opinion or making a factual statement that was also in writing. Dowling was a firm believer in the idea that friends become jealous of others' opportunities, and friends often offer bad advice that stops others from getting ahead.

Dowling's swift move to the kitchen table established immediately that he was in charge. He placed the couple to one side so he would not get "middled." A salesperson knows that a sale is lost for sure if both prospects aren't visible at all time. They can signal each other with facial expressions or gestures otherwise.

"I'm not so sure about this. People will laugh at us for being such fools," Harry Hanson said. "Do you have to use our names?"

"Yes, we have to warn people that this is happening to real people like yourselves. I know it is not easy, in fact, it is brave on your part to go on the record, but people will recognize you are not doing this for yourselves. You are doing it for them—to protect everyone by warning them."

The faces of the Hansons glowed when the photographer started clicking away. They were changing their attitude toward themselves. They were no longer cheated fools; they were now national heroes. Dowling got the story. It was time to write.

Did the reporter cross the line by using high-pressure sales tactics?

Yes: For shame! A reporter is using sales tactics that would be sharply criticized if done by a salesperson! Dowling must know that people will laugh at the victims in his story, and his heroic-act speech is so much bull it is not acceptable.

No: It is neither written nor suggested that a reporter is bound to certain behavior when conducting interviews. The reporter must use all means within standards of conduct to get a story as long as no promises are made that are not kept and no one's safety is jeopardized.

It was time to write, and Dowling used a suitable device in organizing the beginning of his rather complicated story about the land sales. He chose to lead with the experience of one of the victims. He wrote, in succeeding paragraphs, about what they were promised and then what they got:

> "Harry Hanson and his wife Vera remember the idyllic scene in the video about Sweetwater Valley: abundant water, recreation, convenient shopping, swimming pools and 'the good life.'
>
> "Life hasn't been that good for Hanson, a retired electrician from Ridgeland, who bought into the idyllic dream five years ago.
>
> "The Hansons live in a mobile home on scrub land that is scorched by blistering heat in the summer and raked by freezing winds in winter."

Dowling then recounted each point in the language of the narrator in the video and followed each one with a comeback from the couple. He hoped to capture the interest of the readers and found no problem in writing further to explain how this unfortunate situation happened to the Hansons and many others.

The story resulted in getting more people to come forward and report their experiences. Dowling knew, though, that he could pretty much write the same story every year and find new victims, new locations, but the same old pitch.

Memorandum

- Promises of highly promoted land developments need careful scrutiny.
- Reporters at times need to employ proven sales techniques.
- Elderly people are most often the targets of consumer fraud.
- A slick sales presentation that covers a consumer fraud scheme is not easy to detect.

How Not to Do It

Chip Shotten was given one last chance to shape up or be asked to find a new profession. His record as an investigative reporter was fraught with missed stories, errors and lawsuits. He wanted to make a big splash with a story, and he saw the opportunity when an informant came to him with an allegation that she had had an extramarital affair with the governor. She would give a sworn statement, but she wanted $100. Shotten paid her. "Call it expense money," Shotten told her.

Two days later, she called and said that the *Daily Metro* had called her about the story, and she needed $100 more to keep it exclusive. Shotten scraped up the money and left it in an envelope at the reception desk. Soon after, the informant was on the phone and told Shotten the *Daily Metro* had bid the price up. Shotten was getting irritated, but he wanted the story. "You know, you haven't given me any details. How do I know you got good stuff," Shotten said, talking out of the side of his mouth as he had seen reporters do in old, old movies.

"My lawyer is filing a lawsuit this afternoon, and I'll give you a jump on the story for $500," she said. Shotten told his editor to hold the front page open, then he got a payday loan and came up with the money. The story his paid-for source told was indeed shocking. She gave graphic accounts of rendezvous at midnight under the Capitol dome.

Shotten wrote it up in breathless prose. He met his editor at the elevator and was all smiles. "I've got the story. It's the biggest story this paper ever had." Then he saw his source waiting in the lobby. She asked for more money, but he told her to come back later.

"I see you chased Polly out of here. I told the guards downstairs to never let her in the building," the editor commented. "She used to come here and try to sell imaginary stories. She hears voices. Once she tried to sell us a story that she was a secret lover of Lou Gehrig. We all got a good laugh out of that one. Now what is the story you have?"

Question for discussion: What did Shotten do wrong?

Answer: Everything.

Chapter Recap

Protecting consumers is a difficult role for a reporter. It is easy enough to write a warning in a publication or go on TV and tell of a fraud, but an investigative reporter will get out of the newsroom and deal with the victim of fraud who may not be easily persuaded to go on the record. The reporter must also confront those he believes are responsible for the fraud. Another difficult assignment is to determine how to react when information turns up that is private or forbidden in some other way but is a blockbuster revelation that the public should know about. We will tackle that assignment in the next chapter.

Class Assignments

1. Find the listing of help wanted advertisements in a Sunday edition of a local newspaper, or go on the Internet and punch up "direct sales representatives" and perhaps another word like "commissions" or "closers." You will find ads for people who are wanted to take jobs selling products or services, and the ads sometimes give a hint about what kind of sales tactics will be used to strong-arm consumers. There will be a phone number to call for the sales job. You may be able to identify the person who placed the ad by putting that number into an Internet search at www.whitepages.com. This is called a backwards phone directory because it tells you the names and addresses of the persons who have that number.

   If you can match up a product with the help wanted ad, you will have taken the first step toward an investigation, by identifying companies that advertise blatantly for high-pressure sales tactics. Another approach, if the number is not listed in an Internet phone directory, is to look in the same newspaper classified section to see whether the number matches the number to call for some get-rich-quick investment scheme, a so-called business opportunity, or a deal on buying resort property.

2. Have you ever felt that you were cheated, swindled, defrauded or ripped off? Write about your experience. Submit your story to the class for discussion about how that particular consumer problem could be investigated and exposed. Then write and outline showing how you would proceed with an investigation.

Notes

1. National Consumers League, www.stopseniorscams.org/art_priz.htm.
2. William Gaines and Ray Mosely, "At Work with Some Slick Salesmen: Insurance Firms That Feast on Fears of the Aged," *Chicago Tribune,* September 29, 1978.
3. "Abuses in the Sale of Health Insurance to the Elderly in Supplementation of Medicare," Staff Study of Select Committee on Aging, U.S. House of Representatives, November 28, 1978.

C h a p t e r   1 0

Investigating Health Care

INVESTIGATIVE REPORTERS who take on issues involving health care have to learn a new area of terminology and law and be ready for a counterattack from representatives of health care providers. The work is a formidable challenge, but the results can score with readers and viewers.

An example of a reporter delving into the mysteries of medical care is the award-winning 2003 TV report by Stuart Watson at WCNC-TV in Charlotte, North Carolina.[1] Watson went where few reporters have dared—the dentist's office. He reported about dentists who drilled the teeth of children as young as four years old, for as long as four hours. The children came out of the ordeal with mouths full of silver-capped teeth. Watson told viewers the Medicaid reimbursement system rewarded dentists for fast work on as many teeth as possible in one sitting.

Watson was able to find local people who complained about the treatment their children received. He took copies of X-rays and dental records to outside experts to see whether the dental work was necessary. They said it was not.

"The citizens pay for this treatment through their tax dollars—tens of millions of dollars," Watson said.

His organization of the elements of the story fit a pattern that is often seen in investigative reports. First he interviewed people who told of their experiences with the dentists, then he talked with experts who said the treatment was wrong, then he showed documents to bolster his own argument of wrongdoing and, finally, he ran a rebuttal from the target of the investi-

Source: WCNC-TV in Charlotte, North Carolina

gation. The first report on the 11 p.m. newscast took four minutes and 40 seconds, an enormous slice of the time budget for news. Nothing is missing. The report has the same quality as network investigative broadcasts.

Children are pictured, but parents do the talking. The emotion shows in their faces and voices, an advantage that TV has over the print media.

The argument is immediately stated: taxpayers are paying for unnecessary dental work.

Starting the documents trail, Watson tells of the court record of one of the doctors.

Watson asked for viewers to tell him of their children's experiences in the dentist's chair in his first broadcast, and he was able to find enough complaints to sustain reports from July until December 2003.

The WCNC-TV dentist story touched on two prime areas: unnecessary suffering of patients and inflated costs. People want the highest quality and safest medical practices at any cost, so investigative reporters will emphasize safety, but they also do not neglect the area of overcharging. The *Los Angeles Times* story about dangerous drugs, the *Chicago Tribune* hospital surgery and health insurance stories, and the *Seattle Times* story about research—each challenged medical practices. Many other reports have been published,

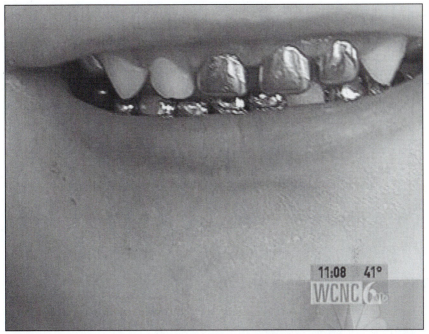

Source: WCNC-TV in Charlotte, North Carolina

and many await being researched in the areas of medical professionals, medical institutions and the regulation of the medical industry.

The Medical Profession

The medical profession is made up of professional staff as well as institutions and infrastructure.

People

Most people think first of doctors and nurses when they think about medical professionals, but the range of careers in the medical field is broader than that.

> Physician. Is the medical doctor properly licensed? Has the doctor ever been expelled from a hospital or professional membership organization? A word of caution: As a reporter working on a story, you might feel as if the doctor you are investigating is suspicious, but a reporter cannot correctly call a licensed medical practition-

225

er a quack even if the doctor touts worthless medical remedies. A quack is an unlicensed person who sells medical cures thought to be worthless.

Chiropractors and podiatrists. These medical professionals are licensed separately, and their practice is limited to their specialty. Do they adhere to the limitations?

Pharmacists. They can get in trouble by deviating from a prescription, and big trouble awaits them if they exceed the dosage of a controlled substance.

Nurses. They bear a weighty responsibility. State laws define what they can and cannot do.

Lab technicians and ambulance attendants. Some states license these professionals also.

Veterinarians. In a 2006 poll, these medical professionals were shown to be among the most trusted of all professionals. Do they have proper respect for animals or a brutal lack of compassion?[2]

Infrastructure

Medical infrastructure comprises the various institutions that make up the medical system in the United States.

Hospitals and nursing homes. These are the medical institutions most often encountered by the public.

Mental care facilities. These can also include treatment centers for alcohol and substance abuse.

Research laboratories. Research labs are sometimes affiliated with an institution such as a university, with the government or with a pharmaceutical company. The subject of an investigation might be a federally funded project for testing a drug or a medical process.

Insurance. So much of the cost of medical care in the United States is paid by insurance companies or by public assistance that patients often lose track of the actual costs.

Medical Licensure, Discipline and Privacy

Doctors and other medical professionals leave both a paper and an electronic trail because they receive payment for treating patients in government assistance programs, they are licensed by the states and they sue or get sued. The records come from the courts, state licensing hearings and state vouchers for payment of patient bills. The courts have been friendly to reporters in declaring most of these documents public record.

In the early 1990s, a doctor tested the system of public records in an Oklahoma court.[3] The Oklahoma Board of Medical Licensure and Supervision in 1993 heard charges that the doctor had been convicted of getting payments from the state Civilian Health and Medical Program by filing fraudulent claims. Although the board suspended the doctor's license for six months, a federal court reversed the criminal conviction for insufficient evidence. The doctor then wanted the records of his suspension expunged.

The appeals court upheld a lower court decision that the records would not be expunged and would be available for the public:

"We find no authority, either expressed or implied, for (the) board to expunge records of disciplinary action taken. To the contrary, the legislature had mandated such records be preserved and maintained. . . . [R]eports of disciplinary action imposed by (the) board are expressly required to be available to the public upon request. All of [the] board's meetings are to be conducted under the Open Meetings Act. The Open Meetings Act requires written minutes, which shall be an official summary of the proceedings, including actions taken, and also requires those minutes to be open to public inspection."

Other states have similar laws and similar rulings.

Some records that lead to stories about doctors are not so obvious. How about doctors who warn against smoking and yet own tobacco farms? That surprising finding was made in 1998 by Allen G. Breed, a reporter for the Associated Press, who wrote "Healers Raising the Killer Weed." He found that 760 medical doctors were granted federal allotment quotas for growing tobacco. Breed covered North Carolina for AP and thought it would be a good idea to look at the government database showing permits to grow tobacco and then match the permits with a database of licensed medical doctors. Some doctors in interviews with Breed said they told their patients not to smoke; one doctor was even a regional director of the American Cancer Society. Breed produced data the reader could absorb. He wrote that the doctors were licensed to produce enough tobacco for 193 million packs of cigarettes a year.[4]

Personal medical records are private, but they are valuable for studying medical treatment received. A reporter can use them after getting permission of the patient.

Government Inspections of Medical Facilities

Nursing homes may be the most inspected facilities in America. They are required to open their doors to building, fire, food and health care inspectors. In addition, state and federal auditors look over their shoulders at the financials. That means they leave an accessible trail of documents that give the overall picture. Some nursing homes are well-run and attractive with dedicated staffs and the best food. Some are not.

Investigative reporters often check on local nursing homes and keep the spotlight on them so they will be prodded into providing good care. Reporters may listen to complaints of residents and try to check them out, or they may make a more formal study.

A reporter can start an investigation into nursing homes from a computer terminal. In most states, the regulators place their inspection reports on the Internet. States that have not usually provide a summary of the inspections. A study of those reports can be startling. They sometimes reveal abuses of patients who are roughed up, neglected and teased. Some nursing homes are short-staffed, and often reports mention residents wandering away.

In only one month sampled at random in Illinois,[5] 17 nursing homes were fined for breaking the rules. Three were fined for allowing patients to wander away from the facility. A mentally impaired resident at one was found in the middle of a busy road. At another home, a resident who was wearing an electronic monitoring device left the facility without staff knowledge. A concerned citizen contacted police after encountering the resident, who looked lost, approximately one mile from the facility. At the third home, a resident who was recently admitted with notation of a history of leaving another facility left the building. Staff notified police who later found him, wearing slippers and no coat, about two miles from the nursing home.

Other reports by the state showed even more serious problems. In one home, a resident died from positional asphyxia, which was the result of getting caught in a bed rail. At another, a resident who had a history of heart problems was improperly supervised and suffered a grand mal seizure and later died. A third home was cited for failure to initiate cardiopulmonary resuscitation on a resident as the doctor had ordered; this failure resulted in the resident being found in cardiopulmonary arrest when the ambulance crew arrived.

In another area of patient abuse cited by the state, a nursing home failed to prevent the ongoing sexual relationship between a resident and a staff member. Another failed to follow its abuse prohibition policy by allowing the staff member to continue to work after allegations of patient abuse were reported to the director of nurses. Another home, by failing to thoroughly investigate allegations of physical and verbal abuse by a staff member against a resident, was alleged to have placed 24 residents at risk of abuse by a staff person. The nursing homes have been given an opportunity to appeal the fines.

A summary of the violations found in the inspection reports would be an important story that could be written immediately. But we do not want that. As investigative reporters we do not accept the investigation of public agencies and report on them. We have to investigate the nursing home as well as the agencies that inspect them. We will have to find a method to carry out our own independent probe.

One step is to analyze the state reports and make new disclosures. By looking at the citations against a nursing home during a certain time period—let's say three or four years—and placing them in a simple database, we can determine which homes have repeat violations. These repeat problems might be in the kitchen or because they allow residents to wander away. Or perhaps an investigative study might focus on how the local nursing homes rank compared with the rest of the state.

Phillip Reese and Nancy Weaver Teichert of *The Sacramento Bee* undertook such a study of California state inspection reports in 2005.[6] They then carried their reporting to a higher level by thoroughly investigating those local nursing homes that did not fare well. They wrote:

> Sacramento nursing homes failed to meet minimum federal and state standards more often than facilities in the rest of the top 10 largest cities in California during the last two years, according to a *Bee* analysis of state inspection reports.
>
> Local facilities also were cited for more deficiencies than facilities in nearly all cities of comparable size across the nation during 2003 and 2004.
>
> Sacramento's federal and state shortcomings—all pinpointed by state inspectors—range from poor food preparation to not giving residents the medicines they need. Some mistakes were relatively benign; a few caused serious health problems, even death.

The *Bee* reporters got full reports on the violations, and they interviewed experts, former employees and residents. To take this story to another level of investigative reporting, we would want to see for ourselves what is happening by getting inside the nursing homes.

Getting an undercover job is not an option. Not only does it have many strikes against it, but it is not workable in this investigation because we want to make a broad survey, not report on one or two bad homes. We discussed several alternatives in an early chapter of this textbook. A reporter could ask a patient whether a visit is possible, and then the reporter could drop in unexpectedly and ask for a tour; or the reporter could formally request a tour. Bill Baskerville, Associated Press reporter, said that to gain entrance to a state mental hospital, "I strolled in. It is a public building after all. The door to the second floor stairs was unlocked and so I went up." [7] He was soon ordered out.

If the reporter can legally gain entrance to the hospital or nursing home, it would be easy to refer to the state inspection reports to see whether the problems cited there have been corrected.

Aside from violations that take place in more private areas of a facility, some conditions are in plain view. The Illinois Department of Public Health provides a list:

Is the general atmosphere of the home warm, pleasant and cheerful?

Are residents allowed to wear their own clothes, decorate their rooms and keep a few prized possessions on hand?

Is there a place for private visits with family and friends?

Is the nursing home clean and orderly?

Is the home reasonably free of unpleasant odors?

Are toilet and bathing facilities easy for disabled patients to use?

Is the home well-lighted?

Are rooms well-ventilated and kept at a comfortable temperature?

Is the nursing home free of obvious hazards, such as obstacles to residents, hazards underfoot and unsteady chairs?

Do bathtubs and showers have non-slip surfaces?

Are there smoke detectors, an automatic sprinkler system and portable fire extinguishers?

Are exit doors unobstructed and unlocked from inside?

Are nurse or emergency call buttons located at each resident's bed and in toilet and bathing facilities?

Is the kitchen clean and reasonably tidy?

Does the nursing home have a varied program of recreational, cultural and intellectual activities for residents?

Does each resident have a reading light, a comfortable chair, and closet space and drawers for personal belongings?

Is there fresh drinking water within reach?

Is there a curtain or screen available to provide privacy for each bed whenever necessary?

Do bathing and toilet facilities have adequate privacy?

Insurance Claims and Fraud

Departments of insurance or insurance commissions in the states monitor the financial health of companies and hear complaints from consumers about companies and salespersons. They may extend their responsibility into the regulation of health maintenance organizations and workers' compensation insurance. Their records are important to a reporter doing a story that follows up on the effects of a disaster such as a hurricane, flood, tornado or earthquake. State agencies require financial information and routinely audit companies; that information is then usually posted on the agency Web site. Annual financial reports that must be filed are harder to come by online, but many official Web sites have summaries of the reports posted and searchable. Some Web sites even post details of disciplinary actions against agents, brokers and companies.

When investigating costs, reporters can look at a hospital, clinic or individual practitioner in much the same way as they examine the finances of a professional football team or a local government.

Not-for-profit hospitals, nursing homes and their associated services must file an IRS 990 financial statement; that is usually where a reporter starts. To be thorough, the reporter will search an online list on the licensing board's Web site for the names of all medical practitioners, not only the medical doctors, who are associated with a given health facility.

The hospital or nursing home will probably have government-assisted patients. These facilities must bill the state for those patients' care, and everything but the names of the patients will be public record. It must be understood that Medicare is not a public-assistance program; Medicare is an insurance plan administered by the government. Although the federal government conducts audits of Medicare and facilities that work with Medicare, records of an individual's treatment are not available.

Medicaid, known by other names in some states (Medical in California, for example) is also known as public aid. Half of the public assistance money for Medicaid comes from the federal government and half from the states. The state pays the money to health care providers.

An investigative survey might be the result of a comparison of public-assistance bills from different hospitals for specific procedures. To compare costs in the private sector, a reporter is often able to get hospital bills from cooperative patients or from the discovery process in a lawsuit. Medicare does not cover all medical costs, however, and participants often turn to other, private insurance to supplement their coverage.

The insurance industry is an example of private companies that are regulated by the government in a special way. The federal government does not make rules for insurance companies or monitor their financial statements; instead, each state has a unit of government that handles that. Investigative reporters can find detailed information about complaints, officers and assets in state insurance departments. Because the states want to make sure that the insurance companies have enough assets to be able to pay claims, they require the insurance companies to set aside assets in a special account. This financial information is disclosed.

Case Study

Investigating Licensed and Unlicensed Medical Professionals*

Anne Fortunato, feature writer for the *Great Forks (Wis.) Herald-Times,* was tipped off to a story by an old and reliable source at the local hospital.

"Have you heard about Great Forks Retreat, the new cancer clinic that's opened up in the building that used to be the old municipal hospital? It looks just like a medical hospital, but there's not a licensed doctor who will go near the place."

The tipster was a nurse who had helped Fortunato on a previous scandal that exposed administrators who were stealing supplies from the hospital. That was Fortunato's first attempt to write an investigative story on her beat, which was medical and scientific features. Fortunato might have laughed off the idea of a "pirate" hospital in Great Forks if she had not had a high regard for the source of the information. At least, it deserved checking out.

Fortunato needed someone quotable who had an impressive title, and she caught up with the medical director of a state hospital.

"Yes, I've heard of Great Forks Retreat," he said. "Everybody in the medical field is talking about it, and they are bouncing around some crazy stories. They say they are administering coffee enemas and treating patients with foot reflexology and dosing them with ground-up plant leaves from Brazil. All of this is legal, I guess, but those remedies were discarded many, many years ago. The fellow who runs it has got some mail order diploma and calls himself Doctor Cornucopia, Doctor of Unencumbered Methodology. I guess that's legal, too."

Legal? That was a question for Fortunato to relay to the attorney general's staff.

"I'm not going to say anything about Great Forks Retreat," an assistant attorney general told Fortunato. "But I can talk about quackery in general. Now, don't misquote me as to connecting Great Forks Retreat to quackery. Quackery is not a term to be taken lightly. People say a bad doctor is a quack, but you can't call him a quack if he's got a license. And if he has no license, you can't call him a quack

---

*The cases are based on real investigative stories, but the names and places have been changed to protect reporters, their sources and the secrets they have. Some are actual stories told in a step-by-step reconstruction and others are composites.

unless he is practicing medicine. If a person does not break the skin with shots, write prescriptions, or hang out a sign saying he is a medical doctor, you can't call him a quack, and you can't arrest him for practicing medicine without a license. I mean, after all, how many times has your mother told you to have some chicken broth and lie down? We can't prosecute her for practicing medicine."

"It sounds like you've had encounters with this kind of thing before," Fortunato inserted.

"Yes, and anyone who has tried to close down these fellows is in for a hard time. The guy who runs this Great Forks Retreat place is suing a newspaper in Coastal City. Good luck."

Fortunato went online and found the Coastal City lawsuit. She learned that Cornucopia was suing because the Coastal City newspaper had written a story reporting that Cornucopia had been barred from operating in their state. Fortunato soon also discovered that the state attorney general's news releases were online, and they showed that Cornucopia had been enjoined from practicing medicine in the state—just as the newspaper had reported. Cornucopia, however, based his lawsuit on the argument that he had appealed the court ruling and it was not final. It seemed to Fortunato that it was a nuisance lawsuit, filed merely to allow him to say he was suing over the story. She found the reporter in Coastal City who had written the story.

"I'd like to tell you about it but we are being sued," she said. "The editors won't let me write anything about him anymore. Everybody is running scared. Good luck!" It was time for Fortunato to go to her editors. She wrote out her presentation:

TO: Metropolitan Editor
FROM: Anne Fortunato

RE: Story Outline: "Great Forks Retreat"

Subject: A clinic has been opened in an old hospital building in Great Forks and has been made to look like a medical facility, but actually it is a center for unlicensed practitioners of questionable remedies and unproven treatments.
Scope: We can show the background of the persons involved in its operation, thoroughly check on its claims of cures and either establish that they work or debunk them as frauds.
Need: The medical establishment, law enforcement and press have been unable to respond to the claims the

clinic makes because what the clinic does seems to take advantage of loopholes in the laws. We need to at least warn people and let them decide.

Methods: We can watch the hospital building and learn the patients' names by taking down license plate numbers and then talking to them. We can inquire about the clinic's claims of cure-alls by asking, as any person might.

Documentation: Several lawsuits could give us some leads. I will check the state for revocation of licenses for any of the practitioners who may have previously had licenses. I will look for billing to the state for Medicaid. They do not qualify for public-assistance or insurance payments, but I will look for some indirect way they may be getting the payments.

Presentation: We have two related parts to this story. One is a description of Great Forks Retreat and what it offers, with profiles of the practitioners there, showing their backgrounds and history of complaints. Another is the health care practices themselves, explaining them and quoting experts in traditional medicine about their effectiveness.

Follow-up: The state wants to shut the clinic down, and it may do so if we can come up with more information.

The memo sparked a heated debate among the editors at the end of the morning doping session the next day. Twice a day, the top editor meets with staff members; the managing editor; and editors of the metropolitan, national, international, features, editorial, business and sports news. They review the news that was in their morning paper and the competition press and TV, and they plan for the next day's coverage. The editor introduced the subject of Great Forks Retreat:

Editor: Did everyone see the Fortunato memo? What do you think?

National: I think we had better stay away from this one. They haven't done anything wrong. Let's wait until something happens, and we can put a strong lead on it.

Metro: This is not a routine story. It's investigative. We will come up with the facts and have our own lead.

National: But there's nothing there yet. Anne doesn't even know what she will find.

Metro: She has done a lot of work on this, and she knows there is an important story there—the same as I do.

Managing: I agree with National. It's all a fishing expedition at this point. Let's not get too excited about it.

Metro: Well, you can see from this memo that Anne is cautious, too. She's a good reporter, and she knows how to work the story.

Editor: Okay, there's no harm in having her continue on the story, and we will see what she comes up with.

At the very time the editors were meeting, Fortunato got a call from her source at the AG's office. "Don't let anybody know I told you this, but I just got a call about Great Forks Retreat from your competitor, a fellow by the name of Shotten."

Fortunato felt sick. She knew Shotten never did anything right but that he would put a cheap shot in his paper just to ruin her story. She told her editor, and he assigned Claude Payton, an experienced investigative reporter, to work with her. Her editor suggested they rush the story to completion.

Although the reporters were working full throttle to get the story, they were determined not to miss a step in the investigative process. They would not cut corners and, instead, would work harder. Fortunato called Cornucopia immediately and got an appointment to go visit him that afternoon to get the official version about Great Forks Retreat.

"I'm always willing to help out a young reporter," Cornucopia said. "I understand you wanted to ask about my Great Forks Retreat. We haven't publicized it in the general media because word-of-mouth has kept us busy."

"It is a rather unusual place, I've heard," Fortunato said.

"Yes, it's the first of its kind and a breakthrough in health care." Fortunato noted that he did not say medical care, and she realized he was being very careful. "I expect to have similar clinics up and running in several states before the end of the year. We offer, at a low rate, such services as full-body heating and my nationally acclaimed cancer therapy." Fortunato noted once more that the doctor was careful in his word choice. He did not say "cancer cure."

"This clinic appears to be a hospital, but I understand it is not staffed by any licensed physicians."

Cornucopia sat back in his chair and laughed. "The only reason it may look like a hospital is that it is in an old hospital building. There is no sign that suggests it is a hospital. And I thank the Good Lord that the staff is not licensed." Fortunato had been told that Cornucopia often mixed religion with his health remedies. "If they were licensed, they would be a part of the medical establishment that we do not want to be associated with. It is they who are suppressing my revolutionary treatments," he told Fortunato.

"Like feeling the soles of people's feet to tell if they have heart disease, giving them coffee enemas and prescribing food supplements and vitamins instead of drugs?"

"I have many success stories to prove that those things work, but only if they are integrated into the dietary and health care system I have developed. It is structured around my patented formula known as Xyphicolo."

"How do you spell that?"

"Here, read all about it in my brochure," he said as he handed her a very colorful and expensive information packet.

"Do medical doctors elsewhere test the patients before you admit them?"

"We test them. We have a unique diagnostic machine that I designed that can analyze saliva and urine and come up with a set of numbers that locates and identifies any human illness, including cancer. We bring their numbers in alignment with our treatment," he said.

At that point, Fortunato broke a self-imposed rule of not arguing with the subject of an investigation. "I'm afraid I find that hard to believe. If there is such a machine, I would think that everyone would be using it."

"The medical establishment will not allow it. How could they? Think of all those expensive tests they would not be able to give. You know, the doctors have these secret corporations, and they own all the labs and all the machines. When you have the power to treat cancer successfully, as I do, they are going to gang up on you. I have many patients who walk away without a trace of cancer, and you'll find them today living happy, normal lives. I've got some letters here that are testimonials to the healing power of my discovery and my regimen. If you are going to write a story about me or Great Forks Retreat, you will want to include them. Otherwise, I will know you have malicious intent, and it will be a matter for the attention of my attorneys. I already have them working overtime in several states. I have to protect myself because I am being persecuted by the Establishment."

Should Fortunato accept the explanation Cornucopia has given?

Yes: He has a right to deviate from the establishment views and procedures and try anything that may help the patients. If the patients are stimulated by coffee enemas and because of them find relief from pain, they should be able to be treated with them even if they are a placebo. The public has grown weary of the restrictions placed on medical care.

No: He is spouting typical quack defenses. He says everyone is out to get him because he is smarter than they are. Placebo or not, those patients had better not be refusing proven medications and procedures when they turn to him, or we are talking about a matter of life or death.

She asked for a tour of the facility and was impressed with its cleanliness. When she was shown the miracle machine, she noted the name of the machine had been scraped off, but she saw a product number from the manufacturer, which she jotted in her notes.

Fortunato hurried back to the newsroom and found Payton. He had been working the phones and the Internet. "Anne, I found out the Florida attorney general rapped them for using some crazy machine that is supposed to diagnose every possible illness. Well, they found out that it was a soil-testing machine and was U.S. Department of Agriculture surplus that Cornucopia bought off the Internet. I'm trying to find the auction documentation on the Internet.

Fortunato found in her national search of lawsuits that several complaints had been brought against Cornucopia by family members of his patients who had died. The families alleged that Cornucopia's people had abandoned proven and accepted methods of treatment to follow his unproven and discarded remedies. Some patients had been diagnosed elsewhere as having terminal cancer, and they had come to Cornucopia as a last resort. If they died, he could dodge the blame because they were already terminal.

Once again, Fortunato had to treat the many lawsuits, which were all unsuccessful or still pending, as mere allegations, but she contacted the families' attorneys for details. Some attorneys replied and sent her documents attached to e-mails. Now the story could be built around the fact that the miracle diagnostic machine cited in the lawsuits was merely a soil tester.

They had to be sure. They were able to get the specifications of the machine, which had been abandoned by the USDA, and now they could say with absolute certainty that it was the very same machine the clinic was using.

Fortunato started calling patients on the phone. She had the letters from Cornucopia, but she chose not to use them. Instead, she sought fairness and balance by talking with patients she had found on her own by looking up the license numbers of cars parked outside of Great Forks Retreat. (After an initial stay in the clinic, patients returned as outpatients once a week.)

Getting the names from license numbers in Fortunato's state required a letter in advance, but because she was a member of the press and often filed such requests, the department of motor vehicles kept a letter on file for her and responded immediately. It was a favor she and Payton accepted with the full understanding that it would not induce the newspaper to write favorable reports about the department in any story. Some of the cars were from out of state, and the ownership was not public record. In a few cases, she was able to find the patients from the phone listings on the Internet.

Should Fortunato ignore the names the doctor gave her?

Yes: These are people who have been selected by Cornucopia to testify in his behalf. It is not a patient list; a patient list would be confidential. These people have apparently agreed to be revealed and are expecting a call. The reporter chose people from other sources who have not been prompted.

No: Cornucopia's list should not be ignored because ignoring it smacks of the malicious intent the doctor mentioned in his threat of a lawsuit. The reporter has not given the target of the investigation a fair chance to reply; in fact, the reporter has ignored his best argument. If she uses only the critical former patients, Cornucopia has every right to hold a press conference, demand a retraction or even sue.

Fortunato introduced herself over the phone to the patients and explained that she was looking for stories about the retreat and Cornucopia. She got the same strong endorsements that she might have gotten from the list.

"He's a wonderful doctor! Why, he cured me of cancer! He found that my numbers on his machine were out of line, and he kept giving his special drug—I never can remember the name, and . . ."

"Xyphicolo?"

"Yes. And he doesn't believe in the foods we eat today. You know, he says the insecticides and the food coloring they put in our food are giving us cancer and all kinds of diseases. He wouldn't touch them. He says everybody should eat and drink in purity. He has me on a diet of sesame seeds and artichoke stems."

"Where do you get those things?"

"His mail order house. They're blessed you know. He is a very religious man."

"Are you sure you had cancer? Did other doctors diagnose you as having cancer?"

"I don't need other doctors. What do they know? His machine said I had cancer and he is curing me. I hope you are not out to write some nasty story about him. Because the press is in league with the commercial medical dynasty, and they are out to get him. If you write bad things about him, remember, he has many friends who will go to his aid."

Fortunato could add the lady to her growing list of warnings. Fortunato has also been warned by the Coastal City reporter, the assistant attorney general, and Cornucopia himself.

Should the reporter heed the warnings?

Yes: She should not be asking people questions if she is going to ignore what they say. She is going to get herself in big trouble if she writes a story. After all, the patients swear by him, and he may be within the law. Also, Fortunato is beginning to encroach on people's religious beliefs. Just because the machine was used to test soil doesn't mean it can't test human excretion. The only group of people complaining is the medical establishment and that is because he is challenging them. Can they say that all their remedies work?

No: Fortunato sees warnings as a challenge. Her mother warned her not to take the job at the newspaper and advised her to get a nice job with a pension, maybe at the post office, instead. Fortunato is not about to believe in the soil tester because she has good common sense. Although she is not a full-time investigative reporter, she knows from journalistic instinct that a soil tester is not to be applied to humans. Once revealed, the public will be on her side.

Note that according to the Missouri Group—a project of the University of Missouri School of Journalism—one of the obstacles to investigative reporting is, quite frankly, a lack of courage. "This is the great inhibitor. It means poking into dark corners, asking hard questions about controversial, sensitive affairs. Fortunately, investigative reporting is so important and the rewards are so substantial that more reporters than ever are finding support to do it." [8]

The lady who said the doctor would have many friends was correct. As Fortunato made more calls, she found that patients' loyalty to him had a religious fervor. One woman was an exception:

> "Somebody ought to do something about him. He's got this worthless pill that is a food supplement, and he makes everybody go on a strange diet. I got sick eating some peapods from Nepal. My medical doctor said I don't have cancer, but Cornucopia said my numbers were out of whack when he put drops of my perspiration in some machine after he gave me a heat treatment."

Fortunato decided to drop in on Cornucopia and this time confront him with the hard questions. She was sure his patients had told him about the calls they had received from her and her line of questioning. She saw that his car was not parked by the retreat, so she waited for him in the parking lot, working on her notes and writing parts of the story while she waited. It would be best, she decided, to catch him outside rather than deal with a receptionist. After no more than 10 minutes, he drove up in his car, got out, and walked toward the door. He was carrying a small paper bag. Fortunato headed him off at the door, shouting out, "Doctor, I have a few more questions for you."

When he saw her, he tried to hide the bag, but there was no way he could. "I'm not going to answer any further questions," he said.

Then Fortunato saw what was in the bag. It was a cheeseburger and fries from the Boomburger Fast Food Place. A large spot of grease stained through the paper bag.

"Your patients would be a bit surprised to see what you had for lunch," she said.

"Well, you have to treat yourself once in a while," he said sheepishly. He turned away and opened the door.

Fortunato knew she would have to give him a chance to explain the soil tester, so she shouted, "The diagnostic machine. It's a soil tester!" He did not respond, but Fortunato was satisfied that he heard her and had been given a chance to answer to the most telling evidence against him.

She got back to the newspaper and continued to write and rewrite. Then the word came to the center desk in the newsroom that the competition was promoting on its Web site a big next-morning story about a miracle cure clinic. Both editors and reporters at the *Herald-Times* went into high gear to pull their story together and write as quickly as possible. A plan for extensive graphics had to be reduced to a map showing the location of Great Forks Retreat.

The news story had a straight lead, starting off with the soil machine:

"A device touted as a detector of cancer at Great Forks Retreat in Great Forks is no more than an agriculture soil tester, the *Herald-Times* has learned.

The story gave a balanced account of the claims of the often discredited doctor and the opposition medical authorities who would go on the record.

But the real topper was the burger and fries.

Should the burger and fries be used?

Yes: It is the one undisputed example of the insincerity of the so-called doctor. He might really believe in his treatments and diets, but Fortunato caught him with greasy hands on a Number Four Triple-Pattie Super Cheese Meal.

No: It does not fit. This is a story about medical care, and suddenly it branches out into a critique of fast-food meals. The doctor has a right to eat anything he wants. It is his private business and does not affect patient care. It is frivolous and silly.

The burger stayed in the story. At the least, it would be one thing that the competition would not have. Shotten's story ran at the same time as the *Herald-Times* story. To the surprise and delight of everyone at the *Herald-Times,* Shotten believed the pitch of the doctor and the clinic, and Shotten's story was a glowing tribute to the operation. He extolled the value of the miracle machine without knowing it was a soil tester. The story comprised one interview, with Cornucopia, who said the same things he had told Fortunato. Shotten also used the testimonials and the fancy brochure. His story ran in only one edition before it was pulled out of the paper by his editors.

Fortunato and Payton were a step ahead of the attorney general, who got an injunction and closed down Great Forks Retreat. Cornucopia moved his operation to New Jersey. Fortunato and Payton received many thanks for their story, but Fortunato also got a call from the clinic's most ardent supporter.

"I don't believe a word of your story, especially that part about the burger and fries. It just couldn't be."

Memorandum

- State insurance regulators keep financial reports of medical, auto and life insurance companies.
- TV reporters are called upon to report on a wide range of subjects.
- Patient care and overpricing are usually separate investigative stories.
- Allegations of medical quackery are difficult to prove.

Reporter as Ombudsman

Investigative reporters who write about waste and corruption in government and fraud in the business sector also become a sort of ombudsman for the public. People sometimes keep a reporter busy on the phone and by e-mail, asking what can be done about a problem, and, in return, the reporter tells them where they might get help. Based on what has been covered in this textbook, here are some questions a reporter can answer:

1. A woman says her elderly mother is being seen by a doctor who is 86 years old and still makes house calls. He uses techniques from the 1950s and will not let her see another doctor. She is loyal to him because he was her family doctor.

The doctor has a right to keep practicing until any age, and there are no grounds to file a complaint just because he is thought to be too old. It is apparent, however, that he is not keeping up with new discoveries and procedures and that he is advising a patient to not get a second opinion. Therefore a hearing before the state medical licensing board could be requested. Do not expect the American Medical Association to resolve the issue. The AMA is a membership organization and can only revoke the doctor's membership. This doctor probably is not a member anyway.

2. A caller relates how a bill collector calls a person at work and complains to anyone who answers the phone about an unpaid credit card bill. He has called every five minutes for an hour as well as after midnight, harassing the debtor.

People who are in the business of collecting bills for other people are licensed in many states and must comply with a set of rules that prohibit the conduct that the debtor is experiencing. The debtor can file a complaint with the state licensing agency, or, if the bill collector is working across state lines, the debtor can complain to the Federal Trade Commission, which could issue a cease-and-desist order.

3. A caller advises that a pharmacist with an office across the street from the police station is selling recreational drugs to university students without prescriptions so the students can stay awake in class.

Even if the pharmacist is properly licensed, selling a controlled substance without the proper controls of a medical doctor's prescription is a criminal offense. The police or the county prosecutor should be informed. If they take no action, the Drug Enforcement Administration—part of the U.S. Department of Justice—can act. Do not confuse DEA with the Food and Drug Administration (FDA), which oversees drug testing.

4. Patients in a skilled-care nursing home say the food is so tasteless they go to the fast-food restaurant down the street for a burger and fries.

Institutional food seldom pleases all the residents, and taste is hard to measure. Nursing home inspectors measure portions and judge whether food is safe and nutritious. The problem in this nursing home is that the staff is allowing seriously ill patients to wander around the neighborhood. They have lost their control over the patients' special diets, and state health inspectors should be aware of the violation.

5. A caller reports that her uncle is a health food advocate and buys food at the health food store. He bought some eucalyptus leaves that the clerk said would cure his gout. Instead, they made him sick.

The store is not selling drugs, merely herbs, making the FDA and the DEA not the best places to handle the issue. What we have here is a store clerk practicing medicine without a license by selling something and claiming it has curative value. Should we tell the state licensing board? No. All it can do is take away a license, and the proprietor does not have one. Instead, we tell the police or county prosecutor because a law has been broken.

6. A source reveals by e-mail that officials—the judge, prosecutor and county commissioners—in a remote county in the state extort money from visitors and tamper with election machines. Their influence is powerful in the state capitol. No one on the local or state level can be trusted, and none of their crimes are committed outside the state boundaries.

The FBI can investigate because election fraud is a federal crime. Candidates for Congress are on the same ballot as local candidates, so there is good cause. The FBI can take over an investigation for many reasons, such as a violation of civil rights or the robbery of a federally insured bank. Also, almost every local government receives federal funding for at least some of its programs, and this could cause the U.S. attorney general to act. Rather than call in the FBI, though, an investigative reporter will want to work on the story personally to see whether it can be proved.

Chapter Recap

Investigations of medical care are important to readers because medical care directly affects their physical well-being. But what about their automobiles? They are an extension of the body, and people rely on them to get to work, to school or to the doctor's office. Who is checking on the people we entrust with our autos? Reporters, that's who. They can help keep auto mechanics, truck drivers and other private for-profit entrepreneurs honest. But keeping such people honest may take more than documents. Some special techniques are the subject of study in the next chapter.

Class Assignments

1. The numbers in the Medicare supplement insurance story in Chapter 9 are dated. You can update these numbers and make a flat-out comparison of all insurance companies in your state if you have access to their financial information on the Internet or if you make a trip to the state office building and read them. Remember, there are different kinds of insurance, and you cannot mix auto, life, fire and health insurance statistics. Look for the overhead costs, such as the sales commissions, and figure the percentage of return for each

company. Which is worst and which is best from the viewpoint of the policy holder? Show your results in a chart.

2. Search on the Internet and find the nursing home inspection results in your state that are posted online by the department or agency of government that regulates them. Also, a basic list of all nursing care facilities that are approved for Medicare or Medicaid reimbursement is searchable online at www.medicare.gov/NHCompare/Include/DataSection/Questions/HomeSelect.asp.

If the local inspection reports are not online, you will have to go to the state office that inspects the facilities. There should be no question that they are public record, but the names of patients will not be shown.

List the nursing homes in your region, then note the type of violation cited, using a code letter of your choice. An abusive staff might be A, for abuse; allowing a patient to wander away is lack of security, an S; inadequate medical care might be M; and poor housekeeping, H.

In much the same way as we suggested checking on judges with the most reversals, count the number of similar letters. It is likely that one home will stand out in patient abuse and another in letting the patients wander. This kind of a survey will cause many questions. Why does this happen time after time? The answers might be found in a follow-up visit to those nursing homes.

Another approach is to use a computer spreadsheet and produce a thorough study. For the purpose of illustration, we used a Microsoft® Excel work sheet to create an internal database. Reporters have for many decades used chronologies as they gather information for a complicated report. Before computer record keeping was available, notations were made on file cards and kept in order; in that way, new material could be inserted in the proper place.

When computers became common, a chronology could be put on a work sheet, line by line, and new material could be inserted and the sheet could be re-sorted. A worksheet has more advantages. The lines can be shuffled and searched by date, alphabetical order or subject matter. The spreadsheet is not the whole of an investigation, but it is a valuable resource for organization.

Excel is called a limited database system, but the limits are that there can only be 16,384 rows and 256 columns, which presents no problem for an investigative database. Although spreadsheets were originally designed for numbers and accounting tasks, an internal database works well for students in a classroom investigative journalism project because students can gather information in identical, preset formats and then bring it to class and combine it with information gathered by other students.

You will need to know how to click on a cell to open it, and then insert information in that cell by typing it into a cell at the top of the form and hitting "enter." First, pull up an empty worksheet from Microsoft Excel, then add column headings across the first row. As a very basic example, we listed Institutions, Date, H (Housekeeping), S (Security), A (Abuse), M (Medical) and Notes as the topics for seven columns (see Table 10.1). Next, write the names of all the nursing homes included in your range of investigation, which would be all of the nursing homes in your circulation or broadcast area. You might want to reduce the numbers by including only skilled nursing homes or for-profit homes, but to be a meaningful survey the list must be all-inclusive, not a selection you made. You can also control the size of the survey by adjusting the number of years surveyed.

Then go to the inspection reports and write the date of each inspection in the second column. The computer, in its great wisdom, will recognize that it is a date and treat it accordingly.

TABLE 10.1 Nursing Home Spreadsheet

INSTITUTION	DATE	H	S	A	M	NOTES
Central City Care	8/30/2007	3	2	2	1	staff taunts resident for poor bladder control
Founders Skilled Nursing	11/3/2007	0	1	1	2	unpleasant odor
Garfield East	12/13/2007	3	0	1	0	patient walks from facility
Maison House	9/10/2007	1	0	0	1	wrong prescription
Pointe Drift Care	8/28/2007	2	1	2	1	bugs near ice machine
Post Road Nursing Center	9/1/2007	2	2	1	2	lack of privacy
Ridgelander Care	9/11/2007	1	2	2	2	lack of recreation
St. Villa Vista	12/13/2007	3	1	2	3	bugs in janitor closet
Tri-Cities Retreat	10/15/2007	1	3	2	1	patient falls
Brier Park Home	11/1/2007	2	4	1	2	poor kitchen cleanliness
Buchanan Riverview	10/2/2007	2	2	0	2	no recreation

Read the reports and mark the number of violations in each category under the types of violations in each column. You will want to insert notes in the right-hand column. Notes can be lengthy. Adjust the width of the columns by clicking with a mouse on the line that separates the columns at the very top of each column and dragging the line to the position that will give you the width you want.

Table 10.1 is an example of the first step in a searchable work sheet that uses realistic but fictional information.

The second step is to insert more rounds of reports applicable to the same nursing homes but taken from other inspection dates. As the information piles up, you can click on "sort" and choose differ-

TABLE 10.2   Sorting Nursing Home Findings

INSTITUTION	DATE	H	S	A	M
Central City Care	8/30/2007	3	2	2	1
Central City Care	9/28/2007	1	1	1	0
Central City Care	10/26/2007	1	1	0	1
Central City Care	11/2/2007	3	2	2	0
Central City Care	12/18/2007	1	1	2	0
Central City Care	1/19/2008	2	1	3	1
Central City Care	3/11/2008	2	2	2	0
Founders Skilled Nursing	9/23/2007	1	1	2	0
Founders Skilled Nursing	10/12/2007	2	2	1	2
Founders Skilled Nursing	11/3/2007	0	1	1	2
Founders Skilled Nursing	12/3/2007	0	1	2	0
Founders Skilled Nursing	1/3/2008	1	2	1	1
Founders Skilled Nursing	2/16/2008	2	0	1	0
Founders Skilled Nursing	3/8/2008	2	2	0	1
Garfield East	9/13/2007	2	1	1	0
Garfield East	10/13/2007	4	0	2	0
Garfield East	11/7/2007	3	1	1	1
Garfield East	12/13/2007	3	0	1	0
Garfield East	1/10/2008	3	2	2	1
Garfield East	2/13/2008	2	1	2	0
Garfield East	3/13/2008	3	0	1	0

ent ways to display the information. You can sort according to any of the columns, which helps to identify clusters (see Table 10.2).

For ease of interpretation, you could even mark the rows with different colors for each home. Central City has 12 abuse complaints; Garfield, 10; and Founders, eight. But look at Garfield's 20 housekeeping violations—almost three times as many as Founders. That means that you will be able to report that Central City Care has more incidents of patient abuse than any other nursing home in the area, and you can cite your survey and the state reports as your source. Then you can flesh out the story with specific incidents taken from the state reports. You can refer to your notes in the far-right column, and they are searchable. But your numbers will be more important.

Remember to talk to the administrators of the homes and also to give a nod of approval to the place with the best records. Nursing homes sometimes have similar names, so do not confuse the entirely fictional nursing homes in this exercise with any real nursing homes anywhere.

Notes

1. Stuart Watson, "The Investigators: Medicaid Dental Centers Making More Money on Baby Root Canals," WCNC.com, December 18, 2003, www.wcnc.com/news/topstories/stories/wcnc-121803-al-medicaid.b4d99017.html.
2. The nursing profession is the most trusted profession in the United States, and automobile salespeople are the least trusted, according to a *USA Today*/Gallup poll taken in 2006. The telephone poll of 1,009 people nationwide found 84 percent of people considered nurses' ethics as "very high" or "high" compared with 7 percent who felt that way about people who sell cars. Pharmacists scored second to nurses, with 73 percent, while veterinarians had 71 percent trust, the poll said. Clergy and college teachers tied at 58 percent on the ethics scale, while police officers managed just 54 percent trust. See www.usatoday.com/news/polls/tables/live/2006-12-11-ethics.htm for details.
3. Board of Medical Licensure v. Miglaccio, 917 P.2d 483 (1996 OK Civ App 37), www.oscn.net/applications/oscn/DeliverDocument.asp?CiteID=4597.
4. Jerry Schwartz, *Associated Press Reporting Handbook* (New York: McGraw-Hill, 2002), 199.
5. "Nursing Homes in Illinois," Illinois Department of Public Health, www.idph.state.il.us/webapp/LTCApp/ltc.jsp.
6. Phillip Reese and Nancy Weaver Teichert, "Watchdog Report: Nursing Homes Pile Up Citation: Centers in City Lead California in Fines," *Sacramento Bee*, October 2, 2005, http://dwb.sacbee.com/content/news/projects/watchdog/nursing_homes/story/13703019p-14500090c.html.
7. Jerry Schwartz, *Associated Press Reporting Handbook* (New York: McGraw-Hill, 2002), 184.
8. Missouri Group, Brian S. Brooks et al., "News Reporting and Writing," 8th ed. (Boston: Bedford/St. Martin's, 2005), 403–404.

C h a p t e r   1 1

Investigating Businesses

$\mathbf{A}$N INVESTIGATIVE STORY IN 1978 involved union management, transactions of an internationally known financier, records of an insurance company and the failure of state and federal regulatory agencies. It was probably the most complex type of report investigative journalists can be called upon to write. But by amassing hundreds of documents, talking to experts and untangling financial reports, the reporters were able to write this lead:

> "Aided by what appears to be a near total collapse of law enforcement . . . a holding company which had as one of its apparent backers missing former Teamster boss Jimmy Hoffa, has managed to dismantle the huge Blue Coal Company in Ashley, Lazerne County."

The reporters told this story of private, for-profit businesses not for the readers of the *New York Times* or *Wall Street Journal,* but for the *Pottsville (Pa.) Republican,* a newspaper serving a mountain town of 15,000. Reporters Gilbert M. Gaul and Elliot G. Jaspin won a Pulitzer Prize for their work on the story.

This classic example led local reporters elsewhere to wade into the deep waters of investigating private businesses. They learned that information on these companies was available and stories could be told in easily understood language.

A private businessperson is hardly private at all. After some thought, one could conclude that the two words in fact do not fit together. To be in business means to deal with the public—to sell your skills and products to people. In the United States, a so-called private businessperson is weighted down with government forms that are for the most part public record. The private businessperson deals with the government as both a customer and an overseer. This situation has evolved because of the large role the businessperson has been asked to play.

In many countries, even those we call Western democracies, the government plays a more direct role. The government may own the banks and the airlines and the broadcast stations. In the United States, government yields to individuals to perform these functions but asks in return—to keep people honest and not bickering—that businesses be licensed or regulated. In licensing, the government exercises ongoing supervision of a business owner by extending a license to run a business, making sure the owners and employees are qualified, and requiring them to obey rules in order to keep that license.

Regulation, in contrast with licensing, is not as domineering. Agencies that regulate enforce rules but do not require a test or college degree before a person can open a business such as a restaurant. If a restaurateur wants to remain open, though, a sneeze guard has to be placed over the food cart and the bar has to close on time.

The investigative reporter has two distinct areas in which to work in gathering information about for-profit businesses:

- Documents. The target of an investigation, especially if the target is an officer of a for-profit firm, is usually surprised at the amount of public information earlier assumed to be private.
- Surveys. Reporters not only use documents to create the investigative report; sometimes reporters actually create the documents on which the final investigative story is based.

Document-Based Investigations of Privately Held Companies

In previous chapters we examined how *The Orange County Register* used a Securities and Exchange Commission (SEC) filing to document a story about for-profit companies buying and selling human body parts, how the *Austin American-Statesman* exposed carelessness by companies pumping oil through pipelines, and how the *Los Angeles Times* showed that drug companies were marketing drugs without adequate testing. These stories were based on documents for the most part.

In the following case study, a financial portrait of a family-held, for-profit company was created by the reporter with no help from the company and no inside source.

Case Study

Sports Equals Big Business*

The major league football team in Middleton was considered an asset to the city, and residents—most were avid fans—were able to excuse the team for its losing ways. The team for many years played in General Stadium, a city-owned facility. The stadium was a bit run-down, and if it had not been city-owned, city inspectors would have shut it down many years before. But the city rented it to the team for its games and also to others for concerts and revivals.

The owners of the team announced one day that they were going to relocate to Landers, a small city just outside the metropolitan area. There was a possibility, the team executives said, that they could be persuaded to stay in Middleton if the city built the team a new stadium. The people of Middleton were confused. They wanted the team to stay, but they also did not want to feel they were being shaken down as taxpayers by the team owners. The team owners said General Stadium had become so inadequate it was losing them revenue at a time when executive suites and sports bars at football games were in demand.

What was the financial condition of the team? The editors sent a sports reporter who had a close relationship with the owners to ask specifics about their financial condition. He came back empty-handed.

"They said they never give out financial information," he reported. The situation fit the definition of a subject waiting to be investigated. Someone was trying to hide something that was of public concern, and the story needed original research by a reporter. The editors gave Charles R. Miller the assignment.

Miller wanted to get the official version of how much money the team owners made or lost and perhaps compare Middleton's team with another team in the league that played in a better stadium. It might be that the owners deserved a better location, and the taxpayers would have to foot the bill. He approached the team business manager with the idea of cooperating, but once again the newspaper was turned away. The team was a private, family-owned compa-

---

*The cases are based on real investigative stories, but the names and places have been changed to protect reporters, their sources and the secrets they have. Some are actual stories told in a step-by-step reconstruction and others are composites.

ny, he was reminded, and family members did not have to disclose financials. There was nothing wrong with the city building a new facility because it was not a direct subsidy to the team; instead it was good business for the city to have a better sports facility, the team spokesperson said.

Miller checked for previous stories and found that the owners never gave out the least bit of financial information. He learned that monopolistic practices by sports teams were tolerated by the law—an unusual treatment. In fact, a sports league is not really a monopoly; it is more like a cartel. A cartel exists when a group of separate companies get together and make rules for themselves. The arrangement is considered worthy of exemption from some rules governing other businesses because a sports league would certainly have to have binding rules about what percentage of the proceeds goes to the visiting team, the size of the playing field, and standardized equipment, for example.

But Miller knew how to start digging for information about the team. He knew that because the team rented from the city, there would be a public contract on file. Miller contacted the city attorney's office where such contracts were negotiated and kept. The city was more helpful than usual because officials understood that Miller was investigating the team and not the city. He found that the contract required the team to pay a percentage of its ticket sales as the rental charge; therefore, there was a financial report of income in the city controller's office. It showed that the team had sold $19 million in game tickets during the most recent year. If it had not been in the contract, Miller could have figured it out by counting the seats at different prices and multiplying by the admission price because every game at General Stadium was a sell-out. He learned from the contract that the team got no money from the sale of food or from the parking concession, which was handled by city employees.

Miller then interviewed the league secretary, who explained that 40 percent of the proceeds of the ticket sales is claimed by the visiting team.

The big item for sports teams is the revenue from broadcasting. The league had negotiated the broadcast contracts, and every team received the same amount no matter how small their advertising market. Miller learned from the league office that it was $54.5 million for each team. "Did you say $54.5 million? What do they have to do for that?"

"They don't have to do anything. It's for broadcast rights," a league spokesperson said. They don't furnish the play-by-play or the blimp. The network does that. A check comes in the mail for $54.5 million, and all they have to do is cash it."

On the expense side, the big item was the players' salaries: $36.5 million. Miller learned about this from the players' union. Because the league was a cartel, all of the teams had the same costs for team equipment, from towels in the shower to the area of grass they had to cut. Miller was fortunate to have found that one team in the league, at Coastal City, was publicly traded, and it published an annual financial report. Miller adopted its figures to his balance sheet. The team in Middleton showed a clear profit of $26.3 million. Miller wrote this out, walked across the newsroom to the fax machines and faxed it to the Middleton team's business office (see Figure 11.1).

As he arrived back at his desk, the phone was ringing. It was the business manager, and he wanted to make some corrections. "These operating expenses are too low and some of the income is overstated," he said.

"Okay, what are the figures?" Miller asked.

"Well, the operating expenses are about $1 million too low, and the income from promotions is about a million too high," he said.

"What about the other figures? Is it possible that there is more income than I have found and lower expenses for some items?"

"Oh, I can't tell you that. I can't reveal anything about the finances of the company."

Miller realized he had been snookered.

Should the business manager be able to get away with telling only what supported the team argument?

Yes: Miller can yield to the demands of the manager without hurting his story. What does it matter to a reader if the team made $26 million or $24 million? That is a lot of money for one family in one year, and another $2 million is not going to matter.

No: Miller has no obligation to use the information about the $2 million margin of difference. Miller can go ahead with his own figures. The manager is playing games besides football and is out of line.

The story ran, and the team stayed in Middleton. Maybe the story had some influence on public opinion. The city agreed to modernize the stadium, and the team owners were satisfied, but they still finished dead last in the league standings. Miller was unhappy with himself because he had forgotten something important. The ticket sales are a season in advance, and the broadcast money comes in long before the games start, so the team coffers have all those millions that draw interest for almost a year before they need to be spent on salaries and other costs.

Case Memorandum

- Scaled down to the basics, financial stories can be told in elementary school math,

Figure 11.1 Letter requesting comment

```
Edward Swanson
Business Manager
Middleton Major League Football, Inc.

Dear Mr. Swanson:

Please reconsider your decision not to comment about the
finances of the team. I am sending the figures we have
compiled and need to know whether they are correct.

Charles Miller
Reporter
Middleton Daily News
_____  —
```

Estimate of Annual Income/Profits

Revenue (in millions)

```
Ticket Sales—football games at General Stadium:
    Source: City contract in City Controller office $ 19.0

Share of ticket sales from away games:
    Source: Coastal City financial report               9.5

TV rights:
    Source: League office                              54.5

Logos, promotions:
    Source: League office                               8.0

Total revenue                                        $ 91.0
```

Expenses (in millions)

```
Visiting team share of ticket sales
    Source: League, Coastal City                      $ 7.6

Rent for General Stadium
    Source: City Controller                             3.9

Player salaries
    Source: Players' union                             36.5

Operations:
    Source: Coastal City financial report              15.0

Amusement tax
    Source: City Treasurer Office                       1.7

Total expenses:                                      $ 64.7


    Net profit                                       $ 26.3
```

- Companies that are privately held still leave a trail of public documents,
- Sports stories are not only for the sports pages.
- Local investigative reporters can expand their horizons far beyond city hall.

Document-Based Investigations of Publicly Held Companies

For-profit companies that sell stock across a state line have to file financial information with the Securities and Exchange Commission (SEC). The name means the commission regulates both the sales of securities and the exchanges that facilitate the sales. Corporations that qualify have to file electronically, and the SEC becomes merely a conveyer of this information straight from the companies and signed by the corporation officials. Those reports on file are documents that investigative reporters can pull up from computer terminals. The companies are not filing these reports for the convenience of investigative reporters, of course; the purpose of the filings is to inform stockholders and potential stockholders of the company's financial condition.

Any financial activity the company undertakes must be reported individually and in a timely manner; therefore large corporations often file many documents. The most comprehensive is the annual report, which is filed on form 10-K. As an example, we found the 2006 annual report of the Gannett Corporation, a large multimedia corporation. That year, the company was active in buying and selling newspapers and television stations. Gannett did nothing to cause us to look at its filings—we are not investigating the company—but they make an interesting study because they are important to journalism. Gannett filed a 72-page annual report.

One sore point among investors is the benefits that companies provide their top officials, and these can be the subject of a newspaper investigation. In the Gannett report, some of these perks are explained:

"In 2004, as a part of a new compensation agreement, the Board of Directors awarded the Chairman restricted stock units related to the company's common stock. Effective July 1, 2004, and for a 12-month period, the Chairman received a restricted stock unit award that vests with respect to 1,603 shares per month of Gannett's common stock. If the Chairman remained in the company's employ on July 1, 2005, which he did, he received an additional restricted stock unit award that will vest with respect to 1,603 shares of common stock per month for an additional 12-month period. Upon vesting, the value of the shares is contributed to the Chairman's account under the Gannett Deferred Compensation Plan. Any portion of the restricted stock unit grants remaining unvested will be forfeited upon the Chairman's termination for any reason. The awards are charged to expense as they vest. Also during 2003, a restricted stock unit grant of $150,000 was awarded to the company's Chairman, which was deferred under the Deferred Compensation Plan and converted into 1,913 shares of company common stock. The award was charged to expense when granted. In December 2005, the Board of Directors awarded 3,085,350 stock options and 247,250 SIRs. The stock options have an exercise price of $60.29. Other stock options and 12,500 SIRs were awarded earlier in 2005, including 225,000 options in July granted to the newly named President and Chief Executive Officer at the then-current market price of $71.94. The Executive Compensation Committee may grant other types of awards that are valued in whole or in part by reference to or that are otherwise based on fair market value of the company's common stock or other criteria established by the Executive Compensation Committee and the achievement of performance goals. The maximum aggregate grant of performance shares that may be awarded to any participant in any fiscal year shall not exceed 500,000 shares of common stock. The maximum aggregate amount of performance units or cash-based awards that may be awarded to any participant in any fiscal year shall not exceed $10,000,000."

(Stockholders are supposed to be relieved that there is a limitation of $10 million as a bonus for the company chairman.)

One revealing aspect of a form 10-K is the section labeled "Commitments, contingent liabilities and other matters." This is the section that shows pending lawsuits. For this section, the Gannett report said in part:

"Litigation: On Dec. 31, 2003, two employees of the company's television station KUSA in Denver filed a purported class action lawsuit in the U.S. District Court for the District of Colorado against Gannett and the Gannett Retirement Plan (Plan) on behalf of themselves and other similarly situated individuals who participated in the Plan after Jan. 1, 1998, the date that certain amendments to the Plan took effect. The plaintiffs allege, among other things, that the current pension plan formula adopted in that amendment violated the age discrimination accrual provisions of the Employee Retirement Income Security Act. The plaintiffs seek to have their post-1997 benefits recalculated and seek other equitable relief. Gannett believes that it has valid defenses to the issues raised in the complaint and will defend itself vigorously. Due to the uncertainties of judicial determinations, however, it is not possible at this time to predict the ultimate outcome of this matter with respect to liability or damages, if any."

The lawsuit is significant enough for the company to mention it, but if the company officials in anticipating the results of a lawsuit do not believe it would endanger the company's bottom line significantly, they have the option of not listing them.

"The company and a number of its subsidiaries are defendants in other judicial and administrative proceedings involving matters incidental to their business. The company's management does not believe that any material liability will be imposed as a result of these matters."

The company also decides which factors about its business are a risk, and Gannett warned its investors in the following words:

"Item 1A. Risk Factors

"In addition to the other information contained or incorporated by reference into this Form 10-K, prospective investors should consider carefully the following risk factors before investing in our securities. The risks described below may not be the only risks we face. Additional risks that we do not yet perceive or that we currently believe are immaterial may also adversely affect our business and the trading price of our securities.

"Advertising produces the predominant share of our newspaper and broadcasting revenues. With the continued development of alternative forms of media, particularly those based on the Internet, our traditional print and television businesses are facing increasingly stiff competition for advertising revenues. Alternative media sources also affect our ability to increase our circulation revenues and television audience. This competition could make it difficult for us to grow our advertising and circulation revenues, which we believe will challenge us to expand the contributions of our online and other digital businesses. If we are unable to meet these challenges successfully, we may have difficulty increasing revenues to offset the additional expenses we expect to incur as a result of rising employee benefit and other labor costs, newsprint prices and interest expense, not to mention stock compensation expense which must be reported in the financial statements for the first time in 2006 in accordance with a new accounting rule. Our future results also depend on economic conditions in our principal newspaper and television markets, including the United Kingdom, where a softening advertising environment may affect our ability to increase revenues from our Newsquest operation. Any weakening of the British pound-to-U.S. dollar exchange rate further could adversely impact Newsquest's earnings contribution."

The vicissitudes of the media are also enough to cause Gannett to warn stockholders:

"Our newspaper and broadcasting operations are subject to government regulation. Changing regulations, particularly FCC regulations which affect our television stations, may result in increased costs and adversely affect our future profitability."

The company describes its goals for the future but warns the public of any possible misfortune:

"We intend to continue our efforts to identify and complete strategic investments, partnerships and business acquisitions. These efforts may not prove successful. Strategic investments and partnerships with other companies expose us to risks that we may not be able to control the operations of our investee or partnership, which could decrease the amount of benefits we reap from a particular relationship."

The examples above do not indicate a need for investigation, but they serve as an example of what is available. A for-profit firm may be going to the government for special tax breaks, and the reporter will want to look at its SEC filings that show it is possibly not in as dire a financial condition as it claims; or, quite the reverse, when a company—like Enron at the turn of the century—is flying high and luring investors, a reporter could examine the SEC filing with the hope of finding the true story of the company's financial condition.

The reporter might be interested in the company because of its association with a major political candidate. The SEC filings could then be the springboard to other documents, including, for example, a lawsuit of the nature mentioned in the Gannett filing, which could be tracked down. Such a lawsuit might also be found on the Internet, and chances are good that it will be found if it is a federal court case or a case that is under appeal.

Another approach that investigative reporters often use is to make comparisons of similar companies, just as reporters in the case studies in this textbook compared city budgets. How does the Gannett compensation package for its executives compare with other companies its size?

Original Surveys

An investigative survey is not the kind of survey a newspaper makes of voter public opinion prior to elections, but it has many of the same aspects of those surveys because a designated group of people or companies is going to be checked and specific rules will be created to make sure everything surveyed is tested equally. The result is a finding by the reporter of an important fact that otherwise would not be known. A survey could indicate what percentage of auto mechanics make unnecessary repairs, which school foods are the most nutritious, and which companies are more generous when insured persons file claims. If the story is about speeding trucks, the survey might involve timing them along the roadway. A story of racial discrimination—called redlining—is accomplished by surveying different areas of the community and comparing availability and cost of services such as banking and insurance.

A survey for such purposes requires that the reporter make specific plans and stick to them. In a survey of auto repair garages, one would not change the planned locations to be visited because more interesting results were being realized at auto dealers than at back-alley independent garages. If some results do not go the way the reporter had hoped, those incidents cannot be removed from the story and disregarded. The newspaper would not be able to hold out the report as a fair survey if that were done. In the resulting story, the reporter always has an unspoken agreement with the reader that the reporter reveals the parameters of the study. The reader would discount the findings if the survey were tampered with.

Case Study

Survey: Auto Mechanics, Routine Checkup*

In Metropolitan Kastleton people relied on their cars to get them to work and out and about on their errands. It was a sad moment for sure when any Kastleton driver turned the ignition key and got no response or when a banging started in the engine. The car was in need of repair, and the driver was at the mercy of an auto mechanic.[1]

Roberta Carter, writer for the *Kastletonian,* an alternative newspaper, recognized that auto repair mechanics consistently ranked high on the lists of the complaints received by consumer protection groups. Carter went online and read stories about auto repairs that newspapers in other cities had done, and she talked to the reporters who had written the stories. Then she wrapped up her thoughts in a memo to the editor.

TO: Metropolitan Editor
FROM: Roberta Carter

RE: Story Outline: "Auto Mechanics, Routine Checkup"

Subject: Whether auto mechanics do unnecessary repairs
Scope: We will make a survey of the skill and honesty of auto mechanics in Kastleton and in the suburbs by taking to repair garages a car that has been found by an expert to have properly operating transmissions,

---

*The cases are based on real investigative stories, but the names and places have been changed to protect reporters, their sources and the secrets they have. Some are actual stories told in a step-by-step reconstruction and others are composites.

starters and brakes, and reporting on what the garages said or did when they examined it.

Need: A car is a necessity for any working person in Kastleton, and it could even be considered an extension of the person's body. It becomes almost an emotional experience when it breaks down. The car owner then has to rely on a complete stranger in a greasy, noisy building somewhere. The driver is without protection, but we can help.

Methods: We will rely solely on a well-planned tour of garages picked at random and will insert no information other than our findings, so that each garage is treated the same. Unlike most other newspapers that undertake such efforts, we will not stop at getting estimates of the cost. We will actually pay for any work done. If we do not follow through with the repair and pay, the mechanics could say it was only an estimate and they would not have charged what they had estimated after they set about doing the work and found nothing wrong. Our survey will be extensive, we will use four cars driven by reporters, checked by our expert and dropped off at a repair garage on the way into work. I believe it will be necessary to go to 52 garages to make the survey complete.

Sources: The sources will be our own experiences, and the documentation will be our receipts and the notes of our expert.

Presentation: We will tell of our findings in a four-day series of articles. Each day will feature a different type of garage; the selection will be evenly balanced in our at-random survey. Each day will feature a different kind of auto repair business: independent side-street operations, franchises, gas stations and the big retailers. We expect we will encounter some dishonesty, and we will explain that in detail; but we will also feature the mechanics who did the best jobs.

Follow-Up: If we find that shoddy and unnecessary work is widespread, the legislature might get involved with testing and licensing auto mechanics, who now are completely unregulated.

As an alternative newspaper, the *Kastletonian* was expected to be more freewheeling than the big newspaper of record in the metropolitan area. The editors tended to take chances, look for stories missed by the competition and give those big display. The paper was free of charge and distributed only on working days. It had been started only five years before by some editors and reporters from the bigger paper who were being laid off during a cutback by the big paper. The reporters got start-up money and a loan from some local investors who had learned that such enterprises were successful in other cities. The editors of the *Kastletonian* were interested in the auto repair story, but they had many questions.

Q: — What if there is no unnecessary repair, no overcharging?

A: — Then we have a story that says the fears of car owners about mechanics are unfounded.

Q: — If we agree to pay for the repairs, can we put a limit on the amount that would have to come out of the newsroom budget?

A: — Even if all of the repair shops made unnecessary repairs, the total cost would probably not exceed one or two out-of-town-expense trips. We cannot have a limit because that would compromise the study. Once committed, we would have to pay for all the repairs.

Q: — Are we going to ask for the old parts when we drop off the car?

A: — That is one of the best ways for a consumer to avoid being cheated, but if we do that, the mechanics will be suspicious because few people think to make such a request. We could ask for the used, supposedly defective part after the work is done and after we are presented with a bill.

Q: — How much will the expert cost?

A: — We can't pay the expert. The expert will have to be a volunteer. If we pay the expert, people can say we bought the opinion, that the expert was our agent and not an outside authority.

Q: — Can we trust the expert?

A: — The expert will not know where we are taking the car. That way, people will not be able to argue that the expert influenced the results of the survey.

Q: — Are we going to be accused of entrapment?

A: — We are not going to suggest that the mechanic do specific work; in other words, we will not say, "I think I need a new transmission." We will only say that we think something is wrong.

The questions answered, the reporters started by seeking an expert. The best person to hold out as an expert would be an instructor in automotive repair at a school. Carter found that instructors at local vocational schools were reluctant to cooperate although the examination of the car would not take much time. One said that he was afraid he would alienate the local garage operators by criticizing them, and he needed their help in placing graduates in jobs. Carter kept looking and finally found an ideal candidate who agreed to take part in the study. He was an instructor in a community college that was 50 miles from downtown Kastleton. That might create a problem because, after he approved the condition of the car that was to be taken to a mechanic, the driver would have a long drive back home. The distance helped the security of the newspaper study, though.

The reporters set out with the cars on the first day, wondering whether they had set up a perfect and fair plan. The very first stop yielded a new transmission. From then on, it was surprising to find, day after day, that about half of the repair shops overcharged and carried out unneeded repairs. They found that the male and female reporters were cheated equally, which dispelled a preconceived notion that a woman was more likely to be cheated. Mechanics very seldom returned the used parts, saying their pricing was based on the assumption that they could take them as trade-ins; also some said they had mixed them with other parts and could no longer identify them for certain.

The editor was near panic as he saw his budget drained away as the repair bills began to pile up. At final count, exactly half of the shops—26—had charged for unnecessary repairs.

When it came time to write, Carter drafted an outline and wrote a draft of the first story. The results of the visits to big franchised operations, retail stores with auto repair, so-called back-alley garages and, finally, gas stations were set out in each day's report. An editor was blunt:

> "This will never work. All this about going from one place to another, having mechanics examine the cars for this and that. It's all too confusing. You have to explain each one of these malfunctions. You have to write about one malfunction a day, explain it thoroughly, and we will make a graphic design of a car to illustrate that malfunction."

But the lead to the story stood up: "A motorist has a 50-50 chance of getting a fair deal from an auto mechanic in Kastleton."

No question about it, the editor was right about the organization of the writing, and the story was well told. The series became a local sensation. All the TV stations reported on it. It was the subject of discussion in coffee shops at lunch. It had such a good run that the editors called for another day to be added to the series, which is almost unheard of because most series are cut back. The tacked-on day consisted of interviews with lawmakers and experts. The consensus was that auto mechanics should be regulated.

On the last day of the series, Carter was stunned when she picked up the *Kastletonian* on her way into work. An editorial writer for the paper was challenging the conclusions of the auto repair stories. He praised the work of his reporters and lauded the response of the readers, but he warned that the survey was too small to cause any important change in the law. He wrote that there were too many rules and regulations and layers of governmental bureaucracies already, and to license auto mechanics would create an army of inspectors, all of whom would be exposed to the temptation of bribery. The auto mechanics should clean up their own acts and build reputations individually, based on performance, he wrote.

Did the reporters entrap the auto mechanics?

Yes: The reporters came to the garages with trickery in mind. By rigging a car they set a trap. Also, because they didn't reveal the real purpose behind having the car examined, they were guilty of misrepresentation, which is not sanctioned in journalism. If a mechanic asked where the reporters worked, they probably would not have told the truth.

No: The reporters did no more than what any person could do. They were careful to not suggest which repairs might be needed. Yes, they set a trap, but entrapment means to suggest a crime. They did not instruct the repair person to fix the car even if it didn't need it.

Is a formal survey necessary?

Yes: The series will command more attention and respect if it is done the right way. The readers then can be told how it was done. If someone considers suing the newspaper, they will have to realize that the reporters took every precaution to be fair.

No: Why not forget all these formal survey preparations and take a car to a few places thought to be bad. The story will have the same impact on the reader.

Was the editorial writer correct?

Yes: He took a realistic look at a problem that was only superficially covered by the reporters. In the excitement of the moment, people responded with the first solution that came to mind without proper consideration. The editorial brought them back to their senses.

No: The study was not superficial, it was representative. The sample was large enough that we can safely conclude that if it were done elsewhere the results would be similar. People need protection. They know there will be a cost in tax dollars to regulate auto mechanics, but it is much less than a transmission that was not needed.

Nothing ever happened on the legislative front, but Carter got calls every day for about a year from people who wanted to know where to find an honest auto mechanic. She had to tell them they were at risk no matter where they went. The expert mechanic who had driven 100 miles to participate became a celebrity and was in demand on the speaking circuit. There was talk of him running for the state legislature.

The series was such a success that the editors asked Carter to do another series that would be equally well received. It happened that Carter had received a very good lead from a very good source. It was exactly the kind of story she needed. The tipster was a former employee of a major automaker who had inside information on the design and manufacture of automobile shock absorbers. He was adamant in his attack on the automakers, claiming the shock absorbers were shoddily constructed from the cheapest of materials. Carter learned that a shock absorber was a relatively simple device— it was just a big spring in a tube. Attached above the four wheels, the shock absorbers bounced and took the brunt of the impact when the car hit a bump or a pothole.

The editors were excited about the idea and were already think- ing of graphics and display. They hoped the investigation would have the impact of Ralph Nader's landmark exposé of auto manufacturers and their lack of concern for safety. Carter sought out statistics and victims of faulty shock absorbers. She found neither. She learned that shock absorbers were not a safety factor; in fact, without them the driver was in for a bumpy ride but had more control over the vehicle than if the shock absorbers were the biggest and most expensive available. The U.S. Department of Transportation, which keeps detailed statistics on auto accidents, had recorded absolutely none attributed to shock absorbers. This seemingly great idea could not pass the test and was abandoned. This was not a worthwhile story if the public safety was not at risk, and such a story would never get by the keen eye of many an editor.

Carter still had to satisfy the request to top her previous effort, so she settled on the idea of auto insurance. This time, she found plenty to write about. She found the auto insurance business was rife with problems. Some companies specialized in insuring people who could not get insurance from major companies because of their poor driv- ing records; these companies were notorious for not paying claims. Carter found many stories of victims who had been hit by drivers insured by these companies. These victims experienced frustrating delays and heard absurd excuses for nonpayment of claims. Carter's lead example was a worker who lost his job because he lost his car when it was hit by one of their drivers.

The series was comprehensive, and it detailed bizarre stories. Carter was asked to testify to a state legislative committee about her findings. She had done good work, and she awaited the response of the readership. But the public ho-hummed the story. It was difficult to understand why, but it could have been that the readers believed they would not be victims of such poor luck as her examples had been or that, simply put, auto insurance or a lack of it does not bring out the same emotional concern as an automobile in need of repair.

Case Memorandum

- Public response may be far more or far less than expected.
- Investigative reports can be done with few documents if the reporter carefully creates first-person documentation.
- Editorial writers are independent of reporters and editors.
- A survey needs to be set up to create documentation, not to confirm a premise.
- The best of documentation is meaningless if the story is not an important public issue.

Case Study

Survey: Speeding and Tailgating Trucks*

Gary Hammond, a reporter-producer for the Tri-Cities TV Probe Team, liked stories about big things with wheels. He always thought of possible visuals when he put together an investigative piece, and if the piece was about big things with wheels, it was sure to have built-in action. The subject might be the safety of school buses or the efficiency of ambulance drivers. So when Hammond looked up into his rearview mirror on the highway and saw a speeding truck bearing down on his convertible, he felt both terror and relief because he had time to get out of the way. Calming down, he realized there was a story to be told. He would design a project to find out how many trucks were speeding and tailgating on the highways.

He knew such a story had good elements for TV, and so Hammond gave it a try. Hammond would be producing what is usually called a package—a story that is taped and edited to be inserted in the broadcast; it is not told live on camera. A package usually

*The cases are based on real investigative stories, but the names and places have been changed to protect reporters, their sources and the secrets they have. Some are actual stories told in a step-by-step reconstruction and others are composites.

features a live lead-in by the anchor. As a reporter-producer at the station, Hammond works with a cameraman and Hammond himself is the on-the-air personality. A larger operation would have a reporter, a producer and a cameraman, but Hammond was happy with the simplicity of his arrangement.

Hammond tested his theory that most trucks were speeding and tailgating cars. He borrowed a hand-held radar gun with a digital number that lit up on the back and showed the speed of an approaching truck. If the cameraman stood behind him, pointing the camera at the number on the back of the radar gun, the screen would display the speed of the truck as it approached. On a busy highway they got good shots showing trucks were going 70 and 72 miles an hour in a 55-mph zone. They had the best kind of pictures for an investigative report—those that help prove the premise.

Should a story be given preference because it has good pictures?

Yes: The TV reporter must look for a subject that provides good possibilities for pictures, just as a print media reporter looks for ways to tell the story in words and graphics. If the reporter believes the subject is exciting, the pictures will convey that excitement. A print media person who objects is jealous of the power of TV.

No: If important stories are being pushed aside for frivolous stories because they have better picture possibilities, then the public is not being served. The viewers are sophisticated enough to sit through an important story without being entertained with manufactured excitement.

Hammond went to a truck stop without the camera and talked to truckers. He identified himself and asked why they were speeding and tailgating. They agreed that they drove over the speed limit at times, and some said it was because the trucking companies for whom they worked made impossible demands on their schedules. They worked long hours and were in need of sleep. Then they started to gather around Hammond and talked about their problems. One of the main concerns of the drivers was that the trucking companies were skimping on repairs. They let trucks go on the road with mushy brakes and loose wiring, the drivers said, and they allowed the tires to get dangerously thin. Hammond was excited about the twist in the story. It seemed that not only automobile drivers were terrorized by speeding trucks, so were the truck drivers. The drivers' comments were off the record, but Hammond got the phone numbers of a few of the most talkative for contact later.

Somebody in the government must have the job of enforcing the laws for trucks, Hammond surmised. He talked to the state police captain at the local post who said the police did their best to ticket speeders but they had limited resources. He also pointed out that truckers had antiradar devices in their trucks, making it possible for them to spot a trooper. Hammond asked what the police did about unsafe trucks and was told that the police were constrained from stopping trucks because of rights built into the U.S. Constitution: If trucks have mushy brakes or thin rubber, there isn't sufficient visual evidence of a violation for the police to make a legal stop. But a federal government unit within the U.S. Department of Transportation routinely examined trucks for safety, he said. Federal inspectors sometimes went to weigh stations and carried out surprise inspections when the trucks were weighed. Hammond contacted the federal agency and was elated to be invited to come and watch federal officials examine trucks at weigh stations. He expected to get action pictures.

He outlined his idea for the news director.

TO: News Director
FROM: Gary Hammond

RE: Story Outline: Survey: Speeding and Tailgating Trucks

Title: Why Trucks Speed and Tailgate
Scope: We will examine the reasons truck drivers speed and tailgate on the highways and will reveal that many of the trucks are in dangerous disrepair.
Need: We will be able to generate enough concern from enforcement agencies to actually take unsafe trunks off the roads, saving many lives.
Methods: This will be a two-pronged attack. We will conduct two at-random surveys. To show that trucks are speeding, we will station two reporters at each of two points 25 miles apart on the highways coming into Metro City. As a truck passes point A, a reporter will write a brief description and the exact time. Then the team 25 miles down the road will do the same for about two hours. That way, we can determine the exact speed and the number of speeders. We will have video to prove it. The other survey will be in cooperation with the federal safety inspectors. We will go with them at random and score how the trucks fare.
Sources: The most important source will be the results of our surveys. Other sources will be film clips of

```
truck accidents and files of investigations of truck
accidents from the federal transportation agency. We
will talk to truck drivers, confronting them at the
weigh stations if their trucks come out looking bad.
We will also attempt to talk to officials of the
trucking companies.
```

Presentation: I believe we will be able to put together a compilation of truck accidents for my voice-over
telling what we did. We should be able to get three
strong segments that will build on one another. The
first day will be the accidents and complaints, then
we prove trucks are speeding and then on the final day
we show the shabby condition of trucks.

Although the news director complained that it would take time and personnel to carry out, he recognized that there was little risk in making the commitment. They had on good authority that trucks were speeding and were unsafe. The timing along the highway was a great success. In that two-hour period, at three different highways, the count showed that every truck that made the trip was speeding.

In contrast, the reporters evaluated the trip to the weigh station as completely unsuccessful. They went out with the federal safety crews and stayed all day. All they got to show for it were pictures of a few dirty taillights and a loose rearview mirror. It was a sad showing for the reporters' premise, and it appeared that the idea of unsafe trucks would have to be dropped. Hammond called one of the trucker sources and told him that the situation was not as bad as he had thought. The man gave out a hearty laugh over the phone.

"Come on, now, you don't think that we would bring an (expletive deleted) truck into a weigh station with those guys there," he said. "Why, as soon as they go out in the morning, the word goes out about where they're going. We watch them and report it on the CB radio or call our friends on their cell phones. We say, 'there's smokies in the chicken coop.' Then we just bypass the weigh station. They sell maps in truck stops that show all the weigh stations and how to bypass them."

Hammond went out and checked for himself. In the area of a weigh station where the inspectors had set up for the day, he could see a line of trucks exiting the Interstate at the last interchange before the weigh station. He saw the trucks snake along an access road and then turn back onto the highway at the next interchange. The line of trucks could be viewed from an overpass, and Hammond got pictures. This was important for showing how the truckers were avoiding safety checks, but it did not illustrate the actual condition of the vehicles. One trucker told Hammond that the most vigilant police department when it came to truck safety enforcement was in a suburb nearby. Hammond tagged along with a police officer in that jurisdiction and got pictures of many violations.

The story was edited and ran for three nights as a segment on the news. Hammond dropped the idea of showing serious truck accidents. The footage they got of trucks speeding behind cars on rainswept roadways was much more relevant to the story, and the footage didn't blame the truckers for every accident that could be found.

While the investigative piece was running, Hammond got a call from a trucker who said the series was unfair, that it did not consider the fact that automobile drivers speed as much as truckers and possibly have cars in poorer repair. The caller added:

"Hey, you guys ought to be looking at those rental trucks on the road. Do you know, anybody can drive one of those. They don't even need a trucker license. You got an inexperienced person behind the wheel and the truck is in bad repair. I had to rent one once, and it had loose steering and soft brakes. I told the guys at the rental place when I took it back, and I hope they fixed it."

Hammond had to agree, and he followed up with a new idea. The reporters could rent these trucks and take them to an expert to be examined. The experts could be the beleaguered federal inspectors. The reporters would then return them to the truck rental office and report the poor condition of the trucks. They would have to use a hidden camera. They might have the camera across the street and try to carry out the transaction outside the building. Hammond worked in a state where it is illegal to tape a conversation without the permission of all persons in the conversation, but he could make silent videos from public property.

After they rented the trucks and they were in their possession, they drove them off private property and had them examined. After the examination, the clerk at the rental office was given a list of necessary repairs. The next step made the report a special one: One week later the reporters went back and rented the same trucks again and took them to the same expert who found the same problems. Not one of the trucks had been repaired. For the rebuttal, reporters went to the workplaces of the employees of the rental companies and confronted them with their findings. Not one employee would talk; they referred all questions to their supervisors.

The request for an interview arrived at corporate headquarters, and the reporters received a call from a corporate lawyer. The lawyer would not talk for attribution but agreed that the national safety director of the company would go on camera from his office if he received questions in advance. He would answer questions generally, the lawyer said, not about any particular incidents. Fairness was important to Hammond and the TV news department, so they— Hammond and a cameraman—agreed and showed up at the car rental office. The camera was rolling when the safety director—coming off as a rather pleasant fellow—answered a few questions about his job. Then Hammond told him about their survey and asked for his comments.

"Wait a minute. Stop right there. I don't remember our agreeing to that question," the lawyer said.

"Okay, I'll rephrase it," Hammond said. He tried again, but the lawyer stopped him.

"This is not getting us anywhere. You have broken our agreement, and you are going to have to give me the film you shot and leave this office."

The cameraman looked at Hammond for guidance. "Okay, you have a right not to answer the questions," Hammond said. "We were doing this so you could respond to the facts we are going to broadcast. We will use your refusal to talk about it, which we have on tape, and we are not going to give it to you."

"I'm afraid you have to," the lawyer said with a confident smirk. "You entered these premises with an oral contract. You broke that agreement. Those pictures then were shot on private property, which you entered illegally, retroactively. Please give them to me now so this does not become a police matter."

Does Hammond have to give up the pictures?

Yes: The interviewee has a lawyer, and the lawyer has warned the TV reporter that he is in violation of an agreement. The pictures were taken on private property and belong to the company. This is a small story and not worth going to jail.

No: Nobody is going to jail. A lawyer is not the law, he is merely serving his client with the best argument he can muster. The idea of a contract being retroactive is mumbo jumbo. The tape does not belong to the company just because it is on their property. Should Hammond turn over his wallet? That is on their company property, too. It is the lawyer who should go to jail if he took something that did not belong to him.

The story was broadcast; it included shots of the lawyer stopping the interview. Reaction again was good, and Hammond got the reputation of doing stories about big things with wheels. Soon after, Hammond read the auto mechanic series in the Kastleton paper that Roberta Carter had done and thought he might try such an investigation for TV.

Case Memorandum

- Investigative reporters will look for and confront the government agency that is supposed to regulate the for-profit area of business the reporter is researching.
- A reporter is more likely to get a story if the story is viewed from all aspects.
- TV reporters seek stories that have movement and conflict in addition to relevance.
- A reporter or editor attempts to detect early whether an investigation is on or off the mark.

Chapter Recap

The local, family-owned company that prides itself on its privacy can be held up to the light through public and private documents. At the other end of the spectrum, the giant corporation provides even more available documentation through the SEC, which we have shown in previous chapters to be at the fingertips of a reporter sitting at a computer terminal. We have seen that a survey works when examining for-profit services that have few documents. Other organizations can tempt a reporter, too—especially those with special rules, like schools and religion. In the next chapter, we will learn how to pursue their stories and about some special documents that can provide breakthroughs for investigators.

Class Assignments

1. The U.S. Small Business Administration directs its efforts to helping local businesses with few resources to survive in the midst of competition from the giant conglomerates with deep pockets. It lends funds to start-ups. One of the problems for the recipients of the loans is that they have to repay the government. Go to the listing of defaults on the SBA Web site (http://search.sba.gov/query.html) and find a loan that is in default in your local area. You will have a rare opportunity to research a private business. The SBA will have posted an audit of the business directed toward determining why it failed. You can expand on that information by finding lawsuits directed against the business or its owners. Possibly a bankruptcy filing can be found online. If so, that filing will list all

the pending litigation. Why did the business fail? If the business went belly-up, can blame be determined?

2. Another approach to the same kind of story is to get a list from the SBA Web site (http://search.sba.gov/query.html) of all small-business defaults for either your state or for companies in a particular business—such as restaurants—and cross-check them with the list of bankruptcies in order to learn what percentage has failed. The results would be similar, but you would have more timely stories because you would not have to wait for the SBA audit. After documents have been gathered, organized and interpreted, you will want to contact the principal owner for an interview. It may seem like a tough interview to undertake, but often the failed small-business operator has had no opportunity to be heard and is eager to tell the story of the business.

Notes

1. The case study on auto repair was modeled after a *Chicago Tribune* series published in 1976; the lead paragraph was borrowed from the series.

C h a p t e r   1 2

Special Topics and Tricks of the Trade

EVERY INVESTIGATIVE STORY IS AN ADVENTURE for the reporter and the reader or viewer. Who knows into what area of society the next investigation will delve? It could be the secrets of a church or the glamorous life of a riverboat pilot. The next investigation could be surprising even if the subject is as common as school lunches or speeding trucks. A reporter who is looking for an easy investigation will learn that there is no such thing in journalism. Every subject will present new challenges and will call for new tactics. Journalists in this chapter show they can rise to the occasion.

Religion

It started with a routine mention in a court file—Cardinal Bernard Law acknowledged having been warned that the Rev. John J. Geoghan had molested children before he assigned Geoghan to a position in a Massachusetts parish. Reporters and editors at the *Boston Globe* wanted to know whether other such cases existed in the Boston Archdiocese. But the court case files had been sealed. The *Globe* went to court to get them opened and, meanwhile, used other investigative tools to chip away at the story.

Using a computer database that included a directory of priests, the *Globe* reporters dug out other court cases and hit the pavement looking for interviews with victims of sexual abuse by the clergy. They were able to write: "Since the mid-nineties, more than 130 people have come forward with horrific childhood tales. . . ." It was not the end of the story, it was merely the end of the beginning. The *Globe* ran two parts to the story and asked others to contact the paper if they had similar experiences.[1]

After more than a year of newspaper stories, the court files were opened and the widespread abuse of children was revealed. Cardinal Law resigned, and a new state law was passed that requires the clergy to report sexual abuse.

The *Globe* won another Pulitzer Prize and also the Selden Ring Award, which is of great importance to investigative journalism because investigative reporting is its only category, it has only one winner and it pays the handsome sum of $35,000.

Another product of the *Boston Globe* stories was that other journalists pursued the question of abuse by the clergy in their own circulation areas. Those who did found they had to battle in court to get the files.

One battle occurred in Maine, where local reporters also had to file objections to get sealed court records. The appeals court in Maine ruled in favor of opening the files, finding that the public's need to know outweighed the privacy of the priests.

Blethen Maine Newspapers, Inc., owner of several Maine newspapers, requested Maine's attorney general to disclose investigative records related to allegations of sexual abuse by 18 deceased Roman Catholic priests.[2] The attorney general ultimately denied the request because he concluded that disclosure of the investigative records relating to the deceased priests would "constitute an unwarranted invasion of personal privacy." Blethen sought judicial review of the attorney general's decision, and the Superior Court vacated the attorney general's denial of the request and ordered full disclosure of the records. The showdown was in the Maine Supreme Court:

> "We affirm the court's judgment to the extent that it ordered the disclosure of the records, but conclude that the court should have also ordered the records redacted so as to eliminate the names and other identifying information of the living persons who are cited in the records. We therefore vacate the judgment and remand for further proceedings so that the records will be subject to redaction before their disclosure."

The court concluded that the privacy interests of the alleged victims and witnesses and the residual privacy interests of the deceased priests, if any, were exceeded by the public's interest in disclosure of the information because the information pertained to possible criminal activity and the extent to which those activities were investigated by public officials.

Religion is an area that is not licensed, and officers of the church are not required to file financial information for either the public or the IRS. It would seem that anyone could consecrate a garage and cause it to be qualified as a church, call oneself "the reverend" and escape taxation, but the IRS does not so readily agree. To qualify, a "church" has to have members and a regular schedule of gatherings. When churches expand into areas other than religious purposes, like owning radio stations, newspapers or retail stores, they are supposed to spin them off into for-profit corporations.

The *Chicago Tribune* was a finalist in the Pulitzer Prize selection in 1995 for a series of articles about the finances of Louis Farrakhan's Nation of Islam. It showed that Farrakhan had created a series of for-profit companies, including a restaurant, in association with the Nation of Islam. Although it was Farrakhan's public statements that made him a controversial figure, the *Tribune* series concentrated on the financial aspects of the religious institution. The *Tribune* report made an argument that it was wrong for a religious institution to own a for-profit business as it might own stock in a major corporation, and it questioned whether Farrakhan's family members were beneficiaries of the for-profits.

In reports about other religious groups, reporters have shown that people in religious organizations who are in control of the organization or its money may abuse the privilege of their responsibility through excessive personal spending. Other investigative stories have shown that some evangelists have been known to make inordinate claims about their ability to heal ailments.

Nepotism

Religion is only one of the subjects that investigative reporters must approach with new ideas and ingenuity because of the special rules that have been set up that will often protect them from public disclosure. An unlikely group, riverboat pilots, also fall outside the norm, but after some tenacity on the part of a couple of New Orleans reporters the veil of secrecy was parted.

Job selection for riverboat pilots on the Mississippi River was a family secret until Keith Darce and Jeff Meitrodt chased the story and told the readers of the *New Orleans Times-Picayune* all about it. In a four-part series of articles staring November 4, 2001, the reporters told how a group of white, politically connected families maintained a hold on riverboat pilot jobs that paid $300,000 a year to start.

The reporters needed to get copies of the job applications for the pilots to prove allegations of nepotism, in other words, the hiring of relatives. That is where the unusual government structure came into play. The applications were public record but were maintained by the pilots' regulatory board, a quasi-government panel of the pilots themselves. The pilots

were virtually unregulated by the state. They policed and punished themselves and investigated their own accidents. Access to their records
required a FOIA request, but the reporters knew that the FOIA letter
would have to be perfect to make sure the pilots had to respond with the
records.

"There is no wiggle room in an FOIA request," Darce said. "It should
be crafted after careful research." Figure 12.1 shows the letter they sent:

Figure 12.1 Freedom of Information Act request letter, river port pilot review board

July 25, 2001

Board of River Port Pilot Review for the Port of New Orleans
8712 Highway 23
Belle Chasse, LA 70037
By fax: 392-7598

Re: Request for Public Records

To Whom It May Concern:

In accordance the Louisiana Public Records Act, Louisiana Revised Statute
section 44:1, *et seq.*, I request copies of the following records:

1. All rules and regulations regarding pilot misconduct.
2. Records of all fines and reprimands against any River Port pilot, and/or
   member of the Crescent City River Port Pilots Association.
3. Accident reports for each River Port pilot, which under state law are to be
   permanent and detailed and kept for each pilot "for as long as the pilot is
   piloting."
4. All annual reports on accident investigations, which under state law are to be
   filed with the Louisiana Department of Transportation and Development on or
   before Feb. 28 of each year.

The Public Records Act requires that public records be provided for
inspection within, at most, three business days. If any of these requested records
do not exist or will not be provided, you must notify me within, at most, three
business days regarding the reason(s) for the delay or refusal.

I look forward to hearing from you soon.

Sincerely yours,

Jeffrey Meitrodt
Special Projects Editor
The Times-Picayune
Phone: 504-826-3497. Fax: 504-826-3007

Source: Jeffrey Mietrodt, Freedom of Information Act request

The reporters found that of 100 applicants selected to become pilots,
85 were related to another working pilot, and the others were relatives of
state legislators or lobbyists.

They also learned of campaign contribution tactics in which hundreds of thousands of dollars were contributed to elected officials, making the pilots one of the most politically powerful groups in the state.

Labor

The federal and state departments of labor keep on file public documents that are not too often touched by investigative reporters. The U.S. Department of Labor is empowered to monitor and investigate the operations of labor unions, and the unions have to file financial reports that are available for public viewing. The state departments of labor handle unemployment compensation and workers' compensation claims. One document, the LM-30, filed with the U.S. Department of Labor, shows the finances of each local union and the names and salaries of union officials. The salaries seem low until it is discovered that the officers hold positions in more than one local—perhaps in four or five—and their compensation is inordinate. Every officer and employee of a labor organization must file an LM-30 to document economic interests. Workers' compensation and unemployment compensation claims are usually argued in local courts.

Labor is one area where the two sides—labor and management— square off, and investigative reporters will find they are caught in the middle. If there is a story about persons cheating on benefits, labor will accuse the newspaper of taking business's side, and if it is a story about horrendous conditions in migrant labor camps, which are inspected by the labor departments, advertisers will grumble that the newspaper is too liberal in its causes. Reporters often joke that they've done their job if both sides are displeased.

The U.S. Department of Labor also includes the Occupational Safety and Health Administration (OSHA), which is alert to problems in the workplace. OSHA has investigated such major problems as egregious violations involving respiratory protection and injury-and-illness recordkeeping, protection from cotton dust and setting standards for asbestos. The OSHA Web site provides complete reports from OSHA inspections, and although the site is huge and not easy to navigate, a reporter will probably find it worth the time to look up local industries.

Money

Banking, investments and business in general is a beat that encounters federal and state regulation almost every day, but readers of *The Toledo Blade* found that investments in rare coins are virtually unregulated. Reporters for the *Blade,* a publication known for its strong, prize-winning investigative contributions to the community, learned in 2006 that, since 1998, the state government of Ohio had been investing millions of dollars in rare coins— nickels, dimes and pennies. One coin dealer's firm made more than $1 million off the deal in one year, the paper reported.

The agreement to invest the money in rare coins is rare itself. Reporter Mike Wilkenson could find no other instance of a state government investing in a rare coin fund. Wilkenson reported that the Ohio Bureau of Workers' Compensation continued to be the sole government investor in the coin funds despite strong concerns raised by an auditor with the bureau about possible conflicts of interest and whether the state's millions were adequately protected. The state then auctioned off the coins and promised not to do it again.

Schools

Schools present a large challenge to reporters. Student records are private, even those embarrassing grades on final exams. Also, the world of academia is fraught with jargon. If a reporter sees a college professor's curriculum vitae, what would that mean? It really means the professional history of that professor. Students know what a syllabus is, but do all of the readers of a newspaper? And what is this strange thing called a symposium?

Schools come in many structures: Some are governmental operations such as the military academies, others—most major universities—are tax-supported schools with local control. Others are private and not-for-profit, which means they have to file the form 990 annual financial report with the IRS. Some schools are for-profit; these are usually trade schools or correspondence schools. Such schools may get funding from the state or federal departments of education for projects and, thus, have to report their expenditures to those government agencies—but only for the expenses growing out of the government funding.

Like a government or a business, school districts have been known to misspend money that should have gone toward direct education. The head of a federal program for disadvantaged children in the Chicago schools spent money from the program for elaborate dinner parties for his family and friends, and members of a Chicago suburban school district funded family trips to Disneyland with school money. In addition to checking the vouchers, a reporter could survey the school expenditures and compare the percentage of dollars spent on instruction with the percentage spent on noneducational expenses on a cost-per-pupil basis.

Also, schools often transport students by bus and either own buses or contract with a bus company. Schools have to provide lunch and security. They have to clean and repair buildings. Will there be enough money for education? How about the food? No one cares much for institutional food, and a child is likely to discard a lunch and lose all the nutrients that the schools claim the students are eating at lunch.

Case Study

School Food: The Lowest Bid*

The beat reporter for education, Joyce Vale, was asked by her editors to report on the quality of food being served in the St. Dyer city schools. The idea seemed out of line. This was not an education issue, but more of a food story, she argued. Something for the food editor? But she did not protest too loudly because she would not have liked someone coming into her beat and disturbing her contacts.

Although she admitted that many of the school programs she had written about over the years never really worked out too well, she believed the educators had good ideas and could not be put down for trying. But she thought writing about the school lunch was a silly idea. If she were to write about the quality of school food, the newspaper's photographers no doubt would want to take a picture of her sitting in a fifth-grader's undersized seat, eating some bland baloney sandwich, she feared.

The editor told her they had heard complaints about the quality of the food, which was pre-plated and shipped in from a factory, and the editors believed it would be ideal for an investigation on her beat. A survey is needed, the editor said. The schools would have to be asked to let the reporters examine the food and take it to an outside laboratory for testing.

When Vale contacted the school principals about this project, they told her they did not care for outsiders coming into their schools. One principal stated frankly: "I don't want to do this, but if I don't, people will say we are covering up something." When Vale contacted school personnel about the food, she found little interest on the

*The cases are based on real investigative stories, but the names and places have been changed to protect reporters, their sources and the secrets they have. Some are actual stories told in a step-by-step reconstruction and others are composites.

part of professionals. The teachers agreed that lunch was important, but they did not place it in the highest priority.

The lunch program in St. Dyer was let out for bids to companies that produced the frozen meals, and the food had to meet the nutrition requirements of the U.S. Department of Agriculture school food program. The winning bid therefore always ended up being the cheapest food in the smallest quantity that met the minimal requirements of nutrition. Vale was irritated by the idea that so little concern was given the children's meals that the contract would go to the lowest bidder. She then recognized the irony that, although the schools were taking the lowest bids on school food, her own newspaper had just recently rapped the mayor for not taking the lowest bid on pothole filling.

Is this inconsistent reporting?

Yes: How can we believe a reporter who writes that it is wrong to not accept the lowest bid when the reporter's newspaper supports the opposite idea? Such behavior shows that journalists will take whatever stance is necessary to get a good story. This time the hypocrisy is exposed.

No: Every investigative story stands separately and is reported according to the facts surrounding it. It is obvious that accepting the lowest bid is right in some circumstances and wrong in others.

Vale decided that she should visit a school at lunchtime to see how the pre-plated system worked. When she arrived at the school lunchroom, it seemed different from when she had been in school. She remembered hot food being dished out by a nice lady and the clatter of plates and cups and eating utensils. But now she saw children eating out of foil dishes and using a "spork"—a pitifully small, flimsy, plastic combination spoon and fork.

"You will have to get with the 21st century, Joyce. This is the way every school does it," a former teacher told her. "Just get ready to taste the stuff."

Every child got the same food and the same amount of food, whether that child was a tiny first-grader or a hulking athlete about to enter middle school. The portion of ground meat was without flavor of any kind. On the daily list of meals, this same meat showed up as a burger, Salisbury steak, meat balls and sloppy joes. A smattering of whipped potato tasted surprisingly like library paste, and the vegetable was so laden with artificial coloring that it looked like a plastic ornament. The children ate very little and dumped the tray and its uneaten contents into waste buckets at the doorway. "Why set standards for food if it is so tasteless it will not be eaten," Vale thought. Her story was what the children ate, not what they were served.

Vale told her editors that the newspaper should take the food to a commercial lab and have it tested in the tray as it was served to each child; they could figure how much they consumed by averaging the amount of food discarded. A technician at a lab said it could be done at a reasonable cost. By taking one of the waste containers, scraping off all the food and counting the number of trays, they could find the average nutrients rejected per child.

The lab would put the food from the waste container into a giant food mixer, and spin it until it was emulsified and looked like a thick, brown milk shake. The lab would then analyze the mixture for nutrients and subtract that from the analysis of the original meals as served. The report from the lab could read like a cereal box, listing all the vitamins and other chemical ingredients. If the exercise was carried out in several school districts, it would show the amount of waste, and it would show which company had the most acceptable food.

The editors became excited about the prospects of such a story because it would be more than opinion; it would actually be documented.

The managing editor always took great pride in selecting pictures. The paper had limited space, and each picture needed to be an attention getter and carry a message. His solution was to have all the pictures sent to him in his electronic message file, and then he would spin them across his computer screen at such a rate of speed that he would merely get a glimpse of each. If one caught his eye, he would choose it as a finalist on the basis of his belief that, if it stood out to him, it would stand out to the reader, too.

With the hope of satisfying the managing editor, the metropolitan editor always pushed the reporters to think about the pictures for every story. This led to a problem with the story about school food. The schools would not let the newspaper take pictures of children in the school. The editors wanted pictures of children throwing away meals, preferably with disgusted looks on their faces, and they would accept no less. When told they could not get such pictures, the story was not canceled, but Vale could sense it shrinking in importance and being reduced to a cute feature in the back of the paper among the grocery ads.

She then had a new idea. They could invite a group of children to lunch in surroundings that looked like a school, but it would be in a place the newspaper rented for the occasion. The students would receive the same meals, and the newspaper photographer would be able to get good shots of their facial expressions.

Would Vale's work-around be okay?

Yes: This is not a situation of faking a shot. The situation will not be misrepresented because Vale will not write that these are the children we tested. The kids will love it. It is an innocent picture and not such a crucial story. No one has been getting sick; it is only a taste test. Readers will understand that it doesn't matter. We do that all the time. We faked a shot at the beach on an unseasonably warm day and asked some people to go in the water and splash around a bit. After all, no question needs to be resolved here. We know the kids hate the food and are throwing it away, so no matter what expression they show, it will not be an exaggeration.

No: You are right about one thing. The kids will love it and make all kinds of ugly faces. It's not fair to the food providers. It is a faked shot of the worst kind. By the way, there is also no excuse for the picture at the beach. The story about school food is an investigation into which we put much thought. If we fake a shot, people will remember that we faked it and forget what the story revealed. You can be sure we will get caught. The school officials will know, and they will yell loud and long.

Vale gave her idea a full 10 seconds of study and then discarded it. The newspaper printed color pictures of the meals and ranked the meals. For the first time, people started showing some interest in what the schoolchildren were served, and several poorly rated schools changed providers or changed the system of bidding.

Back-Pocket Documents

So many public documents are available that reporters never get a chance to use them all during a lifelong career. Some commonly used documents are mentioned throughout this textbook, but others are kept in reporters' back pockets. Each investigative reporter has favorite back-pocket documents. This fondness may have come about because a certain document rose to the occasion and saved a story for the reporter.

Postal Service Records

One example of a back-pocket document is described in a section of the U.S. postal regulations. This section makes into a public record the names of all persons with access to a particular post office box used in commerce; also public record are the names of persons with bulk mailing accounts. This section of the law is little known, and it has peeled back the layers of many a closely guarded secret.

All a reporter has to do is give the box number to the postmaster. The postmaster is instructed by the postal code to supply the names and addresses of every person or company that rented that box. Such information is provided by the applicant every time someone applies for a box number. If the box number was ever advertised as a place to send money, it is considered as having been used in commerce. This same information is also available for bulk mailing accounts (bulk mail refers to that number on a printed mailer that is placed where a stamp would go otherwise).

The box number is handy for exposing mail-order hoaxes, and the bulk-mailing records can expose mailers of anonymous political literature and not-so-charitable charities. The code states:

"Post office box holder information, from Form 1093, Application for Post Office Box or Caller Number, will be provided only as follows: (i) Business use—The recorded name, address, and telephone number of the holder of a post office box being used for the purpose of doing or soliciting business with the public, and any person applying for a box in behalf of a holder, will be furnished to any person without charge. The postmaster may furnish this information from Form 1093 when he is satisfied from the entries appearing on it, or from evidence furnished by the requester (such as an advertising circular), that the box is being used for such a business purpose. When the postmaster is unable to determine whether a business use is involved, he shall refer the request to Chief Field Counsel for advice.

"The post office also will disclose the names and addresses of customers. Upon request, the addresses of specifically identified postal customers will be made available only as follows:

"(1) Change of address. The new address of any specific customer who has filed a permanent or temporary change of address order by submitting PS Form 3575, (a hand-written order, or an electronically communicated order) will be furnished to any person upon payment of the Fee. . . . Disclosure will be limited to the address of the specifically identified individual about. . . . The Postal Service reserves the right not to disclose the address of an individual for the protection of the individual's personal safety.

"(2) Name and address of permit holder. The name and address of the holder of a particular bulk mail permit, permit imprint or similar permit, or postage meter permit, and the name of any person applying for a permit in behalf of a holder, will be furnished to any person upon the payment of any fees."

UCC Filings

A Uniform Commercial Code (UCC) document may be a favorite of an investigative reporter, and it is not only for use on special occasions. A UCC filing is made by a person who has an interest in the property in another's possession. It might be an expensive copy machine or some factory machinery that is being bought in installments and, just as a bank needs to declare its ownership in real estate, the seller of other property that is being purchased in installments wants its claim of the unpaid amount in the legal records. The UCC filing applies only to moveable property, not real estate, and although the property is defined as moveable, motor vehicle liens are not included because they are handled by state motor vehicle licensing agencies.

UCC filings sometimes can reveal wrongdoing. UCC filings can show whether a judge has an interest in a business that makes parking meters, an alderman has a printing business that gets government contracts, and a minister outfits his office with luxurious furnishings. Reporters can pick up on such stories if they see there is an unpaid amount on certain equipment and a public official is named in the UCC filing. Expensive medical equipment may be leased by a hospital, and the UCC filing might reveal the owners are a group of doctors who are referring patients for tests using the equipment.

Reporters who are familiar with the system will check regularly for UCC filings, whether online or in the state office building, and a reporter working on an investigation should search these files to learn more about the subject of any investigation.

The document displayed here (see Figure 12.2) shows how limited the information in a UCC filing might be, and yet it could provide the first hint of wrongdoing. States keep UCC filings as public records, and state laws guarantee public access. The name, Uniform Commercial Code, is derived from the fact that, although the states control the filings and the release of the information, the forms are uniform everywhere in the United States.

You can see that Asphalt Joe, a business entity owned by Joseph J. Jones, has a lien on property owned by Robert Burge, who we know is the mayor. It might seem absurd that the form shows Burge's address as city hall, but such mistakes have been made. Few people realize when they file the forms that a reporter might look at them. When Betty Maltese, then the mayor of Cicero, Illinois, had city workers doing work on her private properties, their addresses on building reports were stated to be city hall. In Asphalt Joe's filing, the information is sparser than that, but we know from the minutes of the city council meetings that Asphalt Joe has no-bid contracts with the city. It may be that Joe has been given the equipment or been allowed to borrow the money for purchase of the equipment, but Joe has kept a lien on it. The bottom line is that Joe and the mayor are doing business together—a business that has a connection to pothole filling—and the reporter is on to something.

For an example of how to access the UCC filings, we looked at the system in California, where the secretary of state's office maintains for public inspection a searchable index for all UCC records. The index provides for the retrieval of a record by the name of the debtor and by the file number of the initial financing statement and each filed UCC record relating to the initial financing statement.

Figure 12.2 Sample Uniform Commercial Code (UCC) financing statement

UCC FINANCING STATEMENT
FOLLOW INSTRUCTIONS (front and back) CAREFULLY

A. NAME & PHONE OF CONTACT AT FILER [optional]

B. SEND ACKNOWLEDGMENT TO: (Name and Address)

Asphalt Joe
Joseph J. Jones
1771 Buchanan Way
Buchan EW 4632

THE ABOVE SPACE IS FOR FILING OFFICE USE ONLY

1. DEBTOR'S EXACT FULL LEGAL NAME - insert only one debtor name (1a or 1b) - do not abbreviate or combine names

1a. ORGANIZATION'S NAME

OR

1b. INDIVIDUAL'S LAST NAME	FIRST NAME	MIDDLE NAME	SUFFIX
Burge	**Robert**	**Charles**	

1c. MAILING ADDRESS	CITY	STATE	POSTAL CODE	COUNTRY
City Hall	**Buchanan**	**EV**	**4435**	**USA**

1d. SEE INSTRUCTIONS	ADD'L INFO RE ORGANIZATION DEBTOR	1e. TYPE OF ORGANIZATION **construction**	1f. JURISDICTION OF ORGANIZATION	1g. ORGANIZATIONAL ID #, if any ☐ NONE

2. ADDITIONAL DEBTOR'S EXACT FULL LEGAL NAME - insert only one debtor name (2a or 2b) - do not abbreviate or combine names

2a. ORGANIZATION'S NAME

OR

2b. INDIVIDUAL'S LAST NAME	FIRST NAME	MIDDLE NAME	SUFFIX

2c. MAILING ADDRESS	CITY	STATE	POSTAL CODE	COUNTRY

2d. SEE INSTRUCTIONS	ADD'L INFO RE ORGANIZATION DEBTOR	2e. TYPE OF ORGANIZATION	2f. JURISDICTION OF ORGANIZATION	2g. ORGANIZATIONAL ID #, if any ☐ NONE

3. SECURED PARTY'S NAME (or NAME of TOTAL ASSIGNEE of ASSIGNOR S/P) - insert only one secured party name (3a or 3b)

3a. ORGANIZATION'S NAME
Asphalt Joe

OR

3b. INDIVIDUAL'S LAST NAME	FIRST NAME	MIDDLE NAME	SUFFIX
Jones	**Joseph**	**John**	

3c. MAILING ADDRESS	CITY	STATE	POSTAL CODE	COUNTRY
1771 Buchanan Way	**Buchanan**	**EV**	**4632**	**USA**

4. This FINANCING STATEMENT covers the following collateral:

Heavy equipment for pothole repair
1. Deep dipper
3. transport tankers
1 #24 Heavy scoop
5 Filament prongs
1. Convexion extruder
17 tons of unbleached seditive

5. ALTERNATIVE DESIGNATION [if applicable]:	LESSEE/LESSOR	CONSIGNEE/CONSIGNOR	BAILEE/BAILOR	SELLER/BUYER	AG. LIEN	NON-UCC FILING

6. This FINANCING STATEMENT is to be filed [for record] (or recorded) in the REAL ESTATE RECORDS. Attach Addendum [if applicable] | 7. Check to REQUEST SEARCH REPORT(S) on Debtor(s) [ADDITIONAL FEE] [optional] | All Debtors | Debtor 1 | Debtor 2

8. OPTIONAL FILER REFERENCE DATA

FILING OFFICE COPY — UCC FINANCING STATEMENT (FORM UCC1) (REV. 05/22/02)   International Association of Commercial Administrators (IACA)

Search requests in California need to supply the name of a debtor to be searched, in the exact form as it appears on the document. Requests must specify whether the debtor is an individual or an organization. A search request always includes the name and address of the person to whom the search report is to be sent.

Lobbyists

A third back-pocket document is the report of a lobbyist. When legislative bodies gather to design a law, they are supposed to be responsive to the needs of the people the members represent.

Some citizens are more active in presenting their views than others. They may go to the state capitol and wait in the lobby outside the legislative meeting place, hoping to approach a legislator during a recess and talk up their personal argument for or against a law. The fact that these people gathered in the lobby led to them being called lobbyists.

Businesspeople, farmers, union workers, teachers, industrialists and others are not able to take time away from their jobs to hang around the halls of the state capitol, so they hire somebody—an expert—to make the contacts on their behalf with the lawmakers.

Being a lobbyist has a bad connotation, but in reality the lobbyist today merely represents a part of society that wants to be heard. That is, lobbyists doing their everyday work are not usually of interest to an investigative reporter. If things get out of hand, however, and a lobbyist wines and dines the legislators or showers legislators with gifts, an investigative reporter would be very interested.

Lobbyists have to file disclosure statements that show whom among public officials they have contacted and what favors they have done for them. The reporter will try to learn the other end of the quid pro quo. What did the official do in return? Sen. Robert Packwood of Oregon wrote in his diary that he led a very lonely life and that lobbyists were his only friends. The Senate ethics committee brought a complaint in 1995 that Packwood had "solicited financial support for his wife from persons with an interest in legislation in exchange, gratitude, or recognition for his official acts." Among the charges was that Packwood squeezed the arms of a lobbyist and leaned over and kissed her on the mouth in his Senate office. Packwood resigned before hearings were held.

Lobbyists must report contacts with lawmakers. They must file forms with the Office of the Clerk of the U.S. House of Representatives and with the Secretary of the Senate. The equivalent forms on the state level are usually placed with the state secretary of state.

How Not to Do It

Chip Shotten's best source, the ambitious county commission member, was on the phone.

"I'm not going to tell you who this is but you will recognize my voice."

"Wuzz up?"

"It's about Joe Staunch, the school board president. The state pulled his real estate broker license for gross infractions of the law. But here's the good part. He's been carrying on a romantic affair with one of the lady school principals, a widow. He's been seen coming out of her place every afternoon. That's all I can tell you. You're on your own."

Shotten invested some time by positioning himself across the street from the principal's home the next afternoon and saw a man coming out of the door and was able to get a picture. He also noticed a woman sitting on the porch of a house across the street who was watching him and the principal's house. He asked her whether she knew the man whom they both had seen come out of the house.

"I don't know who that is, but there have been some funny goings on over there," she said.

"Like what?" Shotten asked.

"People coming and going. That kind of thing," she said.

Shotten got a picture of Staunch the next day and took it to the woman across the street.

"That's him!" she said.

Shotten knew he had the right man now, but he needed more confirmation. "Who else would have seen him?" he asked.

"Mrs. Rankle next door. She's has been keeping an eye on the neighborhood."

Shotten talked to Rankle and got her to identify the picture of Staunch as the person she had seen come from the house.

Staunch was a part-time board president and a full-time real estate broker. Shotten stopped in at Bond Street Realty, a bitter competitor of Staunch Real Estate. He asked the broker, "Do you know whether Staunch had his license revoked?"

"That's what I hear," the broker said.

"Oh, really? Why?"

"I heard it was for embezzlement of a client's funds. Very serious!"

Shotten wrote an FOIA request and mailed it to the statehouse, demanding information about Staunch's real estate license. Shotten had a copy clerk at the competing newspaper on a cash retainer to spy on the competitor's newsroom. The clerk told him that Lori Benton was also onto the story.

Shotten panicked. He did not have enough solid facts to go ahead with the story, and yet he would not let himself be scooped on it. He decided to call Staunch and close out with him. He got an agent in Staunch's office on the phone and asked for Staunch. The agent said Staunch was not in.

"You tell that sleazebag I'm going to do a number on him," Shotten said and slammed down the phone.

He found an assistant to the deputy day editor and told him that it was an emergency. He said he had two positive identifications of the regular visitor to the principal's house, and although the state had yet to reply to his FOIA, he had the real estate competitor and an anonymous source (the member of the county commission) confirming the loss of the real estate license.

"I'm not sure this is a big story for us," the assistant editor said.

"But, don't you see, this is like what Paula Jones sued President Clinton about. He was the governor, and she was a state employee. It was sexual harassment of a public employee."

"What's that got to do about his real estate license?" the low-level editor asked.

"It's a morals profile. We've got a guy running the school board who is a criminal and a philanderer."

"Did you talk to Staunch about it?"

"He wouldn't come to the phone," Shotten said.

"Okay, the top editors have gone on a sledding trip to Winnipeg, and I have to make the call. You can go ahead with the story if you are sure about it."

The story had no credence at all. The next day, the lawyers started calling, and they called all week. It was discovered that the man coming from the principal's home had been there doing repairs on her air conditioning system. The two neighbors had been wrong in their identification because Staunch had been there earlier in the week to pick up costumes for the school production of "The Merry Widow."

The principal did not have a lawyer, but she called in a sputtering rage and demanded that the newspaper run a prominent correction. "You don't want that," Shotten said. "That will only bring up the matter all over again," he told her.

"I want a big correction in tomorrow's paper," she demanded.

"Listen lady, how do we know it's not true? Maybe we got it wrong this time, but can you prove you didn't do such a thing ever?" he asked.

The real estate competitor said he got his information from the member of the county commission, and the commission member said he overheard it at the coffee shop. The agent in Staunch's office reported that Shotten had called Staunch a sleazebag.

Benton, meanwhile, had received the same tip as Shotten and immediately went online to the state licensing department and searched the list of actions. She found none against Staunch. Then she called the licensing department and asked them to check. They could find nothing. She then checked the index in the county clerk of the courts office for both criminal and civil lawsuits and found none. No FOIA letters were called for; the public's access to the information was provided by various state laws. Not at all interested in a possible relationship between Staunch and the school principal, Benton dropped her pursuit of the story.

Lawsuits from Staunch, the principal and the repairman are pending.

Should Shotten and his newspaper lose a libel suit?

Yes: Shotten wrote an incorrect story with malicious intent and a reckless disregard of the truth. He did not give the target of the investigation a fair chance to reply and made no effort to contact the principal. Then he refused to run a correction.

No: He was not wrong. The ladies in the neighborhood were wrong. He sincerely believed that Staunch was guilty of the allegations against him. Besides, Staunch is a public official, which means it is very difficult for him to win a libel verdict. Shotten fulfilled the obligation for a rebuttal when he called and gave Staunch a warning, telling him he was going to "do a number" on him, but Staunch did not call back.

Should the courts give a break to reporters writing about public officials?

Yes: The right of the public to know is in jeopardy every time a lawsuit is brought against the media. A strict court would have a chilling effect and would cause the media to not pursue investigations in the future. Specific court decisions favor journalists when they expose the conduct of public officials.

No: The story had nothing to do with Staunch's public office, which was only part-time. It was a blatant attack on a private citizen. Staunch's reputation as a private citizen was damaged. Shotten practiced bad journalism from the inception of the story and was poorly supervised by the editors.

Which of the following concepts of good investigative reporting did Shotten violate?

- If a tip does not pan out, throw it out.
- A supervising editor must be kept informed.

- The requirement for a confirmation cannot be satisfied by a remark of a person who has only a passing knowledge of the subject.
- Required steps cannot be skipped to rush a story because of pressure of competition.
- A full retraction of any information learned to be incorrect must be made immediately.
- Informants should not be paid for information about a competitor.
- Reporters do not make derogatory comments about a person they are researching.
- Every possible effort must be made to ensure that the subject of an investigation is provided an opportunity to reply to negative allegations in a story.
- Pictures of people must have positive identification, preferably by the subjects pictured.

The commonsense answer is that all the statements above were abused by Shotten.

Chapter Recap

In this final chapter, we have examined some of the many stories that investigative reporters have found in every area of American society. It is obvious that the field has few limits. Laws protect reporters and the public and enable reporters to serve the public. The media, in constant change, offers new ways to deliver the news and information that the public needs. In this textbook, we have jumped feet first into the vast world of documents—both paper and electronic—and have been able to organize that world and recognize the laws that govern it. We met real reporters who take pride in their work, and we followed fictitious characters who encounter real issues.

Anyone thinking about building a career as an investigative reporter needs to know a few secrets. One is that it is hard work; a second is that, although there is recognition, the work most often goes unappreciated; and the third secret—the most guarded secret of all—is that it can be immensely fulfilling.

Class Assignments

1. How would you vote if you were sitting on a jury for one of the lawsuits brought against Shotten?

2. The public schools have budgets and annual reports the same as municipalities. Locate a copy of each for a local school district; they can often be found on the Internet or by calling on the school superintendent's office. If that does not work, check whether the public library has a copy. Using the techniques studied earlier for working with a city budget: (1) determine whether the money was spent for what had been budgeted, (2) isolate and compare one or two simple functions like bus transportation costs per pupil or hours of training for teachers for at least three similar school districts, or (3) show the ratio of costs for direct classroom instruction in several local and similar school districts.

Notes

1. Matt Carroll, Sacha Pfeifer, Michael Rezendes, and Walter Robinson, "Church Allowed Abuse by Priest for Years," *Boston Globe,* January 6–7, 2002, www.boston.com/globe/spotlight/abuse/stories/010602_geoghan.htm.

2, Blethen Maine Newspapers, Inc. v. State of Maine, 2005 ME 56, A.2d (April 22, 2005), www.courts.state.me.us/opinions/supreme/index.html.

A p p e n d i x   1

Freedom of Information Act

The 1966 Freedom of Information Act (P.L. 89–487) requires executive branch agencies and independent commissions to make available to citizens, upon request, all documents and records—except those that fall into the following exempt categories:

- Secret national security or foreign policy information;
- Internal personnel practices;
- Information exempted by law;
- Trade secrets or other confidential commercial or financial information;
- Interagency or intra-agency memos;
- Personal information, personnel or medical files;
- Law enforcement investigatory information;
- Information related to reports on financial institutions; and
- Geological and geophysical information.

Following passage of the FOIA, studies of its operation noted that major problems in obtaining information were bureaucratic delay, the cost of bringing suit to force disclosure and excessive charges levied by the agencies for finding and providing the requested information. Congress in 1974 amended the act to remove some of the obstacles to public access.

Chief among the provisions of the amendments were those allowing a federal judge to review a decision of the government to classify certain material. Another provision set deadlines for the agency to respond to a request for information under the law. Another amendment permitted judges to order payment of attorneys' fees and court costs for plaintiffs who won suits brought for information under the act.

As amended in 1974, the act:

- Required federal agencies to publish their indexes of final opinions on settlements of internal cases, policy statements and administrative staff manuals—or, if the indexes were not published, to furnish them on request to any person for the cost of duplication. The 1966 law simply required agencies to make such indexes available for public inspection and copying.
- Reworded a provision of the 1966 law to require agencies to release unlisted documents to someone requesting them with a reasonable description. This change was to ensure that an agency could not refuse to provide material simply because the applicant could not give its precise title.
- Directed each agency to publish a uniform set of fees for providing documents at the cost of finding and copying them; the amendment allowed waiver or reduction of those fees when in the public interest.
- Empowered federal district courts to order agencies to produce improperly withheld documents—and to examine the contested materials privately *(in camera)* to determine if they were properly exempted under one of the nine categories. This amendment removed the barrier to court review, which the Supreme Court had pointed out, giving courts the power to hold that a document had been improperly classified and therefore should be released. The government was required to prove that contested material was properly classified.
- Set time limits for agency responses to requests: ten working days for an initial request; twenty working days for an appeal from an initial refusal to produce documents; a possible ten working-day extension that could be granted only once in a single case.
- Set a thirty-day time limit for an agency response to a complaint filed in court under the act, provided that such cases should be given priority attention by the courts at the appeal, as well as at the trial, level.
- Allowed courts to order the government to pay attorneys' fees and court costs for persons winning suits against them under the act.
- Authorized a court to find an agency employee acted capriciously or arbitrarily in withholding information. Such a finding would set into action Civil Service Commission proceedings to determine the need for disciplinary action. If the commission found such a need, the relevant agency would

take the disciplinary action which the commission recommended.

- Amended the wording of the national defense and national security exemption to make clear that it applied only to properly classified information, clarifying congressional intent to allow review of the decision to stamp something "classified."
- Amended the wording of the law enforcement exemption to allow withholding only of information which, if disclosed, would interfere with enforcement proceedings, deprive someone of a fair trial or hearing, invade personal privacy in an unwarranted way, disclose the identity of a confidential source, disclose investigative techniques or endanger law enforcement personnel. Also protected from disclosure all information from a confidential source obtained by a criminal law enforcement agency or by an agency conducting a lawful national security investigation.
- Provided that segregable nonexempt portions of requested material be released after deletion of the exempt portions.
- Required an annual agency report to Congress including a list of all agency decisions to withhold information requested under the act, the reasons, the appeals, the results, all relevant rules, the fee schedule and the names of officials responsible for each denial of information.
- Required an annual report from the attorney general to Congress listing the number of cases arising under the act, the exemption involved in each case and the disposition, costs, fees and penalties of each case.

All agencies of the executive branch have issued regulations to implement the Freedom of Information Act, which may be found in the *Code of Federal Regulations* (consult the general index of the code under "Freedom of Information").

New electronic FOIA provisions. The passage of the Electronic Freedom of Information Act of 1996 amended the FOIA further by expanding coverage to government information stored electronically. In addition, the act specified that federal data should be placed in electronic form when possible. The 1996 act also set about to improve the public's access to government data by speeding up the time government agencies are allowed to take in responding to a request, and by requiring that indexes of government records be made available to the public.

FOIA and the Department of Homeland Security. The Homeland Security Act of 2002, which established the Department of Homeland Security (DHS), granted broad exemption to the FOIA in exchange for the cooperation of private companies in sharing information with the government regarding vulnerabilities in the nation's critical infrastructure. Subtitle B of the act (the Critical Infrastructure Information Act) exempted from the FOIA and other federal and state disclosure requirements any critical infrastructure information that is voluntarily submitted to a covered federal agency for use in the security of critical infrastructure and protected systems, analysis, warning, interdependency study, recovery, reconstitution or other informational purpose when accompanied by an express statement that such information is being submitted voluntarily in expectation of such nondisclosure protection. The Homeland Security Act required the secretary of DHS to establish specified procedures for the receipt, care and storage by federal agencies of such critical infrastructure information and to provide criminal penalties for the unauthorized disclosure of such information.

During the 2002 debate over the Homeland Security Act, many lawmakers voiced concern over the fact that the new law shielded companies from lawsuits to compel disclosure, criminalized otherwise legitimate whistleblower activity by DHS employees and preempted any state or local disclosure laws. On March 12, 2003, Sen. Patrick Leahy introduced the Restoration of Freedom of Information Act of 2003 (Restore FOIA). As proposed, Restore FOIA would

- Limit the FOIA exemption to relevant "records" submitted by the private sector, such that only those that actually pertain to critical infrastructure safety are protected.
- Allow for government oversight, including the ability to use and share the records within and between agencies.
- Allow local authorities to apply their own sunshine laws.
- Not provide civil immunity to companies that voluntarily submit information.
- Not restrict congressional use or disclosure of voluntarily submitted critical infrastructure information.

Legislative action was pending on the Restore FOIA proposal in the 108th Congress (2003–2005).

The following is the text of the Freedom of Information Act, as amended, as it appears in the U.S. Code, Title 5, Chapter 5, Subchapter II, section 552.

§ 552. Public information; agency rules, opinions, orders, records, and proceedings

(a) Each agency shall make available to the public information as follows:

   (1) Each agency shall separately state and currently publish in the *Federal Register* for the guidance of the public—

      (A) descriptions of its central and field organization and the established places at which, the employees (and in the case of a uniformed service, the members) from whom, and the methods whereby, the public may obtain information, make submittals or requests, or obtain decisions;

      (B) statements of the general course and method by which its functions are channeled and determined, including the nature and requirements of all formal and informal procedures available;

      (C) rules of procedure, descriptions of forms available or the places at which forms may be obtained, and instructions as to the scope and contents of all papers, reports, or examinations;

      (D) substantive rules of general applicability adopted as authorized by law, and statements of general policy or interpretations of general applicability formulated and adopted by the agency; and

      (E) each amendment, revision, or repeal of the foregoing.

   Except to the extent that a person has actual and timely notice of the terms thereof, a person may not in any manner be required to resort to, or be adversely affected by, a matter required to be published in the *Federal Register* and not so published. For the purpose of this paragraph, matter reasonably available to the class of persons affected thereby is deemed published in the *Federal Register,* when incorporated by reference therein with the approval of the director of the *Federal Register.*

   (2) Each agency, in accordance with published rules, shall make available for public inspection and copying—

      (A) final opinions, including concurring and dissenting opinions, as well as orders, made in the adjudication of cases;

      (B) those statements of policy and interpretations which have been adopted by the agency and are not published in the *Federal Register,*

(C) administrative staff manuals and instructions to staff that affect a member of the public;

(D) copies of all records, regardless of form or format, which have been released to any person under paragraph (3) and which, because of the nature of their subject matter, the agency determines have become or are likely to become the subject of subsequent requests for substantially the same records; and

(E) a general index of the records referred to under subparagraph (D); unless the materials are promptly published and copies offered for sale. **For records created on or after November 1, 1996, within one year after such date, each agency shall make such records available, including by computer telecommunications or, if computer telecommunications means have not been established by the agency, by other electronic means.** To the extent required to prevent a clearly unwarranted invasion of personal privacy, an agency may delete identifying details when it makes available or publishes an opinion, statement of policy, interpretation, **staff manual, instruction, or copies of records referred to in subparagraph (D).** However, in each case the justification for the deletion shall be explained fully in writing, **and the extent of such deletion shall be indicated on the portion of the record which is made available or published, unless including that indication would harm an interest protected by the exemption in subsection (b) under which the deletion is made. If technically feasible, the extent of the deletion shall be indicated at the place in the record where the deletion was made.** Each agency shall also maintain and make available for public inspection and copying current indexes providing identifying information for the public as to any matter issued, adopted, or promulgated after July 4, 1967, and required by this paragraph to be made available or published. Each agency shall promptly publish, quarterly or more frequently, and distribute (by sale or otherwise) copies of each index or supplements thereto unless it determines by order published in the **Federal Register** that the publication would be unnecessary and impracticable, in which case the agency shall nonetheless provide copies of such index on request at a cost not to exceed the direct cost of duplication. **Each agency shall make the index referred to in subparagraph (E) available by computer telecommunications by December 31, 1999.** A final order, opinion, statement of policy, interpretation, or staff manual or instruction that affects a member of the public may be relied on, used, or cited as precedent by an agency against a party other than an agency only if—

    (i) it has been indexed and either made available or published as provided by this paragraph; or

    (ii) the party has actual and timely notice of the terms thereof.

(3) (A) Except with respect to the records made available under paragraphs (1) and (2) of this subsection, each agency, upon any request for records which (i) reasonably describes such records and (ii) is made in accordance with published rules stating the time, place, fees (if any), and procedures to be followed, shall make the records promptly available to any person.

(B) **In making any record available to a person under this paragraph, an agency shall provide the record in any form or format requested by the person if the record is readily reproducible by the agency in that form or format. Each agency shall make reasonable efforts to maintain its records in forms or formats that are reproducible for purposes of this section.**

(C) **In responding under this paragraph to a request for records, an agency shall make reasonable efforts to search for the records in electronic form or format, except when such efforts would significantly interfere with the operation of the agency's automated information system.**

(D) **For purposes of this paragraph, the term "search" means to review, manually or by automated means, agency records for the purpose of locating those records which are responsive to a request.**

(E) An agency, or part of an agency, that is an element of the intelligence community (as that term is defined in section 3(4) of the National Security Act of 1947 (50 U.S.C. 401a(4))) shall not make any record available under this paragraph to—

    (i) any government entity, other than a State, territory, commonwealth, or district of the United States, or any subdivision thereof; or

    (ii) a representative of a government entity described in clause (i).

(4) (A) (i) In order to carry out the provisions of this section, each agency shall promulgate regulations, pursuant to notice and receipt of public comment, specifying the schedule of fees applicable to the processing of requests under this section and establishing procedures and guidelines for determining when such fees should be waived or reduced.

Such schedule shall conform to the guidelines which shall be promulgated, pursuant to notice and receipt of public comment, by the director of the Office of Management and Budget and which shall provide for a uniform schedule of fees for all agencies.

(ii) Such agency regulations shall provide that—

(I) fees shall be limited to reasonable standard charges for document search, duplication, and review, when records are requested for commercial use;

(II) fees shall be limited to reasonable standard charges for document duplication when records are not sought for commercial use and the request is made by an educational or noncommercial scientific institution, whose purpose is scholarly or scientific research; or a representative of the news media; and

(III) for any request not described in (I) or (II), fees shall be limited to reasonable standard charges for document search and duplication.

(iii) Documents shall be furnished without any charge or at a charge reduced below the fees established under clause (ii) if disclosure of the information is in the public interest because it is likely to contribute significantly to public understanding of the operations or activities of the government and is not primarily in the commercial interest of the requester.

(iv) Fee schedules shall provide for the recovery of only the direct costs of search, duplication, or review. Review costs shall include only the direct costs incurred during the initial examination of a document for the purposes of determining whether the documents must be disclosed under this section and for the purposes of withholding any portions exempt from disclosure under this section. Review costs may not include any costs incurred in resolving issues of law or policy that may be raised in the course of processing a request under this section. No fee may be charged by any agency under this section—

(I) if the costs of routine collection and processing of the fee are likely to equal or exceed the amount of the fee; or

(II) for any request described in clause (ii) (II) or (III) of this subparagraph for the first two hours of search time or for the first one hundred pages of duplication.

(v) No agency may require advance payment of any fee unless the requester has previously failed to pay fees in a timely fashion, or the agency has determined that the fee will exceed $250.

(vi) Nothing in this subparagraph shall supersede fees chargeable under a statute specifically providing for setting the level of fees for particular types of records.

(vii) In any action by a requester regarding the waiver of fees under this section, the court shall determine the matter de novo: *Provided,* That the court's review of the matter shall be limited to the record before the agency.

(B) On complaint, the district court of the United States in the district in which the complainant resides, or has his principal place of business, or in which the agency records are situated, or in the District of Columbia, has jurisdiction to enjoin the agency from withholding agency records and to order the production of any agency records improperly withheld from the complainant. In such a case the court shall determine the matter de novo, and may examine the contents of such agency records in camera to determine whether such records or any part thereof shall be withheld under any of the exemptions set forth in subsection (b) of this section, and the burden is on the agency to sustain its action. **In addition to any other matters to which a court accords substantial weight, a court shall accord substantial weight to an affidavit of an agency concerning the agency's determination as to technical feasibility under paragraph (2)(C) and subsection (b) and reproducibility under paragraph (3)(B).**

(C) Notwithstanding any other provision of law, the defendant shall serve an answer or otherwise plead to any complaint made under this subsection within thirty days after service upon the defendant of the pleading in which such complaint is made, unless the court otherwise directs for good cause shown.

[(D) Repealed. Pub. L. 98-620, title IV, Sec. 402(2), Nov. 8, 1984, 98 Stat. 3357.]

(E) The court may assess against the United States reasonable attorney fees and other litigation costs reasonably incurred in any case under this section in which the complainant has substantially prevailed.

(F) Whenever the court orders the production of any agency records improperly withheld from the complainant and assesses against the United States reasonable attorney fees and other litigation costs, and the court additionally issues a written finding that the circumstances surrounding the withholding raise questions whether agency personnel acted arbitrarily or capriciously with respect to the withholding, the Special Counsel shall promptly initiate a proceeding to determine whether disciplinary action is warranted against the officer or employee who was primarily responsible for the withholding. The Special Counsel, after investigation and consideration of the evidence submitted, shall submit his findings and recommendations to the administrative authority of the agency concerned and shall send copies of the findings and recommendations to the officer or employee or his representative. The administrative authority shall take the corrective action that the Special Counsel recommends.

(G) In the event of noncompliance with the order of the court, the district court may punish for contempt the responsible employee, and in the case of a uniformed service, the responsible member.

(5) Each agency having more than one member shall maintain and make available for public inspection a record of the final votes of each member in every agency proceeding.

(6) (A) Each agency, upon any request for records made under paragraph (1), (2), or (3) of this subsection, shall—

   (i) determine within twenty days (excepting Saturdays, Sundays, and legal public holidays) after the receipt of any such request whether to comply with such request and shall immediately notify the person making such request of such determination and the reasons therefor, and of the right of such person to appeal to the head of the agency any adverse determination; and

   (ii) make a determination with respect to any appeal within twenty days (excepting Saturdays, Sundays, and legal public holidays) after the receipt of such appeal. If on appeal the denial of the request for records is in whole or in part upheld, the agency shall notify the person making such request of the provisions for judicial review of that determination under paragraph (4) of this subsection.

(B) (i) **In unusual circumstances as specified in this subparagraph, the time limits prescribed in either clause (i) or clause (ii) of subparagraph (A) may be extended by written notice to the person making such request setting forth** the unusual circumstances for such extension and the date on which a determination is expected to be dispatched. No such notice shall specify a date that would result in an extension for more than ten working days, except as provided in clause (ii) of this subparagraph.

(ii) With respect to a request for which a written notice under clause (i) extends the time limits prescribed under clause (i) of subparagraph (A), the agency shall notify the person making the request if the request cannot be processed within the time limit specified in that clause and shall provide the person an opportunity to limit the scope of the request so that it may be processed within that time limit or an opportunity to arrange with the agency an alternative time frame for processing the request or a modified request. Refusal by the person to reasonably modify the request or arrange such an alternative time frame shall be considered as a factor in determining whether exceptional circumstances exist for purposes of subparagraph (C).

(iii) As used in this subparagraph, "unusual circumstances" means, but only to the extent reasonably necessary to the proper processing of the particular requests—

(I) the need to search for and collect the requested records from field facilities or other establishments that are separate from the office processing the request;

(II) the need to search for, collect, and appropriately examine a voluminous amount of separate and distinct records which are demanded in a single request; or

(III) the need for consultation, which shall be conducted with all practicable speed, with another agency having a substantial interest in the determination of the request or among two or more components of the agency having substantial subject-matter interest therein.

(iv) Each agency may promulgate regulations, pursuant to notice and receipt of public comment, providing for the aggregation of certain requests by the same requestor, or by a group of requestors acting in concert, if the agency reasonably believes that such requests actually constitute a single request, which would otherwise satisfy the unusual circumstances specified in this subparagraph, and the

> requests involve clearly related matters. Multiple requests involving unrelated matters shall not be aggregated.

(C) (i) Any person making a request to any agency for records under paragraph (1), (2), or (3) of this subsection shall be deemed to have exhausted his administrative remedies with respect to such request if the agency fails to comply with the applicable time limit provisions of this paragraph. If the government can show exceptional circumstances exist and that the agency is exercising due diligence in responding to the request, the court may retain jurisdiction and allow the agency additional time to complete its review of the records. Upon any determination by an agency to comply with a request for records, the records shall be made promptly available to such person making such request. Any notification of denial of any request for records under this subsection shall set forth the names and titles or positions of each person responsible for the denial of such request.

(ii) **For purposes of this subparagraph, the term "exceptional circumstances" does not include a delay that results from a predictable agency workload of requests under this section, unless the agency demonstrates reasonable progress in reducing its backlog of pending requests.**

(iii) **Refusal by a person to reasonably modify the scope of a request or arrange an alternative time frame for processing a request (or a modified request) under clause (ii) after being given an opportunity to do so by the agency to whom the person made the request shall be considered as a factor in determining whether exceptional circumstances exist for purposes of this subparagraph.**

(D) (i) **Each agency may promulgate regulations, pursuant to notice and receipt of public comment, providing for multitrack processing of requests for records based on the amount of work or time (or both) involved in processing requests.**

(ii) **Regulations under this subparagraph may provide a person making a request that does not qualify for the fastest multitrack processing an opportunity to limit the scope of the request in order to qualify for faster processing.**

(iii) **This subparagraph shall not be considered to affect the requirement under subparagraph (C) to exercise due diligence.**

(E) (i) Each agency shall promulgate regulations, pursuant to notice and receipt of public comment, providing for expedited processing of requests for records—

    (I) in cases in which the person requesting the records demonstrates a compelling need; and

    (II) in other cases determined by the agency.

(ii) Notwithstanding clause (i), regulations under this subparagraph must ensure—

    (I) that a determination of whether to provide expedited processing shall be made, and notice of the determination shall be provided to the person making the request, within ten days after the date of the request; and

    (II) expeditious consideration of administrative appeals of such determinations of whether to provide expedited processing.

(iii) An agency shall process as soon as practicable any request for records to which the agency has granted expedited processing under this subparagraph. Agency action to deny or affirm denial of a request for expedited processing pursuant to this subparagraph, and failure by an agency to respond in a timely manner to such a request shall be subject to judicial review under paragraph (4), except that the judicial review shall be based on the record before the agency at the time of the determination.

(iv) A district court of the United States shall not have jurisdiction to review an agency denial of expedited processing of a request for records after the agency has provided a complete response to the request.

(v) For purposes of this subparagraph, the term "compelling need" means—

    (I) that a failure to obtain requested records on an expedited basis under this paragraph could reasonably be expected to pose an imminent threat to the life or physical safety of an individual; or

    (II) with respect to a request made by a person primarily engaged in disseminating information, urgency to inform the public concerning actual or alleged federal government activity.

(vi) A demonstration of a compelling need by a person making a request for expedited processing shall be made by a

> **statement certified by such person to be true and correct to the best of such person's knowledge and belief.**
>
> **(F) In denying a request for records, in whole or in part, an agency shall make a reasonable effort to estimate the volume of any requested matter the provision of which is denied, and shall provide any such estimate to the person making the request, unless providing such estimate would harm an interest protected by the exemption in subsection (b) pursuant to which the denial is made.**

(b) This section does not apply to matters that are—

    (1)(A) specifically authorized under criteria established by an Executive order to be kept secret in the interest of national defense or foreign policy and (B) are in fact properly classified pursuant to such Executive order;

    (2) related solely to the internal personnel rules and practices of an agency;

    (3) specifically exempted from disclosure by statute (other than section 552b of this title), provided that such statute (A) requires that the matters be withheld from the public in such a manner as to leave no discretion on the issue, or (B) establishes particular criteria for withholding or refers to particular types of matters to be withheld;

    (4) trade secrets and commercial or financial information obtained from a person and privileged or confidential;

    (5) inter-agency or intra-agency memorandums or letters which would not be available by law to a party other than an agency in litigation with the agency;

    (6) personnel and medical files and similar files the disclosure of which would constitute a clearly unwarranted invasion of personal privacy;

    (7) records or information compiled for law enforcement purposes, but only to the extent that the production of such law enforcement records or information (A) could reasonably be expected to interfere with enforcement proceedings, (B) would deprive a person of a right to a fair trial or an impartial adjudication, (C) could reasonably be expected to constitute an unwarranted invasion of personal privacy, (D) could reasonably be expected to disclose the identity of a confidential source, including a State, local, or foreign agency or authority or any private institution which furnished information on a confidential basis, and, in the case of a record or information compiled by criminal law enforcement authority in the course of a

criminal investigation or by an agency conducting a lawful national security intelligence investigation, information furnished by a confidential source, (E) would disclose techniques and procedures for law enforcement investigations or prosecutions, or would disclose guidelines for law enforcement investigations or prosecutions if such disclosure could reasonably be expected to risk circumvention of the law, or (F) could reasonably be expected to endanger the life or physical safety of any individual;

(8) contained in or related to examination, operating, or condition reports prepared by, on behalf of, or for the use of an agency responsible for the regulation or supervision of financial institutions; or

(9) geological and geophysical information and data, including maps, concerning wells.

Any reasonably segregable portion of a record shall be provided to any person requesting such record after deletion of the portions which are exempt under this subsection. **The amount of information deleted shall be indicated on the released portion of the record, unless including that indication would harm an interest protected by the exemption in this subsection under which the deletion is made. If technically feasible, the amount of the information deleted shall be indicated at the place in the record where such deletion is made.**

(c) (1) Whenever a request is made which involves access to records described in subsection (b)(7)(A) and—

(A) the investigation or proceeding involves a possible violation of criminal law; and

(B) there is reason to believe that (i) the subject of the investigation or proceeding is not aware of its pendency, and (ii) disclosure of the existence of the records could reasonably be expected to interfere with enforcement proceedings, the agency may, during only such time as that circumstance continues, treat the records as not subject to the requirements of this section.

(2) Whenever informant records maintained by a criminal law enforcement agency under an informant's name or personal identifier are requested by a third party according to the informant's name or personal identifier, the agency may treat the records as not subject to the requirements of this section unless the informant's status as an informant has been officially confirmed.

(3) Whenever a request is made which involves access to records maintained by the Federal Bureau of Investigation pertaining to foreign

intelligence or counterintelligence, or international terrorism, and the existence of the records is classified information as provided in subsection (b)(1), the Bureau may, as long as the existence of the records remains classified information, treat the records as not subject to the requirements of this section.

(d) This section does not authorize withholding of information or limit the availability of records to the public, except as specifically stated in this section. This section is not authority to withhold information from Congress.

(e) (1) On or before February 1 of each year, each agency shall submit to the Attorney General of the United States a report which shall cover the preceding fiscal year and which shall include—
  (A) the number of determinations made by the agency not to comply with requests for records made to such agency under subsection (a) and the reasons for each such determination;
  (B) (i) the number of appeals made by persons under subsection (a)(6), the result of such appeals, and the reason for the action upon each appeal that results in a denial of information; and
      (ii) a complete list of all statutes that the agency relies upon to authorize the agency to withhold information under subsection (b)(3), a description of whether a court has upheld the decision of the agency to withhold information under each such statute, and a concise description of the scope of any information withheld;
  (C) the number of requests for records pending before the agency as of September 30 of the preceding year, and the median number of days that such requests had been pending before the agency as of that date;
  (D) the number of requests for records received by the agency and the number of requests which the agency processed;
  (E) the median number of days taken by the agency to process different types of requests;
  (F) the total amount of fees collected by the agency for processing requests; and
  (G) the number of full-time staff of the agency devoted to processing requests for records under this section, and the total amount expended by the agency for processing such requests.
  (2) Each agency shall make each such report available to the public including by computer telecommunications, or if computer

telecommunications means have not been established by the agency, by other electronic means.

(3) The Attorney General of the United States shall make each report which has been made available by electronic means available at a single electronic access point. The Attorney General of the United States shall notify the Chairman and ranking minority member of the Committee on Government Reform and Oversight of the House of Representatives and the Chairman and ranking minority member of the Committees on Governmental Affairs and the Judiciary of the Senate, no later than April 1 of the year in which each such report is issued, that such reports are available by electronic means.

(4) The Attorney General of the United States, in consultation with the director of the Office of Management and Budget, shall develop reporting and performance guidelines in connection with reports required by this subsection by October 1, 1997, and may establish additional requirements for such reports as the Attorney General determines may be useful.

(5) The Attorney General of the United States shall submit an annual report on or before April 1 of each calendar year which shall include for the prior calendar year a listing of the number of cases arising under this section, the exemption involved in each case, the disposition of such case, and the cost, fees, and penalties assessed under subparagraphs (E), (F), and (G) of subsection (a)(4). Such report shall also include a description of the efforts undertaken by the Department of Justice to encourage agency compliance with this section.

(f) For purposes of this section, the term—

(1) "agency" as defined in section 551(1) of this title includes any executive department, military department, government corporation, government controlled corporation, or other establishment in the executive branch of the government (including the Executive Office of the President), or any independent regulatory agency; and

(2) "record" and any other term used in this section in reference to information includes any information that would be an agency record subject to the requirements of this section when maintained by an agency in any format, including an electronic format.

(g) The head of each agency shall prepare and make publicly available upon request, reference material or a guide for requesting records or information from the agency, subject to the exemptions in subsection (b), including—

(1) an index of all major information systems of the agency;

(2) a description of major information and record locator systems maintained by the agency; and

(3) a handbook for obtaining various types and categories of public information from the agency pursuant to chapter 35 of title 44, and under this section.

A p p e n d i x   2

Law that Makes Financial Information of a Tax-Exempt Organization Public

---

The Internal Revenue Service of the U.S. Department of the Treasury has instructed tax-exempt organizations to file financial reports and make them public or risk a penalty. Excerpts from the IRS instructions can be viewed at http://www.irs.gov/instructions/i990-ez/ar02.html#d0e450.

Who Must File

Filing Tests

Organizations exempt from income tax under Internal Revenue Code section 501(a), which includes sections 501(c), 501(e), 501(f), 501(k), 501(n), and 4947(a)(1) must generally file Form 990 or Form 990-EZ based on their gross receipts for the tax year.... For this purpose, *gross receipts* is the organization's total revenues from all sources during its annual accounting period, without subtracting any costs or expenses....

If the organization does not meet any of the exceptions ... and its annual gross receipts are normally more than $25,000, it must file Form 990 or Form 990-EZ. If the organization is a sponsoring organization, or a controlling organization within the meaning of section 512(b)(13), it must file Form 990. However, if the organization is a supporting organization described in section 509(a)(3), it generally must file Form 990 (Form 990-EZ if applicable) even if its gross receipts are normally $25,000, or less. Supporting organizations of religious organizations need not file Form 990 (or form 990-EZ) if their gross receipts are normally $5,000, or less. See the gross receipts discussion in *General Instruction B.*

If the organization's gross receipts during the year are less than $100,000 and its total assets at the end of the year are less than $250,000, it may file Form 990-EZ instead of Form 990. Even if the organization meets this test, it can still file Form 990.

Organizations Not Required To File Form 990 or 990-EZ

The following types of organizations exempt from tax under section 501(a) (section 527 for political organizations) do not have to file Form 990, or Form 990-EZ, with the IRS. However, if the organization chooses to file a Form 990 or Form 990-EZ, it must also attach the schedules and statements described in the instructions for these forms.

1. A church, an interchurch organization of local units of a church, a convention or association of churches, an integrated auxiliary of a church (such as a men's or women's organization, religious school, mission society, or youth group).
2. A church-affiliated organization that is exclusively engaged in managing funds or maintaining retirement programs and is described in Rev. Proc. 96-10, 1996-1 C.B. 577.
3. A school below college level affiliated with a church or operated by a religious order.
4. A mission society sponsored by, or affiliated with, one or more churches or church denominations, if more than half of the society's activities are conducted in, or directed at, persons in foreign countries.
5. An exclusively religious activity of any religious order.
6. A state institution whose income is excluded from gross income under section 115.
7. An organization described in section 501(c)(1). A section 501(c)(1) organization is a corporation organized under an Act of Congress that is:
    - An instrumentality of the United States, and
    - Exempt from federal income taxes. . . .

Use of Form 990, or Form 990-EZ, To Satisfy State Reporting Requirements

Some states and local government units will accept a copy of Form 990, or Form 990-EZ, Schedule A (Form 990 or 990-EZ), and Schedule B (Form 990, 990-EZ, or 990-PF) in place of all or part of their own financial report forms. The substitution applies primarily to section 501(c)(3) organizations, but some of the other types of section 501(c) organizations are also affected.

If the organization uses Form 990, or Form 990-EZ, to satisfy state or local filing requirements, such as those under state charitable solicitation acts, note the following discussions.

Determine State Filing Requirements

The organization should consult the appropriate officials of all states and other jurisdictions in which it does business to determine their specific filing requirements. Doing business in a jurisdiction may include any of the following: (a) soliciting contributions or grants by mail or otherwise from individuals, businesses, or other charitable organizations; (b) conducting programs; (c) having employees within that jurisdiction; (d) maintaining a checking account; or (e) owning or renting property there.

Monetary Tests May Differ

Some or all of the dollar limitations applicable to Form 990, or Form 990-EZ, when filed with the IRS may not apply when using Form 990, or Form 990-EZ, in place of state or local report forms. Examples of the IRS dollar limitations that do not meet some state requirements are the $25,000 gross receipts minimum that creates an obligation to file with the IRS (see the gross receipts discussion in *General Instruction B*) and the $50,000 minimum for listing professional fees in Part II-A of Schedule A (Form 990 or 990-EZ).

Additional Information May Be Required

State or local filing requirements may require the organization to attach to Form 990, or Form 990-EZ, one or more of the following: (a) additional financial statements, such as a complete analysis of functional expenses or a statement of changes in net assets; (b) notes to financial statements; (c) additional financial schedules; (d) a report on the financial statements by an independent accountant; and (e) answers to additional questions and other information. Each jurisdiction may require the additional material to be presented on forms they provide. The additional information does not have to be submitted with the Form 990, or Form 990-EZ, filed with the IRS.

Even if the Form 990, or Form 990-EZ, that the organization files with the IRS is accepted by the IRS as complete, a copy of the same return filed with a state will not fully satisfy that state's filing requirement if required information is not provided, including any of the additional information discussed above, or if the state determines that the form was not completed by following the applicable Form 990, or Form 990-EZ, instructions or supplemental state instructions. If so, the organization may be asked to provide the missing information or to submit an amended return.

Electronic Filing

The organization can file Form 990, or Form 990-EZ, and related forms, schedules, and attachments electronically. However, if an organization files at least 250 returns during the calendar year and has total assets of $10 million or more at the end of the tax year, it must file Form 990 electronically. . . .

If an organization is required to file a return electronically but does not, the organization is considered to have not filed its return. See Temporary Regulations section 301.6033-4T for more information.

For additional information on the electronic filing requirement, visit www.irs.gov/efile. . . .

Failure to File Penalties

Against the Organization

Under section 6652(c)(1)(A), a penalty of $20 a day, not to exceed the smaller of $10,000 or 5% of the gross receipts of the organization for the year, may be charged when a return is filed late, unless the organization can show that the late filing was due to reasonable cause. Organizations with annual gross receipts exceeding $1 million are subject to a penalty of $100 for each day the failure continues (with a maximum penalty with respect to any one return of $50,000). The penalty begins on the due date for filing the Form 990 or Form 990-EZ.

The penalty may also be charged if the organization files an incomplete return. To avoid having to supply missing information later, be sure to complete all applicable line items; answer "Yes," "No," or "N/A" (not applicable) to each question on the return; make an entry (including a zero when appropriate) on all total lines; and enter "None" or "N/A" if an entire part does not apply.

Also, this penalty may be imposed if the organization's return contains incorrect information. For example, an organization that reports contributions net of related fundraising expenses may be subject to this penalty.

Use of a paid preparer does not relieve the organization of its responsibility to file a complete and accurate return.

Against Responsible Person(s)

If the organization does not file a complete return or does not furnish correct information, the IRS will send the organization a letter that includes a fixed time to fulfill these requirements. After that period expires, the person failing to comply will be charged a penalty of $10 a day. The maximum penalty on all persons for failures with respect to any one return shall not exceed $5,000 (section 6652(c)(1)(B)(ii)).

Any person who does not comply with the public inspection requirements, as discussed in *General Instruction M,* will be assessed a penalty of $20 for each day that inspection was not permitted, up to a maximum of $10,000 for each return. The penalties for failure to comply with the public inspection requirements for applications is the same as those for annual returns, except that the $10,000 limitation does not apply (sections 6652(c)(1)(C) and (D)). Any person who willfully fails to comply with the public inspection requirements for annual returns or exemption applications will be subject to an additional penalty of $5,000 (section 6685).

There are also penalties (fines and imprisonment) for willfully not filing returns and for filing fraudulent returns and statements with the IRS (sections 7203, 7206, and 7207). States may impose additional penalties for failure to meet their separate filing requirements. See also the discussion of the *Trust Fund Recovery Penalty, under General Instruction D. . . .*

Public Inspection of Returns, etc.

Some members of the public rely on Form 990, or Form 990-EZ, as the primary or sole source of information about a particular organization. How the public perceives an organization in such cases may be determined by the information presented on its returns.

An organization's completed Form 990, or Form 990-EZ, is available for public inspection as required by section 6104. Schedule B (Form 990,

990-EZ, or 990-PF), is open for public inspection for section 527 organizations filing Form 990 or Form 990-EZ. For other organizations that file Form 990 or Form 990-EZ, parts of Schedule B may be open to public inspection. Form 990-T filed after August 17, 2006, by a 501(c)(3) organization is also available for public inspection and disclosure.

Through the IRS

Use Form 4506-A to request:
- A copy of an exempt or political organization's return, report, notice, or exemption application;
- An inspection of a return, report, notice, or exemption application at an IRS office.

The IRS can provide copies of exempt organization returns on a compact disc (CD). Requesters can order the complete set (all Forms 990 and 990-EZ or all Forms 990-PF filed for a year) or a partial set by state or by month. For more information on the cost and how to order CDs, call the TEGE Customer Account Services toll-free number (1-877-829-5500) or write to the IRS in Cincinnati, OH, at the address in *General Instruction A*.

The IRS may not disclose portions of an exemption application relating to any trade secrets, etc. Additionally, the IRS may not disclose the names and addresses of contributors. See the Instructions for Schedule B (Form 990, 990-EZ, or 990-PF) for more information about the disclosure of that schedule.

Forms 990 or 990-EZ can only be requested for section 527 organizations for tax years beginning after June 30, 2000.

A return, report, notice, or exemption application may be inspected at an IRS office free of charge. Copies of these items may also be obtained through the organization as discussed in the following section.

Through the Organization

Public inspection and distribution of certain returns of unrelated business income. Section 501(c)(3) organizations that are required to file Form 990-T after August 17, 2006, must make Form 990-T available for public inspection under section 6104(d)(1)(A)(ii).

Public inspection and distribution of returns and reports for a political organization. Section 527 political organizations required to file Form 990, or Form 990-EZ, must, in general, make their Form 8871, 8872, 990, or 990-EZ available for public inspection in the same manner as annual information returns of section 501(c) organizations and 4947(a)(1) nonexempt charitable trusts are made available. See the public inspection rules for *Tax-exempt organization,* later. Generally, Form 8871 and Form 8872 are available for inspection and printing from the Internet. The website address for both of these forms is http://eforms.irs.gov. . . .

Public inspection and distribution of applications for tax exemption and annual information returns of tax-exempt organizations. Under regulations sections 301.6104(d)-1 through 301.6104(d)-3, a tax-exempt organization must:

- Make its application for recognition of exemption and its annual information returns available for public inspection without charge at its principal, regional and district offices during regular business hours.
- Make each annual information return available for a period of 3 years beginning on the date the return is required to be filed (determined with regard to any extension of time for filing) or is actually filed, whichever is later.
- Provide a copy without charge, other than a reasonable fee for reproduction and actual postage costs, of all or any part of any application or return required to be made available for public inspection to any individual who makes a request for such copy in person or in writing (except as provided in Regulations sections 301.6104(d)-2 and -3).

How TV, Newspaper and Internet Writing Styles Differ

TV reports have to move quickly, yet tell a complete story, condensing the facts. The viewer has to be told of the importance of the story and won over by being informed about how it was done. TV writers favor the present tense to make news reports seem more immediate. If the school superintendent resigned at the school board meeting the night before, the morning paper will inform readers that the school superintendent resigned last night. The TV news might report on its morning newscast: "Metro City is looking for a new school superintendent this morning."

A TV reporter may also use the more immediate tense for impact. Viewers are informed that there is an ongoing problem in their midst, as the TV reporter relates: "Massive cleanup and rescue efforts are under way this morning in the areas battered by Hurricane Katrina." The print reporter usually abandons the present tense for the historical approach: "Massive clean up and rescue operations were started yesterday in the areas battered by Hurricane Katrina, federal officials said."

The newspaper is recording history, and it will be read in the future. It does not inform the reader of what is happening now because the writer does not know when the words will be read. The broadcaster knows the viewers are listening now and can speak of what is happening now.

Here is how the auto repair story, described in a case study in Chapter 11, would have been presented on TV by Gary Hammond, the reporter-producer for the Tri-Cities TV Probe Team:

APPENDIX TABLE: AUTO REPAIR STORY

VIDEO	AUDIO
ANCHOR:	Tri-Cities residents have a 50-50 chance of getting a fair deal from an auto mechanic, Tri-Cities TV Probe investigative reporter Gary Hammond has found.
HAMMOND 00 10 Seated behind wheel, talks toward passenger seat	When we turn the key on our car ignition, we are at the mercy of a very complex machine. If it doesn't start, we are at the mercy of an auto mechanic.
HAMMOND 00 20 Mechanic in auto garage comes out from under car. "Sol Renich, auto mechanics instructor, Metro College" superimposed across bottom of screen	We have the results of visits to 52 garages. Unnecessary repairs were made or we were over-charged at 26 garages, according to our expert mechanic.
RENICH 00 40 Stands up and wipes hands with rag	Anyone can get a wrench and hang out a sign and be an instant auto mechanic. People have to be very careful about who they trust with their car.
HAMMOND 00 48 Standing with Renich, shows him a bill	Was the work unneeded?
RENICH 00 50 Picture of bill close-up, the total cost is highlighted	Only a small hose was needed to be replaced, but you got ripped off for a new transmission.
RENICH 00 53 Picture of transmission hose; picture of loose wire	A loose wire on a starter might get you a complete overhaul.

HAMMOND 00 59	
Pictures of fronts of auto garages in sequence, stops at Skammer's	At Skammer's Auto Rescuers, Front and Center Streets in Metro City, where they put on a new transmission, the owner would not talk about it.

HAMMOND 01 09	
Following Skammer from his car to the door of the shop	Mister Skammer, I'm Gary Hammond, Probe Team reporter. Why did you charge us for a new transmission when all we needed was a hose?

SKAMMER 01 14	
Turns at door, points at camera	Don't bring that in here!

HAMMOND 01 21	
Camera is outside, lens follows Skammer until he disappears inside	What happens when all that's wrong is a loose wire? Tomorrow night. Gary Hammond reporting.

ANCHOR 01 30	
With Hammond in studio	Is there some agency of government that oversees auto mechanics?

HAMMOND 01 34	They are completely unregulated.

ANCHOR 01 35	Thank you.

The ambush interview adds excitement to an investigative story because the viewer is witnessing the subject's refusal by looking over the shoulder of the reporter. When Hammond is shut out, viewers feel the same way. Hammond and the cameraman knew they could not enter private property once they were specifically told not to go there, so they did their best. Because of their brevity, TV investigations are usually spread over several reports, teasing the viewer with what is to come.

Newspapers and television broadcasts are the outlets for most investigative reporters, but there are others.

- **Internet.** We have shown how the Internet helps journalists gather information. It is also a means of getting the word out about the story, not just in the local circulation area but throughout the world.

- **Magazines.** Magazines offer more space for details than newspapers and certainly more than TV. Some, like *Time* and *Newsweek,* do their own investigations. Others may buy articles from freelance writers.
- **Books.** Because books are no longer hand-copied by monks, they can be produced swiftly and can be timely and investigative.
- **Multimedia.** Multimedia refers to a combination of news delivery outlets under one roof; this can also be called "convergence," which conjures up the coming together harmoniously of diverse communication facilities. This development has been a result of the merger of radio, TV and newspaper ownership and the media companies' expansion into cable and the Internet.

The Internet is more likely to adopt the style of the newspaper because it is being read at some time in the future. But the Internet brings a revolutionary style to journalism called nonlinear writing, which simply means that information on the Internet is not presented in a column from top to bottom. Some say nonlinear information is presented as if someone threw it against a wall and parts stuck there. We might say, though, that it is carefully thrown against the wall.

The online visitor to a Web site is able to choose the portion of the story to read because the parts of the story are spread out across the screen. A main story states the central argument of the investigative report; this will be center screen and encircled by sections of the story. An example worked up from the auto repair series would have, at the center, copy that would summarize the findings of the survey. The screen would offer a place to click on for technical information about brakes, transmissions and starters; then a profile of the expert mechanic and another on how the survey was planned. The Web site could be a stand-alone outlet or a supplement to a newspaper or TV report. There could be a picture gallery and links to helpful journalism Web sites. The copy would also be presented in a more traditional manner with the word "next" inviting a click-on for those people who want their reading organized.

Either way, when multimedia calls for the investigative journalist to produce all media functions, photos are of increased importance. No matter the medium, ideas for pictures are the same. Pictures of people willing to go on camera and make their case, such as victims or experts, are always useful. Some people will not want to go on camera and must be coaxed or tricked. It seems a bit overly aggressive to chase down a reluctant subject and wait with a camera when the subject steps out of a car, but if the person is a public official who is suspected of betraying the public trust and will not appear, no one should complain.

Pictures also aid the investigative reporter in explaining the technical aspects of an investigation. In this case, stock shots weaken the presentation of an investigation. Let's say the investigator learns that a local politician got free airline tickets. A stock shot would be a picture of a busy airport ticket counter that had no connection with the story. Then there would be the drive-by shot of a building. The SEC might be cracking down on a company, so we see a picture of the SEC office building in Washington. The camera moves in on the name of the agency and the entire scene took four seconds. Was it necessary to show the viewer that we know how to find the SEC building?

The ideal investigative picture helps prove the story, like the speeding trucks in Gary Hammond's investigation in Chapter 11 or the bags of unopened letters in the city hall story in Chapter 3.

Web Sites and Readings
to Investigate

Web Sites

Extensive listings of documents available for journalists:
Center for Investigative Reporting
Nonprofit, independent news organization, archives investigations focusing on the subjects of social and criminal justice, the environment and science and technology; the site's "advanced investigation search" is particularly valuable:
http://www.muckraker.org/

Investigative Reporters and Editors, Inc.
Membership organization for persons interested in investigative reporting is a reserve of print and broadcast stories:
www.ire.org/
Resource center contains searchable abstracts of more than 20,000 investigative reporting stories:
www.ire.org/resourcecenter/

The Reporter's Desktop
Web site maintained by reporter Duff Wilson and sponsored by Investigative Reporters and Editors, Inc.:
http://www.reporter.org/desktop/

Information on specific topics:
Aircraft registration inquiry:
Federal Aviation Administration
http://www.faa.gov/licenses_certificates/aircraft_certification/aircraft_registry/interactive_aircraft_inquiry/
Campaign contributions:
Center for Responsive Politics, opensecrets.org
www.opensecrets.org/
Complaints about businesses:
Better Business Bureau
www.bbb.org/

Fraud perpetrated on consumers:
National Fraud Information Center of the National Consumers League
www.fraud.org
Raw investigative FBI reports:
www.fbi.gov

Consumer safety information:
National Safety Council
Membership organization offering information that can help a reporter who is working on a story that affects personal safety. The NSC has a search capacity on its Web site and can supply advice about what to do in an emergency. Because it helps an investigative story to have quotable hints in the form of a sidebar, a story could devote some space to advice from the NSC on a specific topic:
www.nsc.org

U.S. Department of Transportation
www.dot.gov
Links online to the Transportation Safety Institute, which provides instruction about highway, aviation and pipeline safety:
www.tsi.dot.gov/

Books

History, philosophy and role of investigative reporting:
Aucoin, James L. "Evolution of American Investigative Journalism." University of Missouri Press, 2005.
de Burgh, Hugo, ed. "Investigative Journalism: Context and Practice." Routledge, 2000.
Ettema, James S., and Theodore Lewis Glasser. "Custodians of Conscience: Investigative Journalism and Public Virtue." Columbia University Press, 1998.
Greenwald, Marilyn S., and Joseph Bernt, eds. "Big Chill: Investigative Reporting in the Current Media Environment." Iowa State University Press, 2000.
Herbert, John. "Journalism in the Digital Age: Theory and Practice for Broadcast, Print and On-Line Media." Focal Press, 2000.
Pilger, John, ed. "Tell Me No Lies: Investigative Journalism That Changed the World." Thunder's Mouth Press, 2005.
Protess, David L., et al. "Journalism of Outrage: Investigative Reporting and Agenda Building in America." Guilford Press, 1991.
Schwartz, Jerry. "Associated Press Reporting Handbook." McGraw-Hill, 2002.

True stories:
Scandal in Washington:
Bernstein, Carl, and Bob Woodward. "All the President's Men." Simon & Schuster, 1974.
Realistic account of the experiences of a rookie police reporter:
Blau, Robert. "The Cop Shop: True Crime on the Streets of Chicago." Addison-Wesley, 1993.
Extreme example of corruption in the justice system:
Gibson, Edie and Ray, and Randall Turner. "Blind Justice: A Murder, a Scandal, and a Brother's Search to Avenge His Sister's Death." St. Martin's Press, 1991.

Compilation of prize-winning stories:
Fischer, Heinz-Dietrich, in cooperation with Erika J. Fischer, eds. "Local Reporting, 1947-1987: From a County Vote Fraud to a Corrupt City Council," vol. 3 of "Pulitzer Prize Archive." K. G. Saur, 1989.

Help and how-to:
Gaines, William. "Investigative Reporting for Print and Broadcast," 2nd ed. Nelson-Hall Publishers, 1998.
Weinberg, Steve, ed. "The Reporter's Handbook: An Investigator's Guide to Documents and Techniques," 3rd ed. St. Martin's Press, 1996.

Glossary

Here is a list of words and their special meanings for this book or for the field of investigative journalism.

ad lib speaking without written notes

alderman member of a city council

alternative newspaper local news publication that challenges the traditional newspaper of record

ambush (interview) to come upon a person without warning

animated (interview) active facial expressions

anonymous not identifying a person by name

archdiocese geographic division of the Roman Catholic Church

assessor government official who estimates the value of property for taxation

auxiliary secondary persons, used in emergency to back up regular staff

blimp aircraft hovering over football field; it may provide aerial pictures

building commissioner city official who regulates building construction and maintenance

chiropractors persons licensed to perform spinal manipulations

city hall casual name for local government

closers salespeople who are skilled in getting a prospect to sign a contract

conglomerate large group of often unrelated companies joined in single ownership

copyright laws that protect an author from having personal work copied by others

cropping changing a picture by cutting out parts

embezzlement theft of money by an employee, usually over time and concealed by fraudulent bookkeeping

epidemiologists persons of the scientific community

ethics written or unwritten accepted practices

executive branch the offices of government that run the business and enforce the laws

expunged erased

Founders signers of Declaration of Independence and authors of the Constitution

freelance writer works independently and sells articles

kickback money returned to a public official for providing a contract

labor intensive costs heavily weighted with employees

la-de-da! disrespectful sarcastic comeback

litigation filing and pursuing a lawsuit

lobbyist person whose purpose is to influence government officials

M1 military rapid-fire assault weapon

malapropisms incorrect mixing of words

malicious intent meant to do harm

metropolitan editor head of staff that gathers and writes news in a city and suburbs

nepotism preference in hiring given to one's family members

ombudsman official to whom a consumer can go for help

on the record (source of information) mutual understanding that the person being interviewed will be quoted and named in a story

oxygenation air feeding a fire

oxygeneration incorrect term for oxygenation

passing go as in the game of Monopoly

payroll list of employees

periodical publication made up of single issues that are published on a schedule

placebo treatment, which has no curative properties, but it satisfies the patient

plagiarism using someone's artistic work and identifying it as one's own

Ponzi scheme claiming profits are from investments when money is from new investors

Pulitzer Prize most prestigious journalism award

quid pro quo exchange of favors

random selection without a system

ratings period specified times when broadcast listener surveys are conducted

regimen plan to be followed strictly

runaround person requesting assistance is sent to others who are also unresponsive

scams fraudulent conduct in which a person is tricked

scoop reporter gets a story ahead of all competing media

seeing-eye dogs canine escorts for blind people

shopper local publication with advertisements but no news content

smokies in the chicken coop colorful trucker talk for police at the weigh station

snookered tricked, trapped

sour grapes making excuses for losing

tailgate vehicle following another too closely

tipster person who provides information without much detail

undercover job hiding identity to get employment to gather information

unencumbered methodology meaningless term created for this text to illustrate quackery

vacuum trucks vehicles with hoses that suck up water

vouchers bills for services performed

windfall unexpected good fortune

Xyphicolo a meaningless word created for a case study in this text

Index

Abortion, special interest groups, 83
Access to documents and records,
28–30
See also Freedom of Information
Acts (FOIAs)
Accidents, traffic, 103–104
Advertisers' influence, 158–160
Advocacy groups
on abortion, 83
on consumer fraud, 206
Agriculture Department (USDA),
79–80
Aircraft registration information,
325
"An Alderman Who Earned While
He Learned" (Chicago Tribune),
51
Allegations, verifying. *See* Stories,
investigating and pitching
"All the President's Men" (movie),
123–124
"All the President's Men"
(Woodward & Bernstein), 52, 123
Alltheweb search engine, 84–86
All Things Ypsilanti, 87–88
Ambush interviews, 163–165
American Medical Association, 242
Anonymity, 7
Answers to interrogatories, 141
Answer to complaint, 140
Appeals, 142
Arrest records, 139
Ask Jeeves search engine, 84–86
Associated Doctors, 213–214
Atlanta Journal, 178
Attorneys general, 206
Attribution
documents, 42
e-mail, 87
Internet, 86
Austin (Texas) American-Statesman, 101

Awards for reporting. *See* Prizes for
reporting; Pulitzer Prize

Back-pocket documents, 282–287
Balance in stories, 63
Bankruptcy records, 55–56
Bank statements, 24, 25*t*
Baskerville, Bill, 229
Bebow, John, 186
Becka, Holly, 138
Bernstein, Carl, 8, 52, 123
Berry, Steve, 6
Better Business Bureau (BBB), 204,
208
Council of Better Business
Bureaus, 207
Biddle, Daniel, 10, 138
Biographies, 25, 25*t*
Birth records, 53
Bissinger, H.G., 10, 138
Black Hawk helicopter, 174
Blethen Maine Newspapers Inc., 274
Bloggers, 87–88
Blumenthal, Richard, 172
Books
on investigative reporting, 326–327
publishing of investigative report-
ing, 322
Boston Globe, 2, 180, 273–275
Boston Post, 2
Boys Town, 155–156
BRB Publications, 86
Breaking stories, following up on,
7–8
Breed, Allen G., 227
Bribery and extortion, investigating,
133, 181
Budget documents, 25*t*, 26, 39–42
Budget proposal for story, 40*f*
Buildings and structures, safety of,
102–103

Bush, George H. W., 57
Businesses, investigating
  class assignments, 271–272
  complaints against businesses,
    information on, 325–326
  for-profit, 59–60
  letter requesting comment, 254*f*
  not-for-profit organizations, 58
    See also Charities, nonprofits,
      and foundations, investigating
  privately held, 60, 250–255
  publicly held, 60, 255–258
  regulation and licensing, 249–250
  "Sports Equals Big Business" (case
    study), 251–255
  surveys, 250, 258–259
    "Auto Mechanics, Routine
      Checkup" (case study),
      259–265, 320–321
    "Speeding and Tailgating
      Trucks" (case study), 265–270
Business holdings, 56

Campaigns. *See* Elections and voting
Campbell, Ron, 77–78
Case studies
  "The Deal of a Lifetime," 214–220
  "Everybody Loves a Carnival,"
    156–166
  "The Firehouse," 113–117
  "Investigating Licensed and
    Unlicensed Medical
    Professionals," 232–241
  "A Look Behind the Judicial
    Robe," 144–150
  "Mayor Mixes Public and Private
    Business," 34–39
  "Military Guns Sold on the
    Internet," 88–98
  "A Public Document Denied,"
    11–16
  "School Food: The Lowest Bid,"
    279–282
  "Sports Equals Big Business,"
    251–255
  "A Stolen Document," 193–200
  "Survey: Auto Mechanics, Routine
    Checkup," 259–265
    TV reporting of same story,
      320–321

"Survey: Speeding and Tailgating
  Trucks," 265–270
"Waste in City Government,"
  63–75
CBS, 155–156
Center for Responsive Politics, 82,
  183
Certification of work as original, 62
Charities, nonprofits and foundations, investigating, 58, 153–176
  annual financial report, 162*f,* 163*f*
  class assignments, 175–176
  "Everybody Loves a Carnival" (case
    study), 156–166
  flow charts, using, 166–168, 169*f*
  Hale House, 153–154
  law that makes financial informa-
    tion public, 311–317
  online research, 82–83
  regulation of, 154–156
  tax filings by, 311–317
    See also Form 990 or 990-EZ
      (IRS)
    electronic filing, 314
    organizations not required to
      file, 312
    penalties for failure to file,
      314–315
    public inspection of filings,
      315–317
    state filings, 313–314
    who must file, 311–312
  telemarketing complaints,
    169–175
Chicago City Council, investigation
  of, 51
Chicago Daily News, 2
Chicago Sun-Times, 9
Chicago Tribune, 10, 51, 106–109
  Nation of Islam investigation, 275
  police brutality, reporting of,
    134–135
  undercover investigations, 211–214
Child safety, investigating, 118–120
Choosing subjects for stories, 6,
  16–20
Churches. *See* Charities, nonprofits,
  and foundations, investigating
Clark County, Nevada, 188
Claxton, Melvin, 110–112, 131

Clinton, Bill, 57
Cohn, Alan, 169–174
Coins, state investments in, 277–278
Colleagues' observations and story
  ideas, 9–10
Columbine High School, 118
Commingling of funds, 180
Complaints, civil, 140
Confidentiality. *See* Freedom of
  Information Acts (FOIAs); *specific
  types of information*
Conflict of interest, 62–63, 180
Congressional offices and consumer
  fraud, 205
Connecticut State Police, 169–174
Consumer fraud. *See* Fraud against
  consumers, reporting on
Contracts, 24, 25*t*, 26
Convergence of multimedia report-
  ing, 322
Convictions, criminal. *See* Criminal
  records
Copyright rules, 24–25
Corporate filings, 25*t*
Correctional institutions, investigat-
  ing, 143
Corruption of government officials.
  See Government, investigating
Council of Better Business Bureaus,
  207
County recorder of deeds, 197
Courts
  class assignments, 151
  files, records and documentation,
    55–56
    answers to interrogatories, 141
    answer to complaint, 140
    appeals, 142
    complaint, 140
    discovery, 141–142
    disposition, 142
    divorce, 51
    indexes of cases, 140
    interrogatories, 140–141
    motions, 141
    off limits, 142–143
  investigating, 136–137
  judges, 138
  judicial misbehavior, 179
  jurors, selection of, 137–138

"A Look Behind the Judicial Robe"
  (case study), 144–150
  small claims court, 206–207
Criminal records, 55–56, 139
Currency, 277–278

Dahlberg, Kenneth, 123–124
Dallas Morning News, 182
Darce, Keith, 275–277
Database searching, 30–34, 55,
  78–84
  See also specific names of databases
"The Deal of a Lifetime" (case
  study), 214–220
Death records and obituaries, 56
Deeds, researching ownership,
  188–192, 189*f*, 190*f*
Defense Department (DOD),
  174–175, 181
Definitions of investigative journal-
  ism terms, 329–330
Dentists. *See* Health care, investigat-
  ing
Depositions, 141–142
Derogatory writing, 158
Detroit Fire Department, 110–112
The Detroit News, 110, 131, 186
Dickens, Charles, 1
Dillinger, John, 79
Discipline of medical practitioners,
  records of, 226–227
"Disorder in the Court" (Biddle,
  Bissinger and Tulsky), 10
Disposition of court cases, 142
Divorce records, 51
DoctorFinder, 86
Doctors. *See* Health care, investigat-
  ing; Medicine
Documents and records
  See also Courts; Freedom of
    Information Acts (FOIAs)
  access to, 28–30
  attribution of, 42
  case studies, 34–39
  class assignments, 48–49
  flow charts for tracking, 166–168,
    169*f*
  government, investigating,
    181–182
  how to use, 24–25

lobbyists' reports, 286
matching information in, 39–42
medical licensing, discipline and
  privacy, 226–227
medical records, 23–24
meeting minutes, reviewing, 25*t*,
  26, 185–186
news databases, searching, 30–34
operational, 26
parking violations, 143–144
police records, 133–134
political campaign reports,
  183–185
postal service, 282–283
property ownership, researching,
  187–193
public disclosure, 25–26
taxes, 57, 77, 154–156
tax-exempt organizations' financial reporting, 311–317
types of, 25*t*, 26–28
Uniform Commercial Code
  (UCC) filings, 283–286
DOD (Defense Department), 181
Dogpile search engine, 84–86
DOJ (Justice Department), 206
DOL. *See* Labor Department
DOT. *See* Transportation Department
Drug Enforcement Administration,
  242

EDGAR database, 78
Education and schools, 278–279
  bullying in, 118–120
  case study, 279–282
  private persons, investigating,
    54–55
  records from, 25*t*
  religious schools, tax filings by, 312
  "School Food: The Lowest Bid"
    (case study), 279–282
  Web sites of educational institu-
    tions, 83–84
Elections and voting
  See also Federal Election
    Commission (FEC)
  campaign contributions, informa-
    tion on, 25*t*, 325
  documents, 25*t*, 26
  financial disclosure of candidates, 57

investigating, 56–58, 177–178
  Kerry campaign, 80–81
  petitions for candidacy, 57
  pursuing story on candidate that
    could swing election, 13–14
  voting records, information in, 53
E-mail, 87, 207–208, 209*f*
Emergency Planning and
  Community Right to Know Act
  (EPCRA), 86
Environmental issues, investigating
  EPA records, 60–61
  public safety and, 104
  Toxic Release Inventory, 86
Environmental Protection Agency
  (EPA), 60–61, 205
EPCRA (Emergency Planning
  and Community Right to Know
  Act), 86
Ethics, journalistic, 61–63
Evans, Heidi, 153
"Everybody Loves a Carnival" (case
  study), 156–166
Experimental drugs, investigation of
  deaths from, 23
Extortion and bribery, investigating,
  181

FAA (Federal Aviation
  Administration), 80
"Faith Journey," 153
Fancher, Mike, 24
Farrakhan, Louis, 275
FDA (Food and Drug
  Administration), 105–106
Federal Aviation Administration
  (FAA), 80
Federal Bureau of Investigation
  (FBI), 79, 326
Federal Election Commission (FEC)
  filing requirements, 183
  Kerry campaign, 81
  online research, 80
Federal statistics, online research,
  81, 82
Federal Trade Commission (FTC)
  online research, 79, 118
  public safety, investigating,
    118–120
Felt, Mark, 6

Financial reports. *See* Securities and Exchange Commission (SEC)
Fire protection, investigating, 110–111
    dispatcher log, 111*f*, 112*f*
    "The Firehouse" (case study), 113–117
Flow charts, using, 166–168, 169*f*
FOIAs. *See* Freedom of Information Acts
Follow-up questions, 124–126
Food and Drug Administration (FDA), 105–106
Form 990 or 990-EZ (IRS), 58, 77, 154, 311–317
Form 4506-A (IRS), 316
Forms 8871 and 8872 (IRS), 316–317
For-profit businesses, investigating, 59–60
Foundations. *See* Charities, nonprofits and foundations, investigating
Fox, Michael J., 85
Fraud against consumers, reporting on, 203–222
    See also Health care, investigating
    class assignments, 221–222
    "The Deal of a Lifetime" (case study), 214–220
    defense against, 204–207
        advocacy groups, 206
        Better Business Bureau, 204
        congressional offices, 205
        federal agencies, 206
        legal assistance groups, 205
        small claims court, 206–207
        state and local governments, 206
    how not to do it, 220–221
    schemes, 207–211
        by businesses, 210–211
        by e-mail, 207–208, 209*f*
        by mail, 210, 214*f*
        on the street, 208–210
        by telemarketers, 210
    survey and undercover, 211–214
    Web site information on, 326
Freedom of Information Acts (FOIAs), 31–33, 293–296
    electronic provisions, 295

federal act reprinted, 297–310
government, investigating, 181–182
Homeland Security Act and, 295–296
how not to use, 47–48
medical records and, 23
operational documents, access under, 28–30
police records and, 132
public safety, investigating, 110–112
sample letters, 31f–33f, 276f
Freedom of press, 1
FTC. *See* Federal Trade Commission

Gaines, William, 106–109, 134–135, 211–214
Gannet Corporation, 255–258
GAO (Government Accountability Office), 81
Garland, Texas, 181–182
Gaul, Gilbert M., 249
Geoghan, John J., 273
"Ghost payrollers," 141
Gifts and gratuities to reporters, 62
Glossary, 329–330
"Good guy-bad guy" interviewing technique, 123
Google research, 54, 84–86
Government, investigating, 177–201
    class assignments, 200–201
    conflict of interest, 180
    documents, FOIAs and Open Records Acts, 181–182
    local misbehavior, 179–181
        bribery and extortion, 181
        commingling of funds, 180
        conflict of interest, 180
    meeting minutes, reviewing, 185–186
    political campaign reports, 183–185
    property ownership, researching, 187–193
        sample deed, 189*f*, 190*f*
        sample value declaration, 191*f*
    "A Stolen Document" (case study), 193–200
    voting and elections, 177–178

"Waste in City Government" (case study), 63–75
Government Accountability Office (GAO), 81
Grand Rapids Press, 29
Guidestar Web site, 78

Hale House, 153–154
Hansen, Ronald, 131
Harris, Roy J., 2
Haurwitz, Ralph K.M., 101
"Healers Raising the Killer Weed" (Breed), 227
Health and Human Services, Department of (HHS), 80
Health care, investigating, 223–247
See also Medicare and Medicaid
class assignments, 243–247
consumer protection, 213–214
government inspections, 227–230
institutions and infrastructure, 226
insurance claims and fraud, 230–231
"Investigating Licensed and Unlicensed Medical Professionals" (case study), 232–241
licensing, discipline and privacy, 226–227
Medicaid dental fraud, 223–225
medical professionals, 225–226
ombudsman, reporter as, 241–243
worksheets, 245*t*, 246*t*
Heath, David, 23–24
Heinssen, Thomas, 171
Hensel, Karen, 118–120
HHS (Health and Human Services, Department of), 80
Homeland Security Act and FOIA, 295–296
Houser, Mark, 137
Hugo, Victor, 1
Hunt, Everett Howard, 52
Hurt, Charles, 110–112

Ideas. *See* Story ideas
Identification of reporter, revealing when questioning, 62
Independence of reporters, 63

Individuals. *See* Private persons, investigating
Informants, use of, 23
payment to, 62–63
Inspections, government, 25*t*, 227–230
Insurance
See also Medicare and Medicaid
claims and fraud, 211–214, 230–231
records, 82–83
Internal Revenue Service (IRS)
financial disclosure to, 77, 154, 184
online research, 78
tax-exempt organizations, reporting to, 311–317
Internet, use during investigations, 77–100
attribution of sources, 86
bloggers and, 87–88
class assignments, 99
comparison of television, newspaper and Internet writing, 5, 120, 319–323
e-mail, 87
"Military Guns Sold on the Internet" (case study), 88–98
online research and Web sites
commercial, 84
educational institutions, 83–84
not-for-profits, 82–83
official government, 78–82
organ and tissue sales, 77–78
search engines, 84–86
Interrogatories, 140–141
Interviews, investigative, 6, 121–126
ambush interviews, 163–165
follow-up questions, 124–126
print, 122–124
revealing identification as reporter, 62
submitting questions in writing, 38–39
television, 121–122
"Investigating Licensed and Unlicensed Medical Professionals" (case study), 232–241
Investigative journalism
defined, 2–3

purpose of, 3
terms used in, 329–330
Investigative reporters. *See* Reporters, investigative
IRS. *See* Internal Revenue Service

Jackson, David, 134–135
Jaquiss, Nigel, 87
Jaspin, Elliot G., 249
Journalists. *See* Reporters, investigative
Judges, investigating, 10, 138
  See also Courts
  "A Look Behind the Judicial Robe" (case study), 144–150
Jurors, selection of, 137–138
Justice Department (DOJ), 206
  See also Federal Bureau of Investigation (FBI)

Kerry, John, 80–81
Kerry, Teresa Heinz, 81
King, Rodney, 134

Labor, 277
Labor Department (DOL), 104–105, 206, 277
LaFluer, Jennifer, 138
Land records office, 197
Law, Bernard (Cardinal), 273
Law enforcement. *See* Police, investigating
Lawsuits. *See* Courts
Leads, duty to follow up on, 195–197
Legal assistance groups on consumer fraud, 205
Legal issues for reporters, 5
  See also Freedom of Information Acts (FOIAs)
Leopold, Nathan, 2
Letters, personal, 24, 25*t*
Library archives and indexes of newspapers, 30, 34, 84
Library of Congress, 34
License documents, 25*t*, 53–54, 250
Liens and mortgages. *See* Property ownership, researching
Lobbyists' reports, 286
Local governments. *See* State and local governments

Loeb, Richard, 2
Logo for story, 46
"A Look Behind the Judicial Robe," 144–150
Los Angeles Times, 105–106

Magazines
  reporting for, characteristics of, 322
  trade magazines, 25*t*
Mail fraud, 210, 214*f*
Maine Supreme Court, 274
"Mayor Mixes Public and Private Business" (case study), 34–39
McGonigle, Steve, 138
Medicare and Medicaid
  dental fraud, 223–225
  insurance fraud, 212–213
  nursing home care, 231
  online research, 244
  overbidding, 106
  telemarketing fraud, 203
Medicine
  See also Health care, investigating
  experiments, deaths from, 23
  organs and tissues, sale of, 77–78
  public safety, investigating, 105–109
  records, 23–24, 25*t*
Meitrodt, Jeff, 275–277
Mellon Trust bank, 81
Memorandum, elements of, 44–47
Metropolitan Life, 213
The Miami Herald, 177
Michigan Court of Appeals, 29
"Military Guns Sold on the Internet" (case study), 88–98
Minutes of meetings, 25*t*, 26, 185–186
Money, 277–278
Mortgages and liens. *See* Property ownership, researching
Motions in court, 141
Multimedia reporting, 322

Name trace, 52–53
National Abortion Federation (NAF), 83
National Association of Insurance Commissioners, 82–83

National Consumers League (NCL), 204, 207

National Right to Life Committee, 83

National Safety Council, 326

Nation of Islam, 275

NCL. *See* National Consumers League

Nepotism, 179, 275–277

Nesmith, Jeff, 101

New Orleans Times-Picayune, 275

News Channel 8, 169–174

Newspapers

  archives online, 30, 84

  changes in size and coverage of, 4–5

  compared to television and Internet writing, 5, 120, 319–323

  library archives and indexes of, 30, 34

News releases, using, 25, 25*t*

New York Daily News, 153–154

New York Times, 2

9-1-1 calls, 133–134

Nixon, Richard M.

  campaign funds, misuse of, 185

  national security and, 181

  resignation of, 8

Nonprofit organizations. *See* Charities, nonprofits and foundations, investigating

The Northwest Indiana Times, 63

Nursing homes, 231

  See also Health care, investigating

Obituaries and death records, 56

Occupational Safety and Health Administration (OSHA), 104–105, 277

Oklahoma Board of Medical Licensure and Supervision, 227

Ombudsman, reporter as, 241–243

Ombwatch, 86

Online research and sources. *See* Internet, use during investigations

Open Records Acts, 181–182

Opinion, inclusion of, 150

The Orange County Register, 77, 82

Organs and tissues, sale of, 77–78

OSHA. *See* Occupational Safety and Health Administration

"Paper corporations," investigating, 59

Paraphrasing quotation to avoid shocking or explicit language, 95

Parking violations, investigating, 143–144

Partnerships, investigating, 59–60

Payroll documents, 25*t*, 26

Peabody Award, 47

Penalties for failure to file required IRS forms, 314–315

People, places and entities, investigating, 51–75

  business entities, 58–60

  class assignments, 75

  ethics of, 61–63

  for-profit businesses, 59–60

  not-for-profit organizations, 58

  places, 61

  private persons, 52–56

    See also Private persons, investigating

  public officials, 56–58

  "Waste in City Government" (case study), 63–75

Perot, Ross, 57

Personal information. *See* Private persons, investigating

Philadelphia Inquirer, 10, 138

Photographs, 24, 62

Physicians. *See* Health care, investigating; Medicine

Pictures, use of, 266–270, 322–323

Pierce, Steve, 87–88

PINs (Property index numbers), 197

Pioneer Life of Illinois, 213

Pipelines, safety of, 101

"Pipelines: The Invisible Danger" (Nesmith and Haurwitz), 101

Pitching a story idea, 43–47

Places, investigating, 61

  See also Property ownership, researching

Plagiarism, 62

Planned Parenthood, 83

Police, investigating, 132–135

  actions, evaluating, 132–133

  brutality and violence, 134–135

  documents, using, 133–134

  telemarketing campaigns, 169–175

working with, 135–136
Political activities, investigating, 55
Political campaigns. *See* Elections
 and voting
Ponzi, Charles, 2
Ponzi scheme investigation, 2
Postal service records, 282–283
Pottsville (Pa.) Republican, 249
Prisons, investigating, 143
Privacy
 See also Freedom of Information
  Acts (FOIAs)
 licensing and discipline of medical
  practitioners, records of,
  226–227
 medical records, 23, 238
Private documents, 24, 25*t*
Privately held businesses, investigat-
 ing, 250–255
Private persons, investigating, 52–56
 birth records, 53
 business holdings of, 56
 court records of, 55–56
 death records and obituaries of, 56
 licenses, 53–54
 name trace, 52–53
 political activities of, 55
 property records, 53
 published works of, 55
 yearbooks, 54–55
Prizes for reporting
 See also Pulitzer Prize
 Peabody Award, 47
 Selden Ring Award, 274
Probate records, 55
Professional associations, researching, 82–83
Promoting story idea, 43–47
Property index numbers (PINs), 197
Property ownership, researching, 53,
 187–193, 189*f*, 190*f*
"A Public Document Denied" (case
 study), 11–16
Publicly held businesses, investigating, 255–258
Public officials, investigating, 56–58
 campaign documents, 57
 financial disclosure, 57
 official documents, 57–58
 petitions for candidacy, 57

Public records. *See* Documents and
 records
Public safety, investigating, 101–129
 buildings and structures, 102–103
 children, 118–120
 class assignment, 128
 Detroit Fire Department dispatcher log, 111–112*f*
 environment, 104
 "The Firehouse" (case study),
  113–117
 fire protection, 110–112
 how not to do it, 126–128
 medicine, 105–109
 pipeline story, 101
 transportation, 103–104
 Web sites on consumer safety,
  326
 workplace, 104–105
Published works, researching, 55
Pulitzer Prize
 Boys Town investigation (1972),
  155
 Catholic Church, child abuse
  investigation (2003), 2, 274, 275
 Chicago City Council investigation
  (1987), 51
 Chicago health facilities investigation (1976), 106
 coal company investigation (1978),
  249
 Internet bloggers and, 87
 journalists on state payroll investigation (1950s), 2
 judicial misconduct investigation
  (1986), 10
 Leopold and Loeb investigation
  (1925), 2
 Miami mayor election investigation (1999), 177
 Ponzi scheme investigation (1921),
  2
 public safety investigation (2001),
  105–109
Pulling the clips, 30

Questions. *See* Interviews, investigative
Quoting
 attorney as speaker, 157–158

error in original, 116–117
truthfulness in, 62

Records. *See* Documents and records
Reese, Phillip, 229
Regulation of businesses, investigating, 249–250
Regulatory inspections, 25*t*, 227–230
Religious organizations, 273–275
  See also Charities, nonprofits and
    foundations, investigating
Reporters, investigative, 1–21
  class assignments, 20–21
  comparison of television, newspaper and Internet writing, 120, 319–323
  investigative journalism, defined, 2–3
  legal issues and, 5
  "A Public Document Denied"
    (case study), 11–16
  story ideas, 6–10
    breaking stories, 7–8
    colleagues' observations, 9–10
    planned projects, 8–9
    shared experiences, 10
    subjects, choosing, 6, 16–20
    tips, 6–7
  tools of, 5–6
  types of, 3–5
Responsibility of reporters, 63
Right-to-Know Network, 86
Roman Catholic Church, sexual
  abuse scandal, 2, 273–275

The Sacramento Bee, 229
Safety. *See* Public safety, investigating
Saltonstall, David, 153
Scam artists. *See* Fraud against consumers, reporting on
Schemes to defraud consumers.
  See Fraud against consumers,
  reporting on
Schools. *See* Education and schools
Scientific articles, 25, 25*t*
Search engines
  *See also specific names of search
    engines*
  comparison of, 84–86
  use of, 55

The Seattle Times, 23–24
Secretary of state office and business
  records, 56
Section 501(c) organizations. *See*
  Charities, nonprofits and foundations, investigating
Section 527 organizations, 312, 316
Securities and Exchange
  Commission (SEC)
  financial reports filed with, 60, 184–185, 255–258
  online research, 78, 81–82
Selden Ring Award, 274
Senate Special Committee on Aging, 106–109
Shared experiences and story ideas, 10
Sikorsky Aircraft Co., 174–175
Sinclair, Norman, 131
Sinclair, Upton, 1
Skepticism when talking with public
  officials, 67
Skip trace, 24
Small Business Administration
  (SBA), 271–272
Small claims court, 206–207
Social Security Administration (SSA)
  Death Master File, 56
  online research, 80
Society of Professional Journalists
  (SPJ), 62–63
Sources. *See* Attribution
Special interest groups, 83
Special topics for journalists, 273–291
  back-pocket documents, 282–287
    lobbyists' reports, 286
    postal service records, 282–283
    Uniform Commercial Code
      (UCC) filings, 283–286, 285*f*
  class assignments, 290–291
  how not to do it, 287–290
  labor, 277
  money, 277–278
  nepotism, 275–277
  religion, 273–275
  schools, 278–282
"Sports Equals Big Business" (case
  study), 251–255

SSA. *See* Social Security
Administration
St. Louis Post-Dispatch, 2
State and local governments
building departments and inspections, 102–103
consumer fraud protections, 206
environmental regulation, 104
filings by tax-exempt organizations, 313–314
health departments and inspections, 106
licensing agencies, 54
lobbyist filings with, 286
misbehavior by officials, 179–181
"A Stolen Document" (case study),
193–200
Stories, investigating and pitching,
23–49
advertisers' influence, 158–160
attribution, obtaining, 42
class assignments, 48–49
documents, gaining access to,
28–30
documents, using, 24–28, 25*t*
See also Documents and records
classification of, 26–28
disclosure, 25–26
operational, 26
how not to do it, 47–48
"Mayor Mixes Public and Private
Business" (case study), 34–39
memorandum, elements of, 44–47
previous stories, searching databases for, 30–34
sacrificing productive police beat
to cover one story, 12–13
story idea, promoting, 43–47
suppression of story, 11
taking legal steps and delaying
story vs. going forward with story,
14
validating allegations, 39–42, 63
activities statement, 41*f*
budget proposal, 40*f*
Story ideas
breaking stories, 7–8
choosing, 6–7
colleagues' observations, 9–10
evaluating and pitching, 43–47

method of investigating, 18–20,
18*t*
planned projects, 8–9
shared experiences, 10
subjects, choosing, 16–18, 16*t*
Sun Newspapers, 155
Suppression of story, 11
to stay in favor of advertisers,
158–160
Surfing the Internet, 84–86
Surveys of businesses, investigating,
250, 258–259
"Auto Mechanics, Routine
Checkup" (case study), 259–265
TV reporting of same story,
320–321
"Speeding and Tailgating Trucks"
(case study), 265–270

Taxes. *See* Documents and records;
Internal Revenue Service (IRS)
Tax-exempt organizations. *See*
Charities, nonprofits and founda-
tions, investigating
Teichert, Nancy Weaver, 229
Telemarketers, investigation of,
169–175, 210
Television reporting, 5, 155–156,
169–175
compared to newspaper and
Internet writing, 120, 319–323
interviews, 121–122
Terms used in investigative journal-
ism, 329–330
Texas Open Records Act, 182
Thiem, George, 2
Tips, following up, 6–7
confirming validity, 39–42, 63
Title of investigation, choice of
words, 46
Tools of reporting, 5–6
Toxic Release Inventory, 86
Toy safety, 118
Trade magazines, 25*t*
Transcripts of court proceedings,
142
Transportation Department (DOT)
online research, 80, 326
Pipeline Safety, Office of, 101
sidewalk bus stop, report on, 104

Transportation safety, investigating, 103–104, 265–270
Tulsky, Fredric, 10, 138

Undercover reporting, 9, 109, 210–214, 229–230
Uniform Commercial Code (UCC) filings, 283–286, 285*f*
Universities. *See* Education and schools
USDA (U.S. Department of Agriculture), 79–80

Verifying allegations. *See* Stories, investigating and pitching
Veterans Affairs (VA), Department of, 206
Videotapes, use of, 6, 134
Von Solbrig, Charles, 106
Von Solbrig hospital, 106–109
Voting. *See* Elections and voting

Wallace, George, 79
"Waste in City Government" (case study), 63–75
Watergate scandal
   See also Nixon, Richard M.; Woodward, Bob
   breaking story, follow-up on, 8

FBI and, 79
   private persons, investigating, 52
   tips leading to, 6
Watson, Stuart, 223–225
WCNC-TV (Charlotte, N.C.), 223–225
Web sites
   See also Internet, use during investigations
   documents available for journalists, lists of, 325
   government, list of, 78–82
   information on specific topics, 325–326
Whistleblowers, 174–175
"Who's Who in America," 52
Wikipedia, 86
Wilkenson, Mike, 278
Willamette Week, 87
Willman, David, 105–106
Wilson, Duff, 23–24, 84
WISH-TV (Indianapolis), 118–120
Withholding of source, 35–36
Woodward, Bob, 8, 52, 123–124
Workers' compensation, 104–105
Workplace safety, 104–105, 277
Wyatt, Tim, 138

Yearbooks, use of, 54–55